The Internet Guide for the Legal Researcher

Second Edition

by Don MacLeod

The Internet Guide for the Legal Researcher, Second Edition

by Don MacLeod

THE INTERNET GUIDE FOR THE LEGAL RESEARCHER, SECOND EDITION
COPYRIGHT 1997 BY DON MACLEOD

LIBRARY OF CONGRESS CATALOGING-IN-PUBLICATION DATA

MacLeod, Don, 1955-
    The Internet Guide for the Legal Researcher, Second Edition
    p.   cm.
Includes bibliographical references and index
ISBN 0-939486-46-6
    1. Information storage and retrieval systems — Law — United States.
    2. Legal research — United States — Automation
    3. Internet (Computer network)
KF242.A1M3   1997
025.06'34 — dc20

ACKNOWLEDGMENTS

NO BOOK IS EVER WRITTEN ALONE. Each one is a collaborative effort. I have been very fortunate to have had extraordinary support and encouragement from so many people over the years, from the first excited day when I actually made my timid first connection to the Internet to the present when every new day brings some innovation to the always-changing network.

I am most fortunate to work for a supportive and understanding law firm and so my thanks go out first of all to **Chadbourne & Parke, LLP** in New York. Particular thanks go to **Lillian Arcuri** who has been unstinting and gracious in allowing me the time to pursue the necessary research and to speak at conferences with little advance notice. Everyone should be lucky enough to work with someone as patient, supportive and helpful as Lillian.

Also at Chadbourne are my colleagues, from whom I have learned a great deal and to whom I owe a debt: **Jill Porter**; **John Beaumont**, the hardest-working technical guy you'll ever see jimmy open a stuck network drive; and **Anna Smallen**, who was both a willing student and an enthusiastic convert to the 'Net. Thanks also to **Katherine Wolpe, Brenda Pancham, Barbara Oxley, Iyanth Davis** and **Milo Alexander** without whose reliable help I could not function professionally at all.

For prompt and efficient help, Cleveland's own **Ken Kozlowski** gets a tip of the hat.

And of course, I owe a lasting debt to publisher **Arlene Eis** for taking the chance on publishing the first edition and having the fortitude to see another edition struggle into print.

Most of all, I reserve the greatest thanks of all to all the men and women who have worked together at no pay and for no recognition who have made the Internet a fascinating, useful and valuable addition to the world. I would single out **Ken Mortensen** of Villanova University, **Mark Folmsbee** of Washburn University and **Steve McGarry** of Hieros Gamos as dedicated toilers who have given their time and talents without pay or glory to the Internet. And to the thousands of Webmasters and the technology pioneers who built the first generation of the Internet, I extend a heartfelt thanks.

The contributions are theirs, the faults all my own. To all of these, I remain deeply indebted and unceasingly grateful. *-Don MacLeod, August 15, 1997, New York City*

Dedication

This book is dedicated with love to LAK
for astounding patience and understanding.
Just remember what they say in Hoonah:
"Nobu-Po-Jones, Jean-Zoe-Choshi"
What you said.

-DM

TABLE OF CONTENTS

CHAPTER FOUR
Law-Related Index Pages and Search Engines

CHAPTER FIVE
Federal and International Resources

EXECUTIVE AND CABINET OFFICES

EXECUTIVE AGENCIES

LEGISLATIVE BRANCH

JUDICIAL BRANCH

MILITARY RESOURCES

MISCELLANEOUS FEDERAL RESOURCES

CHAPTER SIX
State and Local Resources

CHAPTER SEVEN
Reference Resources

CHAPTER EIGHT
Glossary

CHAPTER NINE
Index

ENDPAGE
About the Author and Publisher

●●●

Introduction

INTRODUCTION

The Internet is really here to stay.

In its first flush of popularity, the global network was dismissed as a fad, criticized as an interesting but passing toy for computer nerds and college kids or oversold and overhyped in one breathless article after another as a spectacular new invention that would usher in an era of world peace and democracy and give all people equal access to the riches of the new Information Age.

What the Internet did turn into was not the land of instant riches and split-second democracy. It did, however, become the biggest and cheapest publishing system the world has ever known. The Internet is where the editorial content of books, magazines, court opinions, news stories, statutory codes and legislative documents converge with television-style color, immediacy and urgency.

The Big Picture

The Internet, big as it is, is only one part of a larger trend called the *digital convergence*. This fashionable phrase refers to a profound change in how information is created, stored and distributed that is literally changing the world.

Simply put, words, pictures, sound and movies can be transformed into digital format, the binary ones and zeroes that comprise the basic language of all computers. Before the digital revolution, different devices had very specific functions: the telephone carried voice signals, television translated broadcast video signals, radios received audio signals and computers created and read files. Although the migration to a completely digital world is not complete, all these separate appliances are blending together on the Internet. All digital data looks and behaves exactly alike: a digital version of *Seinfeld* is not different technically from the digital code that can be translated into Beethoven's *Ninth Symphony* from a compact disk or the digital signal that makes a trans-Atlantic phone call sound as if it were emanating from the next room.

What is the Internet?

Exactly what is the Internet? Millions of words have been committed to describing the Internet, but in computer terms, it's nothing more than a giant network of networks that links up computers by using a common computer language called the Transmission Control Protocol/Internet Protocol (TCP/IP for short.) The Internet is unregulated (so far), uncontrolled (so far) and free to use (so far.)

There are advisory bodies that exist to centralize the cooperative decisions that keep the network running but now, no laws yet exist specifically to regulate the Internet (though many are now wending their way through the legislatures and courts of the United States and are being considered by other governments throughout the world.) No one "owns" the Internet although Internet traffic travels over telephone lines once owned by the U.S. Government.

A Client-Server Network

The Internet is an immense *client-server* network. That's a type of network in which a local computer (the "client") accesses some useful data on another computer (the "server"). The client asks the server for a file and a copy of the requested file is sent to the client computer.

TCP/IP

Perhaps the most difficult technical concept to understand for computer non-experts is packet-switching. There are two ways to operate a network (of telephones or computers or a combination of both) and that is *circuit switched* and *packet switched*.

Circuit switching is familiar as plain old telephone service. I dial a telephone number, you answer and for the duration of that call, the line connecting us is exclusively ours. Except in case of emergency, no one else can use or interrupt that circuit. A circuit connection is an excellent way to carry voice transmissions: I talk, you talk, I talk again and so forth. In a voice call, there is almost always a signal transmitting across the line.

When it comes to transmitting data, however, packet switching is a much more efficient method. In packet switching, the data being sent is first chopped up into tiny electronic "packets." Like a conventional envelope in the real world, that piece of data contains a destination address, a return address, some correction codes and an indication of where that little piece of data fits with the other little pieces of data that comprise the message. An e-mail message or Web page may be chopped into hundreds of thousands or even millions of these packets and dispatched across the network.

Along the network, the packets are read by computers known as routers. Routers maintain lists of the address of every computer connected to the Internet and send the packets along the most efficient path to the destination according to the amount of traffic on the network. In the same way that two drivers can both arrive at Miami from New York via very different routes: one drives straight down Interstate 95 and the other goes through Columbus, OH, St. Louis, MO, Dallas, TX, and Tallahassee, FL -- they both eventually arrive at the same destination.

Once all the packets that comprise the sent message arrive together, they are reconstituted (or *compiled*, to use the Internet term for it) and the message is again made comprehensible.

Packet switching is ideal for data transmission because computers send *bursts* of information. Unlike a phone conversation between humans in which conversation is continuously exchanged, computers usually send a lot of information in short bursts. In between bursts, there is no need for the computers to be connected to one another. Take that New York to Miami metaphor: in circuit switching, Interstate 95 would be used by only one car at a time. No other cars could travel along the highway until that one car was finished with its journey.

In reality, Interstate 95 is more like a packet-switched network. Many cars with different origins and different destinations can use the highway when they need it, for that part of the journey that gets them closer to their destination. The drivers of the car, knowing where they want to go; they can sort themselves out.

So too with packet switching. The packet address, critical to the functioning of the network, is analogous to the driver's destination. Packets with many different destinations and origins travel the paths of the Internet together and are sorted out at the end. Think of the Internet as a fantastically large tree whose leaves are individual computers, who can send messages to any other leaf on the tree -- and even to leaves growing on other trees -- and you've got a clear picture of how the network operates.

Connecting to the Internet

To connect to the Internet, it's necessary to have an account with an Internet Service Provider (ISP) and a means of accessing that provider. Precisely which level of Internet service is adequate depends on the size of your organization and on the expected amount of Internet use. For solo practitioners who need Internet access only for e-mail and for occasional Web browsing, an ordinary dial-up account with a local ISP using a 28,800 bps modem is more than adequate. For a large law firm of more than 350 attorneys who will be using the Internet around the clock for data retrieval, large-scale e-mail applications and transmission of data, dedicated access across a high-speed connection to a national service provider is a more sensible solution. In between these two extremes come many choices that depend entirely on budget and quantity of use.

To connect to the Internet, the minimum requisites are a computer running a GUI such as Windows 3.1 or Macintosh and a modem capable of data throughput of 14,400 bps. Slower modems are not practical for Internet access. Preferable are 28,000 or the latest generation 56,000 bps modems. For dial-up connections, it's necessary to have a TCP/IP "stack" -- this allows the digital packets created by your computer to travel across the local telephone company's analog (non-digital) phone lines. Windows 95 users have this type of stack already installed in *Dial-Up Networking*. Virtually all new communications software offers a similar stack. For older machines, the most popular TCP/IP stack is *Trumpet WinSock*, available from *http://www.trumpet.com/ dusa.htm* Also required is browser software such as Netscape Navigator or Internet Explorer and some additional Internet software for reading network news, e-mail and for performing other specialized online tasks.

Selecting an Internet Service Provider

The most important part of Internet access is selecting an Internet Service Provider. All across the nation, ISPs have sprung up seemingly overnight. To make shopping around for an ISP easier, visit someone already equipped with Internet and look around *The List* at *http://thelist.com* This Web site is a searchable collection of all known Internet Service Providers. It provides details on the services each of them offers, prices, contact information and other information to make comparison shopping online easy and quick.

What should you look for in an ISP?

First is connection reliability. For dial-up accounts, that means the provider should have no more than 8 or 10 subscribers per modem. Any more users than that per modem risks chronic busy signals. Ask the ISP for its points-of-presence. These are local phone numbers in surrounding geographic areas that will connect to the ISP so that dial-up access is practical when traveling within 100 to 200 miles or more from the local area. A good ISP will provide many local points of presence. Subscribers with dedicated, high-speed connections should ask about remote access and multiple user network licensing; the network administrator should be able to negotiate with an ISP to make a compatible connection.

Technical support ideally should be available around the clock, but a good service provider at least will have a human being available to answer technical questions until 9:00 or 10:00 at night and during regular business hours. The ISP should be willing to help with configuration problems, technical setups and advise on storage requirements for mail and Web site hosts. Some provide site design services, other do not. Ask about storage costs if you plan to create a home page and Web site that will be stored on your ISP's machine. A Web site does not have to be installed at the same ISP who hosts you ordinary Internet access, but there is usually a package rate for combining host services and regular Internet access.

Find an ISP the same way you would any other professional service: ask around for recommendations from others who already have access. Review the ads in the local press. Ask a prospective ISP to refer you to some of their satisfied customers and ask about what their plans for upgrades are.

Finally, law professionals should be aware that ISPs, for technical reasons, must have access to all your files maintained on their server including e-mail, confidential or not. Ask about security considerations, who will have access to e-mail files and whether there is some notification when your files are accessed by the ISP's staff.

As more ISPs get into the business, prices are falling. It's a buyer's market for Internet services and safe, reliable and fast access is very affordable for even the smallest law office.

Levels of Connection

In the Internet world, straightforward rules are hard to come by, here's one exception: always equip yourself with the fastest hardware you can afford. Get the fastest processor, the biggest machine and most importantly, the highest bps connection possible.

Internet connections fall into two categories, dial-up and dedicated. Home users and small offices will likely use dial-up connections. Larger firms, government agencies, corporations and other larger entities will require the speed and performance offered by dedicated lines. Of course, with each increase in access speed, cost increases commensurately. When it comes to anything associated with computers, faster is always better.

Speed, however, is a valuable commodity and consequently comes at additional cost. Of critical concern when using the Internet is the data throughput or bandwidth: both terms refer to the amount of data that can be delivered or sent from a terminal across the network in given time, usually measured in bits per second (bps).

DIAL-UP CONNECTIONS

Dial-up connections require a conventional modem to access the Internet Service Provider over ordinary telephone lines. The minimum modem speed for Internet access is 14,400 bps; anything slower than that is impractical for Internet purposes. A modem speed of 28,800 bps was once considered to be the absolute speed limit for data transfers across analog telephone lines; thanks to new compression software, conventional modems promising 56,800 bps data speeds are now commercially available. The higher speed modems are indeed fast and reliable and should be the first choice for dial-up connectivity.

To take advantage of these higher speed modems, subscribe to either a PPP (Point-to-Point Protocol) or a SLIP (Serial Line Internet Protocol) account from an Internet Service Provider. PPP is the new standard service for dial-up accounts and has all but replaced SLIP connections. For the hardy computer user, a simple shell account operating as a line command shell account -- meaning no graphics -- is educational and challenging and, for personal accounts, a good backup system for reading plain e-mail, listservs and newsgroups. Shell accounts are the most inexpensive accounts of all but they are rudimentary and do not offer even a fraction of the functionality of a PPP or SLIP account. For computer enthusiasts, however, shell accounts are fun (fun, that is, if typing strange UNIX commands counts as recreation where you come from.)

ISDN

The next major improvement to dial up connectivity is ISDN service. ISDN is the acronym for Integrated Services Digital Network and is the next great leap to high-speed access that is practical for home or small office use. ISDN presents some significant problems in setup and price and should be carefully considered in light of anticipated Internet use. Heavy users of the Internet will benefit from ISDN's increased speed more than the occasional user who can get excellent service from simple modem connections. Researchers who will be spending more than three hours a day looking at Web sites, chatting or using newsgroups should be connecting to the Web over an ISDN connection.

In technical terms, ISDN is comprised of three telephone lines that each carry separate communications. These separate channels, two "B" channels that carry voice or data and a "D" channel that sets up a call (but can also carry data) allow for effective data throughput approaching or exceeding 168,000 bps.

The speed of ISDN is very welcome, but ISDN suffers from some serious short-comings. Not all ISPs offer ISDN connectivity nor do all local telephone companies supply ISDN service to their customers; check with both an ISP and the local phone company to find out what is available in your area. Obtaining an ISDN account with the phone company can cost more than $350 for the initial installation and monthly bills for service can average more than $150 (as compared to less than $30 per month for a simple 28,800 bps modem connection over an ordinary analog phone line.)

Access to ISDN also requires a terminal adapter (sometimes referred to incorrectly even by its manufacturers as a "modem") that allows a computer to transmit and receive data over the ISDN circuit. Until Motorola introduced its BitSURFR Pro EZ, configuring the terminal adapter was a bearish, hair-pulling task that could try the patience of even the most computer-happy nerd. Newer terminal adapters are taking some of the difficulty out of installation by offering plug-and-play configuration and setup.

ISDN is a very complicated system that can dramatically improve Internet surf speeds. For more information on ISDN services, ask the local phone company for its promotional material or review PacBell's *ISDN User's Guide* at *http://www.pacbell.com/products/business/fastrak/networking/isdn/info/isdn-guide/index.html* which offers a clear, jargon-free tutorial on the subject.

DEDICATED CONNECTIONS

For larger firms and multiple-user access, dedicated Internet access is the most sensible solution. Dedicated access means that computer terminals (or, more accurately, the local area network to which they are attached) are always connected to the Internet; there is no need to establish a connection by dialing up an Internet Service Provider each time an Internet session is required. Dedicated connections are, in ascending order of data speed and complexity: *56K, frame relay, fractional T-1, T-1* and *T-3*. Connections at these speeds are usually established and maintained by network administrators and the details of how they are set up and operate are not of concern to the average researcher. Data throughput ranges from the eponymous 56,000 bps for 56K connections to more than 4.5 million bps for T-3 lines which are used by massive corporations and universities to run their trunk networks serving tens of thousands of end users.

On the horizon are experimental connection protocols that promiseto make Internet access blazingly fast at inexpensive prices. ADSL, X.25, cable modems and wireless Internet connections via satellite all loom as practical solutions to the problem of moving bandwidth-hungry Internet applications like videoteleconferencing and 3-D videos between client and server. They're still not practical in today's marketplace but may soon become the preferred methods of connection as they replace today's fairly crude connection options with their superior speed and presumably cheaper prices.

The Internet and Legal Research

The Internet does two things extremely well. It is a great way to communicate and it is a revolutionary way to retrieve information. Those two functions provide the legal researcher with a unique set of powerful tools that put the expertise of thousands of professionals and organizations at the desktop. Best of all, the Internet is drastically inexpensive.

As the Internet becomes a ubiquitous presence in offices worldwide, its value as a channel for connecting to people or information increases as well.

The essence of legal research is not so much knowing specific law materials but more knowing how to find those materials. It's not necessary to commit to memory the exact wording of the New Hampshire law against drunk driving so long as one knows where to find that language when necessary.

When the age of computer-assisted legal research (CALR) was born in the early 1980s, commercial networks emerged as the middlemen in the information industry. Online services such as Westlaw and Lexis obtained public domain materials from government agencies such as the courts, state and federal agencies and legislatures. Because personal computers were still rare and few mainframes existed to handle the traffic, these services supplied leased equipment to their customers: researchers of a certain age will remember those sleek, Darth Vader-like UBIQ terminals from Lexis and the pale blue WALT terminals from Westlaw.

Since CALR was first introduced, some profound changes occurred in the law office and in American offices generally. In-house networks connecting powerful desktop computers became standard in all but the smallest offices. This sudden and drastic appearance of fast networked computers in law firms, corporations, government agencies and universities created an immense universe of wired professionals, creating an infrastructure that would be ideal for advanced networking tools.

Within the same span of years, the typewriter became obsolete and the word processor rose to prominence. Everywhere, documents were created electronically and stored on servers. Other document transmittal devices like fax machines, optical character readers and overnight delivery all exist to convert paper-based documents into electronic ones. But these are stop-gap technologies. For all practical purposes, all documents are created electronically and can be very easily transmitted across networks.

Internet, Intranet and Extranet

Innovations on the Internet come in waves; "old" technology frequently is pressed into service for new uses unforeseen by the technology's early designers. Within a year of two of the Web's momentous "Big Bang," computer administrators around the world realized that the same software that made the Internet work so well could also work just as well on the in-house network. Thus was born the second-wave application of Internet technology known as the *Intranet*. Intranet is the term-of-art for a computer network within a corporation or law firm that incorporates many Internet-style protocols such as Web-based information and e-mail. Using an Intranet, network users can enjoy the elegance and ease of hypertext linking on their own local area networks as they do on the much larger Internet.

The seeds of an Intranet are already in place in many law firms: internal e-mail systems and shared document systems such as Lotus Notes or PC Docs lie at the heart of Intranets. The Intranet takes local area networking one step further: it combines in-house resources with links to the greater world, providing seamless, desktop access to both local resources like the firm's law library, staff directory or client database and external resources like links to the Library of Congress, the state code or legal news from *Law Journal EXTRA!* The Intranet is the Internet on a law firm's own network.

The Intranet is a fascinating and complex topic in itself; an entire book may be written on building and maintaining an Intranet itself and it is well beyond the scope of this book to explore all the exciting possibilities the Intranet offers the legal researcher. For more information on the Intranet and links to additional Intranet resources, refer to *http://www.intrack.com/intranet/ifaq.shtml*

The third wave of new networking is the Extranet, a term coined by Netscape Communications executives Jim Barksdale and Mark Andreesen to describe the extension of a firm's Intranet to its clients, customers, satellite offices or other geographically distant network users. At a law firm, extranets are ideal for disseminating work product to clients, for providing satellite offices with immediate information at very little cost and extending access to the firm's information resources to colleagues and co-counsel. For additional information about extranets, see *http://www.intrack.com/intranet/extra.shtml*

Reliability

Of great concern to the legal researcher are the issues of reliability and timeliness. There are no hard rules, only heuristic devices, to what is and what is not reliable on the Internet. Reliability depends on common sense and judgment; timeliness depends on the server. The legal researcher will discover that much of the information of professional interest is produced by official sources which produce information that can be confidently relied upon. A Senate bill from the Thomas server, the text of a statute from

Texas or a court opinion from the Third Circuit are all trustworthy. The information is published by reputable sources and the servers on which the materials is archived are professionally and presumably equipped with enough security to prevent vandals from tainting the text.

There are thousands of reliable Web sites from government agencies at the local, state, federal and international level and thousands more that are produced by professional news bureaus, non-profit organizations, educational institutes, private law firms and other entities that have no motive to publicly distribute erroneous or inaccurate information. That's not to say that mistakes don't creep onto the Internet. Like information in the printed world, information obtained online should be accorded the same degree of respectful skepticism; weigh the source and the bias. Factual material from official sources can be used reliably; of course, for critical applications, always defer to the conventionally recognized official sources: reporter, statute, court decision or other authority.

The problems of reliability are more acute the further away from official reports that the Web becomes. The text of a bill downloaded from the Library of Congress is reliable; the same text, downloaded from Joey Pre-Law's Super Cool Web Site and Internet Party Room is not. Judge the material by the source. There is no quality control on the Internet and there is no marketing department to complain to if downloaded material turns out to be bogus. Until the time comes when Web sites are warranted to be accurate and the Webmasters stand behind their service in some meaningful and enforceable way, be wary of any non-official information.

Practical Changes

The advent of the Internet is already changing certain legal traditions. As electronic reports of court decisions becomes standard, the traditional citing standards are changing. Since the 19th Century, West Publishing's citation system has been recognized as the official cites for case citation. The Internet era is breaking West's virtual monopoly on the citing system by providing a practical means of vendor-neutral citation. (Find details on vendor-neutral citation from the Wisconsin State Bar Web site at *http://www.wisbar.org/bar/sbcite.html*) The *Bluebook*, the standard reference work on formal legal citation, recognizes that many resources on the Internet will be cited in briefs and other legal writings and have proposed standard citation rules for referring to Internet-based materials.

Courts have been very slow to adopt new technologies in litigation but there are signs that the electronic revolution will be coming to American courts very soon. Dockets sheets and electronic document submission are now being tested on an experimental basis at some Federal courts, notably the Bankruptcy Court in the Second Circuit in New York and the day of the brief written in hypertext markup language is at hand. (See an exciting example of an HTML brief submitted to the Supreme Court in the case *ACLU v. Reno* at *http://www.shsl.com/internet/186619.html*

About the Internet Addresses Used in this Book

Throughout the book, thousands of URLs are reprinted. Because URLs contain periods -- now known universally as "dots" -- which are critical elements in creating valid Internet addresses, a new rule in copy editing was required. Punctuation such as a comma to set off a serial item or dependent clause or a period to end a sentence has been deleted to prevent ambiguity. As a rule, URLs never end with a period and never contain commas. But to be on the safe side, and to prevent any misunderstandings in the construction of URLs, all sentences in this book that end with the citation to a URL do not end with periods but rather with the URL set in italics and a single space to set the sentence off from the following one. All URLs were valid and operating at the time of writing in early 1997. Each one was tested twice for validity and accuracy. However, addresses and resources can change at a moment's notice and the continued accuracy of any URL cannot be guaranteed.

The Absolute Rule of the Internet

There is only one thing that can be said about the Internet with absolute certainty. Always keep that in mind when using the network:

Things change.

Communication Protocols

COMMUNICATION PROTOCOLS

Introduction

As revolutions go, the electronic takeover of the law office was a quiet one. Remarkable new tools like videotapes, fax machines and teleconferencing insinuated themselves into the law practice with a minimum of fanfare.

Now, after an initial flush of noisy excitement and an equal measure of puzzlement, electronic mail and the Internet are establishing themselves as standard tools in the average law office. Electronic mail is not a new technology -- it's been around in one form or another for more than 20 years -- but thanks to the Internet, e-mail is turning into one of the most extraordinary additions to the law office since the introduction of carbon paper put entire brigades of law scriveners on the unemployment line.

In a quiet way, the communications capabilities the Internet offers the legal professional continues to make dramatic changes to everyday working life. Leading the way are the *communications protocols* that connect people with each other and are changing the way we communicate with one another. Chief among these protocols is ordinary electronic mail. As useful as e-mail is, the Internet now has spawned some innovative e-mail hybrids that are exciting and innovative news tools that provide the legal researcher with genuinely new tools to locate information. These new protocols, each a variation on e-mail basic messaging capability are the *listserv, Usenet* and *Internet Relay Chat*. Each of these new protocols has a special place in the law firm and each of them extends the researcher's ability to retrieve fast, accurate and inexpensive information.

Electronic Mail

Electronic mail is now so common that it's easy to overlook what a powerful tool it actually is. But think for a moment of what e-mail can do. With e-mail, it's possible to compose a message and send it anywhere on earth in less than a second. That message can be sent to one person or ten or a million people simultaneously. What's more, sending that message costs practically nothing. E-mail is easy to use and very reliable. Electronic mail has shrunk the globe, rejuvenated the lost art of letter writing and made sending a message as simple as pushing a button.

E-mail is the most popular feature of the Internet. Even in the teeth of the informational hurricane of the WorldWideWeb, more than half the traffic traveling on the Internet is e-mail. E-mail access is the leading reason people sign up for Internet accounts. And according to recent surveys of Internet users, e-mail is popular precisely because it is fast, cheap and accurate.

Why is Internet e-mail so popular? Sending e-mail across the Internet permits otherwise incompatible e-mail systems to exchange messages with each other. Before the widespread adoption of the Internet protocol offered a practical solution to connecting proprietary e-mail systems, one vendor's e-mail system could not work with another. Thanks to the Internet and its open architecture, corporations, government agencies, universities and individuals can connect to each other seamlessly, no matter what e-mail system is installed locally. That meant that thousands of networks could connect with each other using the same language. It was major step to wiring up the nation's offices and businesses.

If only for its e-mail capability, the Internet would stand as an one of the Twentieth Century's most important inventions, as revolutionary in its way as the invention of the television, the personal computer or the airplane.

Electronic mail in its simplest form, that is, one-on-one communication between individuals, is certainly a useful tool whose benefits are obvious at a glance: for both professional and personal use, e-mail is faster than a phone call; recipients can look at and respond to e-mail at their leisure; plus a record is kept of e-mail transmissions. And until the day arrives when a meter is running on the number of data packets that flow between two points, sending e-mail across the Internet still costs nothing. Because e-mail is free, no thought is given to sending e-mail between New York and Hong Kong or Los Angeles and Paris. That makes e-mail use informal, timely and practical.

As wonderful as e-mail is for simple messaging, more exciting still are new, e-mail-based applications.

The most important feature of e-mail is its ability to *attach* documents electronically. Thanks to the *attachment* feature, standard on all current e-mail software, Internet e-mail pulls double duty as a *de facto* global document delivery service. Most documents in a law office are created electronically using word processing programs or desktop publishing software. With the click of a mouse, electronic documents can be piggybacked with an e-mail message and travel across the same Internet lines with the same speed and accuracy as e-mail and also at no additional cost. The days of paying large sums to document delivery services to carry pieces of paper on an airplane are drawing to a close because the important material -- namely text and pictures -- can be sent instantly for free to the recipients.

In addition to the important services of messaging and document delivery are the fascinating new protocols based on electronic messaging. E-mail has led to the listserv, the newsgroup and in a certain way, to the *chat room*. Because of their importance to the legal researcher, these e-mail based Internet inventions are discussed at length; as we'll see, the listserv and Usenet are some of the most useful features of the Internet for the legal researcher because they make instant communication with many others practical.

Taken as a whole, e-mail-based communication across the Internet is a dazzling, not-to-be missed way of reaching out to the world from the comfort of a computer terminal.

In the age of the Internet, everyone should have access to electronic mail. It deserves a place in every office because it is as important to everyday work as the telephone and the word processor.

How Electronic Mail Works

Internet e-mail relies on two primary protocols, SMTP and POP. SMTP is an acronym for *Simple Mail Transport Protocol* and is the technical standard by which e-mail messages are routed from a server to another *host* computer across the network.

Like all data transmitted across the Internet, e-mail messages are transmitted as data packets. These packets each contain addressee information, return addresses and a small piece of the message, like a real-world letter in a paper envelope. After a single e-mail message is chopped up electronically into many little addressed pieces they are then dispatched across the network and reassembled at the receiving end.

The individual packets that make up an e-mail message may take different paths to arrive at the destination but thanks to modern routers, computers which speed these packets to their destinations, they usually arrive undamaged in their entirety. They are then reliably reassembled and the e-mail message made whole again. Once all the packets have arrived and the e-mail message is completely received, it is stored on the host (recipient) computer until it is downloaded from the host by the addressee using POP, the *Post Office Protocol*.

Getting e-mail from the Internet using the Post Office Protocol is like retrieving conventional mail ("snail mail" to experienced e-mailers) from a rural post office. The recipient accesses the mail host from the Internet Service Provider and downloads it to a local mail box where it can then be read. In the electronic age, the recipient doesn't have to drive through snow, sleet and washed-out roads to get a letter; the software does all the dirty work.

E-mail software can be configured to leave e-mail messages on the server, which is useful when accessing the same mail account from two different places such as from home and the office. Usually mail is downloaded from the server to the client and then erased from the mail host. The choice of how e-mail is handled is controlled in the setup and configuration, discussed later in this chapter.

Security Considerations

Ordinarily, the details of how e-mail travels across the network is primarily a purely technical concern. But in light of the need for the legal researcher to keep client confidences private and because of the constraints of ethical rules bearing on attorney-client relationships, e-mail security is a serious issue for law firms using the public pathways of the Internet to carry private messages.

When dealing with sensitive or confidential materials, it's necessary to take precautions to protect that information. The weakest link in the security chain is the host computer, meaning your Internet Service Provider (ISP). The ISP can access your mail at any time in order to maintain their servers and the internal structure of their directories and files. Employees of ISPs therefore can access any subscriber's account at any time and snoop through e-mail residing on the host computer. Because unscrupulous vendors do exist, it's a good idea to sign confidentiality agreements with vendors as part of a service contract so that there is some recourse in the event of accidental or deliberate breach of e-mail confidence by the ISP.

Most security breaches occur locally when sensitive e-mail or attached documents is accessible on an unprotected computer in the office. Terminals and networks carrying sensitive data should be password protected to prevent unauthorized receipt of private messages and sensible precautions used to prevent eavesdroppers from seeing confidential information on the screen, the printer or in a publicly accessible e-mail file.

Theoretically, unencrypted mail can be intercepted almost at any point in its journey between sender and recipient as it travels through the routers installed throughout the Internet. Such intercepts, known as *packet sniffing*, are extremely rare, however. A dedicated electronic thief would need to take pains to steal one's e-mail, however, and the deliberate receipt of someone's else's e-mail while in transit is rare.

The best way to keep e-mail private while in transit is to use encryption software like PGP (Pretty Good Privacy) or a commercial encryption software program like Puffer. Attached documents can be encrypted. The encryption doesn't have to be anything fancy. Documents can be password-encoded with conventional word processing password codes. (Of course, the recipient will need to know the appropriate password in order to decode the received documents.)

Security concerns are sometimes overblown but taking a simple, common sense approach to encrypting data is generally sufficient to insure safe e-mail.

E-Mail Client Software

To send and receive e-mail, client software that can operate on the Internet is required. The latest generation of Web browsers are equipped with built-in e-mail functionality, but software specially designed for e-mail is still available.

For the casual e-mail user, the software that comes with Netscape Navigator, Internet Explorer or America Online is just fine and should provide all the functionality required. High-volume e-mail users, however, will benefit from the advanced features of dedicated e-mail software.

Dedicated E-Mail Software

The most popular e-mail software programs are Eudora and PegasusMail and they are both widely used. Eudora and PegasusMail are both excellent and offer advanced filters, sophisticated folder management features and technical support.

Eudora, so named because its designer was reading a book by Eudora Welty at the time he was tinkering with the software, is available in two flavors. Install it as stripped-down freeware or as a fully-featured commercial release. The commercial software features spell checker, multiple signature files and coding and uncoding for attachments. For more information on Eudora, refer to the designer's home page at *http://www.eudora.com*

PegasusMail is freeware. To download the software and see all its features in action, including its ability to run multiple lists, visit the Pegasus Web site at *http://www.pegasus.usa.com*

For a lengthy list of other e-mail programs, including reviews and links for downloading, head to Consummate Winsock Apps page at *http://www.stroud.com* or *http://cws.iworld.com*

Bundled e-mail

As the Web browsers of choice of professional researchers, we'll focus on the e-mail software bundled with Netscape Navigator and Internet Explorer. Institutional users with networked e-mail services such as **cc:mail, MCIMail** or other networked services will use whatever e-mail is provided by the network administrators; much of the configuration is already completed by the systems operators. Consult the appropriate technical support staff member for help with networked e-mail software.

CONFIGURING NETSCAPE E-MAIL

No matter which e-mail software is used, it's necessary to configure the software. Configuration is a one-time process.

Internet Explorer 3.0 and America Online users will have installation wizards which guide new users through the configuration process. (A wizard is setup software that prompts the user for a response; the user then fills in the blank with the necessary information.) Wizards require no training: launch them by clicking on the *Mail* button and answer the questions as they pop up. Among the things you'll need to know are your IP address, mail host name and your own e-mail address. Ask your Internet Service Provider for these values -- America Online customers will have this information already filled in for them -- and keep it handy for the setup process.

Netscape users will find the configuration process a little more complicated but not especially challenging. To start, find the configuration menus by clicking on **Options | Mail and News Preferences.**

APPEARANCE

These controls define how mail will be displayed on-screen. Select from a choice of fonts, choose how text from older e-mail messages will be treated and pick an e-mail client. *Pane layout* tells Netscape how to display the three-panel e-mail screen. The display panes are movable. To re-size a pane, place the cursor on the line dividing the panes. The cursor turns into a double line. Hold the right button down on the mouse and slide the divider to adjust the size of an individual pane.

COMPOSITION

To set the technical parameters for how messages are exchanged, use these settings. Select "Allow 8-bit" to permit the widest range of e-mail readers to read outgoing mail. MIME-compliant messages interpret different characters; if your recipient reports receipt of garbled messages, try setting MIME-compliant selection.

Copies of all outgoing messages can be sent, via e-mail, to another address if so desired, to a supervisor, say, or to a colleague who needs to review all outgoing e-mail. Be sure to designate a file for outgoing messages so that a copy is always kept of everything sent.

Last, click on the box to *Automatically quote original message when replying.* That way, all your recipients will know which message you are responding to when you write back.

SERVERS

For these settings, it's necessary to know your e-mail address. The *outgoing mail (SMTP) server* is the mail host at your Internet Service Provider. It is usually the domain name of your ISP, which is the name to the right of the @ sign in your e-mail address. Sometimes the ISP calls their server *mail.domainname* or *mailhost.domainname*. Check with your ISP for the appropriate value.

Incoming Mail (POP3) Server: is your e-mail address.

POP3 User Name: is your e-mail name to the left of the @ sign in your e-mail address.

Mail directory can be any directory you designate.

Maximum message size: should be "none" unless you have a very old and memory-challenged computer.

Messages are copied from the server to the local disk, then: Pick *Removed from the server* if you download messages from the server to the same computer all the time. If you download messages from the same server from different computers, say at the office and at home, select *Left on server.* Some ISPs charge for storage of a certain number of megabytes of e-mail. Check with the provider for storage policy.

Check for mail: every ten minutes. Selecting *Never* requires asking the server for new mail manually.

IDENTITY

By default, e-mail messages carry a great deal of identifying information and also automate the response process by your recipient. Set the following values:

Your Name is your real name.

Your e-mail is your e-mail address.

Reply to Address: leave blank unless you want messages to be sent to an e-mail address other than the one indicated.

Your organization: is the name of your law firm, institution or other organizational name. It's optional.

Signature file is a small text file that can be appended to every outgoing message and acts like electronic letterhead. See below.

ORGANIZATION

Select *Remember Mail Password* so that it's not necessary to type a password every time e-mail is accessed. Leave it blank if others have access to the same computer.

Select the *Thread Mail Messages* so that messages concerning the same subject are automatically related to each other.

Sort Mail by whatever is the most convenient; that's usually *date* but the preference is strictly personal.

Signature Files

The electronic equivalent of letterhead or personal stationary is the *signature file*, a small text file that can be added to every e-mail message. Most signature files (known colloquially as *.sig files*) contain the same information that is routinely contained in printed letterhead: firm name, mailing address, telephone number, e-mail and Web site URL.

By Internet custom, the signature file also usually contains a disclaimer of professional responsibility such as *Opinions expressed in this message do not constitute legal advice nor create an attorney-client relationship.* It's also customary to add a witty slogan or quote to the .sig file. For more guidance on designing a .sig file, see *http://www.useful.com/quick/sigfile.htm* or look at the collection of .sig files from Vicki Robinson at *http://www.pcola.gulf.net/~vbraun/sigs/*

When using e-mail for professional purposes, treat a signature file with the same degree of gravity that would be accorded to a printed letter. E-mail doesn't have fancy typesetting or heavy bond paper to convey a crisp, professional image but a considered choice of signature file can. Keep the signature file, brief (four lines or less) and graphics free, to speed downloading by recipients. A simple ASCII file like this is fine:

Ms. Lisa Kearns, Esq.
ATTORNEY-AT-LAW
123 Hoders Lane, Port Radium, ID 90909
(456) 555-6789

HTML Signature files

Before e-mail software capable of displaying HTML code was common, *.sig* files were composed of ASCII text. With HTML-enabled e-mail clients gaining in popularity, *.sig* files now contain URLs that light up with full-color logos, hypertext links or even audio and video files. But until the entire world has upgraded to the high-tech software, stick with the time-tested, low-tech ASCII .sig file.

Creating an E-Mail Message

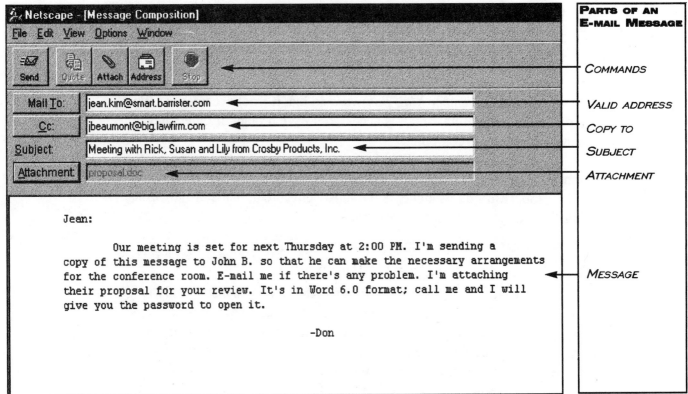

Electronic mail messaging has become so refined that sending an e-mail message is simply a matter of filling in the blanks. E-mail novices can learn how to create and send messages in less then twenty minutes once the e-mail software is properly installed and configured. Once the message has been composed and any necessary attachments included, proofread the message and send it on its way by clicking the **send** button.

E-mail travels the globe instantaneously. Barring major traffic problems on the Internet backbone or slowdowns at the recipients' server due to firewalls, virus checking or other security slow-up, an e-mail message reaches its destination quicker than any other means of written communication. At times, e-mail even moves faster than spoken language.

Receiving an E-Mail Message

E-mail is a two-way street. When an incoming message arrives, a number of things can be done with it. The message can be read and deleted or printed on an attached printer. It can be dispatched to a designated folder. It can be immediately replied to or answered at a later time.

The message can also be forwarded to one or more recipients. Message forwarding is both boon and bane. Messages can and do circle the globe in minutes. (Humorous e-mail messages travel even faster; jokey e-mail messages multiply faster than amoebas in a Petri dish.)

Because e-mail can be forwarded and re-distributed without the sender's knowledge or consent, consider every e-mail message to be a permanent message. It never completely disappears and can, in fact, live on indefinitely. Never e-mail a message that may cause embarrassment or regret in the future when it reappears.

Attaching Documents

After messaging, the most important use of basic electronic mail is to send and receive files as attachments. Those files can be documents in the form of word processing files, HTML files, audio files or any other format a computer is capable of creating.

Present-day document distribution services such as the U.S. Post Office, Federal Express and even fax machines exist to move *paper-bound* words and pictures from one point to another. All these services were created because information -- words and pictures -- is ordinarily stored on paper. Today, the same information is most often created and stored electronically and it can be transported across digital networks. Anything that can be digitized can be transported.

In the past, it was almost impossible to exchange e-mail, let alone documents, between proprietary e-mail systems because of system incompatibility. The use of e-mail for document distribution was limited to those senders and recipients who were attached to the same systems. But now, using the common TCP/IP platform of the Internet, the problems associated with compatibility have been overcome. Internet file attachment is not only practical, it is creating an entirely new way of sending documents from one point to another.

Electronic document distribution works seamlessly. Materials such as briefs, memoranda, affidavits and other legal writings are now routinely created in electronic form by computerized word processing software. Because of that, it's not necessary ever to create a paper copy.

All e-mail software has an *attach* feature. Click on the button or file command for "attach" and a pop-up menu appears to prompt for the requested file. Merely select the appropriate file and send it as one would an ordinary e-mail message. Advanced e-mail software also permits HTML files and URLs to be sent as well as ordinary document files.

There is no simpler or cheaper way to distribute documents and it's likely that in the future, most documents -- from utility bills and contract drafts to love letters and dunning notices -- will be sent via the Internet.

Address Books and Nicknames

As e-mail proliferates, e-mail addresses begin to accumulate too. Like an unwieldy collection of telephone numbers that require a Rolodex to manage, it's easy to collect an unmanageably large number of e-mail addresses too. To alleviate e-mail overload, use some of the e-mail management tools available with all e-mail client software.

The *address book* is the place to store e-mail addresses. To make typing addresses even easier, create *nicknames* for commonly used addresses. Create a nickname that's easy to remember. For instance, if you frequently send e-mail to a client named *eleanor.macintosh@worldwide.globalcorp.com*, create a nickname like "Ellie." That will satisfy the e-mail software's need for a valid address and save lots of typing.

Mailing lists can be created so that a single message can be sent to multiple recipients by grouping them under a single nickname. To send a message to all twelve members of the accounting department, say, make a nickname called "accounting" and enter the e-mail addresses of all twelve individuals. Routing them all the same e-mail is a simple matter of entering the nickname "accounting."

Spam

One of the most common misuses of e-mail technology is *spamming*. Spamming is the practice of sending unsolicited e-mail messages to individual mailboxes, usually as a sales pitch. (Spam also refers to posts sent to Usenet newsgroups that ignore the stated subject matter of the newsgroup.)

The term "spam," according to Internet lore, derives from a Monty Python sketch in which every item on a restaurant menu contains large quantities of the canned meat product. While spam is most obnoxious in listservs and newsgroups, mass e-mailers can now bombard individual mailboxes with junk e-mail. The problem has become so acute that bills have been introduced in the 105th Congress to stem the flow of unsolicited commercial e-mail. (See *http://thomas.loc.gov*)

Until Congress acts, there is very little that can be done to stem spam. But the citizens of the Internet are a resourceful and self-policing bunch and a number of Web sites have been created to finger the most egregious culprits and hopefully shame them into decent behavior. One crusading anti-spam Web site is at *http://spam.abuse.net/spam//rogues.html* where a list of the worst spam offenders is published.

Why is spam so annoying? It wastes time, computer space and fills up private resources, namely one's own e-mailbox with unwanted and unsolicited messages, most of them worthless and some of them illegal.

Spam is usually a sales spiel, flogging some product or service of dubious merit. Like most junk mail, it can be discarded without a second thought; on (rare) occasion, there may even be something interesting in the unsolicited message. Most of the time however, spam is as welcome as ants at a picnic.

This message, typical of most spam, was distributed to millions of e-mailboxes on April 21, 1997:

WIN BIG ON GAME SHOWS LIKE WHEEL OF FORTUNE
(willie@tomboy.com, 4/14/97 3:50)
To: dunvegan@panix.com
From: willie@tomboy.com

WIN BIG ON GAME SHOWS LIKE WHEEL OF FORTUNE
BECOME A GAME SHOW CONTESTANT
RECEIVE WHEEL OF FORTUNE'S PHONE NUMBER

Millions of dollars in cash and merchandise will be given away on various tele vision game shows this year. All of us can easily identify with the contestants on these shows. People from all walks of life become instant national celebri ties with the possibility of achieving, within the incredibly short span of a few minutes' time, every person's dream of instant wealth.

You could be one of this year's lucky winners!

How do I know? Because I have been a contestant on three major network TV game shows! I won terrific merchandise and thousands of dollars in cash just on Wheel of Fortune. Plus much more on two other national network game shows. I was successful because I knew the secrets of how to present myself at an audition and be the kind of contestant the producer was seeking for his game show. I have given these tips to a few of my friends and they too have been selected and have won money and merchandise on game shows.

Netiquette

Spamming is a violation of the rules of *netiquette*, a previously unwritten but now standardized code of online conduct. Since the Internet is a public place with limited resources, some self-generated house rules are necessary to keep the louder neighbors in check. Entire books have been written on netiquette --a bit excessive for a simple topic -- but the appearance of such books indicates the need for a rules-free community like cyberspace to have some stop signs and traffic lights.

The essence of netiquette can be reduced to some simple common sense rules of polite behavior, modified to the unique communications medium of e-mail. They are:

- *Be brief.*
- *Don't flame unless a flame is absolutely warranted. A flame is a very angry e-mail message.*
- *Write clearly and stay on the topic.*
- *Don't spam.*
- *Typing in all caps is considered SHOUTING.*
- *Use smiley faces :-) and common Internet acronyms like*

BTW *(by the way) and* **IMHO** *(In my humble opinion)
sparingly.*
- Write informative headlines.

Managing E-Mail

Mailboxes fill up quickly but the vast majority of e-mail is ephemeral and can be discarded immediately after reading since they are of the "how-are-you-do-you-want-to-go-to-lunch?" variety. However, as e-mail grows in importance to the legal profession, sometimes e-mail messages represent important records of messages and documents sent and received. Keeping an ongoing account of what has been sent and received is a critical recording-keeping function that can be managed with the proper e-mail folders.

Every e-mail software program can be configured to keep a copy of all outgoing messages as described earlier. By default, every e-mail program features an *inbox* where incoming messages are placed, an *out-box* which keeps a record of messages sent and a *trash* file where unwanted messages can be sent. Trash files exist as a temporary holding area for messages that can still be retrieved if the message is needed later. Once the trash file is emptied, however, the message is effectively gone forever.

Users can create folders as the need arises to keep correspondence in a convenient single file for the same client or matter. For example, all e-mail exchanged in the matter of Jones v. Smythe can be moved to a folder called "Jones" thus creating an easy-to-use file system for electronic messages.

Liability and Discoverability of E-Mail

In today's offices, computerized word processing has all but replaced the typewriter. Those documents are stored in electronic media, either locally on a hard drive or floppy disc or on a network system. Every properly run computer network backs up its files every night to save data in case of a system of malfunction due to technical error, human error or deliberate mischief.

In practical terms, that means there is a copy of virtually every document created electronically unless the creator of the document has taken very deliberate steps to erase it. Even then, copies of e-mail can be recovered from back-up tapes and erased files. Erasure is not always permanent.

With the prevalence of e-mail, document production in litigation matters also includes electronic documents. The legal issues of the discovery of e-documents is well beyond the scope of this book but the legal researcher should be alert to the curious paradox that seemingly short-lived e-mail messages and electronically transmitted documents can actually live on forever in a server, computer or floppy disc without one's knowledge and without the consent of the parties to the message.

Closer to home are the ethical issues surrounding the use of electronic mail by attorneys. Among the concerns, especially for lawyers who use listservs, participate in Usenet newsgroups or respond to e-mail inquiries asking legal questions are attorney-client relationships and the limits of legal advertising. The issues are complicated and vary by jurisdiction. For an excellent source of ongoing inquiries into the power and pitfalls of e-mail use by attorneys is the **LegalEthics** Web site at *http://www.legalethics.com* The site features a superb library of articles on the legal issues affecting e-mail and discovery and the ethical problems these new technologies create for the practitioner.

For an interesting series of debates on the use of e-mail by attorneys, review the archives of the **net-lawyers** listserv. Find the archives at *http://eva.dc.lsoft.com/Archives/net-lawyers.html*

❑

LISTSERVS

Here's the scenario: it's 4:30 on a Friday after-
noon and with a court appearance pending on Monday morning, a senior
partner at a large New York City law firm calls the library to ask for a
copy of an article from a medical journal titled *Surgery*, published in
1912. Where, at that hour, under that kind of pressure, could a researcher
find such a rare item?

In days past, it would have been just about impossible to locate
the article. Tracking down such an obscure publication would have
required dozens of phone calls to area libraries, academic institutions and
a thorough search through arcane library catalogs.

What to do? The ideal solution would be to have some means of
requesting this article from librarians around the country to see who, if
any, had the old magazine in their collection.

Such a solution now exists, thanks to the Internet. It's the *listserv*,
a type of electronic mailing list that is transforming how lawyers and
other legal researchers communicate with other.

To find this particular article, the following message was posted
to a listserv called *lawlibref-l,* a mailing list created especially for law
librarians.

> *Greetings all:*
>
> *Does anyone have an article titled "Thrombosis" from the
> Summer 1912 edition of the journal "Surgery"? We need it for
> Monday and we'll be happy to pay the requisite fax and copying
> charges. TIA!* ["Thanks in advance"]
> -DM

In seconds, some 600 law librarians across the United States,
Canada and overseas who subscribe to *lawlibref-l* received that message
in their electronic mailboxes. Among the librarians receiving the request
was one who works at the medical school library at UCLA. After reading
the message, she found the article in her library and faxed a copy of it to
New York long before the close of business. Because of the listserv, it
took only 45 minutes, from the time the request for the article was e-
mailed until the article was received to track down this needle-in-a-
haystack article. The partner, needless to say, was thrilled and the listserv
demonstrated its unique ability to land messages in many laps very, very
quickly.

Of all the innovations produced by the Internet, none plays such
an important role for the legal researcher as the listserv. The unique abili-

ty of the listserv to broadcast a single e-mail message to a designated group of recipients represents a remarkably powerful and astoundingly fast way to deliver messages to select groups of like-minded people.

Named for the most common software program that operates these mailing lists, listservs permit the legal researcher to contact two, two hundred or two thousand other professionals by sending an e-mail message to a single centralized address. The listservs of greatest interest to the legal researcher are public mailing lists, which are open to anyone who wants to join. (Private lists require permission to join.)

As a rule, each mailing list exists to discuss a specific subject. There are hundreds of law-related listservs, which draw together subscribers who share an interest in that legal topic. There are listservs for intellectual property lawyers and lists for law librarians and lists for New Jersey attorneys. There are lists for experts and lists for law professors. Lists exist for law librarians and judges and eldercare professionals. Indeed, it is so easy and simple to set up and run a listserv that every legal topic now either has or shortly will have a list of its own, assuming that three or more people share an interest in the subject.

The listserv, by any measure, is one of the Internet's unqualified and unique success stories. Despite some quibbles, almost every listserv participant has found the listserv to be a useful, informative and timely way to communicate with colleagues very quickly.

A listserv is the place to ask questions of other professionals from around the nation and even the globe. It's not uncommon to find researchers from outside North America posting queries to U.S.-based listservs to ask about points of American law. The groups are ideal for airing opinions on current law topics or new legislation. They're a place to shoot the breeze, tell others about new discoveries, to complain about a new court decision or to talk shop with colleagues across the nation.

One of the most popular law-related listservs, and one that we'll examine in great depth, is called *net-lawyers*; it's turned into the leading forum for lawyers and other legal researchers to discuss how new technology, especially the Internet, affects the practice of law. Net-lawyers is like an electronic town square, where multiple conversations occur all the same time, but no one is drowned out by any other voice.

Whether the listserv is imagined as an online back fence or conference room without walls, it deserves a place in every legal researcher's quiver of research tools. It is an exciting technology made possible by the free-wheeling Internet. Content varies from list to list but the best lists are professionally run and informative. Listservs confer to its participants access to others who share their interests and as such put a body of experts whose brains can be picked on the receiving end of an e-mail message. Every legal researcher should subscribe to at least one listserv. They are invaluable tools.

And the best part of listservs? They're free.

How Listservs Work

Listservs, quite simply, are mailing lists. Software known as *list-server* or *majordomo* receives mail at a central server and then forwards that message -- "reflects" is the technical term -- to any mailbox that has asked the server to receive messages from a specified list. The messages are known as *posts* and the act of sending a message to a listserv is known as *posting*. To participate in listservs, all that's needed is e-mail software. The listserv software installed on the server takes care of the nuts and bolts of distributing messages.

Every listserv has two addresses. The first address is the address of the listserv software and that's the address where commands such as *subscribe* or *unsubscribe* are sent. The other address is the posting address and that is the address to which posts are mailed, once an individual has subscribed to the list.

Listservs all have very specific subject matters. Like newsletters in the print world, listservs are a topical forum intended to link up professionals who share the same professional or recreational interest. Therefore, each listserv clearly defines a topic: one list may be for the discussion of immigration law, one may just be for Ohio attorneys and another may address the emerging law of cyberspace. All that's needed to create a listserv is a host computer operating listserver, listprocessor or majordomo software and some interested subscribers.

Finding Law-Related Listservs

With all the hundreds of listservs in existence, finding a list to match a subject was once a burdensome project. But thanks to the hard work and diligence of law librarians throughout the nation, locating listservs for the discussion of legal topics is very simple; all the law-related listservs can be searched on Web-based indexes.

There are two primary Web sites containing searchable archives of listservs that permit the researcher to quickly and efficiently find details on law-related listservs. Both these sites operate in the same way. The entries usually describe the subject matter of the list and sets forth the list's intended audience. The necessary subscription address and the address to which posts should be made will accompany the description and there's usually an address where requests for additional information can be posted.

Law Lists
http://www.lib.uchicago.edu/~llou/lawlists/info.html

One of the earliest attempts to index all law-related discussion groups resulted in **Law Lists**, a canonical list of lists. Created and maintained by University of Chicago law librarian Lyonette Louis-Jacques, this comprehensive site not only describes in great detail how listservs work and how to use electronic discussion groups in routine legal research, it provides a keyword searchable form for looking up lists by subject matter. International in scope, Law Lists is available in French and Spanish translations.

To locate listservs, enter the subject matter in the search box that appears at *http://www.lib.uchicago.edu/cgi-bin/law-lists* For instance, to find discussion groups created to talk about intellectual property issues, type *intellectual property* in the search box.

First-time users of listservs are encouraged to read Louis-Jacques' *Introduction*, the best online tutorial for getting the most value from listserv technology. Also use this site to search for law-related Usenet news groups.

Louis-Jacques updates *Law Lists* frequently to keep the data current. Like a good Internet citizen, she operates *Law Lists* as a professional labor of love without compensation and she deserves a "thank you" from anyone who has benefitted from her hard work and diligent research.

John Marshall Law School
http://www.jmls.edu/law/lists.html

The John Marshall Law School both hosts and links to a number of law-related listservs. Refer to this page for connections to such general

THE **JOHN MARSHALL LAW SCHOOL**

interest law lists as *lawlibref-l* for law librarians, *lawsrc-l* for Internet law resources and *lawprof* for law professors. Like Law Lists, this is also an excellent site to locate law-related Usenet newsgroups.

Finding General Interest Listservs

Locating listservs for topics that are not strictly law-related, for instance, to find information on a specific industry, product or subject, is a chore that is simplified by using a search engine known as **Liszt** at *http://www.liszt.com* The Liszt directory categorizes thousands of lists from around the global Internet and provides guides to finding additional information, addresses and other helpful data on those lists. Another source for locating listservs is **Tile.net** at *http://www.tile.net/tile/listserv/index.html*

Listserv Commands

A number of commands control how messages are received by and distributed to the members of a mailing list. As stated before, the most important thing to remember is that every listserv has TWO addresses: one address is the command address, where all the messages controlling listserv operations are to be sent. Think of it as the control center. The other address is the e-mail address where messages are posted to the list.

SENDING COMMANDS

BEFORE YOU START

Before you sign up to listservs, get some background information on the list. As a rule, listserv owners provide a help file or a FAQ file to their subscribers and would-be members. Retrieve a copy of this invaluable reference by sending the message *Help name of list* (e.g. *help net-lawyers*) to the command address.

GETTING ON AND LEAVING LISTS

Two commands, with variations, are used, alternately, to join a list or to leave it. To join a list, the commands are *subscribe* or *join*. To end your subscription to a list, the commands are *unsubscribe* or *signoff*.

CUSTOMIZING HOW YOU SEND AND RECEIVE MESSAGES

A number of commands control the flow of messages between your mailbox and the mailing list. These commands can temporarily suspend traffic during vacation periods, determine whether your own posts are sent back to you as a subscriber or send a day's traffic in a single e-mail message.

Acknowledgement

Set ACK; Set NOACK

The colorfully-named ACK/NOACK commands tell the list to either send an acknowledgement of you post, rather than send you a copy (as a list subscriber) of your own post. The ACK command assures that your message has been received by the list. Set NOACK if you receive copies of your own posts or don't need the added confidence of a "message received" notice.

Digest

Set DIGEST

This is an extraordinarily useful command for busy listservs. Commonly known as "digest mode," this command tells the listserv to send one single message a day, rather than forwarding every single individual post as it appears on the list. For lists with high traffic and active subscribers where the number of posts can exceed fifty a day, subscribing in digest mode is a godsend and makes reading and managing lists much simpler.

Vacation Breaks

Set NOMAIL; Set MAIL

Heading on vacation and don't want hundreds of listserv messages to pile up? Send a *set NOMAIL* to the list. That will retain your subscription to the list but temporarily stop distribution of messages to your mailbox. To start receiving messages again, send the command *set MAIL* to the list to nullify the NOMAIL command.

Copies of your own messages

Set REPRO; Set NOREPRO

Presumably you'll keep a copy of a post sent to a list on your own machine and won't need to see a copy sent to your own mailbox. To bounce your own posts, send the command *set NOREPRO*. If, at some later date, you decide you'd like to see your posts as others see them, undo the *set NOREPRO* command by sending the command *set REPRO*.

FINDING OUT WHO ELSE IS ON THE LIST

Subscriber lists generally are available, depending on the policy of the listowner. Most make their subscriber list public; some list owners, especially those that talk about sensitive or controversial subjects, prefer to keep the names of subscribers secret.

Use the following commands to find out who else subscribes to a list and to keep your own subscription either public or private.

Recipients; Review; Who

Depending on the software an individual list uses, these commands will return a list of all known subscribers, if those subscribers have not hidden their identity from public view by sending a CONCEAL command (see below.)

KEEPING YOUR SUBSCRIPTION SECRET

For one reason or another, you may not want your subscription to a listserv known to the Internet public. Depending on the rules of the particular list, you may or may not be able to hide your identity from the commands which reveal subscribers' names. If it's permitted by the listserv owner, hide your subscription by sending the conceal command:

Set CONCEAL; Set UNCONCEAL

Moderated Lists

The best listservs are *moderated*, meaning there is a human being who exercises some editorial control over what material is sent to the list at large. Depending on the purpose of the list and the temperament of the moderator, the moderator may be more-or-less strict about which posts actually appear on the list and which do not. Because of this control, moderated listservs tend to stay focussed on the chartered subject matter and annoying flame wars that can ruin a listserv like a fistfight at a party are squelched before they can begin. At heart, moderators are the playground monitors of the listserv.

A conscientious moderator periodically will distribute to the list a message to remind listserv members of the list's rules and policies. The moderator's message is known in Internet slang as *administrivia*.

Administrivia

Moderated listservs are only as good as their moderators. Net-lawyers is lucky to be moderated by the energetic and thoughtful Lewis Rose who moderates the list when he is not busy with his duties as a partner at the Washington, D.C. firm of Arent, Fox, Kintner, Plotkin and Kahn.

Rose moderates the list without pay , though commercial publisher BNA now pays to publish an unobtrusive ad on the list to help underwrite the cost of maintaining the list. The job takes a considerable amount of time, effort and tact.

The administrivia Rose occasionally posts are sensible and simple guidelines to keep the list coherent and professional. Get the rules for other lists by requesting the same or by searching the list archives for *administrivia*. Below are the rules Rose wrote for net-lawyers and are typical of most listserv regulations.

1. Do not send subscription related commands to net-   lawyers@peach.ease.lsoft.com. Those messages go to the listserv servers at listserv@peach.ease.lsoft.com. To subscribe to the digest, send the message "set net-lawyers mail digests" (without the quotes) to listserv@peach.ease.lsoft.com The digest version simply collects 24 hours worth of net-lawyers email into one large email. It's a good way to reduce mailbox clutter if the volume of messages is too high for you on a realtime basis. To unsubscribe, send the message: "signoff net-lawyers global" to listserv@peach.ease.lsoft.com To subscribe to the regular version of net-lawyers, send the message: "subscribe net-lawyers FirstName LastName" to listserv@peach.ease.lsoft.com

2. Pick a good "Subject" header. Replying to a subject that says "Re: Digest No. 23" is easy but makes it hard for others to find out what you are posting about. The result is likely to be that folks will delete your message without reading it.

3. Watch your "cc" and "bcc" headers. Try to erase the duplicates being sent out.

4. Quote only a line or two of the post that you are replying to. Do not append your post to the entire digest and send that to the list. It will not be approved.

5. Stick to the topic of the list. This list is set up to assist lawyers, librarians, law professors, paralegals, law students, and others regarding how to use the Internet with respect to the practice, research, development, etc. of the law. It is not designed to discuss specific cases, or substantive areas of the law. I will approve the occasional humorous look at the Internet. Sometimes I approve messages that are marginally related to the list topic in the hope that the discussion moves towards the topic. If I don't see that happening, I won't approve more messages. I typically receive about 55 messages a day and approve 15-30 or so.

6.   If you are unhappy with the direction of the list, start a thread on a subject that interests you (but see 5, above, please). The list will become what you make of it, nothing more, nothing less.

7. Not all posts have to have a reply sent to the entire list. Sometimes, it may be appropriate to send a private reply. There have been dozens of sidebar conversations started already on a private basis by this list. That is one of the nicest aspects to a mailing list. If your reply is only of interest to the original poster, send it to the original poster only. If you sent in a post and get lots of interesting replies but see that they have not been sent to the list, summarize them and send them to the list so that all of our subscribers can benefit from them.

8. No ads. I will post interesting CLE opportunities, though.

9. Above all, be nice. We all make mistakes. Courtesy and civility are the hallmark of the Internet. If we remember that, we will all benefit.

10. Listserv automatically deletes subscribes whose mail bounces for four days. If you stop getting mail, please check and see if you are subscribed.

11. An updated version of the net-lawyers FAQ is available by sending the message "getnet-lawyers.FAQ" to listserv@peach.ease.lsoft.com

12. If you do not want to see the [NET-LAWYERS] tag in the subject line, send the message: "SET NET-LAWYERS SHORTHDR" to: listserv@peach.ease.lsoft.com

13. If you think there are other "reminders" I should add to this list, drop me a line (but see 7, above).

> *Thanks, Lewis Rose, Esquire*

Listserv Netiquette

For listservs to function effectively, especially law-related lists, subscribers must be self-policing and adhere to the rules of netiquette. Every attempt should be made to keep the tone cordial, collegial and professional.

Specific to the listserv are such issues of politeness as removing topics of limited interest between two subscribers off the list at large, using appropriate language, refraining from flame wars and writing informative headlines. Much has been made of netiquette; treat the listserv as one would a conference in a public place and the rules of conduct fall naturally into place.

Writing Effective Listserv Messages

Writing effective posts to listservs and newsgroups is a minor craft. The urgency of electronic communications precludes long messages. Messages of 100 to 300 words are the norm, particularly in lists with heavy traffic. Memo-length correspondence is the best format, the briefer, the better. Messages should come to the point succinctly. Avoid wordy, pompous or ill-reasoned posts.

Clearly there are subjects and occasions that require more in-depth treatment to expand upon a point of law or to add substantive material to a discussion in progress. In those instances where longer messages are needed, it's best to rely on the miracles of hypertext and mount the longer message -- consider 750 or more words to be a long message -- on a separate site and then transmit the URL of that message to the listserv at large. That way any of the list participants interested in learning more about the topic can do so without clogging up the list with long treatises that other participants may not care about.

Conversely, refrain from posting messages that are too brief. Posting messages such as "I agree!" or "That's not right" do not add any substantive information to the discussion. Steer clear of messages that are unprofessional in tone; sarcasm, anger and bullying are to be avoided, even when provoked by another's ill-considered post.

Also try to avoid sending unreadable posts. This last category refers to posts containing badly reasoned arguments, messages with factual errors or drastically bad spelling and grammar. Posts to a listserv deserve to be treated with the same level of professional care as any other office communication since one is speaking as a professional to other professionals. An opinion published online is a reflection of professional judgment and expression and bears as much authority as a letter or memoranda printed on paper. Always exercise good editorial judgment.

Lurking

Although it sounds sinister, *lurking* on listservs and other discussion groups is actually a good thing and is, in fact, encouraged. Lurking, in Internet terms, means to read the ongoing threads of a listserv without actively participating in the discussion.

There are a number of good reasons to lurk. Like a conversation at a cocktail party, it is simply good manners to listen to what people are saying before joining in the topical talk. Lurking on a listserv serves the same purpose. It gives the lurker a chance to catch up to the subject matter, to understand the point of view of some of the participants and to see where a topical thread is heading. Lurking for a short time before jumping into a conversation gives the lurker a chance to get up to speed.

Among active listserv participants, newcomers who repeat a subject that has already been discussed or re-hash recent topics are considered rude; it's a breach of netiquette to start "talking" without first seeing what's been said.

With so many listservs available for the legal researcher, each one can afford to appeal to a very narrow, specifically defined audience. Because of that, some listservs that appear at first to be interesting may not turn out to be so. Lurking is a safe way to sample the tone and content of a list to decide whether the tone and content of the list are useful.

In addition to lurking, take some time to review the archives of a prospective listserv. That's usually the best place to find out what people are talking -- and have talked -- about.

Archives

One of the troubling aspects of the Internet is that so much of the traffic across the network is ephemeral. While that's not a problem when the content is a trivial e-mail message or a frivolous Web page, discussions on professional subjects generate interesting and useful bodies of information. The traffic on listservs is recorded to preserve conversations that contain helpful information.

A record of what has been said on a professional listserv is itself a valuable resource, so many listserv owners now *archive* the contents of the listserv on a hospitable server, usually at an academic Web site. To find out where the archive of a listserv is, send a *help* command to the list server. Some lists thoughtfully post a link to their archives.

Archives serve a variety of purposes. In addition to preserving a record of a list's traffic, the archive becomes a repository of that list's wisdom. For instance, a thread may discuss a certain new law at length. Having exhausted that topic, the list at large can then move on to a new topic. But there may be a time when a list participant wants to refer to an old topic or a newcomer wants to see what's already been said on a given topic. That's only possible if an archived record is maintained.

Find archived discussion groups at the following sites:

Law Journal EXTRA!
http://www.ljx.com/forumpages/

LJX hosts a number of law-related listservs. Connect to them and the respective archives from this page. (Also see the reprint of an article by attorney Guy Alvarez, *"Mailing Lists and Newsgroups, the Real Treasures of the Internet,"* which highlights the value of discussion groups to the legal researcher.)

Legal Domain Network
http://www.kentlaw.edu/lawnet/lawnet.html

Chicago-Kent Law School maintains what it calls a "rolling archive" of its **Legal Domain Network**, where a number of law-related listservs are hosted. Refer to this page for the retention policy of archives and for connections to the discussion group there.

Legal Information Institute (Cornell University)
http://www.law.cornell.edu/listservs/

Cornell has reduced the number of listservs it archives; the site keeps messages as a convenience for subscribers who may have missed a few posts. These archives are explicitly not intended to be comprehensive nor are the archives meant to serve as historic archives. Cornell currently archives these lists on a "convenience" basis:

CYBERIA	INTLAW	MAALL
DISPUTES	LAWSRC	TEKNOIDS
EUROLEX	LEGAL-WEBMASTERS	OLDTOOLS

Washburn University Listserv Archives
http://lawlib.wuacc.edu/archive.html

As the most ambitious host of law-related listservs on the Internet, it's only natural that the archives kept here are equally broad in scope. Find the archives to some 40 listservs here.

Big Ear

An unfortunate byproduct of proliferating listservs is information overload. One solution to mastering the ceaseless flow of information coursing through the leading law-related listservs is to tune in to **Big Ear: Current Legal Resources on the Net**. Big Ear is the *nom-de-guerre* of Cornell University's Tom Bruce. Big Ear lurks on six listservs, paying special attention to announcements of new Web sites and the release of software that would interest to the legal profession. Bruce re-publishes a weekly cumulative listing of new sites on an easy-to-search page at *http://barratry.law.cornell.edu:5123/notify/buzz.html*

Currently, Big Ear monitors **lawsrc-l, net-lawyers, teknoids, law-lib, legal-webmasters** and **int-law**. For each of the announcements printed in Big Ear, Bruce typically provides the name of the new resource, the URL, the date, time and list where the announcement appeared and the full text of the announcement.

Archives of Big Ear postings from previous weeks are available as a searchable archive from the home page. This is an excellent service for staying current with new law resources for those researchers who are too busy to subscribe and review multiple listservs themselves.

One Day on a Listserv

Part question-and-answer center, part town hall meeting, part marketplace, *net-lawyers* is a busy, informative and very lively group. For first-time listserv users, this is a good place to become acquainted with how lists work.

The atmosphere is professional and collegial and Lew Rose is a judicious moderator. Reprinted here is the *digest* of a single day of traffic on net-lawyers. Rose stitches individual posts together into a single e-mail message which is then forwarded once a day to those subscribers who have chosen to receive their messages in the convenient digest mode. Other subscribers receive each e-mail message individually. Rose adds headlines and picks and chooses which messages will appear on the list. To subscribe to **net-lawyers**, send the message *subscribe net-lawyers yourname* to *listserv@peach.ease.lsoft.com*

NET-LAWYERS Digest

15 May 1997 to 16 May 1997
(Automatic digest processor , 5/17/97 0:00)
To: Recipients of NET-LAWYERS digests
<NET-LAWYERS@PEACH.EASE.LSOFT.COM>

There are 5 messages totalling 224 lines in this issue.

Topics of the day:

   1. ethics and online research - suggestions?
   2. Domain Name Registration
   3. Newsletter - The Extended Intranet
   4. Online Admission?
   5. SUBJECT HEADINGS

Listowner: Lewis Rose, lewrose@arentfox.com
Archives: http://eva.dc.lsoft.com/Archives/net-lawyers.html

BNA invites you to try BNA's Electronic Information Policy & Law Report, a service devoted to the emerging law of cyberspace. Email rstearns@bna.com for a 5-week free print trial subscription. Or visit http://www.bna.com/newsstand for free electronic trial. (Assistance: 1-800-452-7773, 202-452-4323)

Date: Thu, 15 May 1997 17:14:53 -0700
From: Peter Krakaur <ils@LEGALETHICS.COM>
Subject: Re: ethics and online research - suggestions?

>At 12:37 PM 5/13/97 -0500, you wrote:
>
>>I am in the process of collecting information on the topic of attorney
>>malpractice in legal research. Main point is that failure to use online
>>resources when representing a client could be/should be grounds for
>>malpractice. The mere raising of your question gives me goose-

bumps.

Agreed. If that is your main point, I'd suggest an alternate tack. I do not believe you will find anything out there coming close to what you propose. I am not aware that anyone has even issued an opinion stating that the failure to use westlaw or lexis is a grounds for malpractice. I certainly would think long and hard before establishing such a rule or even proposing it.

>While this is an issue that attorneys may be beginning to think
about,it
>would first have to be determined whether the Model Rules or any
>state bar has placed this obligation into the Rules of Professional
>Conduct. I practice law in California and am aware that the State Bar
>of California (Committee on Professional Responsibility and
Conduct) >is beginning its process of considering the effects that the
new
>technologies are having on the practice of law, but this is only in the
>"considering" stage.

It is, but looking only at web advertising if I am not mistaken. Unless something changed very recently, you should assume that they will not be addressing the main point noted above.

>>Is anyone on the list aware of/involved in any research on this topic? >>I have searched resources on Westlaw, Lexis and the Internet. I was >>just curious if anyone here had some personal rec-ommendations for >>sources to pass on.

I guess you could say I've looked into the Internet ethics issue a bit. Try my site, Legalethics.com (URL below). You could also review the ABA/BNA Manual on Professional Conduct. A couple of chapters on electronic mail and internet use, though you will not find anything suggesting a failure to use the net as a grounds for malpractice.
If you want to get an idea of whether any authorities have addressed the issue of online research and malpractice, try posting your query to the Webethics forum at LegaEethics.com. Alternatively, try the legalethics listserv (again, URL at legalethics.com).
The only authority which I think came close to suggesting a duty to browse(but did not do it) is <underline>Whirlpool Financial Corporation v. GN Holdings, Inc.</underline>, http://www.law.emory.edu/7circuit/sept95/95-1292.html, 1995 U.S.App. LEXIS 27600 (9/28/95)). A reach in the securities context and probably more so in the malpractice realm.

>Recommend that you contact State Bars and the Committees on
>Professional Responsibility and Conduct to see what rules may have
>been enacting including this issue. Further, you might want to see if
>any State Bar Opinions have been issued. Additionally, you might
>want tocontact the ABAto see whether this issue has been addressed
>in the Model Rules of Professional Conduct.

I am not aware of any state or local authority even thinking about establishing a rule requiring online use as part of an attorney's ethical responsibilities. Your time might be better spent reviewing law review articles to see if the issue came up that way. I offer at my site a list of existing ethics opinions and references to changes in ethics rules dealing with the Internet . As you might guess, you wont find any rules or opinions that would help make a case for the main point above.

I do not think the issue of a duty to conduct electronic research is addressed in the Model Rules (probably would be in Rule 1.1). You can search the Model rules and the comments at LII. See LegalEthics.com(EthicsSites/Legal) for the link to the Model Rules.

<bold>Peter Krakaur
<color><param>0000,0000,FFFF</param>Internet
Legal Services</color>   ils@legalethics.com

</bold><smaller>Legalethics.com: http://www.legalethics.com/

INTRALAW(sm): http://www.intralaw.com/

The Practicing Attorney's Home Page: http://www.legalethics.com/pa/

</smaller>

Date: Thu, 15 May 1997 21:49:26 -0400
From: Enrique Gili <elawyer@INTERPORT.NET>
Subject: Domain Name Registration

A few weeks ago there was an extended thread about register-ing domain names outside the United States. There is a service that can accomodate your request, they have compiled an extensive resource on filing exotic domain names and alternative names such as .firm and .web.
But, I'm not sure how stringent they are on clearing trademarks. http://www.netnames.com

----

Date: Thu, 15 May 1997 23:05:33 -0400
From: "M. Sean Fosmire" <fosmire@MAIL.PORTUP.COM>
Subject: Newsletter - The Extended Intranet

Superior Information Services has posted the latest in its irregular series of newsletters. This one is "Using the Internet as an Extended Intranet", found at http://www.afss.com/sis/extranet.htm

==

M. Sean Fosmire   fosmire@portup.com
Marquette, Michigan

Fosmire, Solka & Stenton, P.C.
http://www.afss.com

Superior Information Services, Inc.
http://www.afss.com/sis
==

Date: Thu, 15 May 1997 18:03:31 -0800
From: amansfield@INTERNET.OMM.COM
Subject: Online Admission?

Can an online statement be used as an admission? Does the fact that the message was sent by someone with a User ID and password suffice? What about computers that are "logged into" and left on and unattended? Does anyone know of any case law on this topic?

Date: Fri, 16 May 1997 00:50:32 -0500
From: MATTHEW CORCORAN <SZED92A@PRODIGY.COM>
Subject: SUBJECT HEADINGS

Hi,

I've been lurking on this list serve for almost a year now. I find some of this info pretty useful and that other postings totally unrelated to my work or interests. My one gripe with the list is that with VERY few exceptions NO ONE uses subject headings.

Please, out of common curtesy for those of us who recive large quantities of e-mail, post subject headings along with your messages. That way, threads which are unrelated may be quickly deleted and messages which are important to someone will be read. I can't tell you how many times -- with hundreds of messages in my box, i've deleted all NET LAWYERS posts because i know that only a few are pertenant to my interests and i don't have the time to plow through the rest.

Thanks

MFC

End of NET-LAWYERS Digest - 15 May 1997 to 16 May 1997
****

Usenet

Introduction

After e-mail itself, no other Internet application
has so captured the imagination of the online public as the 15,000+ newsgroups known collectively as Usenet. Usenet is the *vox populi* of the
Internet. It's the place where millions of messages are both posted and
read by an equal number of online authors. As the Third Circuit wrote in
its June 11, 1996 decision in *ACLU v. Reno,* published online at
http://www.aclu.org/court/cdadec.html, the Internet itself is "the most
participatory form of mass speech yet developed." At the center of this
participation is Usenet.

While no hard data exists to quantify the exact number of messages that are posted each day to the newsgroups of Usenet by any anec-
dotal measure, Usenet is wildly popular and generates immense quantities
of e-mail traffic. Some Usenet analysts estimate that a single day's
Usenet traffic would fill the equivalent of 400 textbooks. No reliable service has ever accurately measured Usenet activity, but one thing is certain: after the WorldWideWeb, Usenet is the Internet's most popular
application. Think of Usenet as a huge arena than can hold millions of
people who collect themselves into little groups according to their interests and who then send messages to a central server where everyone in
that group can read and respond to the message. That's a pretty fair picture of what Usenet does and how it works.

Newsgroups

Each one of the thousands of newsgroups that comprise Usenet
has a distinct topic. Those topics represent an entire spectrum of human
interests. There are newsgroups for hobbyists and newsgroups for scientists. Religious believers have theological groups, atheists have another;
every political stripe has a forum to air their views. Fans of the TV show
The Simpsons have still another, as do tropical fish enthusiasts.
Newsgroups exist to discuss politics, science, sociology, sex, travel, education, disabilities, computers and Usenet itself. The topics discussed in
Usenet range from the sublime to the unspeakable and are restricted only
by the imagination of Usenet's users. Newsgroups are chaotic, unregulated, uncensored, unlicensed and gloriously free. In short, Usenet is an
online microcosm of the real world. In Thomas Jefferson's imagined marketplace of ideas, Usenet is the biggest bazaar in the world.

The newsgroups of Usenet were once known as *bulletin boards*
and, in large measure, they still function like a physical bulletin board.
Within the parameters of the stated subject matter, participants can send
messages to a central server where that message can be read by others. If
others so choose, they can comment or elaborate on the post. This back-
and-forth theoretically can go on forever.

Listservs and Usenet

Usenet bears some similarity to the listserv in that it is a way for one person to communicate with others who are interested in the same topic. And while it's true that both depend on the humble e-mail message as the basic unit of currency, there are significant differences between the listserv and the newsgroups of Usenet.

Like the bulletin board in the real world and the listserv on the Internet, the newsgroup is an online "place" where one person can write a message for others to see. On the bulletin board, others can respond or elaborate on the original post, the same as in a listserv. Where Usenet parts company with the listserv is in technical structure and in its degree of formality.

Usenet is distinctly casual. Anyone can drop in to a newsgroup at any time, to post or simply lurk and read what's been posted. Listservs require a subscription. Whereas many listservs are almost always moderated, Usenet groups rarely are. Where the listserv tends to be more formal and professional in tone, Usenet is relaxed and breezy. No special software is necessary to access a listserv. Usenet requires a newsreader.

Turn to Usenet for informal or timely discussions or to talk about topics that are not covered in an existing listserv.

How Usenet Works

Usenet newsgroups are broadcast across the Internet from large servers to local Internet Service Providers. This distribution is called the **newsfeed.** The technical protocol defining how mail is transmitted is the NNTP or *network news transport protocol*. NNTP moves mail between servers; the newsreader negotiates the transmission of messages between the client and the local host.

The quality and quantity of newsgroups accessible to a subscriber is a measure of how good an Internet Service Provider is. The Internet Service Provider acts as a local host for receiving messages to the newsgroups, which they then transmit to the newsfeed.

The latest versions of the leading Web browsers feature built-in newsreaders. The newsreader is designed to retrieve the lengthy list of newsgroups, to access a particular group and then to read the messages posted within the selected group. The newsreader also has an e-mail message editor for writing messages.

Hierarchies

Newsgroups are organized into *hierarchies* which define, in the most general way, the subject matter of the newsgroup. Within each of the hierarchies are any number of sub-groups. There are hundreds of upper-level hierarchies; the most common are:

> **alt:** sexually-explicit, strange or bizarre subject matter
> **bio:** biology and health sciences
> **biz:** commercial services
> **comp:** computer discussions
> **court:** court-related information
> **misc:** miscellaneous topics, usually tamer than the *alt.* groups
> **rec:** recreational topics and hobbies
> **sci:** scientific and technical subjects
> **soc:** social issues and political discussions

Newsgroups from outside the United States -- and there are thousands -- are usually prefixed with a national abbreviation such as **np.** for Japanese groups, **de.** for German groups, **nz.** for New Zealand, etc. When retrieving active newsgroups from the local news host, they are retrieved in alphabetic hierarchy order.

Moderated Groups

Newsgroups can be *moderated* or *unmoderated.* Moderated groups, in which a human editor filters out posts that are repetitive, off-point, offensive or inappropriate in some other fashion, deliver a much more professional environment in which to discuss the group's topic than the unmoderated groups. Unmoderated groups frequently meander off-track or degenerate into pointless and time-wasting *flame wars*, which are insulting posts intended solely as personal attacks between newsgroup participants. Stick with moderated groups, if possible, or better, subscribe to a moderated listserv that speaks to your topic.

Charters and Acceptable Use Policies

Almost all newsgroups are *chartered*. The charter is the state-ment of purpose created by the group's owner to define the purpose of the group and to set out rules of what is and is not acceptable on the group. To obtain the charter and acceptable use policy for a newsgroup, request a copy of the same from the list at large or the list's moderator. Also check with a Usenet archive such as Liszt at *http://www.liszt.com* to locate newsgroup charters.

Usenet Software

Until Netscape bundled a newsreader with its latest release of Netscape Navigator and Netscape Communicator, separate newsreader clients were required to access Usenet. Dedicated newsreaders are still readily available but the current releases of Netscape and Microsoft's Internet Explorer 3.0 and higher already have a perfectly adequate newsreader. To access the Netscape News newsreader software, select **Window |Netscape News**; Internet Explorer users, follow **Go | Read News**.

Very active Usenet participants will want to use a dedicated newsreader which makes lengthy sessions online more comfortable. Ded-icated newsreaders have more mail management features and the displays are easier to read and use.

For separate newsreaders, head to one of the leading software archives like Stroud's Consummate Winsock Apps page at *http://www.stroud.com* or TUCOWS at *http://www.tucows.com* On those sites are descriptions, reviews and access to the leading newsreaders.

Among the most popular shareware and freeware newsreaders available there are **Agent** and **FreeAgent**, respectively. Other newsreaders are **Gravity, NewsFerret for Windows 95, News Xpress, WinVN** and **News for Windows NT** and all of them are completely detailed on Forrest Stroud's reviews at *http://cws.iworld.com/32news-reviews.html* Macintosh and Windows 3.x users should, of course, refer to the flavor of newsreader appropriate to their operating system.

No matter which newsreader software is selected, the software will all share certain capabilities. All newsreaders are able to *retrieve* all the newsgroups to which your ISP subscribes and can arrange those newsgroups into a searchable and well-organized group. By clicking on the name of the newsgroups -- *courts.usa.supreme.court* for example -- the messages that have been posted to that group can be read and responded to.

Newsreaders can all pick and choose among all the thousands of newsgroups; for infrequent news reading, it's possible to subscribe to only a handful of interesting newsgroups. That reduces the amount of mail that will need to be reviewed. All newsreaders are designed with a feature that will permit only the retrieval of posts that have appeared since the last time the newsgroup was accessed. That way only new posts to those groups need to be retrieved and read.

Use the *find* or *search* command installed on your newsreader to locate a particular newsgroup by its keyword name.

Finding Newsgroups

The Liszt Web site at *http://www.liszt.com* provides the most complete, searchable list of newsgroups on the Internet. The interface is simple to use and covers tens of thousands of individual newsgroups. Check with Liszt to see if there are interesting newsgroups which your Internet Service Provider does not receive from their newsfeed.

Configuring the Newsreader

Configuring a newsreader requires a one-time setup. Once the reader has been configured, there is no need to change the settings. The important values to know are the name of your ISP's local mail host (called the NNTP server) and the news RC directory on your local machine. Obtain these from your Internet Service Provider.

Other configurations can be set to increase or decrease the number of new posts retrieved at one time, to sort messages by date, subject or sender and to look over only new posts since last viewing. Refer to the help file on your selected newsreader to set additional configuration parameters.

A Typical Newsgroup

A typical newsgroup has a name that intuitively clues a would-be reader into the subject matter of the newsgroup. For example, a news group that is chartered to discuss legal issues generally called *misc.legal*

To join in the discussion, first select the newsgroup from the list of all newsgroups. Once the group itself has been selected, use the newsreader command to *show all messages*; the exact name of the command varies but every newsreader has a similar command. To read individual messages and respond to them, simply click on the post. The complete message will then appear.

To respond to the message, write out the message in the built-in mail editor and dispatch it with the *send* command. Newsreaders indicate threads, that is, a response to a previously posted message, by a graphic flag, a chevron or by stacking the threads in a hierarchy.

To respond to a post, click on the newsreader command to *post* or *reply*. Your message will be sent automatically to the appropriate newsgroup.

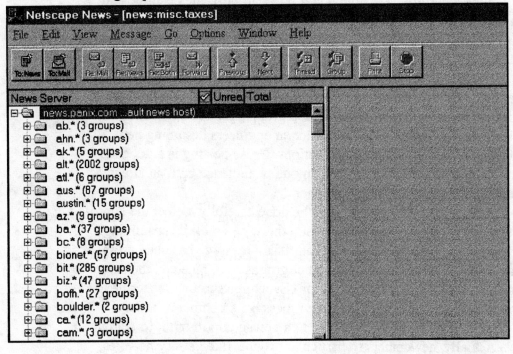

THE LIST OF ALL NEWSGROUPS AVAILABLE FROM YOUR INTERNET SERVICE PROVIDER CAN BE REVIEWED AND SEARCHED IN HIERARCHICAL ORDER.

SELECT A
MESSAGE
FROM THE
LIST.

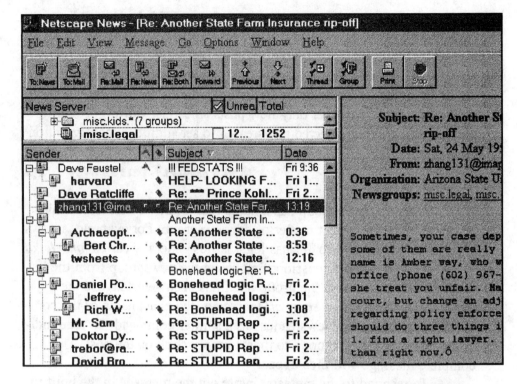

Posting, Cross-Posting and Lurking

Of course, it's entirely possible to initiate a line of discussion on a newsgroup simply by posting a query, announcement or other message to a newsgroup. Use the *post* or *send message* command on your newsreader to pull up a message box. In the message box, enter the name of the newsgroups to which you'd like to post, the headline and then the text of the message itself.

A single messages can be sent to more than one newsgroup at a time, a technique known as *cross-posting*. Cross-posting is a sensible and practical way to query related groups with similar interests; for instance, a question about the Americans with Disabilities Act might be successfully cross-posted to law-related groups, groups discussing disabilities and a newsgroup for construction engineers designing new buildings to comply with new regulations. Cross-posting is a good way to locate information quickly from an online audience with an already-expressed interest in the subject matter.

Cross-posting should always be done carefully. Select the appropriate newsgroups for your cross-post, otherwise you'll be spamming. It's also courteous to announce upfront that a message has been cross-posted and let readers know what other groups have received the same message. Many times, avid readers of Usenet newsgroups subscribe to many similar groups. They'll see your message a number of times.

It is never mandatory to post to a newsgroup in order to read the posts. Actually, newcomers to particular groups, like listserv newbies, are encouraged to lurk, Internet-ese for reading posts and monitoring newsgroups without actually participating. Lurking gives newbies a feel for the tone and content of a newsgroup and brings the novice up to speed with ongoing threads of discussion.

Subject Headings

Like all e-mail messages, it is of great importance to write brief, informative and on-point headlines in the e-mail Subject field so that recipients can tell at a glance if they want to read your post.

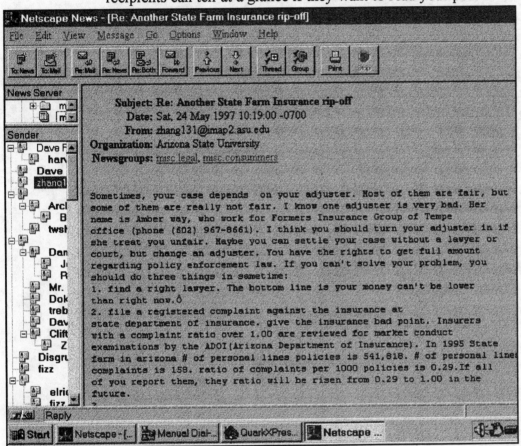

DISPLAY THE FULL TEXT OF THE MESSAGE. THE BORDERS OF EACH FRAME ARE ELASTIC AND CAN BE MOVED WITH THE CURSOR.

And like all good headlines, Usenet headlines pack a lot of information into a very little space. A reader will respond to a headline that contains concrete nouns and vivid verbs more readily than an informationally-flabby headline.

For instance, a headline like *Request for Information* tells the reader nothing; a better headline is *Good treatise on NJ UCC?* or *Need trust forms for Nebraska*. A punchy headline brings in readers.

Effective Usenet Messages

Brevity is appreciated in newsgroups. Keep messages short and to the point. The rule of thumb is that a post should not exceed 300 to 500 words. For lengthier posts, keep a copy of the longer message on your own Web site or computer and tell readers how to retrieve the message or better, offer to take your conversation private through an exchange of e-mail.

A Warning

One online guide to writing well offers the opinion that "subtle-ty is not communicated well in written form." (If that's so, we should all be grateful that Ernest Hemingway, James Joyce and William Shakespeare pre-dated the PC!) What the well-meaning author of that sentence was trying to say is that many people who read Usenet news are not always perceptive readers.

The audience for Usenet is not always well-educated and does-n't always grasp literary devices as irony, wit, allusions and humor. They instead rely instead on a sophomoric system of tilted punctuation collectively called smiley-faces -- :-) to denote happy, :-(for sadness, etc. -- to make their clever points. Before wading into the waters of Usenet, please be warned that fine writing, sorry to say, is a rare com-modity in the newsgroups. Many Usenet newsgroups, in fact, are tedious and some are flat-out stupid. Enter Usenet with a healthy degree of skepticism, patience and open-mindedness.

Even with Usenet's shortcomings, it is still useful as source of insight to what other people are talking about. It represents an interest-ing and imaginative use of basic e-mail capability.

Threads

Like listservs, Usenet newsgroups are capable of message threading. Threads are continuations and elaborations of the original post. An original post may offer one opinion or question; a subsequent posting answering or commenting on that original post begins the thread. Additional posts adding to the online "conversation" extend the threads.

As a thread develops, most Usenet software can sort threads so that the individual posts which comprise the thread can be retrieved as a coherent group. This is handy for swimming back upstream to see what's been said on any given topic. And the netiquette of newsgroups requires a newcomer to become acquainted with the recent history of a thread so that comments are original and not merely repetitions of material that has been posted previously.

Archives

Messages on most newsgroups are deleted frequently, especially on groups with heavy traffic. Typically, a posted message will remain "live" for 48 hours to two weeks, after which messages are either removed permanently or transferred to an archive. The most convenient archive for zipping through Usenet messages is **DejaNews** at *http://www.dejanews.com* There the researcher will find a slickly designed search page that makes finding groups and posting to them absolutely simple. The page features links to newsreader software, classified ads and handy tutorials for new users. Most of the major search engines, notably Infoseek at *http://www.infoseek.com* and AtlaVista at *http://www.altavista.digital.com* also can look through Usenet newsgroups as a searchable archive, distinct from the WorldWideWeb.

Professional Applications

Unfortunately, the otherwise remarkable technology of the news group hasn't yet been fully exploited for professional applications. Unlike the listserv, which has been tamed to provide controlled, responsible discussion groups, the wilderness of Usenet still overflows with uninformed opinions, illiterate posts, unreasoned arguments and flat-out stupidity.

There is no technical barrier to preclude Usenet from evolving into a useful tool for the legal researcher. Moderated news groups, in fact, offer promise to be a central service of the Internet. Well-run Usenet news groups which filter out irrelevant and unprofessional posts are wonderful resources for the researcher, in the same way listservs are.

Newsgroups are more informal than the listserv, they don't require constant attention and, for the casual researcher who doesn't need to be continually updated on a specific topic, can deliver fast answers to the occasional question. But wade into these waters with caution, patience and a finger poised at all times over the *delete* key.

❏

INTERNET RELAY CHAT

Introduction

One of the most curious Internet protocols is the *Internet Relay Chat* in which two or more participants can type messages to each other in real time. While 90-wpm typists may find online conversations stimulating, those of us who still hunt-and-peck on the computer keyboard may find the charm of this utterly-90s style of communication somewhat elusive. IRC is like a three-way marriage of the telephone party line, the ham radio and a computer keyboard.

IRC is the technical term for the *chat room*, in which computer users can gather together and tap out messages to each other across the network. IRC is primarily recreational; however, Washburn University is trying to get professional chat rooms off the ground with something they call the "tea rooms" that will be operated for the legal profession. Even though the professional applications for IRC are elusive, as another Internet innovation based loosely on the e-mail message, IRC deserves at least passing mention.

What IRC Does and How It Works

What are known variously as *chat rooms* or *virtual conversation places* are, in technical terms individual channels on a server. Using specialized software to access the IRC server, individual users can send and receive messages from any number of other users at the same time over that selected channel. Using IRC client software to connect to your Internet Service Provider, you will be switched to a local IRC server computer. That IRC server is networked to other IRC servers, creating a huge interconnected chain of real-time connections.

There is no practical limit on the number of channels that can be supported on an IRC server. Any server, hosting hundreds or thousands of chat channels can also be connected to other servers in turn, creating a vast beehive of typed-out conversations on every subject the mind can conceive in as many languages as there are keyboards to type them in.

IRC requires specialized client software because each message sent to an IRC channel needs to be treated with certain commands to make it acceptable to the server. So far, none of the major browser designers, with the exception of America Online, has succeeded in bundling chat software.

Each command in IRC is preceded with a forward slash (/); find a complete list of all IRC commands from the IRC server by typing */help* once IRC client software has been installed and configured. The commands permit users to join and leave channels, to send messages and to kick other participants off a channel if their behavior becomes obnoxious.

IRC Client Software

Among the half dozen or so IRC clients available, the best one is called **mIRC.** Get details on downloading and installing mIRC software from the home page at *http://www.mirc.co.uk*

A collection of other IRC clients can be found at the Consummate Winsock Apps page at *http://www.stroud.com* for online ratings and connections to other software. Directions for installation will be included with the software. Be prepared to enter such items as your own IP address and server name -- available from the Internet Service Provider -- and be ready with an alias.

The alias, known in IRC terms as a "nickname" or a "nick" is handy for fast connections but does not confer any real anonymity. Any selected nickname can be *fingered*, that is, checked against your e-mail account. Your real name (and rough geographical location) can be determined from that information. Because many IRC channels are occupied by hyper-hormonal males who do not always act like gentlemen, some women users prefer to use a gender-neutral alias to avoid unwanted attentions from online Romeos.

Using IRC

It's difficult to recommend IRC use except as a curiosity or recreational activity. As more than one IRC devotee has explained it, in much earthier terms, IRC is fundamentally an online singles bar. It's a favorite among people who have too much time on their hands: insomniacs, the lovelorn and college students.Still, the idea of people who have never met face-to-face (or *F2F* in IRC slang) talking to each other from points all over the globe is romantically compelling. IRC is a very modern take on pen pals.

Much of the online conversation is utterly banal but the technology itself does not preclude two or more intelligent people typing out discussions of greater importance that what each other had for breakfast (or things of a far more personal nature.) And the occasional international shooting-of-the-breeze also has its charms on the country channels.

Anyone seriously using the Internet should at least try IRC chatting at least once. At the worst, it's harmless fun -- you can always quit --and at best you may connect with some online colleagues, clients or IRC-pals.

To access a chat room, first request the IRC client to connect to the active channels. To connect to a channel, select the *join* command. A list of other chatters who also are logged on the same channel appears onscreen. Follow the conversation as each participant types out a phrase or says something. Your own posts first appear in an "on-deck" circle that you can review before posting.

Because IRC is heavily dependent on quick typing, an entire lexicon of abbreviations to speed messaging has developed. Learn the lingo online; it keeps changing.

Legal Applications of IRC

The leading examples of IRC usage within a the legal context are the "tea rooms" for law librarians at Washburn University in Kansas and the groups created by the commercial service Counsel Connect.

For real-time discussions, find the tea rooms at *http://aall.wuacc.edu/cgi-bin/chat* Washburn hosts four rooms for online chatting: *Public Area*, *LawLibDir* (for directors of law libraries), *Library Reference* and *Law Librarians*. As already noted, IRC technology allows the use of nicknames, so a law librarian with an unscratched itch to call herself "The Goddess of the Card Pocket" can feel free to indulge the fantasy.

The commercial service Counsel Connect at *http://www.counsel.com* provides discussion groups and private areas for its subscribers. A password is required to gain access. These services are discussed in greater detail at the home page.

Internet Relay Chat is undoubtedly interesting. It's also goofy. IRC is one of the biggest selling points for recreational use of the Internet since it allows individuals to talk to others anywhere on the globe without ever having to meet F2F (face-to-face), that is, in person. IRC has also made a name for itself in the tabloid newspapers where breathless headlines have found ready-made sensationalism in those instances where face-to-face meetings of individuals who met in chat rooms have resulted in criminal activity like robbery, assault or worse.

Emerging Communication Protocols

On the horizon are some exciting communications technologies that are not quite ready for practical use that will, in their own ways, take the Internet revolution to a new level. This 21st Century software itself is still undergoing tune-ups in the lab but will soon be mature enough to implement in the office.

What is holding back the widespread distribution of these experimental technologies are the speeds of conventional Internet connections. Most of these new tools are only effective with a high-bandwidth connection. Ordinary 28,880 bps modems or even ISDN dial-up connections are not fast enough to support such emerging protocols as video teleconferencing, voice communications (telephone connections using the Internet as the network), 3-D simulation and other experimental protocols. These programs promise a wonderland of electronic tools that will soon change the way law offices operate: real-time videoconferencing replaces travelling to depositions in distant cities; three-dimensional recreations of crimes or accidents are introduced to explain complicated stories to a jury; and long-distance phone bills join the endangered species list.

The big *however* in this rosy picture of a wired nirvana is that the problem of universal fast access is not even close to being solved. When fast connections -- data through-put rates exceeding a million bits per second or faster -- are the norm, these protocols will take the starring role away from the Web.

But for those who already enjoy high-speed access and regularly connect to others with similar capabilities, there is enough experimental software to play with. The applications for the law office haven't yet been explored but the adventurous and imaginative legal researcher will find a use for these very interesting innovations. Get the software from either TUCOWS at *http://www.tucows.com* or the Consummate Winsock Apps (CWA) page at *http://www.stroud.com*

Please note: these apps all require special hardware installations. Refer to the accompanying review notes at TUCOWS or CWA for details on what additional hardware is required to operate these new applications.

TELEPHONE APPLICATIONS

Phone apps work like conventional telephones except that computers are both the caller and the recipient. Calls are free. Among the software that will turn your computer into a free long-distance telephone network are **Internet Phone for Windows 95** at *http://www.vocaltec.com* **TeleVox** at *http://www.voxware.com* **WebPhone** at *http://www.netspeak.com* and **VDOPhone** at *http://www.vdo.net*

TELEVIDEO AND VIDEOTELECONFERENCING

First promised to the public at the 1964 World's Fair in New York City, televideo is becoming a reality. The pictures are still balky except across very high-speed connections and the image is small, but the first generation technology is breaking through the technological barriers that have until recently precluded the popular use of the long-imagined tool. The leading video software is **CuSeeMe** which allows one-on-one video conversations or multiple user conferencing capabilities. See their home page at *http://www.cuseeme.com* for background and software.

3-D IMAGING

The newest graphic invention to seize the Internet's imagination is VRML or *Virtual Reality Markup Language*. Most VRML is experimental and the tools to create and edit these remarkable, three-dimensional images are still under construction. Advanced (and expensive) computer-aided design (CAD) software has been available for years now, offering engineers and industrial designers 3-D images but VRML breaks through the limitations of cost and ease-of-use and puts the power of 3-D design in the hands of individuals and non-specialists.

The best 3-D browser for viewing BVRML images is WIRL from Vream. Their home page, with downloadable software, demos and sales materials, is at *http://www.vream.com*

❑

Retrieval Protocols

RETRIEVAL PROTOCOLS

Introduction

The muscular communication power of the Inter-net is just one part of the network's remarkable capabilities. Important as the communication functions of the Internet are, more important still is the network's capacity to *retrieve* information.

As a connection of networks that share a common computer language, the Internet solves an immense computing problem: it makes it possible to <u>move</u> files from one computer to another.

It's one thing to be able to write a law review article or to take a picture of a crime scene or to draft a memo on a point of law and store it on one's own computer. But it's another thing to be able to move that file almost instantly to another computer anywhere else on Earth. To state it plainly, *anything that can be created in digital format can now be moved electronically.* The implications are enormous: today's technology can digitally store text, music, software, motion pictures, photographs, documents, audio files and a myriad of other information. The Internet represents the most efficient distribution system ever invented for delivering digitally stored information and puts access to that data within affordable reach of anyone with a computer and an Internet account. The ability to transfer files is what gives the Internet its remarkable power.

On the Internet, a series of technical standards have been developed to make it possible to move files between machines attached to the network. These standards are called *transfer protocols.* As described in Chapter 2, the mail transfer protocols POP and SMTP move e-mail files from one site to another and so provide communication protocols. For obtaining words and multimedia information from a server, a series of additional retrieval protocols have been developed to move text, graphics and files.

Of the retrieval protocols, the most important and the most well-known is the *hypertext transfer protocol* (HTTP) which governs the technical rules for the transport of files that have been created in hypertext markup language (HTML). Other transfer protocols are the *file transfer protocol* (FTP) which permits entire, unopened files to be moved across the network and the *gopher* protocol. Gopher is the non-graphical, text-only precursor to the WorldWideWeb that allows fast retrieval of files from a hoerarchical menu.

Transfer protocols are nothing new; they have been used by commercial databases for many years. When a case is printed from Westlaw or a news story is downloaded from Nexis, what is happening technically are file transfers. The Internet takes that capability one step further by allowing graphics-rich HTML files to be retrieved and downloaded, using the hypertext transfer protocol.

UNIX, HTML, HTTP and the WorldWideWeb

Before HTML and the WorldWideWeb came to domainte the Internet with the introduction of the Mosaic browser in 1993, the Internet was a computer network that was run almost entirely on the UNIX operating system. UNIX, like DOS and Windows, is a powerful computer language. It is a superb computer language but it's difficult for inexperienced computer users to master. Both DOS and UNIX rely on strange arcane commands that must be typed in at a prompt to make the computer perform any meaningful task. The commands are not intuitive and learning them is a difficult and time-consuming task.

A little computer history: With the introduction of the personal computer, some computer pioneers realized that ordinary people had neither the time nor inclination to learn an entire series of weird commands to make their computers work. What Steven Jobs and Steve Wozniak at Apple and Bill Gates and Paul Allen at Microsoft created were *graphical user interfaces (GUIs)* that cured the problem of typing out commands to the computer. Their solution was to replace commands with graphical elements. A user could then simply point at an icon, click on it and issue commands to the computer that way. The point and click system to operating computers revolutionized the computer world and made their inventors immensely wealthy men.

Point and click operating systems do not do away with the underlying commands. What they do is make those commands invisible -- *transparent* is the computer term -- to the user. For instance, the DOS system still is running under Windows. In Windows-based systems, the user clicks on an icon, the icon in turn issues a DOS command to the computer and the computer does something useful. Graphical systems *overlay* line command systems.

The same thing type of invention that transformed personal computers from hard-to-use to point-and-click also turned the Internet from a sleepy, UNIX-based academic network into the world's biggest online system. At the Center for Supercomputing Applications at the University of Illinois Urbana/Champaign, computer scientists were working on a system to overlay the funky commands of UNIX with a graphical user interface in the same way Bill Gates overlaid DOS with Windows. The object of their research was to invent some way of giving the casual computer control over *networked* computers without having to learn strings of weird computer commands of UNIX. Where the Mac and Windows designers developed a way to make standalone computers work better, the team at Urbana wanted create a way to make moving files between networked computers easier, in particular to exploit the newly invented WorldWideWeb, which had just been developed by Tim Berners-Lee in Switzerland at the Center for High-Energy Physics in Bern.

The software that came out of the University of Illinois was first released in December 1993 and was called Mosaic. It is was an absolute and instantaneous success. Because it had been developed by people using taxpayer money, Mosaic's developers gave the software away for free. Within a year, millions of copies of Mosaic were in the hands of users and the Web as we know it today had its beginnings. By January 1994, no more than a dozen law firms had Web sites; within three years, conservative estimates say there are 2,000 or more Web sites for law firms and solo practitioners with more added every working day.

One of the computer scientists who worked on the Mosaic project was a young graduate student named Mark Andreesen. Andressen foresaw just how huge the Web would eventually be and left the Midwest for Silicon Valley. Once there, Andreesen founded a company to improve on the original Mosaic software and to create a commercial version of a Web browser. The company he founded is Netscape Communications and the original Mosaic software has since evolved into the advanced browser software Netscape Navigator. (At this writing, Netscape had just released its latest suite of Web tools, Netscape Communicator 4.0) With the introduction of Netscape, the Web simply exploded.

The present-day popularity of the WorldWideWeb can be attributed to the convergence of many factors. The first is the ubiquity of personal computers at the office and at home. The second is the immense universe of electronically created and stored information created by those personal computers using word processing programs. Third is a computer-literate population. Last is the invention of an easy-to-use software like Netscape and the availability of faster data connections. All those factors reached critical mass and the Internet took over the literate world as the greatest improvement to the dissemination of the printed word since Johans Gutenberg five hundred years earlier.

The WorldWideWeb

Technically, the WorldWideWeb is the entire universe of HTML files that can be accessed and retrieved by a Web browser. In practice, the Web is first and foremost a giant publishing medium. As a publishing medium, the Web is unique. It merges the text and graphical power of the magazine with the immediacy of television and the fluid, up-to-the-second flexibility of radio. The Web fulfills the early promise of desktop publishing: not only can virtually anyone publish text and pictures at very little cost, whatever is published can then be distributed at nominal cost across the Internet. Web publishing does not require ink, paper, binding, trucks, warehouses or any of the other expenses normally associated with professional publishing. Access to the Web means that anyone who wants to publish something can. Off-the-shelf software can electronically create catalogs, brochures, individual documents, magazines, books and every other type of publication that can ordinarily be produced by conventional printing and distribute those publications to readers in minutes.

A TYPICAL HTML PAGE

One of the best examples of effective HTML design is the home page for CNN Interactive at http://www.cnn.com *The CNN Webmasters exploit all the capabilities of HTML.*

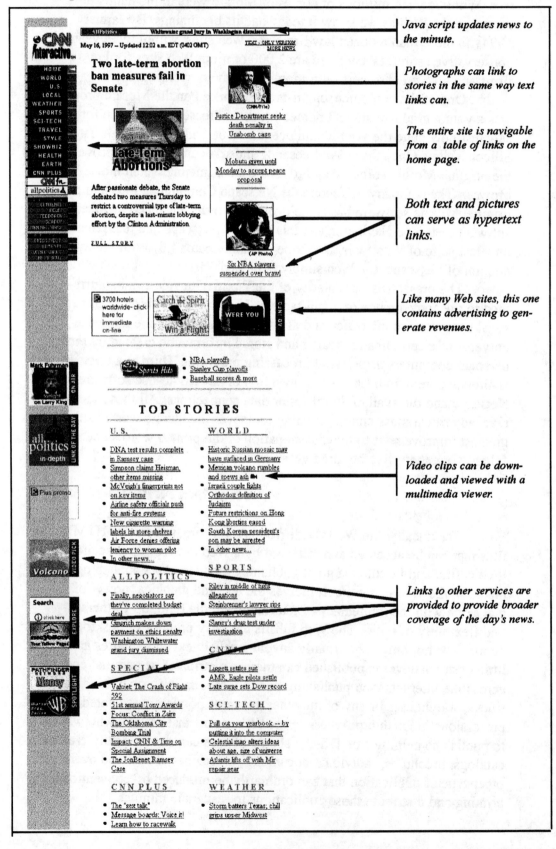

Who publishes material to the WorldWideWeb? Just about everyone. The Web is overflowing with information, the vast majority of it free. For the legal researcher, there are statutory compilations like the *U.S. Code* and state codes and collections of administrative rule-makings like the *Code of Federal Regulations*. Most Federal courts now publish decisions online. Law firms publish newsletters on their home pages. Law schools distribute law reviews. There are thousands of newspapers online as well as magazines and wire services. Corporations publish financial information and businesses print brochures. Airlines put their flight schedules on the Web; schools reprint their curricula; professional associations mount white papers and provide contact information for experts. The Web is Everybody's Publisher.

As more and more information producers mount their data on Web sites, the universe of available information continues to explode. The WorldWideWeb is poised to be the world's first truly global system for moving information between people.

There is no secret to the Web's extraordinary success and its importance in information retrieval. HTML files pack an extraordinary amount of information into easy-to-use formats that can be moved instantaneously around the globe. The science fiction of ten years ago is the WorldWideWeb of today.

It is a marvellous time for the legal researcher. The Web is way to hook into thousands of disparate information resources using the same tool and the same search techniques. Since the introduction of computer-aided legal research in the early 1980s, the researcher has been dependent on third-party vendors like Lexis and Westlaw to provide electronic access to public documents like court opinions and statutes. Now, with the Web, the researcher can access and search those same resources -- in color with hypertext links and interesting fonts -- directly from the desktop without the need for a high-priced middleman. Lexis and Westlaw changed the face of legal researcher by selling fast electronic access to public documents and proprietary editorial services. Now the Web can access and search many of the same data sources for free that once were only available from the commercial services for a fee. Because of that, the Web is turning out to be the most important online tool in legal research.

Hypertext Markup Language

The building blocks of the WorldWideWeb are individual files created in *hypertext markup language* (HTML). With one profound exception, HTML is very similar to conventional desktop publishing languages. Using HTML editor software, individual pages can be created containing text, headlines and graphical materials like pictures, drawings and video links.

The killer application that makes HTML such an important new computer language is its ability to add *hypertext* links within documents. Hypertext is a means of electronically connecting one file to another.

HTML Source Code

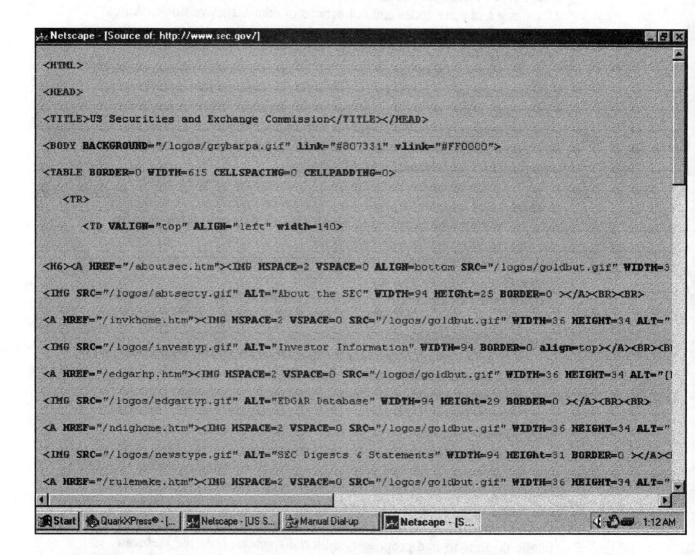

The HTML Code of the home page for the Securities and Exchange Commission. The HTML code is what is actually stored on the SEC's server. See how text and headlines are modified by HTML tags contained within the requisite angle brackets. Tags tell the Web browser how to display text, tables, graphics and multimedia files like video, audio or specialized files like ShockWave applications. Before the advent of HTML editors, now widely available, each tag had to be typed out manually to create a page using HTML. Now HTML editors can automatically add the necessary tags.

HTML pages can be created in minutes and then uploaded to a server where they will be available to anyone with access to the WorldWideWeb. Please note the code continues to the right and is not wrapped; the code is cut off in this printed display. The entire code for this page can be viewed online at *http://www.sec.gov* by selecting the "View Document Source" command on your Web browser. ❏

HTML Souce Code
Displayed by a Browser

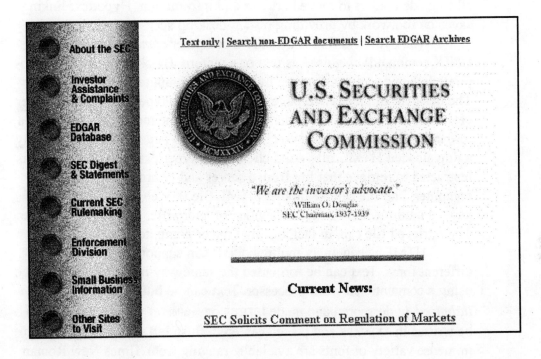

The page as displayed by a Web Browser. All Web browsers are designed to read the tags of HTML language and to translate those tags into graphic images, colors, text and links. The browser is no smarter than the page designer; it can only display what it is instructed to by the source code. The tags control where items are displayed on a page, at what size they'll appear and determine the "look and feel" of a page.

The source code is actually the "real" file of any Web page and therefore the most important material on the WorldWideWeb. Protecting the source code from vandalism by hackers is a serious security problem. In June 1996, hackers obtained access to the source code that created some of the Web pages at the Department of Justice and added obscene slogans, swastikas and other offensive electronic "graffiti" to the source files. Internet researchers accessing the site thought they were seeing official publications of the Department of Justice; the site was immediately shut down, the vandalism corrected and presumably security to prevent access to source code was beefed up. ❑

The idea underlying hypertext linking is not new. Before the electronic link was available, the print solution to "linking" was to print footnotes, bibliographies and annexes that pointed to "additional information" all to guide readers to related articles and information. Hypertext linking saves on footwork by providing instant desktop access.

The hypertext link is actually a computer *command* (usually a UNIX command) disguised as text or a picture. By clicking on the appropriate link, a command is given by the client computer to retrieve a file. The designer of the HTML page indicates in the hypertext link the name of the file and gives the browser the address of the indicated file. When a researcher, using a Web browser, looks at a Web page -- which is actually a downloaded HTML file -- and clicks on a hypertext link, the browser is instructed to retrieve that file from a server and return it to the client computer. The file can be another HTML file (a Web page), a gopher page, a multimedia file such as a video or audio file, or a simple text file. The retrieved file can, in fact, be any type of computer file at all.

HTML is genuinely multimedia. It can support color and text of different fonts. Text can be formatted the same way in HTML as it can be using a conventional word processor. Text can be **bold-faced** or *italicized*, underscored and made larger or smaller at will. Headlines can be written in ALLCAPS and placed centered, flush left or flush right. An immense variety of fonts are available, ranging from Times New Roman to Arial to Courier to specially designed fonts.

What also sets off HTML from ordinary word processing is the ability to drop in *inline graphics* and *interactive tools*. Inline graphics can be ordinary pictures -- digital photographs, scanned-in flat images, drawings, electronically-created graphics made by a digital graphics program -- or motion pictures. Video clips are commonly included on HTML pages. Audio files, in a variety of formats, liven up computers with music and sound. The toolbox of interactive tools gives HTML designers the means to drop in scroll boxes, search pages and graphics that double as hypertext links. All these features make HTML a dynamic and exciting way to present information and account for the explosive popularity of the WorldWideWeb.

Writing HTML and HTML Editors

HTML is comprised of a series of computer codes called *tags*. Tags are written instructions which are interpreted by the *browser*. The leading Web browsers are Netscape Navigator produced by Netscape Communications (*http://www.netscape.com*) and Internet Explorer from the Microsoft Corporation (*http://www.microsoft.com*). Proprietary online services such as America Online and CompuServe have their own browsers that are not as effective as software from Netscape or Microsoft but which do a passable job of reading most HTML files from the Web.

TAGS

The HTML coding language depends on *tags*, which are commands embedded within a page that tell the browser exactly how to display the page. The tags of HTML language are still evolving but the existing language is powerful and flexible. With the availability of HTML editors, HTML files are not more difficult to create than an ordinary word processing document.

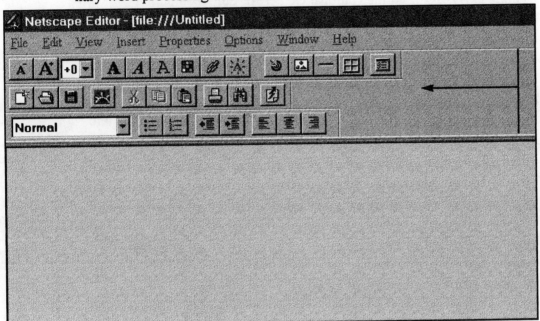

ALL THE CONTROLS NEEDED TO CREATE PROFESSIONAL-STYLE HTML DOCUMENTS ARE AVAILABLE ON NETSCAPE'S BUILT-IN HTML EDITOR. THE EDITOR PROVIDES A WAY TO ADD HYPERTEXT LINKS TO AN OTHERWISE CONVENTIONAL DOCUMENT.

HTML tags are "toggle" commands meaning that one tag begins an operation and a second matching code preceded by a forward slash ends that operation. Tags control text size, the position of graphics, the placement of boxes and frames, colors and all the other features of the Web page.

All text, picture or multimedia files that make up a single HTML file (Web page) must be tagged so that the browser can read it. Tags are always enclosed in angle brackets. Every HTML file begins and ends with the standard tags **<html> </html>** and the contents of the HTML file must appear between these two all-important tags.

There are hundreds of HTML tags, each with a very specific job to do. The most commonly used tags define headlines, body text, inline graphics, tables and colors.

Writing HTML Files

Before the advent of HTML editors, all HTML tagging was done manually; programmers needed to type out all the tags by hand to control how HTML language looked on the page. Editing software can now drop in the tags automatically, with practice, creating HTML files is now no more difficult than writing a document using a word processing program.

In fact, the latest versions of Netscape feature a built-in HTML editor that allows users to write HTML files on the fly. Most word processing software today also have HTML options that allow files to be saved as hypertext documents.

HTML is growing into a complex computer language all its own and the details of writing vivid HTML are a subject for an entire book. For a thorough look at the basics of HTML, pull up *The Beginner's Guide to HTML* from the National Center for Supercomputing Applications at *http://www.ncsa.uiuc.edu/General/Internet/WWW/HTMLPrimer.html* To get a behind-the-scenes look at how very glitzy HTML files are created, look at a page titled "How Do They Do That With HTML?" The page is located at *http://www.nashville.net/~carl/htmlguide/index.html* Webmaster Carl Tashian describes how fancy graphics, backgrounds, sounds and information management tools like

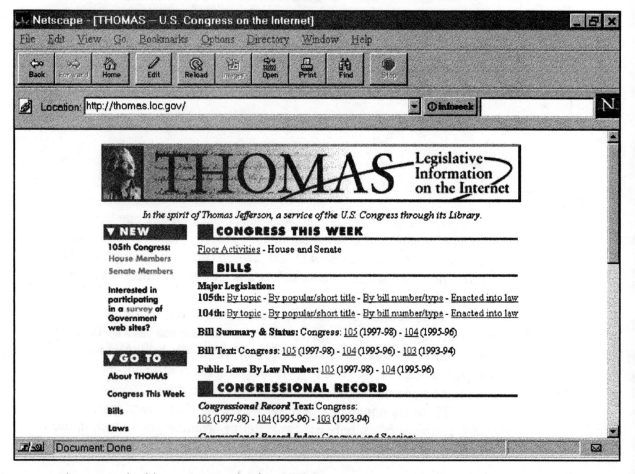

columns and tables are created using HTML.

FRAMES

A popular way of cramming the most information into the smallest possible space is the Web frame. The frame conjoins three Web pages into a single display; each frame operates like a separate Web page with its own navigation tools and its own content. Frames, initially very popular when first introduced, are dropping out of vogue among Web page designer simply because framed pages can be cluttered and hard to read.

ACTIVEX AND JAVASCRIPT

The current generation of Web tools support JavaScript "applets" and Microsoft's ActiveX pages. These are HTML add-ons that provide constant and streaming updates of data on an HTML page. In practical use, JavaScripts and ActiveX pages update news and stock price tickers, provide scrolling headlines on Web pages and make otherwise two-dimensional and flat files move. They enliven the page with color and motion and move the computer world one step closer to television.

FORMS

The researcher will encounter hundreds of *forms* on the Internet. Forms allow the researcher to order goods and services over the Internet, to subscribe to online services and to communicate with the remote data-bases. Late generation Web browsers are required to fully exploit the Web's many forms. To use forms, click on the *Tab* key from one fill-in-the-blank box to the next. Forms encourage online commerce and make it easy to reply interactively with a Web site.

MULTIMEDIA

HTML language charges into the future with a passel of new imaging technologies that make computer pages sing. For computers equipped with soundboards and speakers, audio files can play back music or recordings of speeches. Video files can replay brief video clips. This latter function is frequently used by news services to reproduce news videos.

HyperText Transfer Protocol, URLs and Domain Names

Creating files in hypertext markup language is useful, but the real power of the Web is its ability to move HTML files across a network from a server to a client computer. The protocol which sets out the technical standards that all IP-equipped computers must follow is the *hypertext transfer protocol* better known by its now ubiquitous acronym *http*.

To function properly, a browser must know where to look for a specific file. Each Web page is an individual file that resides on a specific computer on a specific network attached to the Internet. Each file, like the machine it resides on has a specific, unique address and it reports its location on the Internet in a single string of characters. These Web addresses are called Uniform Resource Locators and are always called the URL or the address.

Internet addresses are all-important because they organize the Internet. Browsers can find sites because there is a central registry of addresses maintained by the Internet Network Information Center (InterNIC at *http://rs.internic.net*)

Each network connected to the Internet is assigned to a domain. The current upper-level domains are: *.com* (Commercial); *.edu* (education); *.gov* (government); *.mil* (military); *.net* (network-related) and *.org* (non-profit organizations).Non-U.S. sites all bear country domains, a two-letter abbreviation such as *.ca* for Canada, *.uk* for the United Kingdom, *.ru* for Russia, etc. In May 1997, an international agreement was signed that will expand the number of upper-level domains to provide for an anticipated worldwide expansion of URLs and will soon be adopted.

Within each domain, each network has an assigned address. The address is actually a lengthy number that is machine-readable. This address tells the Internet routers where to send packets addressed to that specific network. These numeric IP addresses also are assigned a name to make it easier for human beings to remember. This unique name, which, when typed out, is translated back to a number so that the browsers and routers can read it, is the all-important *domain name*.

For instance, the network operated by the Massachusetts Institute of Technology is known as *mit* in the *edu* domain. It's domain name, therefore, is *mit.edu* Anyone with a computer connected at MIT to its computer network uses that as their domain name. To send e-mail to someone named Jane Smythe at MIT, the e-mail address is *jane.smythe@mit.edu* which identifies a specific mailbox at an address that is unique to MIT and its network.

In the commercial world, where owning an intuitive address for a Web site is a competitive advantage, disputes are beginning to arise as unique addresses become more rare. International Business Machines has exclusive use of the address *www.ibm.com* to identify its home page; other businesses are precluded from using it because addresses must be unique, even though Irv's Better Menswear might benefit as well from the same domain name.

Web addresses can be lengthy because there are so many individual HTML files on the Web. The forward slash, so common in many URLs, tells the browser to look for a file in a sub-directory. URLs can sometimes be unwieldy but they efficiently pack a great deal of instruction into a single string of characters As an example, the fictitious URL *http://www.lawfirm.com/newsletter/bankruptcy/automaticstay.html* tells the browser to use the hypertext transfer protocol to retrieve an html file named *automaticstay.html* which is stored in the sub-directory *bankruptcy* in the directory *newsletter* on a server in the commercial domain called *lawfirm*.

The legal issues surrounding domain names and disputes arising from the domain name dispute policies of InterNIC are interesting. For more information on this critical service, refer to the *Registration and Database Services* at InterNIC's home page at *http://rs.internic.net*

Browsers

The Swiss-Army knife of the Internet is the Web browser. Built originally to translate the tagged texts of HTML files, the latest versions of the leading Web browsers are remarkably versatile and flexible tools that can be accessorized to handle an eye-popping variety of online tasks. The Web browser is a tireless workhorse, as adept at displaying graphical materials like photographs and artwork as it is in shuffling text between computers.

For the legal researcher, the choice of Web browser is between Netscape Communications' Navigator or their suite of Internet tools called Communicator or the competing software from Microsoft known as the Internet Explorer. Both browsers function perfectly well, but Netscape offers a greater number of features that make it the preferred software for the professional legal researcher. Most new Web-based software is designed to work with both browsers, but Netscape seems to be more aggressive in making its browser more functional and expandable.

Netscape Navigator

It's no exaggeration to say that first-time users can master the use of Netscape within fifteen minutes. The software is about as user-friendly as software can be. Chunky buttons control navigation around the Web. *Back, forward* and *home* are self-explanatory. The *edit* control pulls up an HTML editor on the spot for quick creation of Web pages. Enter URLs by clicking the *open* button; print a displayed page by punching the *print* button and search for specified words within a document using the *find* command. The *stop* button crash-lands a download. The only key that novices may find baffling is the *reload* button which will go back out to the Internet and fetch the same page; the tool is useful for resetting forms or displaying a page that did not load properly.

Netscape tells the user a great deal about what it's doing at the bottom of the screen . A message bar displays the URL of the page being displayed and provides an update of the number of bytes flowing into the browser when accessing a server. The envelope icon in the right corner offers point-and-click access to the browser's built-in e-mail software. In the left corner are the security icons: a broken key indicates that the browser has accessed an unencrypted or otherwise unsecure site; conversely, a secure site displays an intact key and indicates that transmissions between the client and the host are secure.

CONFIGURING NETSCAPE NAVIGATOR

Before Netscape can be made to perform its hypertext tricks, it's necessary to configure the software. To start the configuration, click on the Options selection from the command bar. The drop-down menu offers a selection of preferences. Start with General Preferences...

GENERAL PREFERENCES

APPEARANCE

Toolbar These parameters define how Navigator will display the browser software. Netscape newbies should select the choice to display both text and pictures until the toolbar menu becomes familiar.

Startup The default setting for Netscape is to fire up the Web browser when starting Netscape. Inveterate e-mail readers or Usenet news junkies can select mail or the newsreader to pop up first instead.

Browser starts with Minimalists can select to see a blank screen when the browser starts, but ordinarily it's a good idea to set a search engine, a law-related index page or another frequently-used Web site as the default home page. Netscape comes with its own home page as the default setting but that can be changed in a trice by entering your own preferred URL.

Link styles The default setting is underlined and that is the conventional way links are displayed. The choice is strictly a matter of personal preference, however. Links that have been visited automatically change color; tell Netscape how long you'd like the color change to appear with this setup selection.

Fonts For English speakers, the setting for the Latin1 font will display text appropriately. As software that's intended to be used worldwide, Netscape also supports non-English fonts. Select from the pulldown list of other characters sets to display Japanese, Chinese, Greek, Cyrillic and other languages. Non-English character sets must be loaded optionally. Select the proportional and fixed fonts you find most graphically appearing.

COLORS

The Web is a very colorful place. Customize the browser color scheme here with a selection of colors for links, followed links and text. Select contrasting colors for maximum readability. Use the default colors or select colors from the wheel to make Netscape look like you want it to.

IMAGES

Depending on the monitor and the drivers installed on your system, select *dither*. Dither is the command that tells the computer to display the closest color to the one it is instructed to display.

Display images is a critical setting for anyone dialing in with slow modem connection. By displaying images *after loading*, you'll be able to see the textual portions of a Web without waiting for the pictures to download. Anyone accessing via ISDN, T-1 or other fast connection can allow the images to load with the text.

APPS

To function effectively as a legal research tool, the Web browser must also be equipped with software to telnet into databases. Get telnet software from one of the major software archives discussed below, install it and then set the path to the executable here. It's not necessary to have a TV3270 client, but it's helpful. Most researchers can leave the *view source* box empty. And in the box for *Temporary Directory,* define where you want temp files to be stored after downloading.

HELPERS

Add an extraordinary number of bells and whistles to Netscape by installing helper applications. (Similar software called plug-ins, which automatically start themselves when needed and run inside Netscape as if they were already built-in to the software install themselves and do not need to be configured.)

When Netscape comes across a specialized type of file it cannot read, it will look for software to run the unknown file type. Among the most useful helper apps that the legal researcher should install are:

Adobe Acrobat to read Portable Document Format files (.pdf)
MPEG Viewer to read a variety of video files (.mpg; .mpeg)
PKUnzip to unzip compressed files (.zip)
RealAudio Player to read Real Audio files (.ra)

Once the helper applications have been installed and set up, return to this page in Netscape, add the file extension the software is designed to read, click on *Launch the Application* and then set the path to the software in the dialog box so that Netscape can find the executable. (e.g. *c:/adobe/acroread.exe)*

LANGUAGE

Users who want to browse HTML files created in non-English character sets can install those optional character sets and then select the languages that the browser will accept.

Internet Explorer

In its own bid to capitalize on the Internet, Microsoft has plunged into the competition for the hearts and minds of the Web researcher with its own browser, the *Internet Explorer.* In look and feel, it operates much like the Netscape Navigator.

Internet users who remember the progression of Web browsers from the graphics-free LYNX to the the early release of Mosaic and the unsuccessful careers of some other proprietary software such as *Cello* from the Legal Information Institute at Cornell University and Pipeline have a sentimental attachment to Netscape Navigator. Many netizens resent Microsoft's ham-fisted attempts to make their browser the dominant software. It's simply not as elegant as Netscape and does not support as many plug-ins and accessories.

But is it a good browser? Yes. Internet Explorer can used by professional researchers with excellent results. Many of the functions are standard HTML commands. Like all Web browsers, the Explorer can

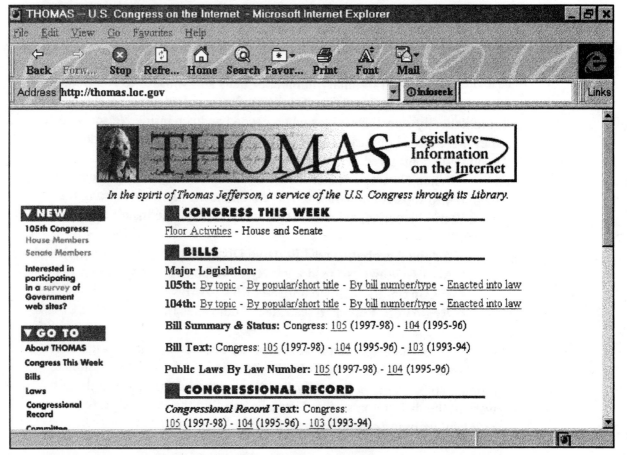

load pages, move back and forth between loaded pages, find words within a displayed document and print.

The Explorer is bundled with Windows 95 software; Microsoft encourages Windows 95 users to subscribe to the Microsoft Network in an attempt to make Microsoft everyone's Internet Service provider. Choose the service if you like -- it is as effective as any other -- and use the Explorer if the look and feel is appealing. On the Internet, strident arguments erupt over the relative merits of the two leading browsers. Netscape is the sentimental favorite but the Internet Explorer is also a trustworthy browser that comes with excellent technical support.

CONFIGURING INTERNET EXPLORER

To set up Internet Explorer, click on View|Options ..

GENERAL

Multimedia controls videos, audio files and graphics (called "pictures.") To speed the loading of pages, turn off multimedia.

Color can assign the default color configuration of your Windows setup or you may select custom colors.

Links may be underlined or not; select link colors here.

Toolbar adds or deletes items from the browser display.

Font settings changes the font display.

CONNECTION

Dialing sets the preferred method of access. Select your dial-up program if you have a dial-in account; network users will have this item set for them by the network administrator.

Proxy server is for networked users; the setting is determined by the network administrator.

NAVIGATION

Page allows the default page to be changed to a specific page, a search engine or any other URL. A search engine like Infoseek or AltaVista is always a good choice for a start page. The default setting is Microsoft's home page.

Name displays the name of the selected page.

Address is the URL of the selected start page.

History displays the URLs you visited. Set the length of time to keep the history list.

PROGRAMS

Mail and *News* equips the client software to retrieve mail and news.

Viewers is one of the most important options. Click on File Types... to display a pulldown menu of file types that require separate software to run. This is the place to add the optional Adobe Acrobat reader and other multimedia software to enable Internet Explorer to read those files it does not natively support.

SECURITY

Content advisor provides an online rating service that's handy when children have access to the terminal.

Certificates offer a way of authenticating sites to prevent criminal impersonation that is useful when money is transmitted online.

Active content turns moving applications on and off. Some Java applets represent a security threat and should be shut off if high security is a priority.

ADVANCED

Warnings alert the surfer about security status. Use the default settings unless the constant warnings become annoying; shut them off at our own risk.

Temporary Internet files are Microsoft's version of caching. Define how much space on the drive you'd like to dedicate to the cache. This is where Web pages are stored temporarily; when asked for a URL, Explorer will check to see if the page is already loaded in a local drive since it's much faster to retrieve a local file than one from the Internet. Set how often Explorer checks the cache by clicking on S*e*ttings .. Manage the files held in the cache here with the commands to view, move or empty folder. Leave the other settings in the default positions.

Cryptography settings can be left on their default settings.

Bookmarks and Favorites

For the researcher, the bookmark function is a godsend. It's a way to maintain a list of frequently visited sites that can then be accessed again with a click. The bookmark is like speed-dial for the Internet.

In Netscape, to add an address to the bookmark file, click on *Bookmarks* and then hit *Add bookmarks*. Use the *Go to bookmarks* command to access the tools needed to arrange bookmarks in logical folders. Click on the command for *Item* to display the options that control the creation of folders and separators.

Sometimes the sheer number of bookmarks becomes unwieldy and the list needs to be weeded. Delete unused bookmarks by highlighting the condemned link and then pulling down the command menu underneath the *Edit* command. Click on delete and the bookmark is zapped into oblivion.

The Internet Explorer calls bookmarks "Favorites." Add favorites under the command bar for F*a*vorites | *A*dd to favorites and manage them with the command F*a*vorites |*O*rganize Favorites ...

Intranet Applications

The Internet revolution is also storming the law office, in-house network with the *Intranet*. The retrieval, communications and organizational power of HTML can also be applied to the local area- and wide area- networks now installed at most medium to large law firms.

Intranets are a subject worthy of an entire book and there is not enough space here to discuss them in depth. To locate general information on Intranets, click on the link to Intranets from Infoseek's home page at *http://www.infoseek.com*

Other Retrieval Protocols

Gopher

As the non-graphical precursor to HTML and the Web, the utilitarian *gopher* was the first widespread means of mounting information on a hierarchical menu. Although the gopher protocol has been eclipsed, for

the most part, by HTML and the Web, gophers are still in use at many
Web sites, particularly ones that are filled with textual information that
doesn't require many graphics.

Gophers stack up links on a menu. Each link in the gopher menu
represents either a file or a directory; files and directories are defined in

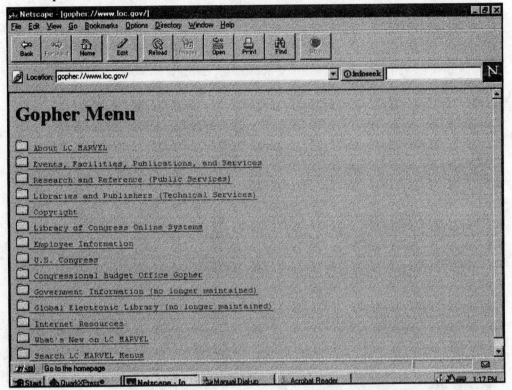

DESPITE ITS
LACK OF
GRAPHIC
PIZAZZ, THE
GOPHER IS
STILL AN
EFFECTIVE
WAY TO
ORGANIZE
INFORMATION
ON A SERV-
ER.

most gophers by a separate icon or change of color. Clicking on a file
item will retrieve that file; selecting a directory link will open the gopher
to another gopher menu.

Gophers were named for their ability to "go-fer" information on a
computer. The software was developed by the University of Minnesota
whose team mascot is, not surprisingly, the gopher.

FTP AND ANONYMOUS FTP

Unlike the fading gopher protocol, FTP is still very much alive. It
is a simple, graceful way to move files, as it name implies. FTP is an
acronym for *file transfer protocol* and is the standardized means for
accessing a directory, hunting for a file and then moving that file in one
piece across a network.

On the Internet, *anonymous FTP* is a common way of allowing
the public to access files that are stored on a privately-owned network.
Most privately-owned networks require users to have a password to log
in to the service; anonymous FTP allows users who do not have network
privileges (say students and faculty at a university, staff members at a
government server or the attorneys at a large law firm) to access certain
public files on the network.

Before search engines and the Web took over the Internet, the
only way to locate files on the network was to use a UNIX command

called *archie*. Archie was a protocol to search through archives of publicly-accessible servers -- archie is "archive" minus the "v" -- that would
return a list of where certain files were located. Now that the Web and
HTML are so prevalent, most files can be located using a browser.

The transfer of documents is still controlled by the file transfer
protocol. This is what a browser uses when it retrieves software files or
documents that are archived in PDF, Word, WordPerfect or other format.

TELNET AND HYTELNET

An early protocol for accessing simple servers, telnet and
hytelnet are still in widespread use on the Internet to access older databases. Telnet allows your computer to act like a terminal attached to a
remote network and that's why it's referred to as a "terminal application."
Telnet is also known as an "emulation protocol" for the same reason: the

TELNET CLIENTS
CAN ACCESS
OLDER DATABAS-
ES. IT DOES NOT
SUPPORT GRAPH-
ICS BUT IT IS A
USEFUL TOOL
FOR LOOKING UP
MATERIALS IN
LIBRARY CATA-
LOGS.

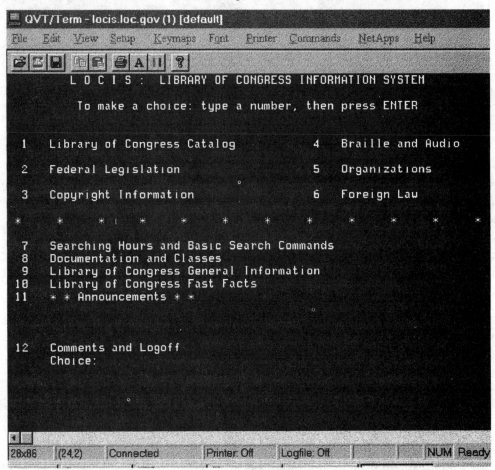

client machine dials into a network using telnet and then can emulate a
local terminal. Using telnet, it's possible to connect to the main catalog of
the New York Public Library and then browse through the catalog as if
your computer were physically attached to the network at the library's
main branch on Fifth Avenue in midtown Manhattan. Telnet is extremely
simple. It has no graphics and it still relies on line commands to navigate
remote servers. The commands themselves are clunky and, with local
variations, usually are created using a combination of the **control** key and

a single letter. Each database uses its own commands, so there are no general rules when telnetting except to read the local help file.

Despite its simplicity, telnet is an effective protocol for browsing large databases, in particular, library catalogs. Hytelnet is of special interest to the legal researcher because it was designed especially to access library catalogs worldwide. Most Web browsers do not support telnet natively.

To empower your browser to telnet to remote servers, install telnet client software and then configure your Web browser to point to the telnet software. To obtain telnet software, refer to the redoubtable collections at Forrest Stroud's site *//www.stroud.com*) or TUCOWS at *http://www.tucows.com* The most popular telnet software is EWAN (*Emulator Without A Name*) at *http://www.lysator.liu.se/~zander/ewan.html* the *TRMPTEL* freeware from Trumpet Software International at *http://www.trumpet.com* and QVT/Term, available from the Consummate Winsock Apps page at *http://http://cws.iworld.com/*

To access a telnet site after the browser has been configured, type the URL in the browser, preceded in this instance by *telnet://* and not the much more common *http://* prefix. Most telnet sites require visitors to login. Connections from Web sites to telnet sites usually indicate what the required login ID is. Follow the instructions.

HYTELNET

[Search | Suggest | What's New?]

- ***New*** Telnet WWWBoard

- About HYTELNET?

- Library Catalogs, arranged geographically
- Library Catalogs, arranged by vendor
- Help files for Library Catalogs

- Other Resources
- ***NEW*** Sites using the Java(tm) Telnet Applet
- Internet Glossary
- Telnet tips
- Telnet/TN3270 escape keys

- Link to "webCATS": web-based catalogues
- Link to Publishers' Catalogues Home Page
- HYTELNET web usage statistics

HYTELNET on the world wide web

HYTELNET PROVIDES EXCELLENT ACCESS TO HUNDREDS OF LAW LIBRARY CATALOGS WORLDWIDE AND IS A STANDARD TOOL FOR LAW LIBRARIANS.

Get Sponsored

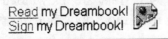
Read my Dreambook!
Sign my Dreambook!

Hytelnet software can be downloaded and run locally. Find information about this shareware on the home page of its creator Peter Scott at *http://www.lights.com/hytelnet* Even without local client software, hytelnet can still be used in its Web version at *http://library.usask.ca/hytelnet/*

In addition to its ability to browse library catalogs, arranged by geographic region, hytelnet can also look through WAIS databases and connect using the TN3270 protocol.

Utilities

For testing lines, querying servers and tracing the path the data packets are taking to arrive from the server to your client computer, make sure to have on hand some Internet utilities. These are tools to perform diagnostic tests on the Internet connection. Network connections to the Internet will have a system administrator who is responsible for maintaining the connections and for running these diagnostic tests. Users connecting from a dial-up account who are experiencing connection trouble can draw a precise bead on the likely cause of connection problems using these tools.

PING

The *ping* utility will send a signal to a known server and ask that server to echo the signal. Ping serves to determine if a connection to the Internet is operating properly. Ping will record how long it takes, in milliseconds for a signal to make a round trip from the client machine to the server.

TRACEROUTE

As the packets of information that make up the Internet are handed off from one router to another across the network, it's possible to recreate the path those packets take using the *traceroute* utility. The tool is of greatest interest to network administrators who need to troubleshoot network traffic problems. For more information on traceroute, look at *http://fnord.tlg.net/NOC/Tools/trace.html*

PDF Files and the Adobe Acrobat Reader

One of the most useful accessories for the legal researcher is the Adobe Acrobat Reader. The reader is required to decode documents that have been stored in the Adobe's Portable Document Format (PDF). Many documents, especially government forms, reports from organizations, booklets and other graphics-rich documents are very often archived using PDF format. The format retains all the fonts, headlines and colors of the original document. PDF is essentially an electronic "photograph" of a document and documents stored in PDF cannot be easily edited.

The Adobe Acrobat reader is freeware. Download the copy appropriate to your operating system from the Adobe Software Corporation at their home page at *http://www.adobe.com* ❑

Law-Related Index Pages and Search Engines

Law-Related Index Pages and Search Engines

Tracking down information on the Internet was once an aggravating, hit-or-miss exercise in futility. Even though there was only a fraction of the information online in the early years of the Internet compared to the unending cornucopia of information available now, finding files or data was a tough task. When data began pouring online in earnest after the invention of GUI Web browsers, the problem of locating and searching information became acute.

But Internet users are a resourceful bunch, and at the same time that the Web began to explode, computer scientists also saw the need to address the very real problem of navigating the rising sea of information. The two solutions that simplify finding information on the Web and other areas of the Internet are the *index page* and the *search engine*.

Index Pages

The index page -- alternately known as a "jump station" -- is a specialized Web page that is designed specifically to link to resources without providing substantive information of its own. Rather than publishing news articles, for instance, the index page instead collects links to news articles and mounts those links on its own one-stop shopping Web page.

The idea of an index page is perfectly simple. It uses the standard techniques of Web design to collect links according to a specified subject. At first, index pages evolved as the work of dedicated amateurs as one Web enthusiast after another began to share the fruits of their research with the Internet at large. These index pages are still excellent sources of information for specific, narrowly-defined subject areas. Of even greater interest are the large-scale law-related index pages that accumulate links and regularly prowl the Internet in search of the latest additions. Usually, the major index pages are sponsored by universities and law schools though three excellent index pages -- *Hieros Gamos*, *FindLaw* and *American Law Sources Online* -- are unaffiliated with any college.

As a rule, index pages are comprehensive collections of links to the information resources most frequently required by the legal researcher. The best sites are updated daily or, at minimum, weekly. The larger sites have the staff and dedication to maintain up-to-date and accurate links and it's rare to hit on a dead or deleted link.

Index pages impose organization on the oft-times unruly info sources of the Internet. For the legal researcher, the index page is a one-stop-shop for legal information; every researcher should be familiar with the leading index pages and consult them first for any research project. Most of the time, the grunt work of finding relevant information sites has already been done by the hard-working Webmasters.

American Law Sources Online

http://www.lawsource.com/also

Highlights This newcomer to the world of law-related index pages, American Law Resources Online (ALSO) is already making a splash, thanks mostly to its links to Mexican and Canadian law resources. The connections for U.S. law resources are extensive too and the Webmasters have ambitious plans for expanding their coverage.

A marvelously simple home page greets the visitors with links that can be figured out in under two seconds. Hook up with law, commentary and both federal and state resources in flash. While there's nothing here for U.S. resources that can't be found elsewhere, researchers who require materials from the other two NAFTA signatories will do well to plug in here. The Canadian links concentrate on provincial law materials such as legislations and statutes and, where available, forms and court information. The same is available for Mexican states, but is extremely limited in scope.

ALSO is still not as comprehensive as the other leading legal index pages, but if the first effort is any indication of what's to come, the site may in time become another welcome addition to the world of easy-to-search index pages for the legal researcher.

Compatible with MSIE 3.0 / 3.01 and Netscape 1.22 / 2.0 / 3.0 / 3.01 / 4.0

This is *ALSO!* . . .

AMERICAN LAW SOURCES ON-LINE

THE ESSENCE OF LEGAL RESEARCH IN TWO WORDS . . . SEE ALSO!

[United States] · [Canada] · [Mexico]

The purpose of *ALSO!* is to provide a comprehensive, uniform, and useful compilation of links to all on-line sources of American law that are available without charge. The source documents are stored, in various file formats, in many separately maintained databases located in several countries. New users should read about using *ALSO!* the first time. Some users should read about finding a lawyer and getting legal advice.

NEW We will add a search function. Please answer a four-question survey on what you would search for.

UNITED STATES

FEDERAL GOVERNMENT

LAW	COMMENTARY	PRACTICE

Alabama	Hawaii	Massachusetts	New Mexico	South Dakota
Alaska	Idaho	Michigan	New York	Tennessee
Arizona	Illinois	Minnesota	North Carolina	Texas
Arkansas	Indiana	Mississippi	North Dakota	Utah
California	Iowa	Missouri	Ohio	Vermont
Colorado	Kansas	Montana	Oklahoma	Virginia
Connecticut	Kentucky	Nebraska	Oregon	Washington
Delaware	Louisiana	Nevada	Pennsylvania	West Virginia
Florida	Maine	New Hampshire	Rhode Island	Wisconsin
Georgia	Maryland	New Jersey	South Carolina	Wyoming

American Samoa · District of Columbia · Guam · Northern Mariana Islands · Puerto Rico · Virgin Islands

Interstate, Multistate, and Boundary Compacts · Uniform Laws

Law Schools · Law Reviews and Periodicals · Law-Related Listservs

FindLaw

http://www.findlaw.com

Highlights First created as a work-shop project for the Northern California Association of Law Librarians, FindLaw has grown into a superb legal reference site. Using a sleek and elegant interface from Yahoo!, FindLaw presents a searchable index of laws, codes, law reviews and legal organizations as well as news and law school information.

FindLaw features a searchable database of Supreme Court decisions and excellent links to state law resources. FindLaw's collection of international resources is second only to those at Cornell University.

For the busy researcher, FindLaw offers a unique (and free) by-subscription mailing list of that reports on new law sites, updates existing sites and reports on law news.

An affiliated site, the Cyberspace Law Center at *http://www.cybersquirrel.com/clc* is run by Stacy Stern, one of FindLaw's three founders. The Cyberspace Law Center publishes substantive information on the emerging law of cyberspace. Links are available for resources on such issues as *commerce, privacy, freedom of expression, intellectual property* and the new area of *cybercrimes*.

FindLaw is also home to the *LawCrawler*, a search engine whose logo is a remarkably ugly spider. Powered by the industrial-strength search engine AltaVista, LawCrawler can search through researcher-defined bodies of data that include *law reviews, U.S. government sites, the U.S. Code, Supreme Court opinions* (from 1906 to present) or the entire *WorldWideWeb*. Searches for foreign law can be restricted to individual country domains.

FindLaw is not yet as comprehensive as Lawlib at Washburn U. or Hieros Gamos, but it is growing quickly. It's also the easiest of the three to search. It's an excellent service.

Internet Legal Resources — Laws Cases & Codes — Law Reviews Search & Services — LawCrawler WWW Search

US Supreme Court Decisions — vol. 200+ 1906+ — Click Here — Free Access • US Reports Citations • Full Text Searchable

[Search FindLaw] [options]

LawCrawler - Supreme Court Decisions - Law Reviews - Legal Minds

Legal Subject Index
Constitutional, Intellectual Property Labor...

Law Schools
Law Reviews, Outlines, Student Resources...

Professional Development
Career Development, CLE, Employment...

Legal Associations and Organizations

Laws: Cases and Codes
Supreme Court Opinions, Constitution, State Laws...

U.S. Federal Government Resources

State Law Resources
California, New York, Texas...

Foreign & International Resources
Country Pages, International Law, International Trade...

Hieros Gamos

http://www.hg.org

Highlights This monster of a law site, produced by a consortium of law offices and overseen by Houston, TX attorney Steve McGarry, belongs in every legal researcher's bookmark file. Promising links to more than 50,000 sites across the Internet, Hieros Gamos is undeniably well-equipped to speed the researcher to all the leading resources on the Web and to archived information. To keep this immense collection of data wieldy, Hieros Gamos is sub-divided into three parts, each with a different body of information.

HG I links to every government site online and more than 6,000 other legal organizations. Select **HG II** for connections to topically-organized subject searches and for links to discussion groups. Also find online seminars under HG II. For advertisements by support services to the legal profession (such as process servers, court reporters, experts and the like), turn to **HG III.**

The site also provides law news, a law library and an extensive collection of electronic law journals.

Hieros Gamos has its own search engine that links to more than 15,000 law-related URLs; for the busy researcher, Hieros Gamos provides more than 9,000 automatic searches that will speed the search process considerably.

For a site this huge, Hieros Gamos is very easy to search, especially by using the left-column menu from the home page. The site won't win any beauty pageants for its graphic design and the frame construction is a nuisance, but because the materials located on this site are as comprehensive as advertised, Hieros Gamos is a must-not-miss index page for the serious legal researcher. Don't miss it. ❑

SEARCH

❖ HG I ❖
DIRECTORIES

The Global Bar
Governments
Associations
Law Schools
Law Firms
Publishers
Services
Vendors
Law Sites
Legal Education
Mediators
On-line Services

❖ HG II ❖
Law Practice
200 Subjects
Discussion Groups

Hieros Gamos - The Comprehensive Legal and Government Site

HG (www.hg.org) is the largest and only comprehensive legal site with over 20,000 original pages and more than 50,000 links. HG I contains information on over 6,000 legal organizations including every government in the world. HG II 's 200+ practice areas, 300+ discussion groups and 50 doing business guides provide free access to substantive information. Now, hundreds of hours of online seminars have been incorporated as well.

HG III's self-listing user-modifiable databases for meetings, publications, employment, law firms, experts, court reporters, ADR professionals, private investigators and process servers provide a free place for the entities within the worldwide legal profession to list information about themselves and for users to be personally notified by e-mail of new content meeting their precise interests. Its other resources, News, the Law Library, the Students' Page, and Journals, are among the most extensive available on the Internet. The new Search feature accesses a database of 15,000 law related URL's. More than 9,000 automatic searches have been defined so that additional materials on the specific subject can be easily found.

Legal Information Institute

http://fatty.law.cornell.edu

Highlights The pioneering Legal Information Institute recently underwent a long-overdue makeover to bring the resources and Web search capabilities up to speed.

Best known for its links to Supreme Court materials as one of the original sites for Project Hermes, the LII is now the best site for finding searchable court rules, New York State materials and for looking through its unique e-mail directory of faculty and staff at U.S. law schools. Cornell maintains a statistical database on litigation in Federal Courts and text-searchable versions of some leading statutes such as the *Uniform Commercial Code, the Copyright Act, the Trademark Act* and the *U.S. Code.*

For keeping up with the latest developments on law-related resources on the Internet, tune in to *BigEar*, the pseudonym for Tom Bruce who monitors and publishes a digest of six law-related listservs.

The LII also reports on important appellate decisions that have been published Net-wide. Resources from around the network are cataloged by legal topic and by source type for state, Federal and international materials. ❑

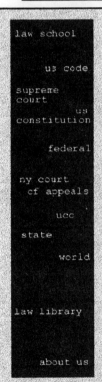

Welcome to the Legal Information Institute

a research activity of the <u>Cornell Law School</u>

This web site holds the Internet publications of the Legal Information Institute, a part of the <u>Cornell Law School</u>

The server offers the LII's collection of <u>recent</u> and <u>historic</u> Supreme Court decisions, its hypertext versions of the full <u>U.S. Code</u>, <u>U.S. Constitution</u>, Federal <u>Rules of Evidence</u> and <u>Civil Procedure</u>, <u>recent opinions of the New York Court of Appeals</u> and commentary on them from the <u>libulletin-ny</u> and other important legal materials -- <u>federal</u>, <u>state</u>, <u>foreign and international</u>. It holds the LII's <u>e-mail address directory of faculty and staff at U.S. law schools</u> as well as contact information on <u>other people and organizations</u> in the field of law. It is host to the *Cornell Law Review,* and offers information about <u>Cornell</u> <u>Law School</u> and <u>the Cornell Law Library.</u>

Internet activity is only one of the LII's activities, which include consulting, software development, and electronic publication on disk and CD-ROM. All electronic products of the LII can be <u>ordered and purchased</u> directly from this site.

- <u>Site tour</u>
- <u>Items of Special Current Interest</u>
- <u>Main Menus (Legal Topics, Sources, Organizations, People)</u>
- <u>About This Site and the LII</u>
- <u>Additional WWW Sources (Law and Other)</u>

Items of Special Current Interest Available via the LII Server Include:

- **New or Newsworthy**
  - <u>LII's Eye on the Courts - Newsworthy Decisions on the Net</u>
  - <u>What LII's BigEar Has Heard on Law-Related Lists</u>
  - <u>Decisions of the International Court of Justice</u>
  - **New From the LII**
    - <u>Immediate Downloading of LII Course Materials</u>
    [LII Disk Publications Now Available in Both Hypertext and Word-Processor Formats For Immediate Purchase and Download]

Villanova Center for Information Law and Polloy

http://www.law.vill.edu

Highlights No other index page provides faster or more comprehensive connections to courts and government sites at both the state and federal level than the Villanova Center for Information Law and Policy. This site can be considered to be a directory of American government; its links form a *de facto* guide to every wired agency on the Internet.

In addition to its remarkable services for American law sources, Villanova has added an equally impressive collection of international law resources that includes full-text statutes of a number of countries

with a comparative analysis. (Only six nations are represented as yet but stay tuned.)

The site is a meta-index page with links to other, smaller law-related index pages such as the *Legal Domain Network,* the *Legal Web* and its sponsor, the commercial newsletter *Legal.Online.*

Tax law researchers will find the *Tax Law Locator* to be the best one-stop Web site for tax law on the Internet.

For government agency research, start here. It's the best site for public Webs. ❑

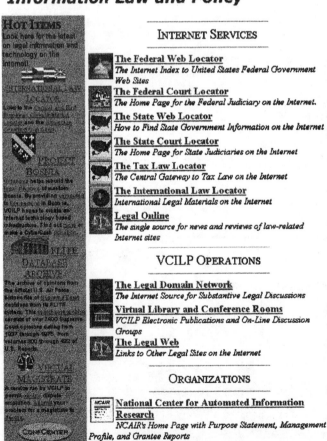

WashLaw Web
Washburn University

http://lawlib.wuacc.edu

Highlights If only one law-related index page were allowed on the Internet, this one would be the one to choose. For the sheer breadth and inventiveness of presentation, WashLaw Web from Washburn University in Topeka, KS is the best all-around law resource on the Internet, period.

It's all-inclusive pull-down menu of links offers a mind-boggling array of law resources that link to every imaginable resource: law firms and directories, bar associations and links for law librarians, commercial sites and listservs are here. Hundreds of topics are cataloged at WashLawb's site; the links are regularly groomed to insure that URLs are fresh and still operating.

In addition to the index frame, the WashLaw Web is fully searchable -- be sure to capitalize connectors for Boolean searching. A customizable form allows researchers to configure the search engine to allow typographical errors, to display links and to dictate the default number of hits.

Washburn is not only a Web site for retrieving information, it is also host to dozens of law-related listservs. And in an effort to find a professional use for Internet Relay Chat functionality, Washburn hosts the chat rooms for law librarians, reference librarians and library directors.

Do not waste a moment -- bookmark this site and use it frequently.

WashLaw WEB

Aallnet
AreaCodes
BarAssociations
BarExams
Books
BusinessDirectory
CaseLaw
Chat
Cities
Codes
CommercialSites
CourseMaterials
Courts
CourtRules
CLE
Directories
DiscussionGroups
Documents
E-MailDirectories
ExecutiveLaw
Experts/Consultants
FacultyForum
FederalLaw
FederalDocuments
ForeignLaw
Freenet
Government
GraduateSchool
HistoricDocuments
Humor
Hytelnet
Indexes
InternationalLaw
Investigators
Judges
Kansas
Law
LawFirms

Welcome!

Washburn University School of Law
1700 College
Topeka, KS 66621
Phone (913) 231-1088, Fax (913) 232-8087
Add your site? .... TERMS and CONDITIONS .... Old Version

WashLaw WEB links you to law related resources on the Internet. In addition to specialized subject areas, you may access information about Law Schools and Law Libraries. You can search "full text" for the law and law journals, as well as browse law library catalogs. The Law Library hosts many law related web servers and listserv discussion groups. Special collections include the Brown vs Board of Education materials, and Kansas Court Decisions.
Join a Discussion, Chat, Table of Contents

Query: [   ] **Submit**

Search WashlawWeb itself

Sample Query: montana AND law (note: connectors MUST be capitalized)

Reset

Help formulating queries?

To use this Broker, you need a WWW browser that supports the Forms interface.

Query Options:

☑ Case insensitive

☑ Keywords match on word boundaries

SEARCH ENGINES

It would be impossible to overstate the importance of the *search engine* to the present-day popularity of the Internet. These specialized Web pages are the network's workhorses, offering a way to quickly locate relevant Web sites, listservs, e-mail, corporate home pages, statistics data, reference materials and every other type of information that can be successfully published on the Internet. The purpose of a search engine is to find Web pages or data archives that contain the words the researcher specifies, but the two dozen or so search engines take slightly different tacks to achieve the same results.

Search engines are the point of entry to the Internet for many researchers and so attract millions of hits per day. The traffic at the leading search engines is heavy enough to support commercial ads and with a steady stream of revenue, search engines can afford to hire professional indexers and to upgrade their search software.

First-generation search engines were little more than string-searchable collections of known Internet sites. With the explosion of Web sites and commensurate increase of data, more advanced search engines use sophisticated software to scan the Internet regularly for new additions to the network.

Generally, search engines are either *indexes* which are manually compiled and electronically searchable indices of data or *robot* databases created by software programs which query every known public archive to locate the metatags of Web pages or the archives of listservs, Usenet groups or other publicly-accessible databases.

Both search systems have their advantages and drawbacks. Manually compiled index sites, like *Yahoo!*, require the editorial judgment of a staff of reviewer-indexers and can never be as current as electronically-generated databases. Likewise, the automated search engines sometimes locate many false hits and are prone to "tag stuffing." (Tag stuffing is way for unscrupulous Web designers to make their page appear on search engines even though the page's content may be irrelevant to the search terms that the researcher enters. Most large search engines have been modified to defeat tag stuffers, but the dedicated tag stuffer can always outwit even the most nimble programmer.)

Search Techniques

There are three ways to search for information on the Internet using search engines: *index searching, Boolean searching* and *relevancy searching*. Most search engines now allow searching using one or more of these strategies so that the widest number of people can use them.

Each search engine provides search tips and advice since each one differs slightly from the others. Even experienced searchers can benefit from browsing the online tips provided on the home page, especially to learn the proper way to string together words to create phrases and how to exclude terms from a search containing common or ambiguous words.

INDEX SEARCHING

Index searching is the easiest way to search. From an index-based search engine like Infoseek or Yahoo!, simply click on the subject terms. Telescoping menus will narrow the search automatically as more restrictive elements are selected. Index searching begins with broad concepts and ends with a narrowly defined set of results that should provide a set of relevant hits, if the terms selected are accurate. Successful index searching requires professional indexing skills to create the searchable database. Both Yahoo! and Infoseek are excellent and reliable indexed sites.

BOOLEAN SEARCHING

Advanced researchers can rely on Boolean searching at the major search engines. Named for the 19th-century English mathematician George Boole, whose theories of logic and set creation form the basis for modern online text searching, Boolean searching uses common phrases to include or exclude information a search.

The most common Boolean connectors are **and, or** and **and not**. Some search engines also support *adjacency* connectors which dictate how close two words must be within relation to one another. For the researcher trained to use Lexis or Westlaw, Boolean searching is a familiar way to search through databases. With a little practice, Boolean searching becomes second nature. It's a simple but powerful way to locate information easily and quickly.

Most search engines allow phrases to be constructed using quotation marks, single quotes or parentheses. To find information on Bill Clinton's policy on trade with China, for example, an effective Boolean search through a search engine like Infoseek might be:

"BILL CLINTON" AND CHINA AND TRADE

Boolean searches are easily modified; an ineffective initial search strategy can be edited very quickly to provide a more precise and on-point query.

There is a knack to writing effective queries. With practice, however, the researcher will be able to construct effective queries almost instantly.

RELEVANCY SEARCHING

The latest generation of search engines offer *relevancy* searching. Also known as *natural language searching*, relevancy searching uses a complicated algorithm to compare an entered search to a known universe of documents. The search software then gives a theoretical score to the search results; the closer a document comes to matching the search terms, the higher the relevancy score.

Lexis and Westlaw searchers will be familiar with relevancy searching through the "Freestyle" and "Westlaw is Natural" searching respectively. Relevancy searching allows the researcher to literally query a database using conversational English. Thus, a relevancy query on the Clinton Administration's policy towards trade with China might be written as

WHAT IS BILL CLINTON'S POLICY TOWARD TRADE WITH CHINA?

Search engines that use relevancy searching return a relevancy "score" that correlates the search results with the search term. A theoretically perfect match receives a score of 100% (or 1,000, depending on the search engine); as hits vary from this theoretical perfect match, the score changes correspondingly.

The software is not entirely dependable. A search may return a document with a perfect score that has no relevance at all to the query and the most relevant documents may bear a score of 90% or less.

Relevancy searching is most attractive to inexperienced searchers, amateurs or researchers who use search engines infrequently. The professional researcher will use Boolean searches more often since the queries are more flexible and use the researcher's imagination to find results, not an as-yet-imperfect search algorithm.

Modern Internet search engines use a combination of Boolean and relevancy searching to serve the largest audience of searchers.

Limitations

For all their power, search engines are still an imperfect means of searching the Internet. Even the most thorough index will miss some pages and the editorial process used to pick and choose Web sites for inclusion invariably leaves out pages that might be relevant to any one search.

Likewise, there is a great of data on Web pages that automated search engines simply do not search and therefore cannot report back. Data that is contained on a Web page in compressed format, for instance, is not searched nor is data that is published as graphical material, such as a statistical table or similar non-text item. The contents of reports that are published in non-HTML format, such as government reports in PDF format or Word 6.0 documents likewise are excluded from the search engine's otherwise all-encompassing grasp.

Search engine programmers are working to cure this problem since an increasing amount of information is hung on the Web in non-HTML format. Smart Web designers understand the limitations of the search engines and index their sites accordingly.

It's also a good idea to run the same search through more than one search engine to increase the likelihood of finding the required information.

Metasearch Search Engines

The Internet has a curious ability to conjoin related information; it can also put together similar services. Search engines that look through other search engines create meta-searches. These metasearch engines can occasionally be helpful when looking for that venerable needle in the always-popular haystack but it's usually just as effective to run a search through two or three of the leading search engines individually. While metasearching is sometimes helpful when looking for information without a clue on where to start, metasearching is slower than searching through most search engines and search queries cannot be readily edited or modified.

The most popular meta-search engine is SavvySearch at *http://wagner.cs.colostate.edu:1969* SavvySearch dispatches searches through some 25 other search engines including such specialized search engines as the Internet Movie Database, the Stanford Information Filtering Tool, LookUp! and NlightN.

Other metasearch search engines are All-in-One at *http://www.albany.net/allinone* and the Internet Sleuth at *http://www.isleuth.com*

Selecting a Search Engine

As search engines continue to improve, selecting a search engine for regular use becomes a matter of personal preference. Infoseek and AltaVista are both search engines of the first-rank. The popular Yahoo! however, is not comprehensive enough to provide support for the professional and should be used primarily for simple searches or when looking for popular, not law-related, topics. Also useful are Lycos and Magellan but because of their power and large-scale retrieval capacity, Infoseek and AltaVista should probably be the search engines in the law office.

Since they're used so often and provide such a useful service to the researcher, it's very common to designate a search engine as a default home page. That way, a search engine is always waiting for any research project that may come along. ❏

AliWeb

http://www.nexor.co.uk/ public/aliweb/ doc/introduction.html

Highlights This U.K. database is sponsored by Nexor, a developer of messaging and directory products. The accent is decidedly English and the search engine is general, not law-related, but it is one of the best tools to use when searching for resources from the United Kingdom.

Described as a "distributed cooperative catalog," AliWeb accepts index submissions from Webmasters to make a searchable database of registered URLs. The database is not as large as the other leading search engines, but AliWeb fills the gap in finding British Web sites.

Nexor also operates a number of other finding tools including *CUSI*, a unified WWW search interface, the last of the remaining archie search engines for gopherized information called *Archieplex*, a searchable collection of Internet standards documents, the *RFC Index* and the *Internet Draft Index*. Nexor also publishes an x.500 *Internet White Pages* directory and for Macintosh users, the *Mac Software Catalog*.

Find the supplementary search engines under the radio button marked *public* from the Nexor home page at *http://www.nexor.com.uk* □

Introduction to ALIWEB

A Public Service provided by NEXOR

The idea behind ALIWEB is very simple.

The World Wide Web is growing too big to find things easily. It is impossible to keep track of all the services other people provide; they change often, and there are simply too many of them.

Therefore ALIWEB proposes that people just keep track of the services they provide, in such a way that automatic programs can simply pick up their descriptions, and combine them into a searchable database.

Because automatic programs cannot understand natural language, these descriptions will have to be written in a concise and standard format.

So the way ALIWEB works is as follows:

1. People write descriptions of their services in a standard format into a file on the Web, by hand or using automatic tools.

2. They then tell ALIWEB about this file.

3. ALIWEB regularly retrieves all these files, and combines them into a searchable database.

4. Anybody can come and search this database from the Web.

Because the database can be updated regularly (currently once a day) the data is very up-to-date. Since ALIWEB does all the work of retrieveing and combining these files, people only need to worry about descriptions of their own services; so the information is likely to be correct and informative. And as only these small description files need to be gathered there is little overhead.

Hopefully this gives you an idea of what ALIWEB is about. If you want to create a description of your services for ALIWEB to include in its database, please see Registering with ALIWEB.

ALIWEB

AltaVista

http://www.altavista.digital.com

Highlights AltaVista, with Infoseek, is the search engine of choice for the professional researcher. It provides a magic wand that can find virtually anything published on the Web or in a Usenet newsgroup. It's fast and comprehensive. Select from a choice between searching the Web or looking through the immense gigabytes of Usenet from the search engine at AltaVista. (Although the name "Digital" still remains in the URL, the site is no longer affiliated with the Digital Equipment Corporation.)

AltaVista supports advanced Boolean searching (*and, or, not, near*) and, what is rare for an Internet search engine, a date restrictor; because of these capacities and its aggressie compilation of Web resources,

AltaVista ranks as one of the best search engines. It's fast, it can pull up immense amounts of information with ease and the interface is both simple to learn and simple to use.

The software that runs AltaVista is available commercially and has been adopted by many other Web sites which require powerful search capabilities. Indeed, AltaVista was developed as a demonstration project to solve the challenge of managing Very Large Memory Databases and it succeeds magnificently in cataloging the millions of pages of the Web.

Click on *Help* from the home page for a guide on constructing pinpoint simple queries. Help for more sophisticated searching is available under the link for *advanced*. ❏

Search the Web and Display the Results in Standard Form

Submit

Tip: To find how many pages point to a site (say, digital.com), try: **link:http://digital.com**

Find files this fast on your PC!

ALTAVISTA TODAY

Hot job openings: join AltaVista!

FREE: E-goodies for Windows users - join the AltaVista Visionary Club.

HOT: The only Active Firewall protects you best.

COOL: Around the World in 80 Seminars on AltaVista Software: Meet us there.

DILBERT: Are you smarter than your boss? Prove it! Play The Dilbert Trivia Game & win signed Dilbert art & other cool stuff!

VISIT THESE SITES POWERED BY ALTAVISTA

Yahoo · CNET's SEARCH.COM · 100hot Websites · LôôkSmart · InfoSpace's Directories · BlueWindow · LawCrawler · PeekABoo · WorldPages · Internet Sleuth · TechWeb · Carrefour.net International · THE ANGLE · Netcreations · WhoWhere · Bigfoot · Webreference.com · Austronaut · 123Link · The Mining Company · Netway Austria · Samara Zimbabwe

ALTAVISTA: USING ALTAVISTA SEARCH SOFTWARE ON DIGITAL UNIX, DIGITAL ALPHA AND DIGITAL STORAGEWORKS

AltaVista gives you access to the largest Web index: 31 million pages found on 627,000 servers (1,158,000 host

Excite

http://www.excite.com

Highlights Excite, like Lycos, is designed to be the search engine of choice for the non-professional user and as such, is of only limited interest to the professional researcher.

There are no features on the Excite service that can't be found on large, better-designed and more powerful search engines. Excite offers such standard links as connections to a *people finder, stock prices, news-groups, airlines, maps* and *shareware*, and a simple search box that relies on relevancy searching. Boolean search-ing is considered "advanced" search-ing and uses the plus sign (+) to add terms and the minus sign (-) to exclude terms. Additional instructions on using Excite can be found under

the link to *Search Tips*. The standard Boolean operators of *and, or, and not* and parentheses to create phrases are available to the researcher.

Excite can search the Web or Usenet newsgroups at large or can be configured to search only those Web sites reviewed by Excite's editorial staff.

The service of greatest interest to the researcher from Excite is *Newstracker*, which promises to search current news articles from more than 300 Web-based publica-tions.

Excite is a good service for ama-teur or occasional users but is not full-featured enough for professional use. ❏

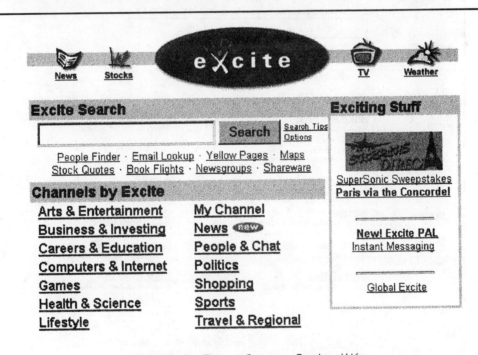

Help · Feedback · Add URL · Advertising · Jobs

Copyright © 1995-1997 Excite Inc. All rights reserved. Disclaimer

Infoseek

http://www.infoseek.com

Highlights Arguably the best search engine on the Internet, Infoseek is both a directory-style index to the Internet and a heavy-duty search engine that will meet the demanding requirements of the professional researcher.

From the home page, even novice searchers can find information quickly with a minimum of training by using the point-and-click connections to the Infoseek index. The search box supports both Boolean and relevancy searches. Click on the button for *Tips* to produce a very brief but immensely helpful tutorial on designing effective queries.

Infoseek is partners with many of the leading directory services, notably Big

Yellow, expanding its already massive database. Infoseek is the first choice for finding information on individuals online and for connecting to business Web sites.

For those researchers who select a non-search engine as their default home page, Infoseek can provide a search tool that mounts right on the Web browser like a directory button. That way, a search engine is always available without the need to access the Infoseek home page directly.

Despite its popularity, Infoseek is very rarely inaccessible, even at peak usage times and the elegant and accurate searching makes this search engine a pleasure to use. ❑

---

infoseek ®
proof of intelligent life on the net sm   BIGyellow   UPS
Yellow Pages Search   UPS™ Services

Type a specific question, **"phrase in quotes"** or **Capitalized Name**.

[   ]

the Web ▾   seek   Tips

● **news center**
Personalized News
World
Business
Technology
Sports

● **smart info**
People & Business
Stocks/Companies
Street Maps
Shareware/Chat
Desk Reference
Infoseek Investor

○ **big yellow**
Find Businesses
Find People
Find E-mail
Global Directories

News Flash: Spam Wars Reach Washington

Click a topic to explore the **Web's largest directory**:

Arts & Entertainment
books, music, games, movies...

Business |News|
business services, small business...

Computers |News|
desktop computers, hardware, software...

Education
colleges, environment, adult education...

Finance & Investment
buy a home, mutual funds...

Getting It Done
find a job, buy a car, your money...

Health
drugs, disease, fitness, women's health...

Internet |News|
intranet, HTML, web publishing...

Kids & Family Fun
Disney, parenting, cool games...

Politics |News|
elections, government, taxes, law...

Shopping
Online shopping, computers, CDs...

Sports |News|
baseball, golf, basketball, hockey...

Travel & Leisure
air travel, food, lodging, cruises...

Click **Ultraseek** to hide directory topics for advanced, streamlined searching.

Infoseek France
Infoseek Germany
Infoseek Italy
Infoseek Japan
Infoseek UK

We're Hiring! Find a Job at Infoseek.

What's New! Add your URL instantly to our index ... and other news from Infoseek.

The Intelligent way to shop on the Net... visit the Infoseek Ultrashop.

Add the power of search to your network, with Ultraseek Server.

Download free software:
Add value to your site with Infoseek Web Kit!
Take command with Microsoft ActiveX Controls!

Lycos

http://www.lycos.com

Highlights Named for the particularly aggressive wolf spider, which hunts down prey instead of laying in wait for it like most spiders, Lycos is most useful for down-and-dirty searching thanks to the plethora of pre-defined links. Lycos is designed primarily as a consumer search engine and does not provide the features required by the professional researcher. The links to *government* and *law* are severely restricted and contain only a handful of links. Lycos features good reference services such as road maps, stock quotes, travel information and a list of the most interesting sites on the Web, but its use for the legal researcher is otherwise of very limited appeal.

Lycos, like AltaVista, can locate graphical material, which makes it handy for Webmasters in need of pictures or for searching data contained within graphics such as tables or charts.

Refer to the informative *Search Help* for tips on creating precise searches through the editorially-groomed archives searchable via Lycos.

Some of the links, such as those for *plug-ins* and *news* may prove helpful in a pinch, but the researcher will do better by relying on bigger and better search engines like Infoseek or AltaVista. ❑

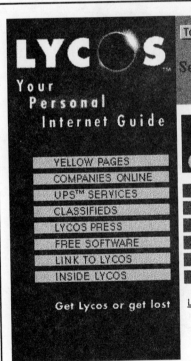

Top 5% Sites | City Guide | Pictures & Sounds | PeopleFind | StockFind | RoadMaps

Search The Web for: [   ] Go Get It

CUSTOM SEARCH

Need Help?
Start Here.

ON LYCOS NOW
- Batman & Robin
- At the Movies
- Gifts for Dad
- Life on the Edge
- Super Lycos Browser
- Take A Trip

YELLOW PAGES
COMPANIES ONLINE
UPS™ SERVICES
CLASSIFIEDS
LYCOS PRESS
FREE SOFTWARE
LINK TO LYCOS
INSIDE LYCOS

Get Lycos or get lost

NEWS | SPORTS | MONEY
TRAVEL | TECHNOLOGY | HEALTH
SCIENCE | EDUCATION | LIFESTYLE
CULTURE | SHOPPING | KIDS
BUSINESS | ENTERTAINMENT | CAREERS
FASHION | GOVERNMENT | AUTOS

Lycos Germany ▪ Lycos Sweden ▪ Lycos France
Lycos UK

City Guide UK ▪ City Guide Canada

New Search ▪ TopNews ▪ TOP 5% ▪ City Guide ▪ StockFind

PeopleFind ▪ Companies Online ▪ Road Maps ▪ Software ▪ About Lycos ▪ Help

Add Your Site to Lycos ▪ Advertise with Lycos ▪ Jobs4You ▪ New2Net

Copyright© 1997 Lycos™, Inc.
All Rights Reserved.
Lycos is a trademark
of Carnegie Mellon University
Questions & Comments

Magellan

http://www.mckinley.com

Highlights In its look and feel, Magellan has a great deal in common with the other general-interest search engines that are designed to attract an amateur audience. Like Yahoo!, Magellan's home page features a telescoping directory of subjects for point-and-click navigation through the database. It is almost identical to Excite in the way queries are constructed and provides the usual links to such common data as stock quotes, e-mail addresses, maps, weather and sports scores.

Magellan is a search engine for amateurs and should be used only for recreational purposes. It is not powerful enough for the professional researcher and the links to law-related information do not even approach being thorough.

Magellan can be used for topical searching or for looking up popular information such as news, shopping and entertainment. The search engine also provides reviewed sites which give an indication of the relative value of the Web site.

Keep Magellan for off-hours recreation or as the search engine for first-time users of the Internet. Otherwise, it's not for the legal researcher. ❏

MAGELLAN
INTERNET GUIDE

HOME | REVIEWS | INFO

[ ] search

○ Reviewed Sites Only   ○ Green Light sites only
◉ The Entire Web   Advanced Search and Tips

WEB REVIEWS

Arts
Photography, Fine Arts...

Business
Companies, Jobs, Services...

Computing
Software, Hardware...

Education
Universities, K-12...

Entertainment
Magazines, Music, Movies...

Health
Medicine, Diseases, Fitness...

Hobbies
Games, Arts & Crafts...

Investing
Investments, Personal Finance...

Life & Style
Celebrities, UFOs...

News & Reference
Newspapers, Libraries...

People Pages
A to Z, Love Stories...

Regional
Travel, Countries, Cities...

Science
Biology, Astronomy...

Shopping
Clothes, Classifieds...

Sports
Basketball, Baseball...

FEATURES

Search Voyeur

Stock Quotes
Sports Scores
City Net
Weather
Maps
Email Search
People Finder

Home | Reviews | Info | Feedback | Add Site

Yahoo!

http://www.yahoo.com

Highlights The well-known index service is indeed a large directory of screened Web sites, but like other consumer-oriented databases, it is not comprehensive enough nor powerful enough to serve as a reliable search engine for the legal researcher.

Its shortcomings as a professional tool notwithstanding, *Yahoo!* is still a good general interest search engine that is unique among the major search engines in that all sites within its database are reviewed; *Yahoo!* is an index, not a genuine search engine that queries Web sites to search for information to add to its database.

Yahoo! is good for news and for its links to reference resources, but the pull-down menu for *Law* under the subject heading *Government* is not nearly complete enough to be regularly used. The *Law* link leads to sub-directories of law information -- the most detailed part of the collection are the links to law schools. Other substantive law materials are not linked here.

Use Yahoo! for non-law research and for quick look-ups. *Yahoo!* is the smallest database of the major search engines, but it is easy to use and rarely inaccessible. It's a good, not great, service that's designed for the amateur. ❑

Federal and International Resources

FEDERAL RESOURCES

Introduction

Just like in the print world, the number one pro-ducer of information for the legal researcher is Uncle Sam himself. The Federal government has aggressively pursued the Internet as a medium to serve the citizens of the United States and the Internet. Rules and regulations, studies and reports, agency contacts and staff directories are all published to the Internet by agencies large and small. Every branch of the government participates equally in the information explosion.

The only major flaw in this otherwise embarrassingly vast ocean of data is that many of the Internet sites here are not comprehensive; there are not enough court decisions online (yet) to make the Internet a reliable tool for case law research in the way Westlaw is. Nor can the current versions of the U.S. Code be entirely relied upon though that will likely change in the near future.

And last, the biggest knock against the Internet is the lack of archives online. While it is hard to quibble with free access to the current and recent issues of the *Federal Register*, for example, the value is diminished somewhat by a lack of older issues that would permit online searching for older administrative rules. Agency decisions and the reports of administrative law judges, informal opinions, letter rulings: all these ought rightfully to be online. The technical means of publishing these types of legal documents to the Internet are simple, practical and inexpensive; the government has done a great service to the taxpayers of America by presenting information they have paid for on a free access system. Would that the government went the extra megabyte and converted their old reports into HTML and put them on a server with a URL! Perhaps that day will come but right now we must be grateful for what is already there. It is a banquet, by any measure, and a boon to the legal researcher.

Common Features of Federal Web Sites

Each Federal Web site has its own personality. There's no graphic uniformity throughout the government and that is an excellent thing. It gives the Webmasters at each agency and bureau the latitude to allow form to follow function in the design of individual sites and gives the researcher the benefit of each Web designer's expertise in the particular information each office produces. Rather than trying to fit a weather bureau satellite image into the same type of Web site that might be otherwise ideal for a corporate proxy statement or a reprint of the spectrum auction of wireless broadcast channels, the government is working more like a private enterprise than a hulking bureaucracy: it gives the Webmasters the freedom to present their information in lively and therefore useable formats. Each Webmaster customizes his or her own office's information to best advantage. Still, there are certain designs that are found on nearly every Federal Web site to help the researcher get around.

SITEMAPS

The Web sites run by government agencies, particularly the Cabinet departments, are immense databases, containing more than 500 individual files in some cases. The Department of Labor for instance, operates a sprawling Web site that publishes statistics, regulations, statutes, *Federal Register* entries and a vast library of other useful data on labor and employment law. A single Web page cannot be designed to link elegantly to all of the resources within the Web. The solution to navigating these Brobdignagian Webs are *sitemaps*, graphic pages that describe how the Web site is structured and how to find information within the confines of the database. Sitemaps are invaluable tools for the large Federal Webs and should always be consulted first when researching on an unfamiliar Web site. Sitemaps orient the visitor and speed up the learning process when wandering in the dark of cyberspace.

SEARCH BARS

Hotlinked pushbuttons or alphabetical bars are common navigational aids. Use them for finding information quickly on a Federal site.

WEBMASTER

Every Federal Web site has a network administrator known as a Webmaster who can be contacted for additional information. Although the Webmaster generally is concerned mostly with technical matters such as correcting dead links, proofreading inoperative or erroneous addresses and tinkering with servers that don't serve, the Webmaster is a good point of contact for asking about the timeliness of information and the reliability of the data if that information is not readily available implicitly on the site. And even if the Webmaster can't answer the questions, he or she is in a good position to locate the appropriate person within the agency who can respond appropriately.

Index Pages for Federal Web Sites

The quickest way to find Federal Web sites is to use an index page containing the necessary links. The best index pages all are operated by universities; one is a government-run Web site. Index pages are frequently updated and can be trusted to zero in on government offices as they are added to the lengthy roster of government sites online. Which index page one uses is a matter of personal taste; each of these servers will deliver the researcher to the government's electronic doorstep in milliseconds.

Federal Web Locator
Villanova Center for Information Law and Policy
http://www.law.vill.edu

U.S. Federal Government Agencies Page
Louisiana State University
http://www.lib.lsu.edu/gov/fedgov.html

WashLawWeb
Washburn University
http://lawlib.wuacc.edu

Government Information Locator Service
http://www.gils.gov

A Note About the Web Sites Selected

With the proliferation of Federal Web sites, selecting which ones
to include in a basic textbook meant ignoring many of the sites maintained by smaller offices and sub-agencies. Because of space limitations,
only those sites with the widest professional interest were selected.
These sites are reliable and accurate and tend not to change drastically.
Each of them has a Webmaster overseeing the maintenance of the site
and the resources mounted on them have a good degree of credibility and
currency.

This collection is deliberately not comprehensive; it's expected
that the legal researcher will be able to connect to a wired sub-agency by
consulting the relevant Cabinet department, independent commission or
other higher-level entity. Links will provide the navigational path to the
smaller office. Refer to one of the index pages for connections to government offices of limited or regional interest.

❏

Office of the President

http://www.whitehouse.gov

Highlights The servers at 1600 Pennsylvania Avenue host an extensive banquet of information from the office of the nation's Chief Executive. The researcher will appreciate the the *Virtual Library* containing White House documents and speeches and the *Briefing Room* where press releases and Federal statistics are on the menu.

The White House Web site is quickly becoming an index page for Federal materials with its extensive links to the most commonly asked-for Federal services which lead to the Cabinet Web sites.

Keep up with the President's hectic schedule with the link to *What's New*. That's the site which publishes the First Citizen's travel schedule and official appointments.

The remainder of this handsome Web site is devoted to virtual tours of the White House, outlines of the President's political initiatives and biographical information. A FAQ file at the *Help Desk* helps first-time visitors navigate the site with ease. ❏

[Text version]

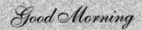

Good Morning

Welcome to the White House

The President & Vice President: Their accomplishments, their families, and how to send them electronic mail

Commonly Requested Federal Services: Direct access to Federal Services

Interactive Citizens' Handbook: Your guide to information about the Federal government

What's New: What's happening at the White House - **President Clinton's Trip to Spain, Poland, Romania and Denmark**

White House History and Tours: Past Presidents and First Families, Art in the President's House and Tours -- **Tour Information**

Site News: Recent additions to our site - **President's Initiative on Race**

The Virtual Library: Search White House documents, listen to speeches, and view photos

The Briefing Room: Today's releases, hot topics, and the latest Federal statistics

Office of the Vice President

http://www.whitehouse.gov/WH/EOP/OVP/html/GORE_Home.html

HIGHLIGHTS The Vice President, with little more to do constitutionally than break ties in the Senate and attend state funerals in distant kingdoms, whiles away his spare time with this politicized but nonetheless informative Web site that highlights the issues closest to the Vice President's heart: the environment and the Internet.

The high-tech home page uses all the tools of HTML programming to produce a site with audio, video clips and special features such as the report on *24 Hours in Cyberspace*.

For the researcher, the most important links are the ones to the *National Performance Review*, the commission created to streamline government and the *Empowerment Zone and Enterprise Community Program* for revitalizing inner cities. All Internet researchers should be acquainted with the National Information Infrastructure -- and the curious claim that Mr. Gore coined the term "information superhighway" in 1980 -- which is a prominent presence and a link on the page. ❏

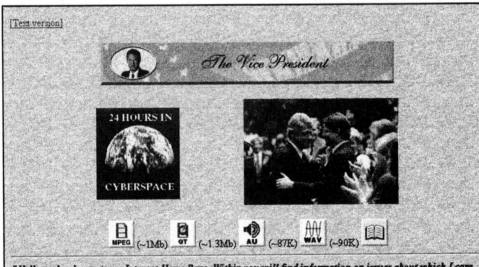

[Text version]

The Vice President

24 HOURS IN CYBERSPACE

MPEG (~1Mb)   QT (~1.3Mb)   AU (~87K)   WAV (~90K)

"Hello and welcome to my Internet Home Page. Within you will find information on issues about which I care deeply including my work to protect and preserve the environment, help revitalize America's communities, reinvent the federal government to make it work better and cost less, support and strengthen families through annual policy conferences, and promote the development and use of technology. Enjoy your visit, and don't forget to take a look at one of my favorite spots -- the cartoon gallery."

♻ Al Gore's commitment and leadership on environmental issues is unparalleled. He has said the protection and preservation of the earth's environment is one of the most important issues facing this generation.

Within two months of taking office, President Clinton asked Vice President Gore to do a comprehensive survey of the entire federal government. Vice President Gore answered the challenge with his National Performance Review: Creating a Government that Works Better and Costs Less report, which produced hundreds of specific recommendations and cost savings reforms to improve the federal government and save taxpayers money. President Clinton and Vice President Gore are leading a revolution to to give you better service from your government.

In addition, Vice President Gore continues his work to rebuild and revitalize America's inner cities and rural areas through his leadership role in the Empowerment Zone and Enterprise Community Program.

Office of Management and Budget

http://www2.whitehouse.gov/WH/ EOP/OMB/html/ombhome.html

HIGHLIGHTS The Office of Management and Budget is charged with the primary task of advising the President on the preparation of the Federal budget; a copy of Uncle Sam's annual outlays is online for public perusal at the OMB's home page.

In addition to the budget, itself a massive undertaking, the OMB discharges other duties under the President's authority: OMB *circulars* are instructions issued to Federal agencies that have an effect of more than two years and OMB *bulletins* which are more transitory and have an effect of less than one year.

The OMB also publishes details of the office's high-priority projects and reports on the regulations and paperwork reduction plans under review. Grants management and submissions to the *Federal Register* fall under OMB's purview; find links to the same from the home page.

Other links lead to employment opportunities and a handful of Federal agencies. ❏

[Text version]

Last Updated: March 5, 1997

Welcome to the
Office of Management and Budget

OMB's Role | Organization of OMB | Federal Budget
OMB Documents | Employment Information | Index
OMB Locator

OMB's Role

OMB's predominant mission is to assist the President in overseeing the preparation of the Federal budget and to supervise its administration in Executive Branch agencies. In helping to formulate the President's spending plans, OMB evaluates the effectiveness of agency programs, policies, and procedures, assesses competing funding demands among agencies, and sets funding priorities. OMB ensures that agency reports, rules, testimony, and proposed legislation are consistent with the President's budget and with Administration policies.

In addition, OMB oversees and coordinates the Administration's procurement, financial management, information, and regulatory policies. In each of these areas, OMB's role is to help improve administrative management, to develop better performance measures and coordinating mechanisms, and to reduce any unnecessary burdens on the public.

Organization of OMB

The Director of OMB is Franklin D. Raines.
The Deputy Director of OMB is Jacob J. Lew.
The Deputy Director for Management of OMB is John A. Koskinen.

The budget and review functions in OMB report directly to the Director and the Deputy Director, while the management and regulatory responsibilities are normally under the supervision of the Deputy Director for Management.

Office of Personnel Management

http://www.opm.gov/index.htm

HIGHLIGHTS One thing politicians of every stripe agree upon: the Federal government is huge and by huge, they mean that it employs a lot of people. Keeping track of all the millions of individuals who draw a Federal paycheck is a task that falls to the Office of Personnel Management, or, as they like to call themselves, the "Federal Government's Human Resources Agency." Whatever they call themselves, this is probably the only personnel agency that reposts Public Laws signed by the President on its Web site to provide a convenient means to alert all its employees about changes to their employment buyouts.

Many regulations are tied to the this home page, most of them clearly of interest to civil servants. There are regs for the *Family and Medical Leave Act*, *Career Transition Assistance* and a *Jobs* list.

Click on the link to the *Index* for a seemingly endless list of agency links to information about pay grades, merit reviews and the like. ❑

United States

Office of Personnel Management

The Federal Government's Human Resources Agency

DC Area Federal Gov't Operating Status

* **Index**
* **What's Hot**
* **What's New**

* **OPM Federal Register Documents**
* **OPM News**
* **USA Jobs**
* **Veterans and Uniformed Services**
* **What is OPM?**

 What's Hot

* 10th Annual National Conference on Federal Quality, July 9-11, 1997
* 1997 Federal Pay Tables
* Employee's Guide to Buyouts Under Public Law 104-208
* FederaLIST
* Final Regulations on Family and Medical Leave
* Satellite Broadcast, Wednesday, April 2, 1997
* Voluntary Separation Incentive Program Guide
* Welfare to Work NEW
* Workshop on the Administration of Family-Friendly Leave Policies, May 15, 1997

Document Accessibility

OPM News

Department of Agriculture

http://www.usda.gov

Highlights The massive Department of Agriculture sprawls across many services, all of which are tied by hypertext links to the Ag Department's home page. In addition to agricultural services, the department also oversees rural development and publishes news of FOIA requests, farm bills and budget summaries. Find the news and current information under the link to the appropriately named *News and Information*.

The Aggies provide speakers for appearances; also find a lengthy list of department publications online.

The link to *About USDA* will provide the researcher with a copy of the *Agriculture* title of the U.S. Code. Look under the same connection for support programs, an organization chart, links to the fraud hotline and strategic plan and details on the department's various support programs.

The materials mounted on the USDA Web site are broad enough to require a search engine. Find it at *http://www.usda.gov/gils/ usdagils.htm* ❑

United States Department of Agriculture

NEWS & INFORMATION   WHAT'S NEW

ABOUT USDA   AGENCIES

OPPORTUNITIES   SEARCH/HELP

Send comments and suggestions about content of USDA's Home Page to Victor Powell at Internet: vic.powell@usda.gov

Department of Commerce

http://www.doc.gov

HIGHLIGHTS The vast reaches of the Department of Commerce with its plentiful bureaus, business and trade offices, statistical services and services to businesses and information providers is an electronic trove of information for the researcher. All of the department's informational largesse is mounted on a simple and graphically ho-hum server that still provides fast links to big data.

The Federal government's newspaper of business, *Commerce Business Daily,* is online and accessible from the home page. So are very useful directories to the thousands of Commerce staffers stationed throughout the world (and cyberspace.)

The frame for *Commerce on the Web* is the mother lode of economic information from the Feds. Find links here to all the leading services, each of which is, in turn,an in-depth source for official statistics and reports on economic matters.

The site is designed well enough that a sitemap is not required. Drill down through the Web pages. ❑

Welcome to the U.S. Department of Commerce

The official seal of the U.S. Department of Commerce; the main entrance of the Herbert C. Hoover Building in Washington, D.C., headquarters of the U.S. Department of Commerce; and William M. Daley, Secretary of Commerce.

General Information...	Commerce on the Web...
Information from the Office of the Secretary	Commerce Web Sites (Arranged by Bureau)
Commerce Email Addresses	Business and Trade
Commerce Telephone Numbers	The Economy and Statistics
Announcements, Bulletins, and Events	Science and Technology
Commerce "Site of the Week"	Information and Business Services

Read the Commerce Strategic Plan

Visit the White House

Visit Commerce Business Daily On-Line (CBDNet)

Visit the Government Information Locator System (GILS)

We want to hear from you. Contact us!

Established on February 14, 1903, to promote American businesses and trade, the U.S. Department of Commerce is the most versatile agency in government. Its broad range of responsibilities include expanding U.S. exports, developing innovative technologies, gathering and disseminating statistical data, measuring economic growth, granting patents, promoting minority entrepreneurship, predicting the weather and monitoring stewardship. As diverse as Commerce's services are, there is an overarching mandate that unifies them: to work with the business community to foster economic growth and the creation of new American jobs.

Date this page was last updated: 06/05/97

Department of Defense

http://www.dtic.mil/defenselink/

HIGHLIGHTS The Cold War is over -- and the military's ARPANet is now known globally as the Internet -- and the military services have turned an eye to online technology.

From the DefenseLINK home page, quickly proceed down the chain of command via the obvious links that lead from the Secretary of Defense's home page through the home pages of the Armed Forces, the Joint Chiefs of Staff to other organizations.

Defense directives and instructions are reprinted on the site and a description of weapons systems. Obvious concerns of national security take precedence over loading these Web sites with information that shouldn't be in the wrong hands: policies of what is acceptable and what is not is set out on this page.

The peace dividend is showing up online with business guides, educational and historical links to help navigate the military's immense bureaucratic structure. ❏

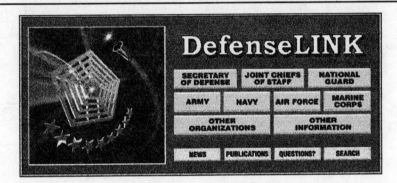

Secretary of Defense William S. Cohen and Deputy Secretary John White would like to welcome you to DefenseLINK, the World-Wide Web Information Service from the Department of Defense.

TOP STORY - Roswell Report - Case Closed

We invite you to visit the American Forces Information Service WWW site for information about the Department's internal news, visual information, entertainment, and educational services; and the American Forces Press Service WWW site to read news and view photographs of Department of Defense activities.

We also invite you to visit BosniaLINK, the official DoD information system about U.S. military activities in Operation Joint Guard. BosniaLINK now includes access to *TALON*, the newspaper serving the soldiers of Task Force Eagle, and to the Stabilization Force (SFOR) fact sheets.

The **Department of Defense** is responsible for providing the military forces needed to deter war and protect the security of our country. The department's headquarters is at the Pentagon.

Under the President, who is also Commander in Chief, the Secretary of Defense exercises the authority, direction, and control over the department, which includes:

- The Secretary of Defense
- The Joint Chiefs of Staff
- The National Guard
- The Army
- The Navy
- The Air Force
- The Marine Corps

Department of Education

http://www.ed.gov

HIGHLIGHTS Energetic and dedicated educational activists operate this Web site and the excitement is almost palpable. The legal researcher is best served with the links from the home page to the *Secretary's Initiatives* where legislation and regulatory action can be found.

The Department publishes a great number of newsletters, research "syntheses," statistics, resource directories and is very forthcoming online about its many major programs to improve American education.

Organizational charts and a telephone directory provide quick access to the department's staff.

The site is equipped with a search engine to speed lookups of stray facts and publications on the extensive Web site. Also find FAQ files and information on grants on the site. ❑

President Announces Education as "Number One Priority", Issues 10-Point Education Plan in State of the Union

Help us improve this site

 # Welcome

What is the Department of Education? Read this brief introduction to learn about the Department, its mission and goals for American education, and also discover some of the special features that this award-winning Web site has to offer.

 # News

What's making the news at the Department of Education? Look here for pointers to the latest information we've added, including: announcements of new funding opportunities, press releases, transcripts of speeches and testimony made by Secretary Richard Riley, and updates on current legislation and our budget.

 # Guides

Whether you are a **teacher**, a **researcher**, or a **student** you have specialized information needs and interests. What resources does the Department make available especially for you? The answer is "lots!" So much, in fact, that we publish three books about what we have to offer -- one for teachers (*Teacher's Guide to the Department of Education*), another for researchers (*Researcher's Guide to the Department of Education*) and for the students we have *The Student Guide to Financial Aid* . We're also starting to collect links to ED-sponsored Internet resources for **parents**.

Department of Energy

http://www.doe.gov

HIGHLIGHTS Recently declassified information joins established online systems to provide electronic access to a deep body of data about the U.S. energy industry.

Links head to labs and field facilities home pages from the department's labs across the country, each of which operates fairly well-detailed servers. Find links on the home page to recent directives and *Code of Federal Regulations* publications.

Directories publish the telephone and e-mail addresses of staff nationwide; keep current on the DOE's latest speeches and public meetings at the home page link to *Department of Energy News and Hot Topics.* ❏

UNITED STATES DEPARTMENT OF

Search Home Page contents

 About The Department of Energy (Learn about the Department of Energy, its mission, plans, organizational structure, and accomplishments.)

 Departmental Resources (Look for information across the Department, connect to other Home Pages, or search for DOE Scientific and Technical Information.)

 Department of Energy News and Hot Topics (Information of current interest such as notices of upcoming public meetings, Secretary of Energy speeches and correspondence, Technology Partnership Opportunities, DOE Directives (includes Orders), DOE Acquistion Regulations (DEAR) and Code of Federal Regulations (CFRs), DOE R&D Tracking Database, training, etc.)

 What's New on the Department's Network (Announcements of new home pages, databases, etc.)

 People, Places and Organizations (Telephone numbers, E-mail and mailing addresses from across the Department and other organizational information.)

 OpenNet (References to the Department's declassified information.)

 Electronic Exchange Initiative (Electronic exchange of scientific and technical documents.)

 THE WHITE HOUSE

 THE UNITED STATES CONGRESS

Department of Health and Human Services

http://www.os.dhhs.gov

HIGHLIGHTS For medico-legal research, an excellent place to start is with the services provided by the Department of Health and Human Services, in particular Pub Med, a database containing links to more than nine-million citations in medical journals and research publications, including the massive Medline.

As one of the largest Federal Web sites, refer to the *Search* button to navigate the lengthy stretches of cyberspace drawing the many Web pages together at this huge site. The search page is sortable and can be restricted by different data fields including *recent laws and executive orders* and *testimony since 1992.* ❏

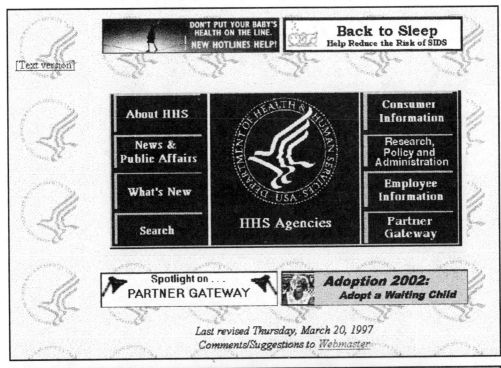

Last revised Thursday, March 20, 1997
Comments/Suggestions to Webmaster

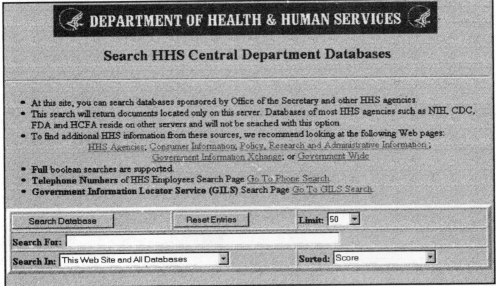

Department of Housing and Urban Development

http://www.hud.gov

HIGHLIGHTS Uncle Sam's home-finders conduct business on the Web by linking up what it calls "citizens" --homeowners, senior citizens, veterans and others -- and "partners," a group that includes academics, attorneys, investors, the media and state and local government. The links to local resources are thorough and are arranged by state. There is enough material stretched out on this Web site to warrant a sitemap; use it to find homes for sale, funding, the HUD phonebook, a research center and news.

There's a link installed to the Inspector General Hotline for fast reporting of fraud, waste and abuse ion HUD programs. Informal complaints are accepted by e-mail. ❑

HOMES and COMMUNITIES

U.S. DEPARTMENT OF HOUSING AND URBAN DEVELOPMENT

NEWS

SITE MAP

SEARCH

COMMENTS

LOCAL OFFICES

VISITORS

1004387

Our job at HUD is to help people find homes and to help our Nation's communities develop and thrive.

against bad landlords. Read more in the News.

For Citizens, we offer tips on home buying, mortgage shopping, and finding affordable rental housing. We list HUD homes for sale and opportunities for you to volunteer to help your community. And you can chat "Over the Back Fence" with your neighbors all over the Nation.

For Community and Business Partners, we have information about funding, technical assistance, best practices, contracting opportunities, major HUD initiatives, and more.

If you aren't sure where to go, check out our site map or use our search. We hope you enjoy your visit!

EQUAL HOUSING OPPORTUNITY

Department of Housing and Urban Development
451 7th Street SW, Washington, DC 20410
Please read our disclaimer.

HUD

Web Site Search Tool

The Web Site Search Tool will allow you to conduct searches of all the documents on HUD's Web Server by term. The results of a search will return the documents most likely to contain the information you desire.

HUD Form Finder Search Tool

The HUD Form Finder Search Tool will allow you to conduct searches on all the forms available on HUD's Web Server. The results of a search will return links to forms you may print and fill out.

Department of the Interior

http://www.doi.gov

HIGHLIGHTS The home page for the Department of the Internet is ergonometrically designed for providing the most bureaucratic information with the least amount of effort. Two side-by-side scroll boxes -- one labeled *Index to Topics* and the other one *Bureaus and Offices* -- are the only paddles required to navigate this info-river. Topically, the site connects to *Policies and Procedures, News, Maps and Spatial Data, Library of Natural Resources, Laws and Regulations (*which are links to sub-agency Web sites) and *Federal Resources* among others.

Other online services include a directory of each of the Department's offices and bureaus and links to the home pages. Also find speeches, policies and the latest news stocked on the home page. ❑

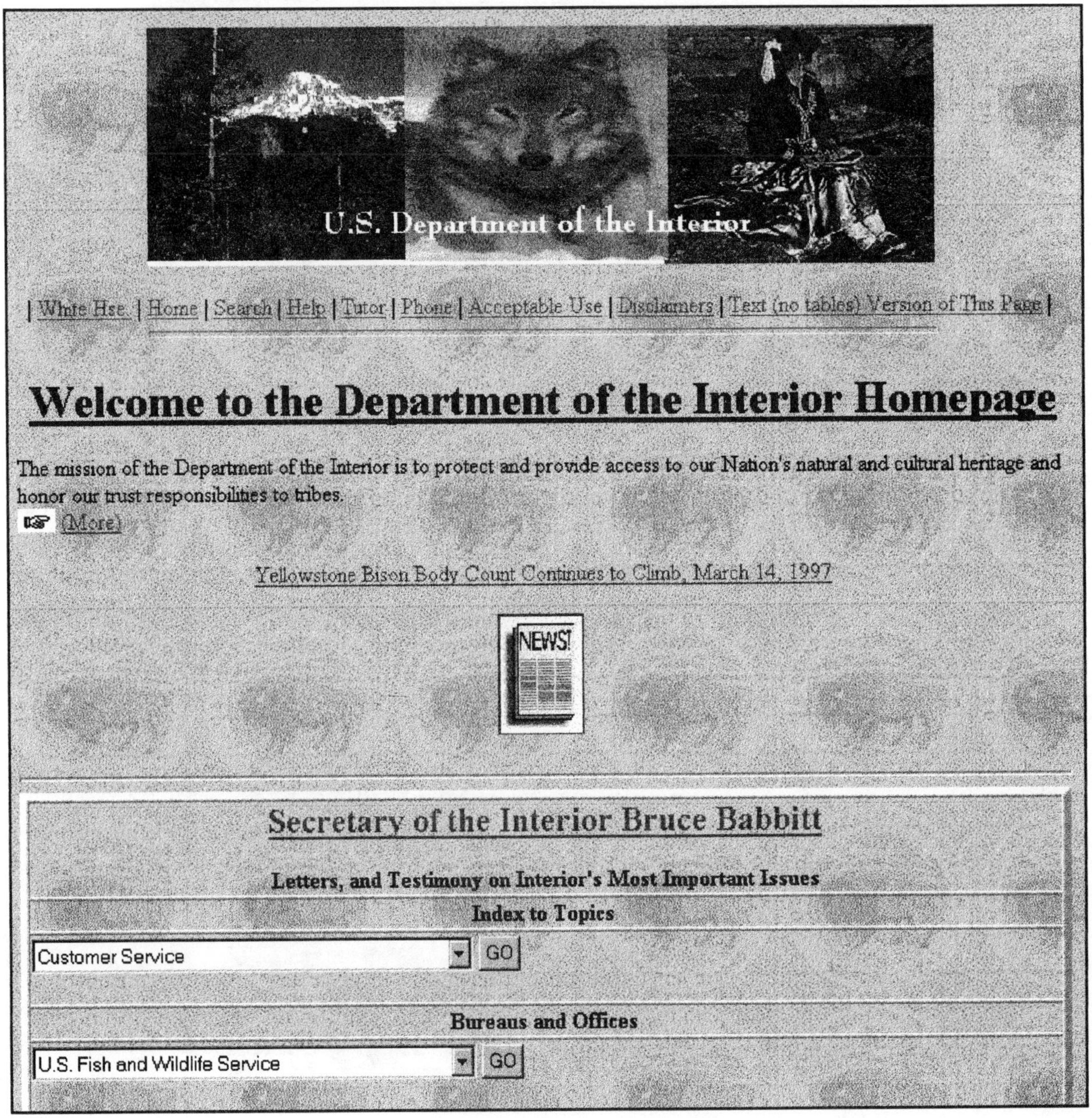
U.S. Department of the Interior
| White Hse. | Home | Search | Help | Tutor | Phone | Acceptable Use | Disclaimers | Text (no tables) Version of This Page |
Welcome to the Department of the Interior Homepage
The mission of the Department of the Interior is to protect and provide access to our Nation's natural and cultural heritage and honor our trust responsibilities to tribes.
(More)
Yellowstone Bison Body Count Continues to Climb, March 14, 1997
NEWS!
Secretary of the Interior Bruce Babbitt
Letters, and Testimony on Interior's Most Important Issues
Index to Topics
Customer Service
GO
Bureaus and Offices
U.S. Fish and Wildlife Service
GO

Department of Justice

http://www.usdoj.gov

HIGHLIGHTS The largest law firm in the nation has the nation's dullest Web site. Certainly restraint and dignity should be the hallmarks of any professional site design but the Department of Justice errs too critically on the side of caution. Still, the links to the various divisions at the Department of Justice are worth the search. The Antitrust Division is a representative example. It mounts press releases and speeches by senior officials, its antitrust guidelines, an archive of briefs, business review letters and bank merger news and Congressional testimony. Similar materials are available from the other divisions as well.

Some three dozen agencies and offices are linked to the Department of Justice site so even if the initial pages prove disappointing, the links to the sub-agencies prove to be more enlightening and much more informative. ❑

United States Department of Justice

Attorney General: Janet Reno

As the largest law firm in the Nation, the Department of Justice serves as counsel for its citizens. It represents them in enforcing the law in the public interest. Through its thousands of lawyers, investigators, and agents, the Department plays the key role in protection against criminals and subversion, in ensuring healthy competition of business in our free enterprise system, in safeguarding the consumer, and in enforcing drug, immigration, and naturalization laws. The Department also plays a significant role in protecting citizens through its efforts for effective law enforcement, crime prevention, crime detection, and prosecution and rehabilitation of offenders.

Moreover, the Department conducts all suits in the Supreme Court in which the United States is concerned. It represents the Government in legal matters generally, rendering legal advice and opinions, upon request, to the President and to the heads of the executive departments. The Attorney General supervises and directs these activities, as well as those of the U.S. Attorneys and U.S. Marshals in the various judicial districts around the country.

Locating Department of Justice Information:

Search the Justice Department WWW Server

Justice Department Organizations - By organizational structure

Justice Department Organizations - Alphabetically by organization name

Topical index

Justice Department Issues, News, Topics of Interest

Justice Department Press Releases

Department of Labor

http://www.dol.gov

HIGHLIGHTS The workers of the cyberworld unite online at the Department of Labor where a plethora of statistics, charts and statutory and regulatory information are now gainfully employed on a hard-toiling server.

Among the information goods supplied by the Department of Labor and its many sub-agencies are the unemployment rate in a number of incarnations, statistics on workplace accidents and injuries and media releases. To help smaller business comply with the myriad regulations governing employment relationships, the department operates a page containing many links to a summary and full text of laws and executive orders and a brief description of the major laws the DoL administers.

The Department is forthcoming about its programs; find descriptions of the agency's activities under the link to the same. Use this site for its statistics, though; it's the best part. ❏

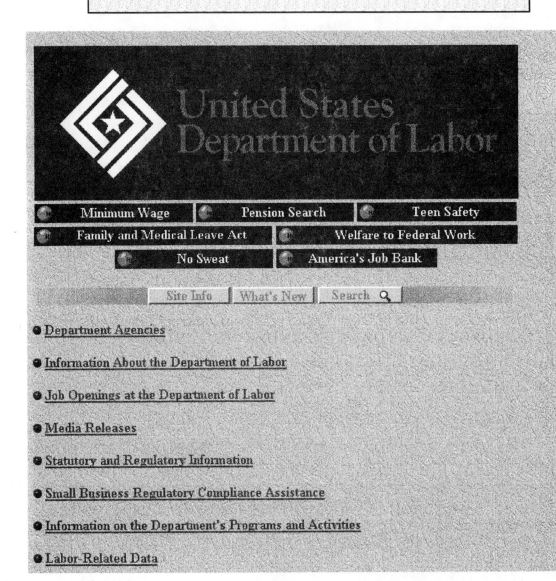

Department of State

http://www.state.gov

HIGHLIGHTS The Department of State does not trifle with graphics; this Web is a no-nonsense and excellent collection of links to its primary public services. Link up with policies from regions around the globe, country background notes and issues of global importance such as countering narcotics traffic, spreading democracy, protecting the oceans and the environment and the status of women.

Ongoing policy issues are published here. So too are press releases from points around the world; find out the official take on international situations from the appropriate regional link. Travel advisories and recommended vaccinations for travelers with itineraries to politically or medically unstable countries are online at the site as well. Librarian alert: a list of the countries of the world is available here. ❑

Text Only Version
Last Updated: Friday, March 28, 1997

Search the U.S. Department of State Web Site

Enter your keywords below at the "Query" prompt to search the **U.S. Department of State Web Site** full-text index to documents 1996-present. [Search tips are available here.]

Query:

| Search with results in table format | Search with text results | Max # documents: 20 |

Search the Secretary of State Web Site (Full-text index to documents 1997-Present)

Search the Gopher Research Collection (Title-only index to files 1993-Present)

Return to the DOSFAN Home Page.
This is an official U.S. Government source for information on the WWW. Inclusion of non-U.S. Government links does not imply endorsement of contents.

Department of Transportation

http://www.dot.gov

HIGHLIGHTS The Department of Transportation moves itself into the Electronic Age with a sophisticated and complex database of information that provide links to all of its sub-agencies, news and statistics and current legislation and regulation. The researcher will be pleased to find a National Transportation Library containing public domain publications linked to the home page which makes looking up articles on transportation issues a fast, one-stop shop. Subjects covered include law, freight, right-of-way, safety,

transit and transportation technology.

The links to legislation end at a unique chart arranged by agency to describe the type of regulation each particular office promulgates: *policy, covenants, regulations, certifications and licensing* are all covered and indicated by easy-to-use links.

Connect to the Bureau of Transportation Statistics for plentiful links to the bureau's library, programs, products and services. This is a good site, well executed. ❑

A Non-Graphical Version

United States Department of Transportation
400 SEVENTH STREET, SW WASHINGTON D.C. 20590

**A message from
U.S. DOT Secretary Rodney Slater**

Welcome message from the Secretary in 3 formats: Video, Audio, and Text.

What's hot @ DOT

COMMONLY REQUESTED SERVICES
- **CONTACTS**
- **NEWS & STATISTICS**
- **LEGISLATION & REGULATION**
- **NATIONAL TRANSPORTATION LIBRARY**
- **SAFETY ISSUES**
- **DOING BUSINESS WITH DOT**
- **QUESTIONS AND COMMENTS**

--Other DOT Services--

 go

Search the entire DOT Web server

 Search

Bureau of Transportation Statistics

Federal Aviation Administration

Federal Highway Administration

Federal Railroad Administration

Federal Transit Administration

Maritime Administration

National Highway Traffic Safety Administration

Office of the Secretary

Research and Special Administration

St. Lawrence Seaway Development Corporation

Transportation Administrative Service Center

United States Coast Guard

Office of the Inspector General

Surface Transportation Board

Links to Outside of the Department

Department of the Treasury

http://www.ustreas.gov

HIGHLIGHTS The Treasury is a jack of all trades in the Federal ontology. In addition to making fiscal and tax policy for the nation and actually making the coin of that same realm, the Department of the Treasury also operates the Secret Service and pays the bills.

This page suffers from a major Web design flaw, however; there is not enough information on the page to permit sensible searching. The researcher can use a search box to find things like releases and speeches but the Webmaster has not provided an index to the site or sitemap that would aid in navigation. Because most of the resources are hidden, it's hard to catalog resources and hard to find published items. Use at your own risk. ❑

Text Only Version

Welcome to the
Department of the Treasury

▶Browse
▶What's New
▶Who's Who
▶Treasury Offices
▶Tours & Treasures
▶Correspondence

Browse / What's New / Who's Who / Treasury Offices / Tours & Treasures / Correspondence / Search / Email Web Master / Treasury Mission

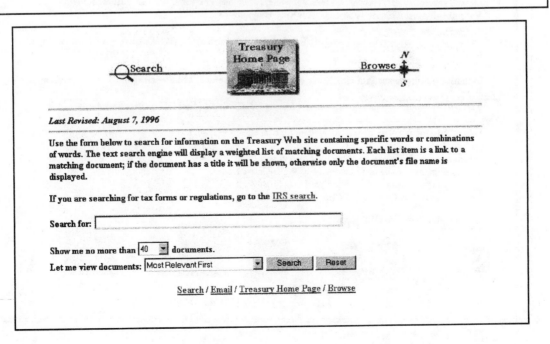

Search — Treasury Home Page — Browse N S

Last Revised: August 7, 1996

Use the form below to search for information on the Treasury Web site containing specific words or combinations of words. The text search engine will display a weighted list of matching documents. Each list item is a link to a matching document; if the document has a title it will be shown, otherwise only the document's file name is displayed.

If you are searching for tax forms or regulations, go to the IRS search.

Search for: [   ]

Show me no more than 40 ▼ documents.

Let me view documents: [Most Relevant First ▼] [Search] [Reset]

Search / Email / Treasury Home Page / Browse

Department of Veterans Affairs

http://www.va.gov

HIGHLIGHTS The quote from Abraham Lincoln provides the *raison d' etre* for this plain but informative Web site from the Department of Veterans Affairs. The benefits available to the veterans of the armed services are provided in detail here. The department offers links to Web sites for special veteran constituencies such as women, minorities and veterans of certain recent conflicts such as Bosnia and the Gulf War. Getting around the sometimes labyrinthine structures of the VA is made easier by the inclusion of a search bar for *Organization* to connect the department's far-flung facilities and operations. Data, medical services, benefits and forms are all online here. ❑

DEPARTMENT OF VETERANS AFFAIRS

TO CARE FOR HIM
WHO SHALL HAVE
BORNE THE BATTLE,
AND FOR HIS WIDOW
AND HIS ORPHAN...
Abraham Lincoln

| VA HOME | WELCOME | WHAT'S NEW | BENEFITS | FACILITIES | SPECIAL PROGRAMS | ORGANIZATION | DATA | MEDICAL | SERVER | LINKS | PROCUREMENT |

* *

⚫ What's New
   Press releases, Announcements for Veterans, List of Veterans Service Organizations, Job Opportunities With VA and the Government, What's New on this VA Server, and more...
⚫ Benefits
   Veterans Benefits, Federal Benefits for Veterans & Dependents, VA Cemeteries, VA Forms...
⚫ Facilities
   Where To Go for Help, Phone Numbers, Bulletin Boards, Medical Centers, Clinics, Regional Offices, Vet Centers, Facility Planning, Construction and Real Property...
⚫ Special Programs
   Special categories of Veterans, Bosnia Veterans, Homeless Veterans, Women Veterans, Persian Gulf Veteran's Illness, Minority Veterans, Advisory Committees...
⚫ Organization
   Structure, Internal Services, Directives/Policies, VA Administrators, CIO Council, VA Procurement, VA Research...
⚫ Data
   Statistics U.S. Veterans Profile, History of Support for Veterans, and Summary of Medical Programs...
⚫ Medical
   Medical Automation, Sharing Innovations Among VA Clinicians, and Informatics Standards...
⚫ Server
   Server Information, Usage Statistics, Free Software...
⚫ Links
   Information for Veterans on other VA Servers and NON VA Servers, Sites of Medical Interest, Internet Search Engines and General Directory of WWW Resources...
⚫ VA Procurement
   Information on VA Contracts (PCHS, PAIRS, ...) and Procurements...

VA's Previous
Home Page

Compliments, Questions,
Complaints, and Concerns

VA Inspector
General Hotline

Administration for Children and Families

http://www.acf.dhhs.gov

Highlights The Administration for Children and Families attempts to keep together the highly-stressed and frequently fragmented American family. The agencies stated mission is to promote "the economic and social well-being of families, children and individuals."

This very simple Web site describes the many programs the agency operates, some of them, like Operation HeadStart, immensely successful. The home page is homely but click on any of the links and the site expands very quickly to provide a great deal of information about each of the programs and each of the sub-agencies, especially from the link for ACF *Programs and Administrative Services*.

To navigate some of the dense thickets of the bureaucracy, click on the family tree for *Organizational Structure and Staff Information*.

The researcher will be particularly interested in *The ACF Press Room* where the most current updates to welfare reform and adoption updates can be found. This link also supports statistical information from the agency, special news items and provides starting points for research into state child support and state welfare agencies.

Additional links to other Web resources concerning welfare, adoption and other issues confronting children and parents can be had at the link for *Other Internet Information Resources.*❑

 US Department of Health & Human Services

Administration For Children and Families

 Oklahoma City April 19, 1995 In Memory

 ACF Programs and Administrative Services
Promoting the economic and social well-being of families, children, individuals and communities is the heart of our mission.

 Organizational Structure and Staff Information
Get to know the people and faces behind ACF's wide range of programs and services.

 The ACF Press Room
Welfare Reform Information NEW April Is Child Abuse Prevention Month! NEW
...flash...this just in! The latest news about the Administration for Children and Families.

 Other Internet Information Resources
Haven't found what you were looking for here? Try the ACF BBS or these Internet resources.

 Questions or comments to WebMaster

 85,483 *Usage Statistics*

Agency for Toxic Substances and Disease Registry

http://atsdr1.atsdr.cdc.gov:8080/ atdrhome.html

Highlights Keep track of the nation's poisons and the most hazardous materials from this site, operated by an agency of the Department of Health and Human Services.

The site is heavily linked to provide thorough coverage of hazmats, including a searchable database of dangerous substances and a "Science Corner" that is a search engine/gateway to environmental health resources.

Toxicology reports outline the 20 most hazardous materials and provide minimal exposure risks for the detailed substances. Of great interest to the first time visitor are the glossary, which define many obscure scientific terms and national alerts that keep the general public posted.

There are enough bureaucratic links to make this site a useful directory for the agency. It also serves as a good index page for environmental sites as it links to leading government sites such as the EPA and to leading private environmental sites.

The annual report reprinted on the site is sadly out of date but the announcements are current and the *ToxFAQs* file of oft-asked questions is a good source for quick answers to the most obvious question. The FAQ can be searched using an alphabetic search bar. ❑

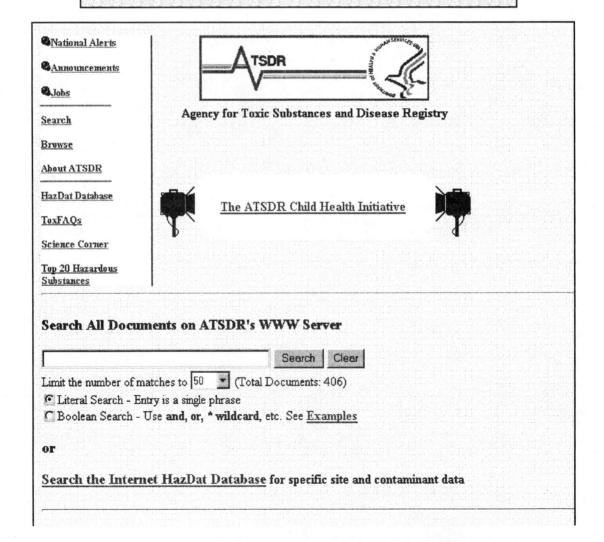

● National Alerts

● Announcements

● Jobs

_____

Search

Browse

About ATSDR

HazDat Database

ToxFAQs

Science Corner

Top 20 Hazardous Substances

Agency for Toxic Substances and Disease Registry

The ATSDR Child Health Initiative

Search All Documents on ATSDR's WWW Server

[   ] Search   Clear

Limit the number of matches to [50 ▼] (Total Documents: 406)

◉ Literal Search - Entry is a single phrase

○ Boolean Search - Use **and, or, * wildcard**, etc. See Examples

or

Search the Internet HazDat Database for specific site and contaminant data

Agricultural Marketing Service

http://www.usda.gov/ ams/titlepag.htm

Highlights The regulated agricultural industries pay for the services of the AMS which exists to help distribute food products from the producer (once known as a "farmer") to the consumer (once known as the "diner.") To do that, the AMS establishes standards for more than 600 agricultural commodities to help maintain agreed-upon quality.

The service helps farmers finance and promote their produce and aids the transportation system to help speed produce from farmland to stewpot. That's all very interesting, of course;

the main draw for the legal researcher will be the directory chart to plumb the depths of the agencies offices, the electronic publication of *USDA Quality Standards*, news and information that includes reports on food purchases and an index of publications from the service's various commodity divisions. Legislative and regulatory review staff publications have pride of place at the Web site.

Click on *Services* for the lowdown on fair trade regulations, grading and certification, food quality assurance and the import/export service. ❑

Welcome to...

USDA's Agricultural Marketing Service

About AMS	USDA	News and Information
Market News		Services
USDA Quality Standards		What's New
AMS Search		Program Areas
Job Opportunities		Comments/Suggestions

Animal and Plant
Health Inspection Service

http://www.aphis.usda.gov

Highlights Agriculture is one of the nation's largest industries and the task of keeping America's livestock and plants free from foreign agricultural pests and diseases falls to the Animal and Plant Health Inspection Service.

By monitoring the borders and airports, the service tries to interdict harmful pests before they can begin ruinous epidemics. They help fight the legal battles from this Web site where the service's regulations are reprinted and where publications detailing the service's mission can be found.

This Web site is also stocked with tips for travelers, information on permits for veterinarians, biotechnologists and for plant protection and quarantine. Businesses with a great deal of import-export can become acquainted with the regulations they face from the materials published on the Web site. It's also a good place for locating forms, general facts about pest control and a directory of the service's staff and offices.

From the home page, link to specialized pages for animal health, plant health, wildlife services, ag biotech and ag trade as well in-depth treatment of bison brucellosis and Floridian medflies. ❑

ANIMAL AND PLANT HEALTH INSPECTION SERVICE

Find out more about the APHIS Mission, Activities, and Organization.

What's HOT in APHIS

●BSE●Karnal Bunt●Missing & Found Pets●Mexican Avocados●Brucellosis & Yellowstone Bison●

Search the APHIS Web: [   ] [Search]

Press Releases	Publications	Regulations	Forms	Jobs
Mailing Lists	Import-Export	Subject Index	Directory	Permits
Travelers' Tips	APHIS Gopher	Fact Book	Guided Tour	Amerinds

NEW! What's New!

❾❿❸❹❻ visitors last year, ❻❶❺❾❶ in 1997 and counting!

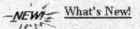

Bureau of Alcohol, Tobacco and Firearms

http://www.atf.treas.gov

Highlights Used to go to the Post Office to see America's Most Wanted. Now even the bad guys are high-tech as the BATF hangs mug shots of the Top Twelve Most Wanted on the bureau's Web site.

Closer to the bureaucratic heart are such useful online services as a lengthy collection of the agency's forms in PDF format for such things as a brewer's permit and tobacco taxes. A press release service keeps the public informed of BATF's activities and a list of publications leads to reprints of the bureau's regulations concerning *firearms curios,* *explosives regulations, gun dealer licensing* and zipped version (in WordPerfect 5.1) of the *Federal Firearms Regulation Reference Guide.*

Other links will give details on the bureau's forensic and laboratory services and proposed rulemakings. The bureau has begun a program known as *Gang Resistance Education and Training* to reduce gang violence and membership; find details under the link to *Outreach.* The most current legal news can be found under the icon for *What's New* where implementation of Public Laws and new rules are published. ❏

ATF

Web Site Updated April 29, 1997

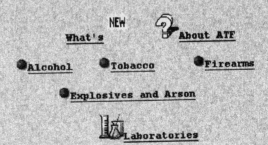

What's NEW   About ATF

● Alcohol   ● Tobacco   ● Firearms

● Explosives and Arson

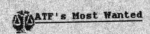 Laboratories

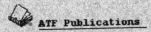 ATF's Most Wanted   Outreach   ATF News

ATF Publications   ATF Forms   ATF Jobs

 Hotline Phone Numbers   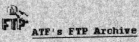 ATF's FTP Archive

Bureau of the Census

http://www.census.gov

Highlights

Counting heads -- all 267,106,767 of them according to the Census Bureau's up-to-the-minute population ticker -- and then painting a statistical picture of the nation is a job that falls to the Census Bureau. On the Census Web site, find enhancements to the data that permit reports to be created or screened for specific demographic information. Search by place name and map or refer to the elaborate *subject guide* to pull down an alphabetic list of census topics to search on: look for vital records such as birth and deaths, divorce statistics, immigration, genealogy, home ownership data, living arrangements and the like. The site is a goldmine of data.

Click on *CenStats* to find subscription info for fee-based online access to reports that until recently only were published on CD-ROM. CenStats also features some free electronic reports that can be downloaded in PDF format. The link for *Access Tools* provides maps and gazetteers for the U.S. and a superb , create-your-own map service known as *Tiger Maps*. ❏

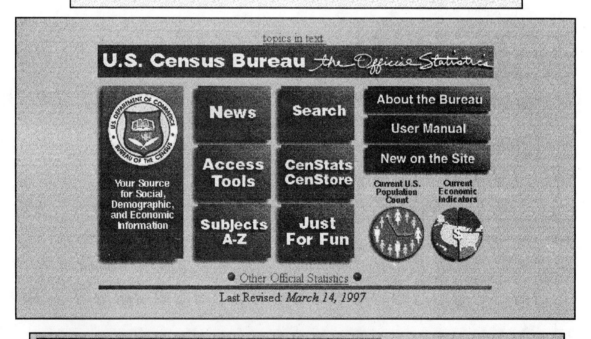

Last Revised: *March 14, 1997*

U.S. Census Bureau *the Official Statistics*

Search the Census Bureau

Word Search

● Search the Census Bureau's continuously expanding library of on-line documents and files by supplying the word or words you would like to find.

Place Search

● Search for information for local areas by place names, zip codes, etc. (Gazetteer)

Map Search

● Search for information geographically by pointing and clicking on your areas of interest. (formerly DataMap)

Bureau of Economic Analysis

http://www.bea.doc.gov

Highlights The BEA's best-seller is the *Survey of Current Business,* a monthly publication which analyzes and estimates the U.S. economy. The electronic version can be downloaded in PDF format at least a week before the print version is available from the BEA's companion site *STAT-USA* at *http://www.stat-usa.gov*

Obtain a copy of the BEA's *User Guide* for a complete review of the bureau's activities. The *User Guide* lists all of the bureau's publications, reports and subscription services and provides a directory of agency personnel to help researchers locate staff members for additional information.

The Web site details the methodology and data sources so that users can see for themselves the logical foundations of the statistical conclusions. There's also a news service that publishes such useful reports as monthly reports on the *gross national product, personal income and international trade in goods and services.* ❏

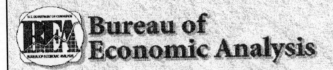

Welcome to the Bureau of Economic Analysis on the World Wide Web! We have developed this system to make it easier for you, our customers, to learn about and access BEA's economic information.

Some of the information on our site is provided in PDF format. Files in pdf format are identified with this symbol: These files can be viewed with free software from Adobe Systems.

ABOUT BEA

WHAT'S NEW?

BEA DATA AND METHODOLOGY

FEEDBACK

USER'S GUIDE

NEWS RELEASE INFORMATION

SURVEY OF CURRENT BUSINESS

OTHER BEA PUBLICATIONS

About BEA | What's New | BEA Data | Feedback

User's Guide | News Release Information | Survey of Current Business | Other BEA Publications

◦Other web sites providing economic statistics

Many excellent sites provide a wealth of economic statistics. Among those you should definitely be familiar with are the following:

- the Bureau of Labor Statistics ,
- the Census Bureau,
- the Economic Research Service of the Department of Agriculture, and
- the Board of Governors of the Federal Reserve System.

BEA joins with these and other agencies to make some of the nation's most closely watched economic indicators available in the Federal Statistics Briefing Room on the White House web site.

Suscribers to STAT-USA/Internet can access data from many providers at a single web site; visitors wishing subscription information are welcome.

Bureau of Engraving and Printing

http://www.ustreas.gov/treasury/bureaus/bep/bep.html

Highlights There's only one genuine license to print money and these guys have it.

The bureau does more than simply crank out pictures of George Washington all day. The BEP also designs and prints such vital security products as postage stamps, Treasury securities, ID cards, naturalization certificates and processes claims for the redemption of mutilated currency.

Clearly, one of the bureau's most important functions is the creation of deterrence technologies to keep forgers at bay. This simple and succinct Web site provides information on public sales of videos and reprints forms for procurement when doing business with the bureau.

Find out here how to redeem smashed cash from the links to *mutilated money* (though, where we come from, money never hangs around long enough to get into any serious trouble.) This Web site certainly won't stop the world from turning but as an informative and brightly lit site for a little government bureau, it's a serviceable and moderately entertaining exercise in online information delivery. Sadly, no samples, in PDF form or otherwise. ❑

Mission statement:

The mission of the Bureau of Engraving and Printing (BEP) is to serve as the Federal Government's most secure and efficient source of vital Government securities.

The Bureau manufactures the financial and other securities of the United States. Accordingly, the Bureau designs, prints, and furnishes a large variety of security products, including Federal Reserve notes, most U.S. postage stamps, Treasury securities, identification cards, naturalization certificates, and other special security documents. All products are designed and manufactured with advanced counterfeit deterrence features to ensure product integrity, and the Bureau advises other Federal agencies on document security matters. The Bureau also processes claims for the redemption of mutilated currency. The Bureau's research and development efforts focus on the continued use of automation in the production process and counterfeit deterrent technologies for use in security documents, especially U.S. currency.

Search / Email / Treasury Home Page / Browse /

Bureau of Export Administration

http://www.bxa.doc.gov

Highlights The busy bureaucrats at the Bureau of Export Administration have taken time from their work helping the republics of the former Soviet Union get on their feet and aiding defense firms that are feeling the pinch of reduced defense spending to mount this very nice Web site.

For the producers of high-tech software, the site delivers a copy of *Commercial Encryption Export Controls*. The *EAR Marketplace* is the place to head for Export Administration Regulations where the researcher can find reprints from the *Federal Register* and connections to subscribe to the EAR database. Subscriptions are $21 per month for unlimited access. For exporters and other companies with significant sales overseas, the bureau links to other government agencies that provide help to internationally-oriented businesses.

There are, of course, press releases and a *What's New* link as well as generous descriptions of what the bureau does and how it operates its programs. There's also a complete directory of offices, addresses, titles, phone numbers and e-mail addresses. ❑

Go to *Menu Choices*

The Bureau of Export Administration

This Site
Updated
March 28, 1997

The Bureau of Export Administration enhances the nation's security and its economic prosperity by controlling exports for national security, foreign policy, and short supply reasons. We administer the Export Administration Act by developing export control policies, issuing export licenses, and prosecuting violators. Additionally, BXA enforces the EAA's antiboycott provisions.

BXA enhances the defense industrial base and assists U.S. defense firms which have felt the impact of reduced defense spending. BXA helps other countries develop export control systems comparable to ours and has assisted enterprises in the republics of the former Soviet Union in converting to civil production. We hope that this web site will help you learn more about us and assist you in working with us.

Bill Reinsch
Under Secretary

BXA ISSUES   *What is happening in BXA?*
Information on important Bureau of Export Administration issues for this week.

WHAT'S NEW   *Website changes*
A chronological listing of changes to this website.

ENCRYPTION   *Commercial Encryption Export Controls*

REGULATIONS   *"EAR Marketplace"*
The Export Administration Regulations are accessible in both online and looseleaf formats through BXA's "EAR Marketplace."

BXA EVENTS   *Special Events*
Information on BXA seminars and special events.

RESOURCES   *What other resources are available to Exporters and Companies?*
Links to other Federal resources to assist exporters and companies.

Bureau of Indian Affairs

http://www.doi.gov/ bureau-indian-affairs.html

Highlights Along with guides to Native American ancestry and information on genealogical research, the BIA Web site is well-provided with substantial legal information including a list of recognized tribal courts appearing on the *list of Federally-recognized American Indian Tribes*.

A map of all Indian land areas, by geographic region, sets out *Indian Land Areas Judicially Established* in 1978. Other links lead to a list of *tribal leaders* and *area offices*. The Branch of Acknowledgement and Research aims to establish claims that Native American groups do exist as Indian tribes. Reports on petitioners for establishing acknowledgement and the summary status of all petitioners seeking such acknowledgment are published on the BIA Web site.

Other items of interest include details on the BIA's Division of Energy and Mineral Resources that help Indian mineral owners manage their resources.

The link for *laws and regulations* reprints treaties, Title 25 of the U.S. Code, Title 25 of the *Code of Federal Regulations* and those U.S. Supreme Court decisions affecting tribal affairs. ❑

U.S. Department of the Interior
On the Web

Bureau of Indian Affairs

Ada E. Deer

☞ Click here for Ms. Deer's Biography
Assistant Secretary for Indian Affairs

BIA Mission Statement

1996 BIA Customer Satisfaction Report
American Indian Heritage Day
Tribal Shares
BIA Press Releases
American Indian Today
Proclamation: Drunk and Drugged Driving Prevention Month -- Lights on for Life Day, December, 1996

Native American Ancestry

Bureau of International Labor Affairs

http://gatekeeper.dol.gov/dol/ilab/

Highlights Trotting the globe to look out for U.S. interests in multilateral and bilateral trade negotiations, the Bureau represents the government on international bodies.

The Web site is stocked with a directory of key personnel and a description of what the bureau does under the link to its *mission statement*.

For reports and publications, check with *What's New* where the researcher can find such titles as *By the Sweat and Toil of Children*, a two-part report on the international use of child labor and *United States/European Union Workshop on Employment Policy and the Promotion of Employability Security*.

Keep current with the bureau's activities by using the links to *Media Releases*. Best link on this otherwise trimmed down and thinly stocked page is the one to *Information Sources Outside DOL* and that only consists of a single link to the *International Labor Organization* site operated by the United Nations.

As government Web sites go, this one is rather paltry and should be used primarily for looking up names and address of the bureau's staff. ❑

U.S. Department of Labor
Bureau of International Labor Affairs

ILAB

● Information About the Deputy Under Secretary

● Information About the Bureau of International Labor Affairs

● What's New

● Media Releases

● Information Sources Outside DOL

--DISCLAIMER--

Send comments to: *Webmaster@dol.gov* Please restrict comments to technical issues. Comments relati content or style will not be acted on by the Webmaster.

 DOL Home Page Top of Document

Bureau of Labor Statistics

http://stats.bls.gov

Highlights As a reference source, the Bureau of Labor Statistics Web site ranks as one of the Internet's great resources. An extraordinarily detailed site generously provides charts, graphs and stacks of numbers to paint a statistical picture of the United States and its workforce.

Click on *Economy at a Glance* for up-to-the-month economic yardsticks like the *consumer price index, producer price index* and the *unemployment rate*. The *Surveys and Programs* publish sophisticated analyses of employment trends, technol-

ogy in the economy, employment projections, compensation and working conditions and other job-related statistics.

The heart of the BLS service lies behind the clickable button for *Data* and that's where the researcher will find the *most requested timeseries* from the bureau's offices, news releases and access to the agency's gopher.

Other links publish international information and connect to leading statistical Web sites within the U.S. government and abroad. ❏

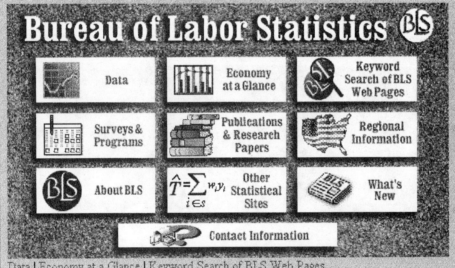

Data | Economy at a Glance | Keyword Search of BLS Web Pages
Surveys & Programs | Publications & Research Papers | Regional Information
About BLS | Other Statistical Sites | What's New | Contact Information

The Bureau of Labor Statistics is an agency within the U.S. Department of Labor.

Jo-Ann L. Yu
Bureau of Labor Statistics
labstat.helpdesk@bls.gov
Last modified: April 4, 1997

Bureau of Land Management

http://www.blm.gov

Highlights   The Federal Government's landlords keep a Web site where statistics on public lands can be had without trespass along with such land management information as surface management regulation, maps of the nation showing areas under the bureau's jurisdiction and a description of exactly what it is that the BLM does.

Instructions for filing for FOIA requests with the agency to ask about mining surveys, grazing rights and something called *cadastral survery plats* are connect-ed to the Web site though electronic means of filing those requests are not.

Office directories take up a good part of the site, along with links to other land management sites of interest within the U.S. government. The bureau publishes materials about petroleum reserves and fire information alerts but the researcher is likely to be most interested in the links to *legislative* and *regulatory actions* which can be located under the link for *Breaking News*.

❑

Click here for a text-only version of this page.

Welcome to the BLM National Homepage

Columbia River Basin Draft Plan Announced

BLM Strategic Plan

- Breaking News
- Accessing BLM Information
- About BLM's New Interim Director
- What is the BLM?
- BLM State Offices
- Other BLM Offices and Websites
- National Map: BLM Points of Interest
- Calendar of Events
- Public Contact Directory
- FY1998 Budget
- Grand Staircase-Escalante National Monument: Images and Information
- Interagency Fire Information
- Information on the National Petroleum Reserve in Alaska
- *Public Land Statistics - 1996* (online publication)

Bureau of Mines

http://www.usbm.gov

Highlights What once was the Bureau of Mines has been transmogrified into the Mining Health and Safety Research Program. In its present incarnation, the agency earns its keep by providing mine operators and mine workers with up-to-date information on how to remain intact during the working day. Among the cheery titles that brighten up this Web site are *Disaster Prevention, Mine Accident Decision Support System* and the less dire *Worker Safety*. The site is well-provided with a database dubbed "CISS" for *Common Information Service System* that provides thousands of publications on mining safety topics in PDF format.

The materials mounted here are primarily informational and serve as reminders that not everyone works in an air-conditioned law office; the rundown on the links to be found under *Worker Health -- respirable dust, toxic fumes from blasting agents* and *diesel emission* -- are the topics are useful for driving home the message that regulations are needed to ensure compliance with basic safety ideas. ❑

Text Only Version

Pittsburgh and Spokane Research Centers
Mining Health & Safety Research

Mission Statement

Our mission is to conduct objective scientific studies, research, experiments, and demonstrations related to the mining and minerals sector in the areas of *worker health, worker safety*, and *disaster prevention*.

The Mining Health and Safety Research Program operates out of research centers located at Pittsburgh, PA, and Spokane, WA.

 | What's New | Mining Health & Safety Updates | Facilities | Don't Miss! |
| Products and Customer Service | NIOSH Vacancy Announcements |
| Free Publication |

Mining Health and Safety Program Areas

- Health and Safety Research Overview
- Worker Health
- Worker Safety
- Disaster Prevention

Bureau of the Public Debt

http://www.publicdebt.treas.gov

Highlights Profligate as Uncle Sam is, he does keep disciplined track of his IOUs. This Web site with a to-the penny calculation of the Public Debt will either freeze the blood with its stupefying number or make the cynical laugh at the ridiculously impossible task of even paying off the vig from a five-and-half *trillion* dollar hole.

There are some practical information resources mounted here, among them forms, interest rates on United States Savings Bonds (quaint as a brass button in the 1990s bull market) and links to the Government Securities Act of 1986. and Uniform Offering Circular Amendments in the CFR.

The debt-minders produce forms that can be downloaded directly from the Web. They also report on upcoming T-bill auctions, publish their rules and regulations and operate *Treasury Direct*, a sort of electronic banking for buying and selling government securities over the wires. The site is completely informative on opening and maintaining an account. ❑

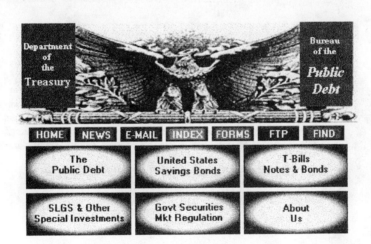

Check out our new Government Securities Market Regulation area.

HOME - Our homepage
NEWS - What's New at Public Debt
E-MAIL - Correspond with us
INDEX - An index of our site
FORMS - Request our forms
FTP - Our downloadable files
FIND - Our search utility
Disclaimers

Department of Treasury's Home Page

Updated April 24, 1997

5:38 THE INTERNET GUIDE FOR THE LEGAL RESEARCHER *Second Edition*

Bureau of Reclamation

http://www.usbr.gov

Highlights Water, water everywhere and some of it is to drink; much of it is to generate electricity, to canoe on or to irrigate crops via a huge network of reservoirs and canals in the American West. The Bureau of Reclamation is, by its own estimation, number six on the hydroelectric charts and so has a considerable control of the scarce water resources of the arid West.

The Web site is not going to make water flow uphill any time soon but there is a fair degree of bureaucratic detail to be found on the site including office directo-

ries, phone numbers, staff information and something the bureau calls *The Book. The Book* is the story of what the Bureau of Reclamation does: to digest, it conserves water, it protects the wet environment, it operates dams, it provides recreation on the top of its reservoirs and it acts as a political referee when competing interests collide.

This is an OK site from a small bureau and despite its lack of regulatory or statutory links, it's helpful to riparian researchers. ❏

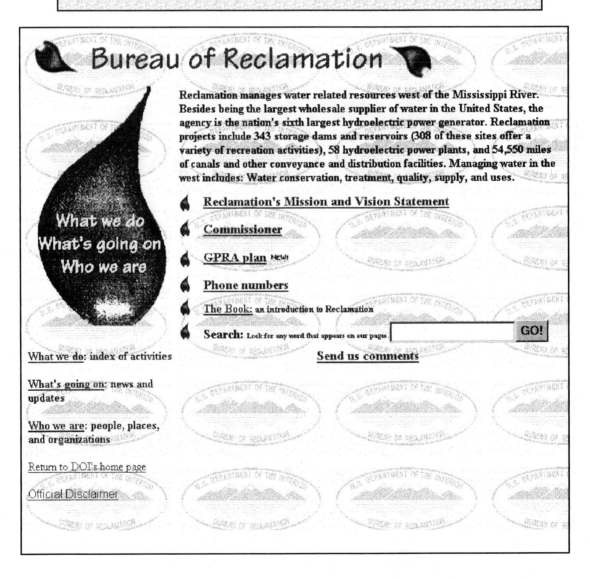

Centers for Disease Control and Prevention

http://www.cdc.gov

Highlights Epidemiologists and medical researchers have a rich library of medical information courtesy of the nation's leading consortium of eleven centers, institutes and offices. The CDC keeps track of such health issues as infectious disease, HIV and AIDS, accidental and occupational injury, women's health, disease prevention and environmental health.

Select from an accessible laundry list of publications including the always amusing *Morbidity and Mortality Weekly Report* which reports on what's killing Americans. The CDC will be happy to e-mail the report to anyone who cares to subscribe.

Rounding out the informational goodies from the CDC are *data and statistics, surveillance data* and *health information*. Travelers will benefit from the CDC's online publication of the *Blue Sheet*, a summary of health info for the international traveler and the *Yellow Book*, which is the complete report. Vaccine recommendations and evaluations of cruise ships also are available from the site. ❑

[Text version]

The Nation's Prevention Agency

SPOTLIGHT ON ... Japanese Encephalitis

CDC
Centers for Disease Control and Prevention

- About CDC
- What's New?
- Health Information
- Travelers' Health
- Publications & Products
- Data & Statistics
- Training & Employment
- Funding

Department of Health & Human Services

SEARCH | SUBSCRIPTIONS | OTHER SITES

MMWR EID

Centers for Disease Control and Prevention (CDC)
About CDC | What's New | Health Information
Travelers' Health | Publications & Products | Data & Statistics
Training & Employment | Funding

Search | Subscriptions | Other Sites | MMWR | EID

In general all information presented in these pages and all items available for download are for public use. However, you may encounter some pages that require a login password and id. If this is the case you may assume that information presented and items available for download therein are for your authorized access only and not for redistribution by you unless you are otherwise informed.

*Centers for Disease Control and Prevention, 1600 Clifton Rd., NE, Atlanta, GA 30333, USA
(404)639-3311*

Central Intelligence Agency

http://www.odci.gov/cia

Highlights   This three-part Web site is surprisingly information-rich, considering the agency's legendary secrecy. Get past the stern warnings and head straight for the list of publications. The most popular item on the menu is the annual *CIA World Factbook*, a compendium of flags, maps, geographical trivia, economic and ethnic data and defense information for all the nations of the world. Our spooks also publish the *Factbook on Intelligence* and offer the public an index of maps that can be ordered via the Web site.

For the diplomatically-inclined, check into the CIA's list of *Chiefs of State and Cabinet Members of Foreign Governments*; for would-be James Bonds, there's a bibliography of literature on intelligence gathering, including a history of the agency.

Take a *Virtual Tour* of the agency or look through the *Exhibit Center for* whatever non-clandestine information the CIA chooses to report about itself. One of the greatest benefits to emerge from the end of the Cold War has been the amount of useful data declassified and subsequently re-published and the CIA site is a shining example of the trend. Find links from the page to recently de-classified satellite images and links to other sites within the intelligence community, primarily military and law enforcement Web sites.

In addition to the link to the Central Intelligence Agency on the home page, it's possible to connect to the *Center for the Study of Intelligence* and general links to the aforementioned *U.S. Intelligence Community*. ❏

Welcome to the
Office of the Director of Central Intelligence
World Wide Web Site

You are entering an Official United States Government System, which may be used only for authorized purposes. Unauthorized modification of any information stored on this system may result in criminal prosecution. The Government may monitor and audit the usage of this system, and all persons are hereby notified that use of this system constitutes consent to such monitoring and auditing.

We currently support three World Wide Web sites here. The Central Intelligence Agency site, the Intelligence Community site, and the The Center for the Study of Intelligence site are all available. Please make a note of the following URLs that identify each of these sites.

- Central Intelligence Agency - **http://www.odci.gov/cia**

- United States Intelligence Community - **http://www.odci.gov/ic**

- Center for the Study of Intelligence - **http://www.odci.gov/csi**

Commodity Futures Trading Commission

http://www.cftc.gov/cftc

Highlights The complex world of futures trading is laid bare in this ambitious Web site containing rules, regulations, enforcement guidelines and even an online mug shot to help track down commodities swindlers. The extensive publications menu offers *annual reports, backgrounders, weekly advisories* and the *quarterly review.* There is a significant amount of financial data and an overview of precisely what the CFTC does.

With all the strange jargon down in the trading pits, the *glossary* of the futures industry will explicate some of the murkier terms of art. For aggrieved customers who have a dispute with a broker, the CFTC offers online guidance for filing a *reparation claim* under the *Reparation Program.*

Use this page to find out about the *commitments of traders* and what banks are participating in the futures markets. Other notable features of the CFTC Web are the reprints of *opinions and orders,* the text of *speeches* made by the commission's senior officials and overviews of both the commission and the markets it regulates. Also find *press releases* and a list of coming attractions under the link to *What's Pending.* ❑

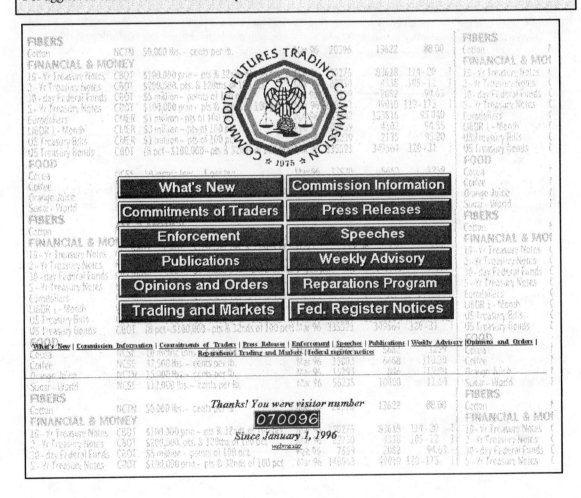

Consumer Product Safety Commission

http://www.cpsc.gov

Highlights *Safety first* -- the consumer product safety commission keeps an eye on the thousands of manufactured products created each year in the United States to make sure that they meet federally-mandated standards for quality and reliability.

The Web site is graphically dull but the links connect to a library of *CPSC Publications* and what they call *Data Relevant to Consumer Product Safety.* (Two reports appear: *Children's Anthropometric Data* and *1994 Residential Fire Loss Estimates.*

The most compelling reason to visit the CPSC site are the monthly *Product Recalls* regularly published as press releases. There's not much material readily available for the legal researcher, the site is geared to providing handy tips to the consumer. (Typical publication: *Organizing a Baby Safety Shower.*) The researcher instead should refer to the plain vanilla *Search* key to look up the CPSC's releases in the *Federal Register* or to retrieve other reports and recall notices. The search engine does a first-class job despite its coach-class look and feel. Researchers in the mood to rough it can click on the gopher link and peruse the gopher links to the *CPSC Hotline, Federal Register* notices, *news* and *publications.* The *Public Calendar* reports on upcoming hearings and meetings of the commissioners and contains dates, time and address of the meetings. ❑

U.S. Consumer Product Safety Commission

CPSC, an independent Federal regulatory agency, helps keep American families safe in their homes by reducing the risk of injury or death from consumer products. Visit us often to share lifesaving information. Go to "Talk to us" to report unsafe products to us.

About us/ Vacancies   Business/ Contracts   Consumer Consumidor   Gopher   Library

News Desk   Public Calendar   Search   Talk to us   What's happening

Site maintained by mcohn@cpsc.gov

Defense Advanced Research Projects Agency

http://www.darpa.mil

Highlights The Internet as we know it would not even exist were it not for the fact that the Defense Advanced Research Projects Agency (DARPA) outgrew its packet-switched command and control network known as DARPANet. The agency turned over the lines which were no longer up to the task of carrying critical information to military posts in the event of attack on the United States to academic and non-military government use, the system which eventually became the Internet.

The circle has closed on itself as the same agency now mounts a simple Web site that describes its projects in as much detail as national security concerns permit. (Read "very little.") The links are mostly polite constructions that allow the public to communicate with the agency and to review the latest appropriations budget. The other links describe the technical and support offices. The most interesting,if not the most useful link is the one for the *Defense Science and Technology Planning Home Page.* ❏

Defense Advanced Research Projects Agency

The Defense Advanced Research Projects Agency (DARPA) is the central research and development organization for the Department of Defense (DoD). It manages and directs selected basic and applied research and development projects for DoD, and pursues research and technology where risk and payoff are both very high and where success may provide dramatic advances for traditional military roles and missions and dual-use applications.

This website is divided into several tracks. Please select from the following list.

- Mission - Describes what DARPA does
- Organization - DARPA's offices and links to their individual web sites
    - A description of each of the Technical and Support Offices
    - A list of the Offices with links to all of the Office Home Pages
- Info - Information available to the public, including how to communicate with DARPA
    - Information for Small Businesses (SBIR/SBSC)
    - DARPA Planned Procurements, May 1997
- News - Recent happenings at the Defense Advanced Research Projects Agency
- Budget - DARPA Budget Information: Upated for FY 1998.
- Solicitations - A listing of current solicitations for the technical offices of DARPA

Hot Topics

● **NEW!** Learn about DARPA's future directions. Visit the DARPATech '97 web page to register on-line for DARPA's biggest conference of the year. **Spaces are limited.**

● **NEW!** Due to recently adopted regulations pursuant to the President's Streamlining Acquisition Initiative, and the Debt Collection Improvement Act of 96, ALL Federal Government contractors desiring to obtain Federal Government contracts or obtain payment for existing contracts MUST register with the Central Contractor Registration Program (CCR) before September 30, 1997. Information regarding CCR registration is available.

Defense Information Systems Agency

http://www.disa.mil

Highlights The fashionable term for serviceman, soldier or sailor is now "warfighter" and that's the catch phrase on this defense site that serves the military. The eponymous Information Systems are fundamentally an Intranet for the Armed Forces; the agency provides a message system like e-mail, an information retrieval system like GILS and inscrutable, hard-to-understand codes like Microsoft tech manuals. If it was the military's intent to confound civilian visitors to the Web site, they have succeeded. The site is of interest to uniformed personnel only. There is little in the way of ordinary legal information for the researcher here but the military researcher in need of DoD-grade software and operating systems can find an online PX for the latest in server and client side codes.

The site is otherwise hard to fathom but the supposition is drawn that commissioned Webmasters will have a field day here. ❑

Defense Nuclear Facilities Safety Board

http://www.dnfsb.gov

Highlights Now that the Cold War is over and the threat of nuclear war considerably abated, concerns about the environmental and social hazards of the facilities where nuclear weapons were manufactured take on a greater urgency. The Defense Nuclear Facilities Safety Board was created to watch over those plants and to make recommendations about the safe operation of those facilities.

There isn't a great deal of information published on the Web site given the sensitive nature of the board's stated mission, but the researcher can locate the *formal recommendations, trip reports, technical document log* of all incoming correspondence to the DNFSB and *weekly reports.*

The board also reprints its *annual report to Congress* on the siteas well as the text of speeches by officials. Links to the full text of the enabling statutes also are provided. ❑

Defense Nuclear Facilities Safety Board

Under its enabling statute, (Public Law 100-456) the Board is responsible for independent, external oversight of all activities in DOE's nuclear weapons complex affecting nuclear health and safety. The Board reviews operations, practices, and occurrences at DOE's defense nuclear facilities and makes recommendations to the Secretary of Energy that are necessary to protect public health and safety. In the event Board reviews disclose an imminent or severe threat to public health and safety, the Board is required to transmit its recommendations directly to the President, as well as to the Secretaries of Energy and Defense.

↖ Board Members ↖ Reports/Documents ↖ General Information

↖ Word Search ↖ Mailbox ↖ GILS ↖ Links ↖ Feedback

Webmaster: Lora Steed
mailbox@dnfsb.gov

Updated: March 13, 1997

You are Visitor:

000010994

Drug Enforcement Administration

http://www.usdoj.gov/dea/index.htm

Highlights The graphic designer for the DEA Web site might have been Jack Webb himself -- it's got a "just the facts, ma'am" feel to it. Click on *The Agency* to get an overview of what the Federal narks do to interdict the importation of drugs. The researcher will be most interested in the publications that the agency produces under the eponymous link. Typical charts include *Heroin-Related Deaths in Florida* (85 in 1995), *Marijuana- Juvenile Arrests* and *Cali Cartel Organizational Structure*. Publications are a cornucopia of press releases, Congressional testimony, magazines, intelligence reports and legalization issues, which suggest strategies for counter-arguments against the legalization of drugs.

Criminal justice researchers will find fruitful materials on *asset forfeiture, aviation operations, intelligence* and the *Organized Crime Drug Enforcement Task Force.*

Additional links lead to anti-drug Web sites and to career opportunities with the agency. ❏

U.S. Department of Justice
Drug Enforcement Administration

★ **The Agency**

★ **Programs**

★ **Publications**

★ **Fugitives**

★ **Statistics**

★ **Employment Opportunities**

★ **Other Internet Sites**

Economic Development Administration

http://cher.eda.doc.gov/ agencies/eda/index.html

Highlights The EDA exists to hustle business for economically-deprived areas of the nation in partnership with local and state governments and regional economic districts. To help promote itself, the administration offers a *Fact Sheet* to outline its plans for community re-development, management initiatives and program tools.

The legal researcher in search of regulations and rules will be gladdened to find a reprint online of the relevant *Code of Federal*

Regulations section and the commission's *Federal Register* notices and dockets.

Other links point directly to the *Office of Economic Conversion*, a list of EDA programs and a directory containing *office contacts*. Outside connections lead to *Other Economic Development Contacts and Resources*. The site is constructed of three frames making navigation occasionally annoying. ❑

U. S Department of Commerce

Economic Development Administration

EDA's Home Page!

To maneuver around our site, just click on any of the items to your left.

Economic Development Administration
U.S. Department of Commerce
14th & Constitution Avenue
Room 7800B
Washington, DC 20230
(202) 482-5081

 To DOC Home Page

If you have comments or questions regarding this page contact EDA's Webmaster (EDAWebmaster@doc.gov).
...... *Updated - February 26, 1997*

Employment Standards Administration

http://www.dol.gov/dol/esa

Highlights The Department of Labor's largest agency enforces legally-mandated wages and working conditions. Its four offices are represented online with compliance information and downloadable graphics of required posters; the links also lead to an overview of what regulations and laws each office administers and provides press releases and special reports to inform the public about the offices' activities.

The Office of Workers Compensation Programs is heavier on the "vision and mission" aspects of its work than on the public disclosure end but there are still informative links for that office and the others.

The most important general interest link is the one that leads to the Wage and Hour Division, the office that spells out and enforces the minimum wage and administers the Family and Medical Leave Act.

Refer to the home page for Statutory, Regulatory and Compliance Information. This is a good site that would be improved with increased reporting of ALJ decisions. ❏

U.S. Department of Labor
Employment Standards Administration

ESA

Hot Minimum Wage   Hot Family & Medical Leave Act   Hot No Sweat

Hot ESA Hammer Awards   Hot Teen Safety

What's New   Search 🔍

● Information about the Assistant Secretary

● Information About ESA

● ESA's Programs

   ● Office of Federal Contract Compliance Programs
Administers anti-discrimination provisions pertaining to government contractors and subcontractors.

   ● Office of Labor-Management Standards
Administers and enforces provisions of the Labor-Management Reporting and Disclosure Act of 1959, as amended (LMRDA), and sections of various other acts (Postal Reorganization Act, Civil Service Reform Act and Foreign Service Act) within the responsibility of the Secretary of Labor. OLMS seeks to promote internal union democracy and financial integrity and to protect the rights of union members. OLMS also administers the Secretary of Labor's statutory responsibilities for the Transit Employee Protection Program and for other employee protection programs.

   ● Office of Workers' Compensation Programs
Administers three major disability compensation programs which provide wage replacement benefits, medical treatment, vocational rehabilitation and other benefits to certain workers or their dependents who experience work-related injury or occupational disease.

   ● Wage and Hour Division
Administers the wage, hour and child labor provisions of the Fair Labor Standards Act as well as several other programs covering farm labor, family and medical leave, immigration and polygraph testing.

Energy Information Institute

http://www.eia.doe.gov/index.html

Highlights Even the researcher with only a tangential interest in energy information regarding petroleum, natural gas, coal, nuclear power or alternative and renewable power sources will find this site fascinating and rewarding as a reference tool.

The electronic shelves are filled with PDF and HTML versions of reports on all those topics, some weekly, some monthly and others annual in their coverage. Typical of the reports are such titles as *Data archive of historical reserves esti-* *mates for United State Crude Oil, Natural Gas, and Natural Gas Liquids* and *Weekly Petroleum Status Report.*

The Institute has hung links to energy groups on the home page that report energy prices and forecasts and state data. The major global complaint with the site is that many of the reports are considerably out of date; the publications contain data that is more than two years old, an eternity in the age of instant information retrieval and analysis. Still, this is a first-rate reference source. ❑

Energy Information Administration

Fuel Groups
- Petroleum
- Natural Gas
- Coal
- Nuclear
- Alternative/Renewables
- Electricity
- Overview

Other Energy Groups
- International
- Forecasting
- Environment
- Energy Prices
- Financial
- State Energy Data
- End Use Consumption

What's New at EIA

Special Features
(Features explained below)
- Email Lists
- Energy Links
- Quiz
- Data Queries
- Energy Calendar

Customer Services
(Services explained below)
- Feedback
- Press Releases
- EIA Contacts
- Government Information Locator Service (GILS)
- Frequently Asked Questions (FAQ)
- EIA Administrator Presentations
- EIA Analysis Agenda

Search (Keyword or Phrase)

[FIND IT]

EIA Publications
A comprehensive list of links
to all the EIA publications

Applications
Downloadable applications,
models, and surveys

Special Features

Email List -- sign up to receive EIA information via Email. Choose from over 15 mailing lists.

Energy Links -- Hundreds of links to other energy related sites. This is one of the most complete lists of energy links available. If you have an energy related web site and would like to be added to our links, please contact the EIA webmaster.

Environmental Protection Agency

http://www.epa.gov

Highlights The giant site requires repeated visits to appreciate fully. The regulations and news hold the greatest interest for the legal researcher; these are models for other government Web sites. Law texts here are the EPA's voluminous CFR entries, *Federal Register* publications, a link to the U.S. Code and e-prints of the major recent environmental legislation.

The link to publications is massive, providing access to more than 5500 titles in both paper and electronic format. Telephone hotlines and agency dockets mean easy retrieval of the leading bureaucratic materials.

Other features of this outstanding Web server are an environmental glossary, news services, data systems and software and information services. The usual directories and leads to offices are here, as are in-depth descriptions of the EPA's programs and initiatives. This all adds up to a remarkable public service in a single, well-designed package. ❏

U.S. Environmental Protection Agency

Message From The Administrator

you and your environment

CONCERNED CITIZENS	STUDENTS & TEACHERS	KIDS
BUSINESS & INDUSTRY	RESEARCHERS & SCIENTISTS	STATE, LOCAL & TRIBAL GOVERNMENTS

a collection of resources

ABOUT EPA	REGULATIONS	PUBLICATIONS
EPA NEWS	CONTRACTS, GRANTS & ENV. FINANCING	DATA SYSTEMS & SOFTWARE
OFFICES, LABS & REGIONS	PROGRAMS & INITIATIVES	INFORMATION SERVICES

browse   what's new   comments   search

About this server
URL: http://www.epa.gov

This page last updated:
February 25, 1997

U.S. Environmental Protection Agency

Search the EPA Server

Use this form to submit a text search on the high level pages of this WWW server. The search is performed by a WAIS server, and there is detailed information available on how to create a WAIS query.

Complete Text: [_____] Submit Query

Search Tips and Instructions | Browse Subject Categories | Search the Web

Other Searches for EPA Information

- EPA Press Releases : full text of EPA Press Releases from 1994 to the present.
- EPA National Publications Catalog citations of EPA publications for ordering from the National Center for Environmental Publications and Information (NCEPI)
- Envirofacts database : a relational database that integrates data extracted from five major EPA program systems: AIRS/AFS, CERCLIS, PCS, RCRIS, and TRIS.
- Federal Register Environmental Subset : search the full text of Federal Register notices pertaining to the environment.
- Office of Air and Radiation Information : for a higher level search on documents from that office.
- Office of Water Information : for a higher level search on documents from that office.

Farm Service Agency

http://www.fsa.usda.gov

Highlights Breaking news and conservation programs are the first stop on this New-Ag database. Other sites that sprout nutritious information are linked to here, in particular the Kansas City Commodity Office that electronically prints a statistical overview and info on the Warehouse Act.

Farmers in need of a loan from the Federal government can find electronic forms to make the application right on the home page. Likewise, a lengthy list of agricultural programs are fleshed out on the site to give the researcher all the informational goods on *Acreage Reduction Programs, FSA Emergency Programs* and other helping farmhands from Washington.

A site map aids in navigating the smaller offices and programs wihtin the big agency. Use it to search the office directory to contact regional offices and employees. Other links connect to Department of Agriculture offices elsewhere on the Web. The site is moderately useful. For an agency this size, the information provided is remarkably modest. ❏

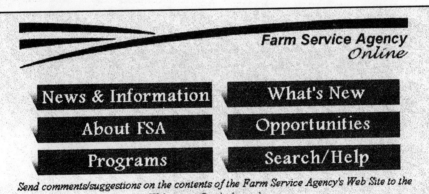

Farm Service Agency Online

News & Information   What's New

About FSA   Opportunities

Programs   Search/Help

Send comments/suggestions on the contents of the Farm Service Agency's Web Site to the
Webmaster@wdc.fsa.usda.gov

Farm Service Agency Online

Search the FSA WEB!

State and Area Office Information

Field Office Search

Employee Phone Book

Federal Aviation Administration

http://www.faa.gov

Highlights The Federal Aviation Administration cruises through cyberspace with a large-scale Web site that combines links to regulation and certification -- flight standards, aviation medicine, rule-making, aircraft certification and suspected unapproved parts links are online -- and technical information for air traffic systems. The overarching word on this site is "safety" and virtually every link serves the higher purpose of making air travel even more safe than it is today.

A smattering of FAA orders are reprinted on the site but the researcher will need to drill down through a lot of links to find them all. To speed the search, connect with the search box at *http://www.faa.gov/ search/iaquery.cgi* The search box will look through a lengthy collection of administrative materials from the FAA's many sub-agencies.

The link to other aviation links connect to weather news, airports internationally, airlines from throughout the world and general aviation links. ❑

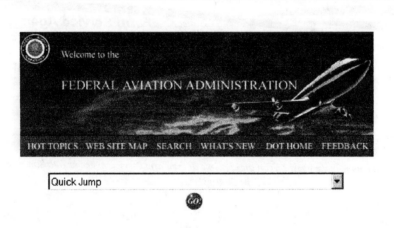

Welcome to the

FEDERAL AVIATION ADMINISTRATION

HOT TOPICS   WEB SITE MAP   SEARCH   WHAT'S NEW   DOT HOME   FEEDBACK

Quick Jump

ABOUT THE FAA

AVIATION SAFETY INFORMATION

HOW DO I ...?

NEWS AND INFORMATION

CENTERS AND REGIONS

FAA-SUPPORTED SITES

OTHER AVIATION SITES

HEADQUARTERS OFFICES

SITE CREDITS

ADMINISTRATION (AAD) provides FAA organizations with the collective ability to acquire, account for and maintain the resources necessary to meet the FAA mission requirements.

AIRPORTS (ARP) provides leadership in planning and developing a safe and efficient national airports system.

AIR TRAFFIC SERVICES (ATS) ensures safety, efficient operation, and maintenance, of the air transportation system.

COMMERCIAL SPACE (AST) regulates and promotes the commercial space and transportation industries.

REGULATION AND CERTIFICATION (AVR) Group, promotes the highest safety standards in the world and provides quality service to the public.

RESEARCH AND ACQUISITIONS (ARA) provides guidance relating to acquisition policy, research, system prototyping, and information resource management.

THE OFFICE OF SYSTEM SAFETY provides access to aviation safety-related databases, safety reports and publications, and information on the Global Analysis Information Network (GAIN) project..

Federal Bureau of Investigation

http://www.fbi.gov

Highlights J. Edgar Hoover meets hypertext as the 1930s-era "Ten Most Wanted List" migrates from smudgy posters hanging on post office walls to color-enhanced and digitally compress .gif files profiling the choicest bad guys *de jour.*

Taking a tip from television, the FBI now enlists the public's help electronically in solving some of the more intractable cases. Find links to major investigations and crime alerts here to wake up the general populace to the dangerous riff-raff that walks among us.

There actually are many interesting links mounted on the Web site; use the subject index to scroll through some of the more professionally useful ones, in particular the Telecommunications Carrier Statement which is of concern for everyone who uses the telephone and the Internet.

For off-time reading, review the FBI files on such celebrities as Elvis Presley, Jackie Robinson and Amelia Earhart released under the Freedom of Information Act. Bookmark 'em, Dano. ❏

Subject Index

Field Offices

Crime Alert

Major
Investigations

FBI's Most
Wanted

What's New

Press Releases

Congressional
Affairs

History

Overview

FBI Academy

FBI Case Files

Programs

Publications

FAQ

Director's
Speeches

Employment

Tour

Radio Show

Proposed
Programs

Mir Aimal Kansi
10 Most Wanted Fugitive
CIA Shooting Suspect Arrested

THE BOMBINGS IN SANDY SPRINGS AND MIDTOWN WERE CARRIED-OUT BY UNITS OF THE ARMY OF GOD
Atlanta Bombing, Army of God Letter

Economic Espionage Arrest
Philadelphia, Pennsylvania

FEDERAL BUREAU OF INVESTIGATION

Use of the NAME, INITIALS, or SEAL of the FBI is restricted by law
and may be used only with written permission of the FBI.
Visit the **U.S. Department of Justice**
and the **Society of Former FBI Special Agents**

FBI Home Page Staff: Office of Public and Congressional Affairs,
Special Projects, & Office of the Chief Scientist
FBI Historical Archives: National Archives

Federal Bureau of Prisons

http://www.bop.gov

Highlights Online head counts for the current week of the U.S. jail population is one of the leading features of this Web site. The bare bones effort tells researchers how to locate inmates in the Federal system (mostly by reprinting the phone numbers of Federal lock-ups) and reprints the bureaus policies on topics of interest to penologists and criminal justice professionals.

Links to the *National Institute of Corrections* gives access to that agency's publications, organizational structure and projects with other Federal agencies.

Links are light from this page, although, in an attempt to lighten up the somber nature of this Web site, a reprint of the 1956 list of rules by the warden of Alcatraz is available for grimly amusing reading.

The *Quick Facts* are useful for scanning very current numbers on the inmate population arranged by gender, race, ethnicity, citizenship, age, type of offense and sentence imposed. ❑

The Federal Bureau of Prisons

Kathleen M. Hawk, Director

- Quick Facts and Statistics.
- Weekly Population Report.
- Program Statements (Policies).
- Inmate Information.
- Employment Information.
  - Special Vacancy Announcement, Duluth, MN
- The National Institute of Corrections.
- Links to Other Pages.

Federal Communications Commission

http://www.fcc.gov

Highlights Few other government sites can compete with breadth of information provided by the FCC on what is the largest federal Web site. To mine this far-reaching site, first turn either to the *Site Map* or the *search page* if only to keep from getting lost in the dense thicket of data.

The FCC publishes its *Daily Digest* here - you can get it delivered right to your e-mail box if you'd like. There's also forms, fees, the text of the Telecommunications Act of 1996, news releases and data on spectrum auctions. Look here for press releases from the commission, agendas for upcoming meetings and -- as you would expect from the leading regulator of new communications technologies, Internet-accessible audio files.

The site is updated daily and is a good source of telecom news on every subject. ❑

Welcome to the FCC. The mission of this independent government agency is to encourage competition in all communications markets and to protect the public interest. In response to direction from the Congress, the FCC develops and implements policy concerning interstate and international communications by radio, television, wire, satellite, and cable.

We are pleased to make the resources of the Commission available to the public and invite you to comment on issues before the Commission.

Sincerely,
Reed Hundt, Chairman

Play Welcome Message
audio file, 25 sec., 200 KB (instructions)

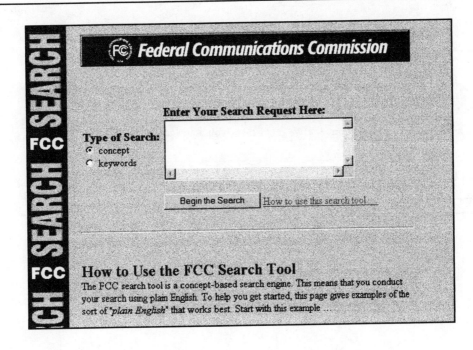

Enter Your Search Request Here:

Type of Search:
⦿ concept
○ keywords

Begin the Search   How to use this search tool

How to Use the FCC Search Tool

The FCC search tool is a concept-based search engine. This means that you conduct your search using plain English. To help you get started, this page gives examples of the sort of *"plain English"* that works best. Start with this example ...

Federal Crop Insurance Corporation

http://www.act.fcic.usda.gov

Highlights Software designers haven't yet convinced Congress to provide a safety net in case the latest beta version of their hot new product withers in the marketplace, but the farmers of America have been at the game longer. The bib overall crowd now enjoy insurance in case Mother Nature turns unpleasant. The Web site is extremely simple -- there are only two links on it -- and phenomenally easy to navigate.

Crystalballing the future of crops in the field is the job of the actuaries who sow the numbers of future results under the link to the *Crop Insurance Actuarial Information Public Access Server*. That's where a series of bulletins and downloaded files containing the latest update on what the months to come hold in store can be found and retrieved for local consumption. Look here for such titles as *Almond Crop Insurance Provisions* and *Revenue Assurance - Loss Adjustment Supplemental Handbook*. Its information only an actuary could love; bookmark it for the applied agrarian statistician on the block. ❏

USDA Risk Management Agency
Federal Crop Insurance Corporation

You have accessed the home page of the Risk Management Agency at the Federal Crop Insurance Corporation of the United States Department of Agriculture. This web site is devoted to making it easier for our customers to access crop insurance and other risk management related information.

Please select one of the following business areas:

- Actuarial Information Public Access Server
- Research and Evaluation Division Home Page

To ensure you are viewing these pages correctly, we recommend you download the latest version of Netscape.

Last modified 10/03/96
rsifuent@rm.fcic.usda.gov

Federal Deposit Insurance Corporation

http://www.fdic.gov

Highlights The banker's failure is the auctioneer's stock and the agency that steps in when the savings and loans head south now pumps the Internet full of news about asset sales, official documents and general news of interest to banking professionals.

The Web site is also an excellent source of statutory codes and administrative rulemakings pertaining to thrift institutions. A databank of statistics offers the researcher *The Banking Review*, *Histor-*

ical Statistics on Banking and the *FDIC Institution Directory System* for looking up information on each FDIC-insured institution.

The link to public information puts official documents in the hands of the public electronically. Also see how the FDIC operates by clicking on *About FDIC*.

The Web site is large enough to require s sitemap. Use it to meander this good information resource. ❑

What's New The most recent additions to the FDIC Web Site

Banking News	Information of interest to the banking industry.	Asset Info	Assets and Products for sale by the FDIC.
Publications	Official documents available now from the FDIC.	Data Bank	Statistical information about banks and banking.
Laws and Regs	Laws and regulations applicable to financial institutions.	About FDIC	Information about the Corporation.
Consumer News	Brochures, Telephone Numbers and other information used regularly by customers of financial institutions.	Site Map	Quick reference to navigating this site.

If you have comments or questions about this site, please contact the Webmaster

The FDIC uses links to other web sites in an effort to assist users in locating information on topics that might be of interest to them. The FDIC cannot attest to the accuracy of information provided by linked sites. Linking to a web site does not constitute an endorsement by the FDIC or any of its employees or the sponsors of the site or the products presented on the site.

Federal Election Commission

http://www.fec.gov

Highlights Money and politicians have an affinity for one another; the Federal Election Commission chaperones the romance to see that affairs remain chaste.

From the FEC Web site, a guide to contributions and the law will provide a non-legal introduction to the subject that will serve as guidance for a client new to the intricate political two-step. More interesting however are the nifty charts and graphs that can be downloaded from the site by drilling down from the home page through *Financial Information about Candidates,* *Parties and PACS* to get to appropriate link.

Get disclosure forms directly from the site; they're HTML forms that can be viewed and printed straight out of the browser. The same associated page also offers raw data from the FEC Campaign Finance Database.

Other items on the cybershelves here are *news and releases,* information to edify those persons and committees subject to FEC regulations (*i.e.* candidates and PACs) on complying with the requisite regulations and a help guide. ❏

FEDERAL ELECTION COMMISSION

Click on the FEC seal above for general information about the Federal Election Commission.
If you're having problems viewing this page, click here to switch to minimal graphics view.

Last updated: March 26, 1997

What's New!

Citizens Guide to Contributions and the Law

Using FEC Services

Financial Information About Candidates, Parties and PACs

Help for Candidates, Parties and PACs

About Elections and Election Administration

Federal Elections and Voting Statistics

News Releases, Media Advisories

NEW! Tools to help you file reports electronically in 1997!!

NEW! Download the National Mail Voter Registration Form now!

Federal Emergency Management Agency

http://www.fema.gov

Highlights Stepping in when disaster strikes, the Federal Emergency Management Agency has been in the spotlight consistently in the 1990s as one natural catastrophe after another befell American citizens. Electronic access is added to the services that the agency now provides before (and presumably during) a disaster occurs. FEMA tries to prepare the public for bad turns of events with a link to *Emergency Preparedness and Training*. A reference library, designed like a blueprint, contains a useful collection of forms, maps, advice on what to do with pets in disasters, telecommunications and legal links.

The agency outlines its mission and powers in the link to *About FEMA*; use the *News Room* and the links to the weather alerts to keep abreast of breaking developments. FEMA also picks its own "Top 5" selections from its own Web site.

The scrolling Java applet gives visitors a heads-up on troublesome but predictable phenomena such as hurricanes, floods and other natural miseries. ❑

FEMA
Federal Emergency Management Agency

es section.... If you suffered losses as a result of a Presidentially-declared disaster,

About FEMA | What's New @FEMA.GOV | FEMA News Room | Reducing Risk through Mitigation | Emergency Preparedness & Training

Spring Flood Watch | Reference Library | GEMS: Global Emergency Management System | Working for a Fire Safe America | Help After a Disaster

DISASTER It strikes anytime, anywhere. It takes many forms -- a hurricane, an earthquake, a tornado, a flood, a fire or a hazardous spill, an act of nature or an act of terrorism. It builds over days or weeks, or hits suddenly, without warning. Every year, millions of Americans face disaster, and its terrifying consequences.

The Federal Emergency Management Agency -- FEMA -- is an independent agency of the federal government, reporting to the President. Since its founding in 1979, FEMA's mission has been clear:

to reduce loss of life and property and protect our nation's critical infrastructure from all types of hazards through a comprehensive, risk-based, emergency management program of mitigation, preparedness, response and recovery.

FEEDBACK
SEARCH

Federal Energy Regulatory Commission

http://www.ferc.fed.us

Highlights The most useful service from the Federal Energy Regulatory Commission Web site is also the most frustrating. It's the GILS (Government Information Locator Service) connection that imposes a search engine on FERC information. Trouble, the Webmaster has not remembered to say just what it is the database searches through -- Orders? Decisions? News? An online hint would go a long way to making this a fine archive of energy-related information. Instead the database is veiled in mystery that is aggravating, not beguiling. Cast your line into these murky waters to see what pulls up in a spirit of adventure; in a spirit of legal research, look elsewhere.

Other links in this ho-hum service take the researcher to an electronic bulletin board service for news and current regulatory releases from the commission. For press releases and the like, try the Office of External Affairs. But until the GILS server gets some online instructions, turn to a commercial service for FERC materials. ❑

Federal Energy Regulatory Commission

The Federal Energy Regulatory Commission, an independent regulatory agency within the Department of Energy:

- regulates the transmission of natural gas in interstate commerce;

- regulates the transmission of oil by pipeline in interstate commerce;

- regulates the transmission and wholesale sales of electricity in interstate commerce;

- licenses and inspects private, municipal and state hydroelectric projects; and

- oversees related environmental matters.

Public Access

A public reference room is available where the public can use FERC facilities for research. The Office of External Affairs provides information to the public and to county, state and federal governmental entities. There are several electronically accessible data processing services that can be accessed from which information can be derived. This includes a system called Remote Public Access (RPA). RPA is a mainframe application which the public and the government can use to access several automated applications on FERC's mainframe. In addition, the electronic bulletin board system provides access to Commission daily issuances and information for other automation applications.

Federal Finanoial Institutions Examination Counoil

http://www.ffiec.gov

Highlights As an umbrella organization tying together the five banking regulatory agencies, FFIEC is singularly situated to deliver one-stop shopping for banking regulations, laws and other regulatory information. It does so smashingly. The *Information Services* is the big attraction here and a click on the link to the same ponies up an index page that leads to the five agencies, educational materials for bank examiners, a breezy title known as the *Uniform Bank Performance Report User's Guide* and FFIEC *Report Forms*

and *Press Releases*.

Compared to the other banking sites, this one is not particularly ambitious nor is it terribly informative. Basic information about bank examination, as would be suspected, is what's available here. There could be more regulatory information, audit results, forms and the like and perhaps they will appear in the future. But in its present form, this lightweight database is a primarily useful as a stepping stone to meatier Webs. ❏

Federal Financial Institutions Examination Council

Mission | Information Services | Examiner Education | Financial / Organization Information
Press Releases | The Five Banking Regulatory Agencies of the FFIEC | Other Links
** Disclaimer **

Members

- Eugene A. Ludwig, *Chairman*
  Comptroller of the Currency
  Office of the Comptroller of the Currency

- Susan M. Phillips, *Vice Chair*
  Member
  Board of Governors of the Federal Reserve System

- Norman E. D'Amours,
  Chairman
  National Credit Union Administration

- Ricki Helfer
  Chairman
  Federal Deposit Insurance Corporation

- Nicolas P. Retsinas
  Director
  Office of Thrift Supervision

- Joe M. Cleaver, *Executive Secretary*
  Federal Financial Institutions Examination Council

- Council Staff
- Examiner Education Staff

Mission

- The Federal Financial Institutions Examination Council (Council) was established on March 10, 1979, pursuant to title X of the Financial Institutions Regulatory and Interest Rate Control Act of 1978 (FIRA), Public Law 95-630. Its mission statement outlines its current tasks.

Federal Highway Administration

http://www.fhwa.dot.gov

Highlights The concrete superhighway meets the information superhighway at this Web site. The Federal Highway Administration is handsomely financed and it shows: the links to statistical information are numerous and a list of annual publications by the agency that keeps traffic flowing more or less smoothly on the Interstates belies their importance as a well-heeled Federal agency. There are reports here on why highways are so vital to commerce and guides on how to de-ice the roadway on inclement weather.

(Whether the legal researcher will find all this riveting reading professionally useful is questionable, but it's *there*.)

Stick to the main entry marked *Legislation and Regulations* to draw a bead on the latest goings-on by the desk-bound drivers in Washington. Locate the text of the National Highway System Designation Act of 1995 here in the same lane as the relevant CFR sections (by section) and appropriations bills. The FHA has its own personal link to the *Federal Register* here as well. ❏

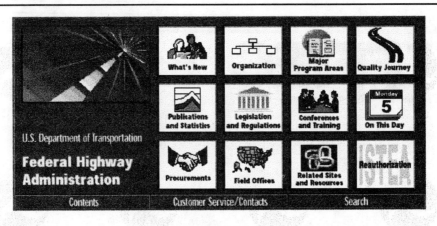

Welcome Message

Text links for users with non-graphical browsers

- Whats New
- Publications and Statistics
- Procurements
- Organization
- Legislation and Regulations
- Field Offices

- Program Areas
- Conferences and Training
- Related Sites and Resources
- Quality Journey
- FHWA By Day
- ISTEA Reauthorization

Contents   Customer Service/Contacts   Search

This page has been accessed `070564` since Friday, January 03, 1997

WARNING: Unauthorized access to this United States Government Computer system is prohibited by Title 18, "Crimes and Criminal Procedure," United States Code, Section 1030, "Fraud and Related Activity in Connection with Computers." Knowingly or intentionally accessing this computer system without authorization or with intent to defraud could result in a fine, imprisonment, or both.

To protect the system from unauthorized use, system administrators monitor this system. Anyone using this system expressly consents to such monitoring and is advised that if monitoring reveals possible evidence of criminal activity, such evidence may be provided to law enforcement officials.

Federal Maritime Commission

http://www.fmc.gov

HIGHLIGHTS Electronic commerce hasn't completely replaced sending goods from point A to point B the old-fashioned way, namely, on a ship. The Federal Maritime Commission sticks up for American shippers by protecting them from onerous regulations by foreign governments. It also has a laundry list of other duties, among them, enforcing the Shipping Act of 1984, reviewing tariff filings between U.S. and foreign ports, licensing freight forwarders, issuing passenger vessel certificates and investigating discriminatory or unfair pricing in the shipping industry. (More details are online under the click for *What We Do*.)

The other connections are straightforward. There are forms here and a directory of the commission bureaus and offices nationwide. Regulations can be retrieved by punching the hypertext link by that name. News releases keep the researcher on the button when it comes to things maritime from this unpretentious but informative site. ❑

Welcome to the

Federal Maritime Commission

Home Page

Today is `05-01-97` The time is `11:22`PM

You are the `002613` person since 3 December 1996.

This Web Page was last modified 21 *April 1997*.

The **Federal Maritime Commission (FMC)** was established in 1961 as an independent government agency, responsible for the regulation of shipping in the foreign trades of the United States. The Commission's five members are appointed by the President with the advice and consent of the Senate. The FMC is headquartered at **800 North Capitol Street, N.W., Washington, D.C. 20573,** with four Area Representatives around the nation.

Federal Railroad Administration

http://www.fra.dot.gov

Highlights The day has arrived when any citizen of the United States -- or the world -- can discover a thorough tutorial on the Gage Restraint Measurement System. Such a welcome quilt of data joins with the latest scoop on high-speed ground transportation, biographies of bureaucrats and an embarrassing photograph of the President for a so-so Web site operated by the people who try to make the trains run on time in a democracy.

Except for the link to *Office of Safety* there is not a great deal here to interest the legal researcher. This site is a curiosity. It has potential, like any other large, sub-Cabinet agency to mount links to regulations, orders and statutes but the site designers seem reluctant to provide the types of administrative reports that would significantly aid the researcher.

Rail buffs might find some recreational pleasure in the site, but for looking up anything more than the tensile strength of railroad tracks when laden with hopper cars full of coal, use alternative info-media. ❑

WELCOME TO THE
FEDERAL RAILROAD ADMINISTRATION (FRA)
WORLD WIDE WEB HOME PAGE

 Biographical Summary of the Administrator

 Biographical Summary of the Deputy Administrator

 FRA - Who We Are And What We Do

 FRA'S Mission And Vision

 FRA Customer Service Plan

 Office of Public Affairs

 Office of Safety

 Asian Pacific American Employees Council

Federal Reserve Board
Board of Governors

http://www.bog.frb.fed.us

Highlights The Board of Governors of the Federal Reserve operate a Web site that should be in the bookmark file of every financial researcher. The hook-ups are both fresh and extensive. The links connect to letters issued by the board and a summary of regulations. The site reprints H.2A applications, e-publishes a lengthy list of current and historical banking statistics. and makes tracks Web-wise to the twelve Federal Reserve Banks.

Use the links to Federal Reserve System's *National Information Center of Banking Information* for Top 100 rankings of banks and bank holding companies and links to institutions within the system.

This full-bodied Web site contains Congressional reports and news releases along with reports from the Federal Open Market Committee including a link to the *Beige Book.*This is an excellent site that is a fundamental resource. ❏

Board of Governors of the Federal Reserve System / Washington D.C.

Federal Reserve Board

Welcome to the Federal Reserve Board
>   About the Federal Reserve System
>   *Purposes and Functions*
>   Members of the Board of Governors
>   Presidents of the Federal Reserve District Banks

Federal Open Market Committee (FOMC)
>   Calendar
>   Members
>   Minutes **UPDATED**
>   Beige Book

Testimony and Speeches
>   Humphrey-Hawkins Testimony
>   Testimony of Federal Reserve Board officials
>   Speeches of Federal Reserve Board members **UPDATED**

Press Releases
>   Board actions
>   Bank holding company cases
>   General **UPDATED**

Reports to the Congress
>   *Annual Report* and *Budget Review* **UPDATED**
>   Report on Funds Availability and Check Fraud (531 KB PDF)
>   Humphrey-Hawkins Report

Domestic and International Research
>   Statistical releases
>   Working papers **UPDATED**
>   Senior Loan Officer Opinion Survey

Federal Trade Commission
http://www.ftc.gov

Highlights Antitrust enforcement and the protection of consumers from unscrupulous manufacturers, retailers and advertisers are the tasks detailed on this excellent Web site. The antitrust links are the best part of the site and lead to advisory opinions, guidelines and Hart-Scott-Rodino premerger notification rules which include the form and instructions and source book information.

Commission actions provides a link to the *Rules of Practice* and *Statutes* in HTML, WordPerfect or PDF format. The actions collection dates from January 1996 to present.

Other links offer transcripts of speeches by senior commission personnel, a directory of regional offices and the *Weekly Calendar* of speeches, commission hearings and testimony and commission meetings.

Remaining links are primarily of interest to the general public. ❏

Federal Trade Commission
6th Street and Pennsylvania Avenue, N.W
Washington, D.C. 20580

http://www.ftc.gov

Welcome to the Home Page for the Federal Trade Commission World Wide Web Server.

- **What's New?**

  - FTC Will Seek to Block Staples/Office Depot Merger
    Submit Electronic Communication

  - "Operation Waistline"
  - Traveler's Advisory: Get What You Pay For
  - Franchise Rulemaking
  - Fortuna-Alliance Update
  - Fair Credit Reporting Act (16 CFR Part 601)
  - Scholarship Scams

- **News Releases**

  - **FYI:** Announced Actions for March 28, 1997

- **FTC Weekly Calendar**

- **Commission Actions**

- **Speeches**

- **Conferences, Hearings, Workshops**

  - Public Workshop on Consumer Information Privacy NEW

- **Staff Reports**

- **Antitrust/Competition Issues**

Federal Transit Administration

http://www.fta.dot.gov

Highlights The Department of Transportation is a sprawling department and within its suzerainty is this administrative service that organizes what little information there is by subject or by office. Subject matter searching leads to a framed Web page for retrieving the National Transit library, directories of the administration's offices, budgets, grants and prints some interesting materials on intermodalism.

Best bet for the legal researcher is the link to *law* wherein such statutory reprints as the *National Economic Crossroads Transportation Efficiency Act of 1997* and the text of *Mass Transportation* from Title 49 of the U.S. Code can be found. Recent releases from the *Federal Register* comprise the administrative publication angle; look here too for studies and guidelines for management.

For insight into transportation trends, refer to the link for *technology.* Other connections represent safety issues and solicitation of public participation. ❑

[Information Organized by Subject]|[Information Organized by Office]
[U.S. Department of Transportation]
[Introductory Information] | [Briefing Room] | [What's New] | [Other Resources]

Search the Federal Transit Administration

[   ] [x Search]

Documentation about making queries is available.

FinanceNet

http://www.financenet.gov

Highlights Hard as it is to believe, someone in Washington cares about running the government efficiently. As part of the Clinton Administration's efforts to improve government functions under the National Performance Review, FinanceNet seeks to make government agencies "stewards" of the taxpayers' resources and to impress upon federal employees that they serve the citizens of the nation. To help achieve this quixotic aim, FinanceNet operates mailing lists for professionals who run the agencies. There are many links for government's middle managers to learn how better to spend the taxpayers' involuntarily rendered dollars.

The real draw for this site is the one-stop shop for information on government asset sales. Access to *Commerce Business Daily* is online here; so is a link to subscribe to the *daily-sales* list to receive an e-mail list of government goods offered for sale. Also see newsgroups on the sale of government surplus.

This is a moderately interesting site whose greatest virtues are brevity and good grooming. ❑

TEXT   HOME   SEARCH   HOTSPOTS   NEWS   MAILLISTS   NEWSGROUPS

FINANCIAL MANAGEMENT IN GOVERNMENT

FINANCENET

ABOUT
WHAT'S NEW
GOVSALES

US FEDERAL
STATE/LOCAL
INTERNATIONAL

TOPICS
JOBS/TRAINING
CALENDARS
SLIDES
SURVEY
BEST OF 'NET
FEEDBACK
STATISTICS
AWARDS
DISCLAIMER

FINANCENET
STAFF

Send technical comments to:
webmaster@
financenet.gov

FinanceNet is the Internet's home for public financial management worldwide. It was established by Vice President Gore's *National Performance Review* in Washington, D.C. in 1994 and is operated by the *National Science Foundation* (a Federal agency) under sponsorship of the *U.S. Chief Financial Officers Council*. FinanceNet reaches across geopolitical boundaries to link government financial management administrators, educators and taxpayers worldwide to catalyze continuous improvements in the productivity of government personnel and in the stewardship and accountability for taxpayer resources. FinanceNet is also the home for Vice President Gore's new International *GovNews* Project to provide a new open access to government information and citizen feedback worldwide.

The GovNews Project A Revolutionary Idea!

Executive Director, FinanceNet
E. Preston Rich
National Science Foundation

TOP

Financial Crimes Enforcement Network

http://www.ustreas.gov/treasury/bureaus/fincen/

Highlights A favorite technique of criminals who have discovered that certain crimes do pay is money laundering. It's up the sleuths at the Treasury Department's Financial Crimes Enforcement Network to finger them.

Using sophisticated detection tools to hunt down washday felons, the FCEN has even moved into the cyberworld where electronic payments are whizzing around from server to client throughout the globe. On the Web site, find a description of what the agency does, how they go about it (without tipping off the bad guys) and forms like the Suspicious Activity Report, Currency Transaction Report and Report of Foreign Bank and Financial Accounts in PDF format.

Advisories and news releases give the Internet world the scoop on money transfers and new overseas players in the money laundering world such as the Seychelles. Links to international law enforcement agencies are also found on this interesting site. ❑

FAQ's

Inside FinCEN

Banks and Beyond

Borderless World

Cyberpayments

OUR MISSION

The Financial Crimes Enforcement Network (FinCEN) is one of the primary agencies that establishes, oversees, and implements Treasury's policies to prevent and detect money laundering. It provides analytical case support, through the use of state-of-the-art technology and intelligence analyses, to many federal agencies as well as state and local law enforcement organizations. FinCEN also administers the Bank Secrecy Act, which is a key component of Treasury's efforts to combat money laundering. In addition, FinCEN is becoming a leader in international efforts to build effective counter-money laundering policies and cooperation throughout the world.

WHAT'S NEW!

[Advisory 8] [Latest News Release]
[FinCEN Notice 97-1]
[FinCEN Top 10 Links]

[Comments to FinCEN]

News Releases

Advisories

BSA Forms

Publications

Financial Management Service

http://www.fms.treas.gov

Highlights The government squander money? Hard to believe. But like all good bureaucracies, there is an agency that tries to prevent some of the more egregious excesses of public purchases of the $50,000-toilet seat variety. The Financial Management Service of the Department of the Treasury fights the good fight with a Web site that notches its successes with links to its own regulations and a published set of guidelines that include instructions on how to file FOIA requests with its information-keepers.

Apparently the FMS Web site is a big hit in Washington because the frame navigation bar provides shortcuts to *FMS's most requested pages*. Those would be the ones containing such delectables as the Standard General Ledger, info on debt collection, consolidated financial conditions, annual report, and electronic benefits transfer.

Heavy-duty FMS users can assure themselves of never missing a morsel of this informational banquet by subscribing to an e-mail notification system that alerts users to new additions to the Web. ❑

QSearch   Treasury Home Page   Browse

THE DEPARTMENT OF THE TREASURY

Financial Management Service

FMS is the U.S. Government's financial manager, central disburser, and collections agent, as well as its accountant and reporter of financial information. Commissioner Russell Morris ensures that FMS promotes sound financial management through its cash management and credit administration programs. These programs help Federal agencies make efficient use of resources and reduce the amount of debt owed to the Government.

Updated February 28, 1997

Search and Browse for Information

Search all FMS Files (includes TFM only search) NEW
   Government Information Locator Records (GILS) at GPO Access
   About GILS

Browse an Alphabetical Index of Major Information Areas
   Accounting Resources
   Activities & Contacts
   Condition of the Federal Government
   Products & Services
   Publications

Fish and Wildlife Service

http://www.fws.gov

Highlights Many home pages from Fish and Wildlife Web sub-agencies link to the FWS home page; they're all connected by a search engine that at last look counted some 1600 HTML pages under management. Among the home pages to be searched are those for wildlife laws, migratory bird management, North American waterfowl and wetlands, the endangered species program and the Service Home Page, FWS's main server.

Link up to a handy reference database by clicking on *searchable databases* where the services include a list of plant species found in wetlands, the effects of fire on ecologies and prescribed burns, maps, news releases and speeches and a fish and wildlife reference service.

To find out a schedule of speeches and meetings sponsored by the service, nick the news button with the cursor to pull a page with the required information.

For an agency with such picturesque charges, the Web site is surprisingly dull; perhaps the Webmaster can get handy with the Leica and enliven the site. ❑

United States
Fish & Wildlife Service

Who We Are | What We Do | Where We Are | Help | Search | News

Welcome to the U.S. Fish and Wildlife Service, a bureau within the Department of the Interior. Our mission is to conserve, protect, and enhance fish and wildlife and their habitats for the continuing benefit of the American people. Our major responsibilities are: migratory birds, endangered species, certain marine mammals, freshwater and anadromous fish, the National Wildlife Refuge System, wetlands, conserving habitat, and environmental contaminants.

We are divided into seven geographic regions, and our headquarters is located in Washington, DC. Regional Offices are involved in regional and local activities. Headquarters offices are involved in nationwide activities. If you are familiar with our internal organization, please visit our Servers Organized by Office page. You are welcome to contact us.

☆ Update your links! The U.S. Fish & Wildlife Service Region 7 web site has moved.

☆ Visit the newest U.S. Fish & Wildlife Service server, the Rock Island Field Office Home Page.

☆ For information on National Fishing Week and a list of states with free fishing days during the week, check our National Fishing Week page.

☆ Get in the Flow for Healthy Streams:
Interested in restoring or managing the streamside environment in your area? Join the U.S. Fish and Wildlife Service, Bureau of Land Management, U.S. Forest Service, and the Natural Resources Conservation Service for an interagency satellite broadcast on riparian restoration and management. Check the Bureau of Land Management's National Training Center for additional information.

Food and Drug Administration

http://www.fda.gov

Highlights The FDA runs a large-scale Web server that is one of the most comprehensive information systems on the Internet. Kick off research by clicking on one of the chunky icons for any one of the FDA's many services. Clicking on *Human Drugs*, for instance, will invoke a free-standing home page for the Center for Drug Evaluation and Research that delivers drug information, regulatory guidance, background on the agency itself and public health advisories. There's also a search bar to aid in navigation. Drilling down even further will connect the researcher to substantial resources: regulatory guidance reprints relevant CFR sections, forms, practice notes, links to the *Federal Register* and the *Manual of Policies and Procedures*.

Most of the links are equally robust. Scientific information is either mounted here natively or linked to non-official sources. The news is current and the links are well-groomed for minimal dead links and 404 lookup errors. ❑

Text Version for Browsers that do not support tables

Welcome to Internet FDA

Your Electronic Source of Information about the U.S. Food and Drug Administration

FDA News

Foods

Human Drugs

Biologics

Medical Devices/Radiological Health

Animal Drugs

Cosmetics

Field Operations/Imports

Toxicology

Foreign Language

MORE CHOICES

Children & Tobacco

SEARCH   COMMENTS

[Department of Health and Human Services Home Page]

Food Nutrition and Consumer Services

http://www.usda.gov/fcs

Highlights Now that the federal government has replaced social welfare programs with its "personal responsibility" act, the agency that once handed out food to hungry children and destitute mothers, the sick, the elderly and others who cannot afford to run for a Senate seat has a Web site to outline their greatly reduced role as pantry to the poor. Find a good deal of information on the Food Stamp program, the WIC (Women, Infants and Children) program and other services from the Web. The site tells agencies and community groups who have come to depend on the USDA for surplus food how to come to grips with the coming reduction in benefits to its clients.

Other links are for talking about issues of welfare reform, food nutrition information and for a library stocked with proposed regulations, fact sheets and

United States Department of Agriculture

Food and Consumer Service

- What's New at FCS

- About FCS

- Welfare Reform

- Contract and Grant Opportunities

- FCS Library of Files
Contains news releases, speeches, proposed regulations, studies, Healthy Kids Hotlines, fact sheets, and

- FCS Research and Evaluation

- Food Stamp Program

- Food Distribution Programs

- Child Nutrition Programs

- WIC Program

- Gleaning and Food Recovery

- Team Nutrition

- Center for Nutrition Policy and Promotion

Foreign Agricultural Service

http://www.fas.usda.gov

Highlights The United States is an immense exporter of food and to keep foreign markets working to the benefit of the nation's farmers, the Foreign Agricultural Service keeps tabs on the transactions. To see how much bulgar goes to Bulgaria, click on *Export Sales Reports* to see weekly and annual reports on the sales of wheat, cotton, oilseeds, feed grain and hides and skins.

World Market and Trade Circulars are forecasts of the market for agricultural products and reports on the competition from around the globe, *viz.* "Uzbekistan's wheat sector is on a bumpy path as it adjusts in the post-Soviet era."

The legal researcher can use this site as a reference service or to track down policy statements under the link to *Trade Policy*. For *GATT Commodity Fact Sheets, NAFTA Facts Sheets* and *FAS Program Fact Sheets,* knock on the link for *News and Information*. A magazine titled *AgExporter* magazine is e-published here for anyone in the grain and hide export business. ❑

U.S. Department of Agriculture

Foreign Agricultural Service

About FAS   Index   Search   E-Mail   Other Links   USDA

Countries

Commodities

Exporter Help

News & Info

Programs

Trade Policy

Expanding Global Markets for U.S. Agriculture

The mission of the Foreign Agricultural Service is to advance the interests of the agricultural community and the general public by working to develop and expand foreign markets for U.S. food and agricultural products.

Welcome to the New FAS Home Page

Welcome to the redesigned FAS homepage. This site, while still under construction, will serve as an interim homepage while we make improvements to the main web server. Please excuse the dust.

FAS FACT FILE

Dollar for dollar, we now export more wheat than steel, more meat than aluminum, and more fruits and vegetables than ships, boats, and trucks combined!

New Items Online!

- Export Sales Report
- World Market and Trade Circulars
- National consultations for the World Food Summit
- Overseas Directory
- FAS Subject Listing

General Services Administration

http://www.gsa.gov

Highlights One of the three central management agencies in the Federal government, the General Services Administration is Uncle Sam's super. They run the office buildings, buy the supplies, furnish the place (peek at the nearest post office to get an idea of GSA's unique eye for interior design), mop the floors and keep gas in the tanks of the motor pool automobiles. Somehow in this flurry of activity, the GSA also finds some time to mount a Web site to tell the wired world precisely how it is that they spend their working day. It is the textbook image of a sprawling bureaucracy, stretching from the Federal Supply Service to Inspector General to the Board of Contract Appeals. The legal researcher can fire this Web site up and thrill to find such rocking good data as the releases from the Office of Governmentwide Policies or the massive collection of offices and rules to be found in the index. Save wear and tear on your mouse and use the search bar to get around this extensive chunk of cyberia. It's a monster of a site with a breathtaking number of links. ❑

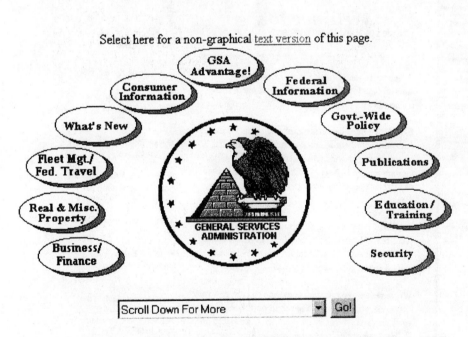

Select here for a non-graphical text version of this page.

GSA Advantage!

Consumer Information

Federal Information

What's New

Govt.-Wide Policy

Fleet Mgt./ Fed. Travel

Publications

Real & Misc. Property

Education/ Training

Business/ Finance

Security

GENERAL SERVICES ADMINISTRATION

Scroll Down For More | Go!

Thank you for letting us help you. You are the **226000th** visitor since January 1, 1997.
This page was last Updated: *1, January 1997*

Health Care
Financing Administration

http://www.hcfa.gov

Highlights The massive agency that administers two of the most critical benefit programs that the government operates -- Medicare and Medicaid -- will become increasingly important as the U.S. population ages. Laws and regulations governing these goliaths are accessible from the home page. Also find a wealth of statistical data about the programs under the eye of the HCFA such as the number of people receiving benefits, health care indicators and other med-

ical analyses and reports.

Publications and forms for the Medicare consumer and professional and technical publications for researchers are mounted on the page.

The services of both major medical programs are considered in easy-to-read Web pages. Use the link *Public Affairs* to locate press releases, fact sheets, the transcripts of speeches and testimony before Congress.

❑

Updated
Apr 01, 1997

| Medicare | Medicaid | Publications & Forms | Local Info. | Stats & Data | Research & Demonstration | Laws & Regs | Public Affairs |

About HCFA
Feedback
Govt. Links
Search
Help

Home Medicare Medicaid Help Feedback Search

Welcome to HCFA
the Medicare and Medicaid Agency
Health Care Financing Administration

Welcome to the **Health Care Financing Administration** (HCFA), the federal agency that administers the Medicare and Medicaid programs.

HCFA provides health insurance for over 74 million Americans through Medicare and Medicaid. The majority of these individuals receive their benefits through the fee-for-service delivery system, however, an increasing number are choosing managed care plans.

In addition to providing health insurance, HCFA also regulates all laboratory testing (except research) in the U.S. through the Clinical Laboratory Improvement Amendments (CLIA) program.

We've revamped our web presence to give you easy access to information you need. In our News Desk, you'll find links to the latest documents available on HCFA's web site. In several subject areas, we provide different tracks to help you find the information you need. Visit us regularly for updated news from HCFA. We look forward to hearing from you.

[About HCFA ▼]
[Quick Navigate]

In the News Apr 02, 1997

❧ HCFA Names New Medicare Carrier for MA, NH, VE, ME

❧ New Home Health Regulations

❧ Medicare AAPCC ASCII Flat Data Files - Annual (ZIP files for 1992-Present)

❧ Medicare Choices Demo. Expanded

❧ HCFA Employment Opportunities Available

❧ Administrative Simplification: Link to the Dept. Data Council (DDC) or Nat'l Comm. on Vital and Hlth Stats (NVHS)

❧ Welfare Reform and Medicaid Fact Sheets

❧ HCFA Initiatives:National Provider Identifier, and PAYERID.

 Department of Health & Human Services

Immigration and Naturalization Service

http://www.ins.usdoj.gov/index.html

Highlights Virtually every legal researcher will need to contact the Immigration and Naturalization Service at least once, if only to retrieve the proper forms for prospective employees, to check on visa status or look up some other stray immigration factoid. The server is a good one and in light of the next-to-impossible task of speaking to a human being at any one of the INS' regional offices -- the lines are always busy -- the preferred first stop for anyone in need of INS regulations or forms. There happens to be a ton of legal information from the agency online: click on the *view or download the latest law* to open an electronic library containing immigration law, regulations, interpretations and decisions in HTML or WordPerfect format.

Employer information is a major resource here and provides FAQs and forms for prospective employers of individuals not born as American citizens. ❑

U.S. Immigration and Naturalization Service

Welcome to the INS Home Page

[TEXT ONLY]

- **The Agency**
  Mission Statement, Organization, Customer Service Initiatives
- **Public Information**
  Statistics, Media-related, Immigration Law and Regulations, Freedom of Information Act and Privacy Act Information, Frequently Asked Questions, Downloadable Forms, Forms By Mail
- **Employer Information**
  Employment Verification Pilot Programs, Employment Eligibility Verification Form I-9, links to frequently asked questions
- **Procurement Notices**
  Base Operating Support Systems (BOSS), Service Technology Alliance Resources (STARS)
- **Federal Government Web Sites**
  Links to Selected Agencies and to Federal Site Locators
- **What's New on the INS Site**
- Site Map

[Search]   Help on Search

NEW!! Read about recent changes to Immigration Law, download the latest Law.

See why we're not finished yet!

Last Modified 4/23/1997

Indian Health Service

http://www.tucson.ihs.gov

Highlights The Public Health Service reaches out to the Native American community with this Web site for explaining the services it provides and the geographic regions in which it provides them. The site comes supplied with press releases, media advisories and transcripts of speeches by the senior officials as well as publications and links to regional offices.

Other than the publications and a smattering of outside links, there is not a great deal on this Web site of interest to the researcher outside of this very specialized subject matter. The links to American Indian sites are interesting and certainly useful to practitioners of Indian law but outside of that, try this Web site out of curiosity rather than for information. Go to the U.S.Code, *Federal Register* or Code of Federal Regulations for that. ❑

Indian Health Service Home Page
An Agency of the Public Health Service
Department of Health and Human Services

[Text Version]

 About the Indian Health Service

 Communications & Publications

 Gateway to CyberSpace

 American Indian Websites

 What's New Apr. 25, 1997

 1996 IHS Trends

Virtual Tour of the IHS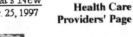

Health Care Providers' Page

Administrators' Reference Page

Job Vacancy Announcements

Customer Information   Publications   Personnel Directories   Information Technology

healthfinder™

is a gateway consumer health information web site from the United States government.

Welcome   Search   DHHS   Award

|| feedback@ihs.gov ||

Institute of Museum and Library Services

http://www.ims.fed.us

Highlights Someone's got to dust the dinosaur bones. The Institute of Museum Services, a miniscule blip on the Federal radar screen, was created in 1996 to help foster cooperation between, well, museums and libraries. The Institute supports these institutions with general operating support, museum assessment, conservation programs to make sure the valuable manuscripts lay-ing in the collections don't turn to dust in another generation and tries to support cooperative ventures between museums and community groups.

The site is most useful for finding out how to apply for a grant from the Institute. There also are links to the U.S. National Commission on Libraries and Information Services.
❑

INSTITUTE OF MUSEUM SERVICES

THE FEDERAL AGENCY THAT STRENGTHENS MUSEUMS TO BENEFIT THE PUBLIC

News from the IMLS Director's Office

The President released the 1998 budget request for the Institute of Museum and Library Services on February 6, 1997.

On October 1, 1996, the Institute of Museum Services became the Institute of Museum and Library Services. A legislative report provides further details.

News from the IMS Program Office

1997 Application and Guidelines Available

1997 General Operating Support application guidelines (132k)
1997 Conservation Project Support application guidelines (561k)
1997 Museum Leadership Initiatives application guidelines(99k)
1997 Professional Services Program application guidelines (111k)
You will need Adobe Acrobat Reader to retrieve the application guidelines from this page. You can download a free copy from Adobe.

1996 Award Announcements

The 1996 awards from the Institute of Museum Services are available on this web site and at the IMS office:

- 1996 Museum Leadership Initiatives awards
- 1996 Professional Services Program awards
- 1996 Conservation Project Support awards
- 1996 General Operating Support awards
- 1996 Conservation Assessment Program awards
- 1996 Museum Assessment Program awards

Internal Revenue Service

http://www.irs.ustreas.gov

Highlights If there is a single government agency that has benefitted most from the advent of the Internet, it is unquestionably the forms-and-instructions heavy offices of the Internal Revenue Service. As one of the few government agencies that touches every single American both personally and professionally and which has created a legal practice area all its own, the IRS has done a great service to the public in building a Web site that is not only packed to the microchips with helpful and in-depth information but also is pleasant (and even amusing) to use.

Get your Adobe Acrobat reader warmed up because the ready access to everything from Form 1040 to electronic filing is mostly in PDF format and it is almost all of it useful.

There's so much material mounted oin this Web site that researchers should use the site tree to locate documents of interest with ease instead of drilling down through dozens of layers of HTML files. This site is a coup for the IRS and an informational boon for legal researchers everywhere. ❑

International Trade Administration

http://www.ita.doc.gov

Highlights Bookmark this heavy reference service for international trade statistics and regional reports on trade. The *Trade Information Center* is a good place to find information on government help with export assistance programs. Use the FAQ file and also refer to *TRADEBASE* directories, announcements of upcoming trade shows and a list of software that will help expedite the export process. *Top Targets for Trade Promotion* give hints on likely markets for U.S. goods.

Trade statistics and reports on market conditions abroad make this the Wall Street analyst report for the Internet citizen. Links here bring forth the *United States Industrial Outlook* and the *Foreign Trade Reference Room* among others. ❑

U.S. Department of Commerce
International Trade Administration

"...dedicated to helping U.S. businesses
compete in the global marketplace..."

Find Info   About ITA   Hot News   Press Room

Information Directory   **Assistance Centers**

Regions and Countries   Trade Information Center

Industries

Cross Cutting Programs   Export Assistance Centers

Trade Statistics   Import Administration

Email

This site is produced and maintained by
the International Trade Administration, U.S. Department of Commerce.

Links to other Internet sites should not be construed as an endorsement of the sites
or the information contained therein.

Maritime Administration

http://marad.dot.gov

Highlights The Merchant Marine keeps shipping operating efficiently and serves double-duty as a back-up to the Navy as an auxiliary sea-going service during time of war.

In its online peacetime incarnation, however, the U.S. Maritime Administration features online tours of its facilities, lists the phone numbers and addresses of its offices and gives its officials a place to write about themselves.

The legal researcher who needs maritime information will find it in the information link that connects to *annual reports* and publications with titles like *By the Capes --A Primer on U.S. Coastwise Laws* and *Maritime Security Program Brochure*.

The news service will never be accused of wordiness: it's fairly slim and contains little more than a few warmed-over press releases and news from the Office of Congressional and Public Affairs. It's not terribly exciting as Web sites go and decidedly light on legal info. ❑

HOME
OFFICES
TOUR
ADMINISTRATOR
NEWS
INFORMATION
GALLERY
LINKS
INDEX

Welcome to the U.S. Maritime Administration

The overall mission of the Maritime Administration is to promote the development and maintenance of an adequate, well-balanced, United States merchant marine, sufficient to carry the Nation's domestic waterborne commerce and a substantial portion of its waterborne foreign commerce, and capable of serving as a naval and military auxiliary in time of war or national emergency.

Contact the Office of Congressional & Public Affairs for general information about the Agency and/or the maritime industry. They can be reached via e-mail at: *pao.marad@marad.dot.gov*

HOME   OFFICES   VIRTUAL TOUR   ADMINISTRATOR   NEWS
INFORMATION   GALLERY   LINKS   INDEX

Merit Systems Protection Board

http://www.fpmi.com/MSPB/ MSPBhomepage.html

Highlights This Web site is operated by a privately-owned business, not the U.S. Government. On the site, find publications from the Board in PDF format addressing such topics as *Fair and Equitable Treatment: A Progress Report on Minority Employment in the Federal Government* and *Removing Poor Performers in the Federal System: An Issue Paper*.

Links to cases decided by the MSPB are searchable and retrievable on the site, using the commercial publisher's search engine. Follow the instructions underlying the clickable icon to *Cases*.

Most of the other information mounted on the site is on the order of directories, mission statements and biographical sketches of the senior officials.

It's a thin site but worthwhile for the case decisions and reports. ❑

- Mission
- Introduction
- Reports
- Chairman
- Vice Chair
- Member

- Regional Offices
- Cases
- Search the MSPB
- Decision Makers
- Information
- Return to FPMI

Mission | Introduction to the MSPB | Reports from the MSPB |
Chairman Erdreich | Vice Chair Slavet | Member Amador |
Regional Offices | Cases from the MSPB | Quick & Easy Search of MSPB Decisions
Decision-Makers at the MSPB | Information and Press Releases from the MSPB

Minority Business Development Agency

http://cher.eda.doc.gov/agencies/mbda/index.html

Highlights Minority-owned businesses get a helping hand from the Minority Business Development Agency but it would be hard to tell from this reed thin Web site. Outside of a quick, five-paragraph writeup of the agency's services and mission and link for additional contacts, there is no other substantive information to be found here. It is one of the smallest Federal Webs; researchers in need of information on minority- and woman-owned businesses would do better to look at the statistics from STAT-USA or browse around one of the many Department of Commerce sub-agencies or the Bureau of Labor Statistics. Bad site. Don't bother. ❑

Welcome to the Minority Business Development Agency

Contents

- Agency Information
- Contact Information

Agency Information

Key responsibilities:

The Minority Business Development Agency (MBDA) is the only Federal agency specifically created to encourage the growth of minority- owned businesses in the United States. MBDA increases opportunities for racial and ethnic minorities to participate in the free enterprise system through the formation and development of competitive minority-owned and managed firms. Established in 1969 by Executive Order 11458, the agency's mission is to:

- Coordinate Federal Government plans, programs, and operations which affect minority business enterprise.
- Promote and coordinate the activities of government and private organizations which help minority businesses grow.
- Collect and disseminate information that will help those interested in establishing or expanding a successful minority-owned firm.
- Fund organizations to provide management and technical assistance to minority entrepreneurs.

Activities and Services:

- Eligibility for MBDA Assistance: The agency provides management and technical assistance, information and advice on starting, managing and expanding a business enterprise to socially or economically disadvantaged individuals including: Hispanic Americans, Asian and Pacific Island Americans, Alaska Natives and Native Americans, African Americans and Hasidic Jews. MBDA also assists public and private sector organizations to increase purchases from minority vendors. MBDA does not provide any grants, loans or loan guarantees to purchase, start. or run a business.
- Business Development Center Program: Minority and Indian Business Development Centers (MBDC and IBDC) increase the number of minority-owned businesses, help existing minority-owned firms to expand, and minimize minority business failures. Centers assist with business and financial planning, management and marketing, bid estimating and construction bonding, loan packaging and other business services. MBDCs and IBDCs are located throughout the country in areas with the largest concentrations of minority populations and the largest number of minority-owned businesses.

National Aeronautics and Space Administration

http://www.nasa.gov

Highlights NASA bagged a homer with the public in July 1997 when it dispatched digital photographs from Mars directly to their Web site, offering a dramatic new application of online technology. The Administration is still heavier on selling science than on connecting the legal researcher to the statutory and regulatory underpinnings of NASA's legal life; the closest this Web site comes to tradi-tional bureaucratic information publication is in the link it offers to *NASA Organization*, an online directory of its far-flung offices and operations.

Enjoy the pictures from outer space and the gee-whiz exhibitions of space science but for more down-to-earth materials like policies and regulations, turn to the paper resources. They're not yet on the Internet. ❏

National Aeronautics and Space Administration

 # The NASA Homepage

- Welcome - This is a good place to begin your journey. Start by reading a letter from NASA Administrator, Dan Goldin, or NASA's Strategic Plan. Check out the User Tips page to find the helper applications you will need to get the most out of what we have to offer. If you're looking for something specific, there's a search engine for the top-level NASA pages.

- Today@NASA - If you've read about NASA recently or seen something on TV, this is place to go for links to more details about breaking news. You can find the most recent Hubble Space Telescope Images, links to the Shuttle Web and the latest news releases. [This site is extremely busy, please be patient.]

- NASA Organization - A list of the offices at NASA Headquarters with links to their Web sites. Below this list, you'll find an extensive subject index of NASA Web sites.

National Agricultural Library

http://www.nalusda.gov

Highlights Look up the legumes in one of the four national libraries, this one a giant server full of maps, images, government documents and other publications.

Browsing for articles and citations is made easier by OPAC access via telnet to ISIS, the Integrated System for Information Services. To get to the *Online Public Catalog and Journal Article Citation* database, telnet to *opac.nal.usda.gov* and

login as ISIS. Links are in attendance here too for the AGRICOLA library, a major catalog of agricultural materials.

This library is so big, stop first at the information desk for *general information* about the NAL's collections, products and services. The library has ten regional centers that can answer many research questions; find a guide on how best to approach those regional sites in the directions reprinted under the link for *Answers to Your Questions.* ❏

Welcome to the

National Agricultural Library

Beltsville Agricultural Research Center Field Day **(June 7, 1997)**

The National Agricultural Library (NAL), part of the Agricultural Research Service **of the** U.S. Department of Agriculture, **is one of four National Libraries in the United States. NAL is a major international source for agriculture and related information. This Web site provides access to NAL's many resources and a gateway to its associated institutions.**

Message from the Director, Pamela Q. J. André

 General Information

A description of NAL's collections, products and services, its mission statement, WWW Policy and Guidelines, visitor information, and staff locator.

National Archives and Records Administration

http://www.nara.gov

Highlights Researchers who enjoy nosing around the musty documents of the past now have a wired playground in which to browse. The caretakers of the government's documentary output are online with links to regional archives, records centers, Presidential libraries and the National Historical Publications and Records Commission.

The best way to work through NARA's holdings is by clicking on the link to the NARA Archival Information Locator (NAIL) which provides an easy means of leafing through the millions of documents held by the agency.

Also turn to NARA's Archives and Library Information Center for an online reference center containing book catalogs and a virtual reference desk as well as links to listservs and discussion groups for archives and library science. ❑

 National Archives and Records Administration

WELCOME!

From the Archivist

NARA's Organization

Building for the Future

Locations and Hours

Washington, DC, Facilities

Regional Archives

Records Centers

Presidential Libraries

Federal Register

NARA Gopher

What's New

Highlights

The Genealogy Page

Welcome to the National Archives and Records Administration (NARA). NARA is the government agency responsible for overseeing the management of the records of the federal government. NARA ensures, for the Citizen and the Public Servant, for the President and the Congress and the Courts, ready access to essential evidence that documents the rights of American citizens, the actions of federal officials, and the national experience.

The Visitor's Gallery

- Online Exhibit Hall: selected NARA exhibitions
- Gift Shop and Bookstore: publications and merchandise relating to NARA and its holdings
- The Digital Classroom: ideas, programs, and publications for the teacher
- Public Programs: conferences, training programs, lectures, films, tours, and other public events

Looking for Information in the National Archives

Genealogy and Individuals

People make history, and the government agencies whose records are preserved in the National Archives of the United States have collected much information on individuals and families. The Genealogy Page provides general information on NARA's resources on individuals, such as **veterans**, as well as guides to the use of NARA holdings. There are only a **very few** genealogical records currently available online .

Historical Records of Government Agencies

NARA makes available to the public the historically valuable records of the three branches of federal government: **executive** (including the President), **legislative**, and **judicial**. National Archives holdings include **textual**; audiovisual; cartographic and architectural; and electronic records.

The Guide to Federal Records in the National Archives of the United States provides general information about holdings for all three branches. You can also search for information about the National Archives in the following databases:

National Credit Union Administration

http://www.ncua.gov

Highlights The National Credit Union Administration supervises and insures more than 7,300 federal credit unions and more than 4,000 state-chartered credit unions. The reference links on the Web site are the best feature of the NCUA Web site; find the text of the enabling statutes, rules and regulations, by-laws and regulatory alerts. Refer to the page for background information on credit unions generally; the agency also provides downloadable software and data files. The download features can retrieve credit union data, call reports or design custom reports. Additional links lead to foreign credit unions, trade organizations, other financial regulators and credit union leagues. Use the sitemap for fast navigation. ❑

NATIONAL CREDIT UNION ADMINISTRATION

Viewing Options

Welcome to NCUA!

About this Web Site

NCUA Lobby (Java)

Frames

Text Only

Site Outline

Feedback

Places to Go

Organization

About Credit Unions

News

Credit Union Data

Reference Information

Other Sites

Download Files and Software

The National Credit Union Administration is an independent federal agency that supervises and insures 7,329 federal credit unions and insures 4,358 state-chartered credit unions. It is entirely funded by credit unions and receives no tax dollars.

NATIONAL CREDIT UNION ADMINISTRATION

Federal Credit Union Act

Federal Credit Union Handbook

Chartering and FOM Manual

Federal Credit Union Bylaws

Federal Credit Union Standard Bylaw Amendments

Rules and Regulations

Accounting Manual

Suspicious Activity Report Forms

Letters to Credit Unions

Regulatory Alerts

Interpretive Rulings and Poli Statements

Legal Opinion Letters

Prohibition Orders

Accounting Bulletins

FFIEC IS Examination Handbook

Financial Performance Repor (FPR) Guide

National Highway Traffic Safety Administration

http://www.nhtsa.dot.gov

Highlights The nation's safety monitors on the interstate provide a Web site that is more for the consumption of consumers than for the dissemination of substantive legal information about the agency. There is, however, a lengthy list of *regulations and standards* for cars and a state legislative fact sheet for easy comparison of state laws. The researcher will also be interested in the databases that the NHTSA puts online containing information about *complaints, investiga-* *tions, non-compliance* and *recalls*. In the same online list is a connection for *technical services* as well as *notices and final rules* promulgated by the Administration.

Other links feature crash test results, analysis of crash avoidance research, injury prevention and a connection to the *National Center for Statistics and Analysis*. This is a good site for legal researchers in need of empirical data on crashworthiness of automobiles. ❑

[General Information] [CARS - Vehicle & Equipment Information]
[PEOPLE - Traffic Safety/Occupant Issues] [What's Hot] [What's New] [Table of Contents]
[Search This Site] [Tools and Utilities]

Information about airbags

NHTSA is responsible for reducing deaths, injuries and economic losses resulting from motor vehicle crashes. This is accomplished by setting and enforcing safety performance standards for motor vehicles and items of motor vehicle equipment, and through grants to state and local governments. The complex relationship between a motor vehicle and its driver is of major interest. Factors influencing this relationship include the driver's physical and mental abilities and driving experience, the nature of driving, the responsiveness of the motor vehicle and its components to the driver's demands, and environmental conditions.

You see in the outline that follows many categories of information. We call your attention especially to the Testing Results for vehicle safety and NCAP crash test results. Safety Problems include databases with data on recalls, technical service bulletins and consumer complaints.

National Institutes of Health

http://www.nih.gov

Highlights For the researcher in need of medical information, health resources, links to clinical research sites or other medical resources should bookmark this site promptly. This is a huge site, made even larger by its generous collection of links to private and quasi-public institutions throughout the world. There is such a wealth of resources that exploring it all would take a day: there are online journals, library and literature resources, news and press releases and links to the other national institutes such as :
 National Cancer Institute

National Eye Institute
National Heart, Lung, and Blood Institute
National Human Genome Research Institute (NHGRI)
National Institute on Aging (NIA)
National Institute on Alcohol Abuse and Alcoholism (NIAAA)
National Institute of Allergy and Infectious Diseases (NIAID)
National Institute of Arthritis and Musculoskeletal and Skin Diseases)

It's a great Web site and first-rate source for online medical research. ❑

National Institutes of Health

Welcome - News - Health - Grants - Science - Institutes - Employees

Can't find it? Try using the NIH Search Engine.
What's New -- The latest information on major additions to the central NIH home page.

Welcome to NIH
An overview and introduction to NIH including an employee directory and maps of the NIH "campus" in Bethesda, Maryland.

News and Events
The NIH Calendar of Events, press releases, special reports, and employment information.

Health Information
A selection of some NIH health resources such as CancerNet, AIDS information, Clinical Alerts, the Women's Health Initiative and the NIH Information Index (a subject-word guide to diseases and conditions under investigation at NIH).

Grants and Contracts
Information on NIH's extramural research and training programs including NIH's funding opportunities (with application kits), grant policy, and award data that includes access to the CRISP database.

Scientific Resources
Intramural (on-site) research news and information including special interest groups, on-line library catalogs and journals, research training information, NIH research labs on the web and computer and network support for NIH scientists.

National Institute of Standards and Technology

http://www.nist.gov

Highlights As a scientific resource, the NIST Web site is both current and thorough, providing the Internet with standard reference materials to help calibrate measurement systems, standard reference data, guidelines for weights and measures (including a fact sheet on metric labeling for consumer products) and standards in trade. This is an authoritative body that produces a wide range of benchmarks for use in industry world-wide. As such, it's an excellent reference resource for the researcher. The institute publishes a bi-monthly *Journal of Research* that can be reviewed online and sponsors a research library, featuring an electronic query system that allows questions to be posted via e-mail to the library staff.

Also use this site to locate offices, link to other scientific Webs and review NIST's programs and services. ❏

Category Descriptions

Text Only Version

General Information	Welcome, intro and fact sheets, plus tours, NIST Boulder homepage, site maps, conference/workshop calendar, NIST in Your House and employment opportunities and other general information
News	Press releases, newsletters, budget updates, congressional testimony, and other newsworthy announcements
Programs	Home Pages for NIST major programs and facilities. ATP, MEP, LABORATORIES, and BALDRIGE
Products & Services	Reference materials and data, calibrations, standards information, and other services
Gallery	Selected images illustrating NIST programs, sites, and research, as well as scientific graphics with captions
Staff Directory	NIST staff listing with phone, fax and E-mail information
Search	Search NIST webspace by keywords, technical activities, or organizational units
FAQs	Frequently asked questions about NIST official time, metric conversions, and more

National Oceanic and Atmospheric Administration

http://www.noaa.gov

Highlights This little-known agency oversees both the National Weather Service and the coastal protection agencies: the National Marine Fisheries Service, the National Ocean Service and the National Environmental Satellite, Data and Information Service. All these agencies and others can be accessed from the NOAA home page.

The programs that NOAA administers are explained in detail on the site but the juiciest information is to be found in the Web sites operated by the sub-agencies. Weather forecasts, satellite images , interactive maps of the coastlines and bulletins to warn about natural and man-made threats to the marine environment make this information quilt a remarkably informative one. The data mounted natively on the NOAA is humdrum; rely instead on the added links to find substantive information. ❏

Select a clickable image representation of this page (140KB).

United States Department of Commerce

National Oceanic and Atmospheric Administration

The NOAA Mission:

- *To describe and predict changes in the Earth's environment, and conserve and manage wisely the Nation's coastal and marine resources to ensure sustainable economic opportunities.*

The NOAA Strategic Plan:

- Executive Summary
- Full Text

The NOAA Diversity Plan:

- Full Text

 NOAA is led by D. James Baker,
Under Secretary of Commerce for Oceans and Atmosphere
and Administrator of NOAA

National Park Service

http://www.nps.gov

Highlights Like many other government Web sites that exist mainly to promote popular services that deal directly with the general public, the Park Service's *ParkNet* is designed primarily as a marketing tool for the keepers of our nation's undeniably majestic park system. The site is light on laws but long on reference materials to guide visitors around the 360+ areas under the stewardship of the National Park Service. Links here will produce pages on which to order an interest-ing array of publications and a park-by-park list of books and other printed materials.

For all the links to educational material, the paucity of legal information is a major drawback to the Park Service's site as is the lack of what might be a spectacularly beautiful catalog of photographs from the parks. Alpenglow in Denali, spring in Yosemite and sunrise in Kitty Hawk should all be here; the Park Service is missing a chance to build good will and we all are the less for it. ❏

Text Version

The National Park Service

ParkNet

FDR Memorial

 Visit Your Parks

 Links to the Past
America's Histories & Cultures

469482

National Railroad Passenger Corporation

http://www.amtrak.com

Highlights The American train system may amuse European visitors but the migration to online scheduling and ticketing bespeaks a willingness to try to move into advanced transportation service. There's not much here directly on point for the legal researcher in the way of regulations, laws or other controlling law, but as a reference and travel service, it's tough to beat. It's of greatest interest to the Northeast Corridor passengers who can use Amtrak efficiently for the Boston-Providence-New Haven-New York- Philadelphia-Washington DC connections.

This is the place to come for promotions and for planning rail travel across the nation. Booking a train trip is a nostalgic exercise even with the utterly modern Web site and database server that cranks out information in the twitch of a mouse. This site is useful as a reference in the travel section of your bookmark file. ❏

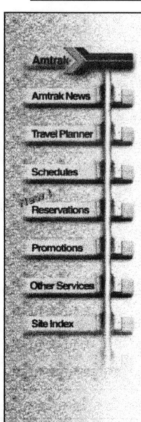

Click HERE For On-Line Reservations, Fares, Ticketing and More !

Experience the Freedom on Today's Amtrak!

Let Amtrak take you to over 500 exciting destinations -- right here on our new Web site.

Plus, try our new on-line reservations and ticketing section, where you can see real-time schedules, make a a reservation, and buy a ticket for the trip of your dreams!

Don't forget to cruise our site to learn about our trains, routes, services, vacation packages and other news. Create your own virtual adventure, then find out how to make your trip a reality!

Amtrak News ‖ Travel Planner ‖ Schedules ‖ Reservations ‖ Promotions ‖ Other Services ‖ Site Index

Questions? Comments? Click Here.

National Science Foundation

http://www.nsf.gov

Highlights As the nominative operators of the Internet, the National Science Foundation and its policies have a significant impact on life online. (The NSF sublets all the Internet operating contracts to private sector vendors; what once were chump-change contracts are soon to be worth a great deal of money in light of the Internet's latter day explosion.)

In addition to its role as "owner" of the Internet, the National Science Foundation's Web site leads to all the best Web sites for Big Science; these links are superb for finding information on any of the cutting edge technological projects funded by the American taxpayer: pick the discipline from the NSF home page to connect with detailed information on biology, computer science, geophysics, mathematics or the social sciences among others.

The NSF site is very large and the external links are considerable. The most useful connection may be the one to *Special Reports*, although the legal researcher may find the regulatory and statutory information to be quite rare. Still, this is a site for reference lookups and connections to scientific information. ❑

Fostering Science
and Engineering
Research and
Education

National Science Foundation

NEWS HIGHLIGHTS

News from the forefront of science & engineering.

PROGRAM AREAS

▷ Biology
▷ Computer, Information Sciences
▷ Crosscutting Programs
▷ Education
▷ Engineering

▷ Geosciences
▷ International
▷ Math, Physical Sciences
▷ Polar Research
▷ Social, Behavioral Sciences

MORE INFORMATION

▷ Special Notices
▷ About the NSF
▷ Grants & Awards
▷ FastLane

▷ National Science Board
▷ Office of the Director

▷ Public Information
▷ Students & Educators
▷ US Science Statistics
▷ Directory & Staff

▷ Visitor Information
▷ External Links

Grants & Awards	Documents Online	Search	Help	Custom News Service

The National Science Foundation
4201 Wilson Boulevard, Arlington, Virginia 22230, USA
Telephone: 703-306-1234 ~ TDD: 703-306-0090

Email: Publications and Program Information,   info@nsf.gov

Comments on Web pages,   webmaster@nsf.gov

Help with FastLane,   fastlane-comments@nsf.gov

National Telecommunications and Information Administration

http://www.ntia.doc.gov

Highlights The NTIA Web site is a must-not-miss resource for the wired researcher and after getting past the goofy graphics, there is a wonderful library of policy statements and National Information Infrastructure reports. Mounted here is information regarding the Internet Domain Names proceeding; the agency is eliciting public comment as the government tries to reduce, if not eliminate, its role as Internet "owner."

Links to the NII provide online access to white papers on privacy issues in the electronic world and the agency's agendas for action and for cooperation.

The *NTIA Facts* page is more of a sales spiel than a reference resource; instead the researcher should use the connection for *NTIA Reports, Filings, and Related Material* where more substantial data can be found. ❏

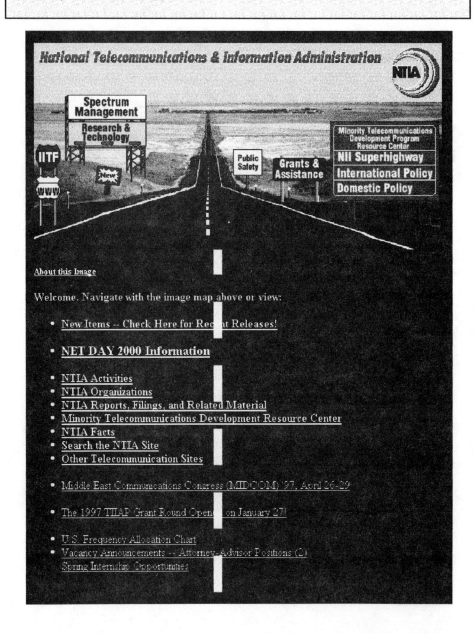

National Transportation Safety Board

http://www.ntsb.gov

Highlights The graphically boring Web site does not reveal the wealth of information waiting for the researcher underneath those yawn-inducing links.

Refer to the links for *Aviation, Highway, Marine, Pipeline/Hazardous Materials* and *Railroad* where many charts and statistical information for the accidents affecting those modes of transportation can be located. For example, the link to aviation leads to *accident synopses, aviation accident statistics* and an online ordering system for obtaining publications.

As of August 1997, the NTSB links were not completely operational but according to "under construction" signs posted on the site, they all should be fully functional soon.

Other information available on the site provides instructions on importing databases from the board and for reviewing accident synopses, arranged by month and year.□

The National Transportation Safety Board welcomes you to its home page.

🔹About the NTSB - History and Mission, Board Members, Organization Chart, Office Locations
🔹Obtaining Information - Sources of NTSB information, Government Information Locator System (GILS) core records
🔹Upcoming Events - Board meetings, Hearings, Symposia, etc. NEW
🔹Speeches and Testimony - by Board Members and Staff
🔹Press Releases
🔹Recommendations - Most Wanted List
🔹Employment Opportunities - Vacancy Announcements - Job Vacancy Hotline: 1-800-573-0937

The NTSB investigates accidents in the following transportation modes.

🔹Aviation - Accidents, Safety Statistics, Publications, Reporting an Accident, CVR and FDR descriptions
🔹Highway - Recent Accidents, Publications
🔹Marine - Recent Accidents, Publications
🔹Pipeline/Hazardous Materials - Recent Accidents, Publications
🔹Railroad - Recent Accidents, Publications

Nuclear Regulatory Commission

http://www.nrc.gov

Highlights Navigating through the complex world of nuclear energy is made simpler on this well-stocked and thoughtfully designed Web site.

Newcomers to the subject can become eleventh-hour scholars by using the handy links to *Nuclear Reactors, Nuclear Materials* and *Radioactive Wastes.* A remarkable amount of material is published on the site, including plant licensing information, information notices and three daily reports from the agency covering the status of plants, current events as reported by plant operators and licensee activities. There are also links to the NRC's *enforcement program* and *geospatial site locations*.

Best feature of the site for the researcher is the link to *Rulemaking* where a description of the rulemaking process resides side-by-side with links to the *Federal Register* and PDF-formatted publications from the commission. ❏

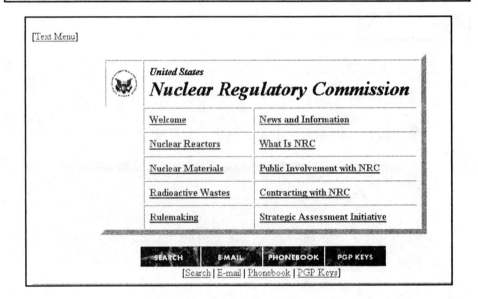

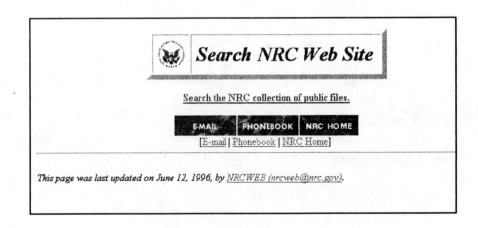

Occupational Safety and Health Administration

http://www.osha.gov

Highlights The most current regulatory information comes to this Web site courtesy of a link to the *Federal Register* but OSHA also is making many of its standards and statistical materials available on the Internet

In addition to the search functions that can look up OSHA information by SIC code, the site also contains a searchable online version of the *Standard Industrial Classification Manual,* which is a useful reference service for all economics-related research and filings made with many regulatory agencies.

Other links on the OSHA site outline the administration's programs and services and reprint the *standards* that employers must follow in the workplace.

There are the standard bureaucratic offerings of office directory and press releases and an interesting, unique link to *Ergonomics,* which provides information for workers who are at risk for developing occupational disabilities from repetitive tasks or from inartfully designed workplace furniture and tools. ❏

- The Assistant Secretary
- Information about OSHA
- **What's New**
- Media Releases
- Publications
- Programs & Services
- Compliance Assistance
- **OSHA Software/Advisors**
- **Office Directory**

- **Ergonomics**
- Federal Register Notices
- Frequently Asked Questions
- Statistics & Data
- Standards
- Other OSHA Documents
- **Technical Information**
- US Government Internet Sites
- Safety & Health Internet Sites

**Download the OSHA Poster
Vanguard & Customer Service**

[Webmaster | OSHA Home Page | OSHA-OCIS | US DOL Web Site | Disclaimer]

Office of the Comptroller of the Currency

http://www.occ.treas.gov

Highlights The Comptrollers' Web site packs a great deal of information into a small space; there are searchable lists of public CRA evaluations and quarterly statistical charts on derivatives. Also see applications online for national bank corporate activities, press releases, and issuances. Among the issuances are *alerts, bulletins* and *advisory letters*, all downloadable in WordPerfect or ASCII format.

The regulators take pains to publish their materials electronically and the researcher can find *significant decisions, applications* and the *Weekly Bulletin* of applications at mouse-length distance on the site.

The links to regulations are equally content-rich and include legal interpretations about the CRA, standards for promulgating regulations and proposals for comment. Additional links contain commonly used forms, economic research and a directory of offices. ❑

 Office of the Comptroller of the Currency

The Office of the Comptroller of the Currency (OCC) is an independent bureau of the Treasury Department. The word currency in the agency's title is a historical anomaly; since the 1930's, the agency has had nothing to do with the issue of U.S. currency. Rather it is the oldest federal financial regulatory body and oversees the nation's federally chartered banks.

Site last updated April 29, 1997

● **What's available** on the OCC website? Search everything on our site by either keyword or concept.

● **What's new** on the OCC Web?

● **What special events** is OCC involved in? - notices of upcoming meetings and conferences and records of past ones.

● **What?** - the national banks, the agency and the industry.

  Statistics and information sources for groups of banks
    ○ Quarterly Derivatives Fact Sheet
  Information available about individual national banks
    ○ Searchable database of public CRA evaluations, list only - no full text.
    ○ List of public CRA evaluations with downloadable full text -- examinations begun after January 1, 1996.
    ○ List of national banks designated wholesale or limited purpose banks under the CRA regulation.
  Help for bank customers
  Electronic money initiatives
  Subject directory
  Other web sites with important information

● **How?** - the work of the agency.

  Mission Statement
  Bank examination
    ○ CRA evaluations coming due
  Community Outreach
    ○ Community and Consumer Organization Database
  Corporate structure
    ○ Availability of applications
    ○ Significant decisions
    ○ Weekly Bulletin of applications -- download or search a Weekly Bulletin or get instructions for fax delivery

Office of Thrift Supervision

http://www.access.gpo.gov ots/index.html

Highlights This terrific, second-generation Web site (it's a complete re-design of the initial site) is a state-of-the-art information delivery system that provides, under the links to *Laws, regs & policies* a virtually complete library of final rules and interim rules, guidance notes, proposed regulations, legal opinions, materials on electronic banking, memoranda and links to search the *Federal Register*.

Click on *Industry and Institution Data* for a page containing a *Fact Book* on the thrift industry, *cost of funds* charts and the *FDIC Institution Directory*.

Other links offer a directory of OTS offices nationwide, news (press releases, speeches and testimony) and a local search engine to browse the OTS site.

Related sites includes links to the FDIC, FFIEC, FHLB and the Federal Reserve Board. This is a model Web site. ❑

Office of Thrift Supervision
www.ots.treas.gov

Welcome to the Office of Thrift Supervision's *New* World Wide Web Site.

home

about OTS

news

key OTS contacts

industry & institution data

public information

laws, regs & policies

related sites

browse the OTS site

e-mail

what's new

Updated:
July 30, 1997

The OTS is the primary regulator of all federal and many state-chartered thrift institutions. The OTS was established as a bureau of the Department of the Treasury on August 9, 1989. The OTS has five regional offices located in Jersey City, Atlanta, Chicago, Dallas, and San Francisco. Its expenses are funded entirely through assessments and fees levied on the institutions it regulates.

This Web site provides access to information on the agency's programs and activities. We hope you find the material informative and helpful. If you have any questions or comments about this web site, please contact the OTS Webmaster at web.master@ots.treas.gov. Please be sure to include your telephone number so we may respond.

Office of Thrift Supervision
1700 G. Street, NW
Washington, DC 20552

The following information is best viewed with Netscape Navigator (2.0 or later) or Internet Explorer.

Notice & Disclaimer

[home] [about OTS] [news] [key OTS contacts] [industry & institution data] [public information]
[laws, regs & policies] [related sites] [browse the OTS site] [what's new]

Pension Benefit Guaranty Corporation

http://www.pbgc.gov

Highlights The ERISA researcher will find this Web site to be useful for such reference applications as monthly interest rate updates, final regulations from the PBGC (including the renumbered regs) and proposed regulations. The link to *Notices* provides current releases from the agency on a variety of timely subjects such as disaster relief and penalties for failure to provide information.

Also online here is a *Pension Search Directory* that's designed to connect deserving pensioners with closed pension plans from more than 600 companies. Family law researchers can find a pamphlet online describing general information on qualified domestic relations orders. Rounding out the online offerings are *press releases, technical updates* and *opinion letters.* ❑

[VIEW TEXT ONLY]

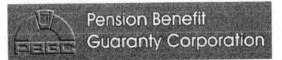

Pension Benefit Guaranty Corporation

UPDATED Pension Search Directory	Your Guaranteed Pension	Divorce Orders & PBGC

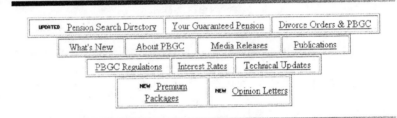

What's New   About PBGC   Media Releases   Publications

PBGC Regulations   Interest Rates   Technical Updates

NEW Premium Packages   NEW Opinion Letters

Information About the Executive Director

Information About PBGC

    Mission statement, programs, benefits, premiums and organization.

Your Guaranteed Pension

    Frequently asked questions about PBGC guaranteed benefits.

Premiums

    Fact Sheet, 1997 Premium Packages

Publications

    Annual Report, Divorce Orders & PBGC, Fact Sheets, Speeches and Testimony

Technical Information about PBGC's Programs and Activities

    PBGC Regulations, Interest Rates, Technical Updates, Opinion Letters

---DISCLAIMER---

PBGC periodically updates this home page with publicly available PBGC information. PBGC's official positions, however, are as stated in the *Federal Register* and other formal publications.

Securities and Exchange Commission

http://www.sec.gov

Highlights The SEC operates one of the most popular government sites on the Internet, thanks mostly to the remarkable EDGAR database of corporate information. This invaluable repository of documents, containing up-to-the-minute filings made by companies regulated under the Securities Act of 1933 and the Securities Exchange Act of 1934 represents an archive worth tens of millions of dollars in private hands; on the Internet, the documents are searchable and downloadable for free for anyone with access to the site. Filings begin in 1993 and are current to the day.

The SEC is one of the best agencies for obtaining rulemakings and the link to current rulemakings provides proposed and adopted rules changes. There are also Commission studies and special reports analyzing the financial markets available on the Web site.

Clicking on the link for *SEC Digest and News* turns up links to press releases and daily summaries of the *News Digest* as well.

From the Enforcement Division come *Litigation Releases, Initial Decisions* issued by administrative law judges and Commission opinions on appeal from the initial decisions. Basically, the only thing missing from this Web site are the No-Action letters.

This is one of the best government sites on the Internet. Use it often. ❑

About the SEC

Investor Assistance & Complaints

EDGAR Database

SEC Digest & Statements

Current SEC Rulemaking

Enforcement Division

Small Business Information

Other Sites to Visit

Text only | Search non-EDGAR documents | Search EDGAR Archives

U.S. SECURITIES AND EXCHANGE COMMISSION

"We are the investor's advocate."
William O. Douglas
SEC Chairman, 1937-1939

Current News:

EDGAR System Open on March 29, 1997 for Filing Only

Chairman Levitt To Speak At Connecticut Investors' Town Meeting

SEC Prepares for Internet EDGAR Database Restructuring

Shareholders Proposal Process Input Due April 7

Social Security Administration

http://www.ssa.gov

Highlights The laws and regulations governing the Social Security Administration are no further away than a link on the Administration's home page. There the researcher will find the text of the Social Security Act, rulings from 1960, legislation, Congressional testimony and a link to the Code of Federal Regulations.

There are links to information about the Administration's fax service for delivering some 175 documents and publications describing benefits. The link to *Facts and Figures* is where the SSA e-

publishes its actuarial data, research and statistical data and *Operational Finances* which tracks the agency's solvency.

Online forms in PDF format include *request for hearing by an administrative law judge, request for earnings and benefit estimate statement* and *Authorization for Source to Release Information to the Social Security Administration.*

A handy link will pull up a FAQ file titled *The Top 10 Most Requested Services from Social Security Online.* ❏

The Official Web Site of the Social Security Administration

Saturday, 29-Mar-97 20:26:44 EST

Did you know Social Security and Supplemental Security Income keep 1.4 million children out of poverty?

Try your:

PEBES available M-F: 8AM - 9PM & Sat: 9AM - 4PM EST

▶ what's new
▶ FAQs
▶ feed back
▶ search the site
▶ site map

About Social Security's benefits --
Publications and other benefit information
Medicare information
Facts and figures
Forms
Our agency and its history
Online transaction services
En Español

International
Financial status of our programs
Services for employers and businesses
Laws and regulations
Freedom of Information
Other sites of interest
Public information resources
How to reach Social Security
How to report fraud to Social Security

what's new | frequently asked questions (FAQs) | feedback | search the site | site map

Stat-USA

http://www.stat-usa.gov/
stat-usa.html

Highlights This by-subscription Web site deserves a spot in the bookmark file of every legal researcher as the leading one-stop shop for thousands of statistical items covering every aspect of the economy. This treasure trove of data contains *Daily Economic News* and statistical releases on such popular economic gauges as:

Gross Domestic Product
Personal Income and Outlays
Foreign Exchange Rates
Consumer Price Index
Producer Price Index
Employment Statistics

The *National Trade Data Bank* offers market research reports, the *Export Yellow Pages* and a list by commodity of U.S. imports and exports.

Even though Stat-USA is produced by the Department of Commerce, it does not rely on taxpayer support which is why a subscription fee is charged. The modest charge is worth it since this site is both very current and remarkably thorough. ❑

Customize This Page | View Your Customized Page
Mostly Text Version

Select From the Most Popular Pages   Go

Home

Index

Order Form

What's New

Other Products

Test Drive

Comments

Help

STAT-USA/Internet

- What's New!
- How to Subscribe

- Daily Economic News
- Frequently Requested Statistical Releases
- **Information By Subject**
    o Export & International Trade
    o Domestic Economic News & Statistical Series
    o Business Leads & Procurement Opportunities
- STAT-USA Databases
- Selected Publications of Interest

- the Newsletter

A Service of the U.S. Department of Commerce

Last Modified: March 26, 1997 | stat-usa@doc.gov | U.S. Department of Commerce

United States Geological Survey

http://www.usgs.gov

Highlights It's the reference materials available on this Web site that make it important, especially the more than 700,000 aerial photographs that the U.S. Geological Survey provides to the Internet. (Special viewer software is needed to view the photos but the software can be downloaded on the spot.)

Other online services of note are the *Geographic Names Information System* that gives Internet researchers access to more than 2 million places names and geographic features; each record contains the Federally recognized name, feature, elevation and population as well as the state and county where the feature is located and the longitude and latitude; the other is the *Global Land Information System* containing data about hydrology, soils, land use, climate and other cartographic information.

Also refer to the *National Geologic Map Database* to search for maps of interest to geochemists, geologists and the like. ❑

Biology	Geology	Mapping	Water

About USGS
Contacts
Ordering Products
Publications and Data
Fact Sheets
The Learning Web
Internet Resources
Search

List of Featured Pages

Ground Water Atlas of the United States - provides detailed data and information on the Nation's important aquifers

List of What's New

"Expanding Sediment Research Capabilities in Today's USGS" - Proceedings of the USGS Sediment Workshop -- Multi-Agency Participation with Papers online!

List of News Releases

USGS Work on Mars and Other Planets

Hazards	Natural Resources	Environment	Information Management	Department of the Interior

U.S. Geological Survey, 804 National Center, Reston, VA 20192, USA
URL http://www.usgs.gov/
 Comments and feedback: USGS Web Team
Last modification: 07-18-97@16:05 (stm)

United States International Trade Commission

http://www.usitc.gov

Highlights The International Trade Commission is a watchdog agency that judges the impact of imports on U.S. industries and also monitors unfair trade practices abroad. To accomplish that, the agency publishes the petitions and complaints it has received from industry groups, its news releases and reprints online its notices which appear in the *Federal Register*.

The link to *Reports and Publications* contains such titles as the *International Economic Review*, factfinding reports, *Industry, Trade and Technology Review* and a series of downloadable reports such as the commission's annual report, statutory provisions related to import relief and *An Introduction to Administrative Protective Order Practice in Antidumping and Countervailing Duty Investigations (2nd edition)*. ❑

Welcome to the United States International Trade Commission

The USITC is an independent, quasi-judicial federal agency that provides objective trade expertise to both the legislative and executive branches of government, determines the impact of imports on U.S. industries, and directs actions against certain unfair trade practices, such as patent, trademark, and copyright infringement. USITC analysts and economists investigate and publish reports on U.S. industries and the global trends that affect them. The agency also updates and publishes the Harmonized Tariff Schedule of the United States.

The information on this server is updated frequently and new sections may be added periodically. While we can't promise to respond, we welcome your comments and suggestions for making this server more useful to you.

- What's new
- EDIS cover sheet and recent petitions and complaints
- Monthly calendar of hearings, deadline dates, and status of investigations
- News releases
- Federal Register notices
- Reports and publications
- Tariff affairs and related matters (includes U.S. Harmonized Tariff Schedule)
- About the USITC and its Commissioners (includes contacts and vacancy announcements)
- Bibliography of trade-related law journal articles
- Trade Resources (trade-related sites)

United States Patent and Trademark Office

http://www.uspto.gov

Highlights One of the best Web servers in the Federal government; the Patent and Trademark Office is one of the largest sites in the government. Use the sitemap to become familiar with the wide range of services available from the site.

Chief among the information services are the *USPTO Patent Databases* that allow free searching of front page information, dating from 1976 to present. There's also an *AIDS Patent* database; both databases can be searched using patent numbers or Boolean searches. Also online is the *U.S. Manual of Classification* and a browseable index of *U.S. Patent Classes.*

In addition to the one-of-a-kind patent search features, many links to regional patent sources such as depository libraries can be found on the site. As for copyrights, a link will connect to the appropriate office at the Library of Congress. This is a great site. ❑

UNITED STATES PATENT AND TRADEMARK OFFICE

- What's New

- About Patents and Trademarks

- US and International Legal Materials

- Information by Topic

- Information by Organizational Structure

- Acquisitions

| SITE INDEX | SEARCH PATENTS | SEARCH AIDS PATS | SITE MAP |
| PTO FEES | DOWNLOAD FORMS | ORDER COPIES | ORG. MAP |

- PTO Museum, current exhibit: *The World of Toys*
- Related Web Sites
- Document Formats and Viewers
- Trademark Registration of Internet Domain Names
- US Copyright Office
- Server Statistics
- *Resources for PTO personnel only*

The PTO is not yet equipped to handle general email inquiries. For general inquiries, call 1.800.786.9199 or 1.703.308.4357 (1.703.308.HELP), or fax to 1.703.305.7786.

Email concerning server content and operation only to www@pioneer.uspto.gov

Last Modified: 5 March 1997

United States Postal Service

http://www.usps.gov

Highlights In the soon-to-be digital world, the U.S. Post Office is facing the unenviable task of re-inventing itself to change with the times. But until the day that utility bills and love letters all arrive by e-mail, the snail mailers are providing some handy services online already.

The best bet here is the *Zip Code directory* that permits looking up Zip+4 numbers for addresses throughout the nation. An additional lookup feature allows association of cities and zip codes. Taking a clue from Federal Express and UPS, the Post Office now provides online tracking of Express Mail packages.

The link to *Change of Address* is not merely a form to tell the letter carrier about a move: there's a well-detailed list of other move-related information that is actually very helpful. The guide helps with packing, changing tax forms, suggests how to move kids and pets and supplies other practical tips. Snail mail will never catch up with e-mail, but the other services make this site a worthwhile one.

❏

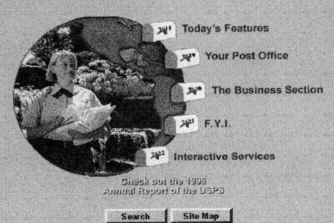

The 1996 Annual Report, titled "On the Move," cites the year's record-breaking financial and best-ever service performance of the Postal Service and uses a competitive theme to illustrate the challenges of a growing marketplace.

STAMPSONLINE

Featuring the latest stamps and stamp collectibles from the U. S. Postal Service. In this site, you will find information on the latest stamps and stamp collectibles.

● Today's Features
    See what's new and exciting at the Postal Service, including the latest information on our Mail Classification Reform case, and new stamp releases

● Your Post Office
    Look up ZIP+4 codes and get addressing tips, get information on stamps, the latest postal rates and products, and check out other useful consumer information. Track your Express Mail.

● The Business Section
    Look here for information to help meet your business mailing needs, business forms and your nearest Postal Business Center. Review our Postal business publications, including Memo to Mailers, for many helpful mailing tips. If you sell goods or services to the Postal Service, look here for the latest procurement information. Track your Express Mail!

United States House of Representatives

http://www.house.gov

Highlights Compared to the paucity of information on the Senate server, the House Web site is the library at Alexandria. The government links to all branches of the Federal government are superb. So are the links to the Representatives. The House reports on its activities with a connection to *This Week on the House Floor* and explains the legislative process to the squeamish.

But like the Senate server, the real legislative goods are to be found at the other end of a mouse click. Refer either to the Thomas server at the Library of Congress -- a link to it is prominently displayed on the home page -- or connect to the *Internet Law Library*, one of the standard law-related index pages. It is a terrific resource that every legal researcher should bookmark and use regularly.

Refer to *House Office Web Sites* for electronic links to legislators and their staff. ❑

[text version]

U.S. House of Representatives
105th Congress, 1st session

What's New
Tour The Capitol
Visitor Information

Organization and Operations

The Legislative Process

Member Pages

Committee Pages

Leadership Pages

Commissions Pages

Other House Organization Pages

House Directory

Annual Schedule

Legislative Branch
Executive Branch
Judicial Branch

Educational Resources

Empowering the Citizen

Comments about our site? Please use this form or send e-mail

This Week on the House Floor

The schedule of bills, resolutions, and other legislative issues the House intends to consider this week. Updated each business day when the House is in session.

Currently on the House Floor

Up-to-date events on the House floor as they happen.

In the spirit of THOMAS Jefferson, the Library of Congress provides you with information about the U.S. Congress legislative process, bills, the Congressional Record, committee information, and historical documents.

Today in Committee

Information on committee meetings are updated hourly. Both open and closed meetings are listed. The public can attend any open committee meeting listed. Some hearings are televised by C-SPAN.

Write Your Representative

Constituents may identify and/or contact their elected Member to the U.S. House of Representatives.

U.S. House of Representatives Internet Law Library

Free public access to the basic documents of U.S. law. Full text searchable copies of the U.S. Code and the Code of Federal Regulations. Over 8,900 links to law resources on the Internet.

United States Senate

http://www.senate.gov

Highlights The Senate site is remarkably simple and takes only a few minutes to explore the entire site online. Start with the link to *legislative activities* where links lead to connections for *committee hearings, pending business* as well as to *treaties, measures, nominations* and an executive and legislative *calendar*.

The Web site is a good place to find information about Senators. From the home page, click on the link to pull up directories of Senators by name or by state and to locate their e-mail addresses. Useful reference sources are the lists of committees and sub-committees, where the real work gets done. The heavy legislative lifting is actually done off the Senate's own Web site. The links to be found as *other resources* lead to other Web servers such as Thomas and the Internet Law Library at the House of Representatives where the most valuable Senate documents are mounted.

As an information service, there is surprisingly little of great interest to the researcher. It all lies elsewhere. Refer to this site only for reference look-ups; otherwise stick to the Library of Congress' Thomas server at *http://thomas.loc.gov* ❏

Legislative Activities | Committees | Senators | Learning About the Senate
Other Resources | What's New | Search | Comments

Last modified on: April 1, 1997

General Accounting Office

http://www.gao.gov

Highlights With all that money flying around Washington, some it sometimes get waylaid in places legislators never intended. Investigating fraud is the job of GAO and indeed, there's even a GAO-sponsored Internet service named *FraudNET* to encourage online reporting of allegations of fraud, waste, abuse or mismanagement of government funds.

The GAO site is where the researcher can find *Comptroller General Decisions and Orders* and reprints of *GAO Policy* *and Guidance Manuals*. Get on the list of GAO reports and testimony published in the agency's *Daybook* by subscribing to the mailing list. (There's also a mailing list to receive Comptroller General decisions.)

The Web site permits researchers to look over special publications and software such as *The Investigator's Guide to Sources of Information* and *Principles of Federal Appropriations Law*. It's a fair site. ❑

GAO   United States
General Accounting Office

Welcome to GAO's Home Page.

The General Accounting Office is the investigative arm of Congress. Charged with examining matters relating to the receipt and disbursement of public funds, GAO performs audits and evaluations of Government programs and activities.

- GAO Reports and Testimony
- Comptroller General Decisions and Opinions
- Reports on Federal Agency Major Rules
- GAO Policy and Guidance Materials
    ○ Assessing Risks and Returns: A Guide for Evaluating Federal Agencies' IT Investment Decision-making
      GAO/AIMD-10.1.13. February 1997.
      (Available in both HTML and PDF versions) New!
- Special Publications and Software
    ○ Year 2000 Computing Crisis: An Assessment Guide (Exposure Draft). GAO/AIMD-10.1.14
      [Available in PDF format] New!
- GAO FraudNET
  Report allegations of fraud, waste, abuse or mismanagement of federal funds
- About GAO

Job Vacancies at GAO

Order Printed Copies of GAO Reports

- By Web Order Form
- By Email

Mailing Lists

- **Daybook** (lists newly released and newly available GAO reports and testimony.)
  Subscribe
  Unsubscribe

- **Decisions** (lists newly released Comptroller General Decisions)
  Subscribe
  Unsubscribe

Frequently Asked Questions

- GAO FAQ
- About PDF (Portable Document Format) Files

Comments and Suggestions

Library of Congress

http://www.loc.gov

Highlights The Library of Congress Web site is simply marvelous. The catalogs are the standards by which almost all other libraries operate, the research services are first-rate and the Webmasters usually have an interesting exhibit on display online at any given time. Pull down the scroll bar to get a bead on what's here for the asking: *country studies, Latin America studies, Global Legal Information Network, copyright records* and links to libraries nigh and far make this one of the richest resources on the Internet, perhaps in the entire wired world.

Certainly every librarian should be professionally familiar with the Library of Congress and its Web site -- even the casual researcher will benefit from repeat visits.

Special programs include information for publishers and standards for bibliographic records and electronic cataloging. Bookmark immediately! ❏

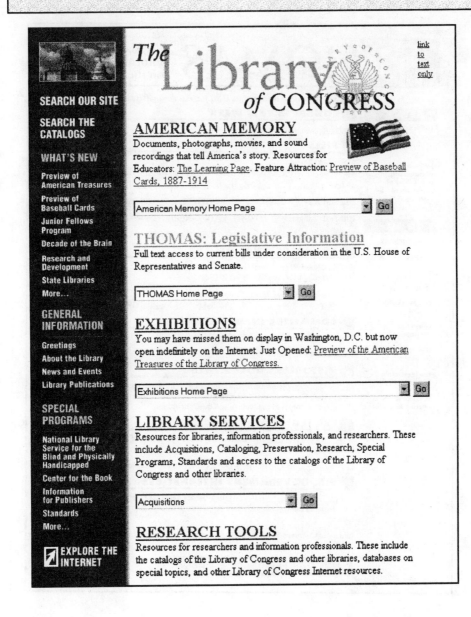

Thomas

http://thomas.loc.gov

Highlights Roll up your sleeves and prepare to dive into the densest legal repository on the Internet. There is no other Web site that provides so much information so quickly in such an easy-to-use package as the legislative server from the Library of Congress known as Thomas. Named for Thomas Jefferson, this experiment in e-democracy brings lawmaking out of the hallways of Washington and into the microchips of every wired individual on the Internet. Bills, legislative histories, *Congressional Record* references, links to bill sponsors and now even reports and accompanying documents stretching back to 1973 are the stock in trade here.

At the risk of hyperbole, this is the best single law-related Web server on the Internet. It is a gloriously successful practical application of the idea that the Internet can transfer intellectual power from a concentrated handful to the great number of literate people.

Thomas, quite simply, is great. ❏

In the spirit of Thomas Jefferson, a service of the U.S. Congress through its Library.

▼ NEW

105th Congress:
House Members
Senate Members

Interested in participating in a survey **of Government web sites?**

▼ GO TO

About THOMAS

Congress This Week

Bills

Laws

Congressional Record

Committee Information

Historical Documents

The Legislative Process

U.S. Government Internet Resources

CONGRESS THIS WEEK

Floor Activities - House and Senate

BILLS

Major Legislation:
105th: By topic - By popular/short title - By bill number/type - Enacted into law
104th: By topic - By popular/short title - By bill number/type - Enacted into law

Bill Summary & Status: Congress: 105 (1997-98) - 104 (1995-96)

Bill Text: Congress: 105 (1997-98) - 104 (1995-96) - 103 (1993-94)

Public Laws By Law Number: 105 (1997-98) - 104 (1995-96)

CONGRESSIONAL RECORD

Congressional Record **Text:** Congress:
105 (1997-98) - 104 (1995-96) - 103 (1993-94)

Congressional Record Index: Congress and Session:
105 - 1st (1997) - 104 - 2nd (1996) - 104 - 1st (1995) - 103 - 2nd (1994)

COMMITTEE INFORMATION

Committee Reports: Congress: 105 (1997-98) - 104 (1995-96)

Committee Home Pages: House - Senate

HISTORICAL DOCUMENTS

Historical documents including the Declaration of Independence, the Federalist Papers, early Congressional documents (Constitutional Convention and Continental Congress broadsides), and the Constitution.

THE LEGISLATIVE PROCESS

How Our Laws Are Made (Revised and updated by Charles W. Johnson, House Parliamentarian)

Enactment of a Law (By Robert B. Dove, Senate Parliamentarian)

U.S. GOVERNMENT INTERNET RESOURCES

Congressional Internet Services (House, Senate, Library of Congress, Government Printing Office, General Accounting Office, Congressional Budget Office)

Library of Congress Web Links: Legislative - Executive - Judicial - State/Local

HOME   FEEDBACK   ABOUT

Federal Court Locator

http://www.law.vill.edu/
Fed-Ct/fedcourt.html

Highlights For judicial research, there is no better starting point than the Federal Court Locator from the Villanova Center for Information Law and Policy. Like its other index pages for legal materials throughout the Internet, the connections here are concise, accurate and kept up-to-date. Navigating the thirteen circuits is made simply by online text links or by clicking on a clickable map of the United States outlining all the jurisdictions.

The link to *Search Cases* gives a circuit-by-circuit list of connections to find cases published in any of the Federal jurisdictions.

Another link, to the FLITE database of Supreme Court cases, provides the researcher with full text search capabilities across official Supreme Court cases from volume 300-422 of the *U.S. Reports*. Opinions can be downloaded in HTML, WordPerfect 5.1 or ASCII format.

Other links lead to the Supreme Court and the Hermes archive at Cornell University's Legal Information Institute where electronically disseminated opinions from the High Court dating from 1991 can be found. ❑

The Federal Court Locator

The Villanova Center for Information Law and Policy

Search Cases S.Ct. FLITE Database Map Jumps Table of Contents

"The Home Page for the Federal Courts on the Internet"™

The Federal Court Locator is a service provided by the Villanova Center for Information Law and Policy. It is intended to give net citizens a means to access information related to the federal judiciary, including slip opinions. This information can be viewed on-line or it can be downloaded.

If you learn of a federal court site on the Internet, please mail us so that we can add a link to it and continue to improve the access to federal judicial information. Also, please visit our page dedicated to *Friends of VCILP*, who have helped keep this the most up-to-date Web page concerning the federal courts.

©1994-1997 Villanova Center for Information Law and Policy

Last Updated: 18 July 1997	
Number of Accesses to Date	669606

CLICK ON THE MAP TO RETRIEVE THE COURT HOME PAGE

Federal Judiciary

http://www.uscourts.gov

Highlights Produced by the Administrative Office of the U.S. Courts, this pleasant Web site is supplied with a variety of reports and statistical information concerning the Federal courts system. Of greatest interest are the documents referring to plans to get the Federal courts wired so that electronic document interchange (EDI) can be implemented. Chief among these is a discussion draft titled *Electronic Case Files in the Federal Courts: A Preliminary Examination of Goals, Issues, and the Road Ahead.*

The administrators also use the Web site to disseminate proposals for public comment. A series of reports are published on the site including the *Directory of Electronic Public Access Services, Optimal Utilization of Judicial Resources, The Long Range Plan for Federal Courts* and an ABA proposal for a standard citation system for the courts.

Other resources on the site are press releases and *Third Branch*, the monthly newsletter of the Federal courts. ❑

WHAT'S NEW | THE THIRD BRANCH | UNDERSTANDING THE FEDERAL COURTS | PUBLIC ACCESS DIRECTORY | FOR PUBLIC REVIEW | PRESS RELEASES

"The judicial Power of the United States, shall be vested in one supreme Court, and in such inferior Courts as the Congress may from time to time ordain and establish."

- Article III, U.S. Constitution

Welcome to the U.S. Federal Courts' Home Page. **This page is maintained by the Administrative Office of the U.S. Courts on behalf of the U.S. Courts.**

The purpose of this site is to function as a clearinghouse for information from and about the Judicial Branch of the U.S. Government.

New:

The final report to Congress by the Judicial Conference of the United States on the Civil Justice Reform Act of 1990 was added 30 June, 1997. These documents are in PDF format.

United States Sentencing Commission

http://www.ussc.gov

Highlights The Sentencing Commission stocks this Web site with a great deal of information of use to the legal researcher. Start with the link to *general information* to become acquainted with the site. The substantive materials begin by clicking on the fat radio button for *Guidelines, Manuals and Amendments.* This is where announcements of new rules and amendments to existing rules are reprinted from the *Federal Register* and where the complete text of the *Guidelines Manual* can be located and downloaded. Under the link for *Publications,* find the *Sourcebook of Federal Sentencing Statistics,* the commission's *Annual Report to Congress* and reports from the staff working groups on money laundering and food and drugs.

Use this site as well to locate Federal sentencing statistics by state and to connect to state sentencing commissions. ❏

UNITED STATES SENTENCING COMMISSION

U.S. Supreme Court

http://supct.law.cornell.edu/ supct

Highlights Project Hermes was the pioneering effort of the Supreme Court and Cornell University to disseminate Supreme Court opinions electronically. Seven years later, the project is a resounding success; cases from the current term can be retrieved by date. The site also provides the oral argument calendar and the current calendar for the current term. Older decisions, dating from 1990 to present, are fully searchable and retrievable by the name of the party. On the page are links to other repositories of Supreme Court decisions prior to 1990, primarily archives held at Villanova (1937 to 1975) and FindLaw (1937 to present) and the USSC+ service which has about 450 much older cases reaching back to 1793. There's also a link to Northwestern University's collection of oral arguments.

This site is a basic tool for every researcher and belongs in the bookmark file. ❑

current | historic | court | search

The LII and Hermes: overview and recent developments

The Legal Information Institute offers Supreme Court opinions under the auspices of Project Hermes, the court's electronic-dissemination project. This archive contains (or will soon contain) all opinions of the court issued since May of 1990. In addition, our collection of over 300 of the most important historical decisions of the Court is available on CD-ROM and (with reduced functionality) over the Net.

During our first four years of operation, the LII simply built finding aids -- such as tables of party names and searching tools -- which in turn pointed to the Hermes archive at Case Western Reserve University. We have now acquired our own Hermes subscription and begun streamed conversion of the decisions into HTML at the time of release. We have also converted the entire CWRU backlist to HTML, and have begun working to fill some long-standing gaps in the Hermes collection.

As the foregoing implies, there are still some omissions and errata in this collection, and a high likelihood that in the process of conversion we've missed a few links here and there. If you run into a problem which is not mentioned in our list of errata and items under construction, do let us know.

Decisions in the LII collection (from May 1990)

First Circuit

http://www.law.emory.edu/ 1circuit

Highlights Emory University is the default host for all Circuit Courts who have not found another academic sponsor. Emory provides very simple Web pages to publish decisions to the Web. There are no earth-shaking enhancements: the pages are utilitarian in design and function. They provide a means of getting to published decisions quickly with a minimum of fuss.

The First Circuit delivers its opinions online dating from 1995 to present; cases can be found by date, party name or by using the keyword search function. Emory is to be applauded for its efforts, but the time is ripe for the circuits themselves to operate their own Web sites where current and historic decisions can be found along with local rules, judicial biographies, directory information and electronic filing of documents. Until then, the servers at Emory are still the best bet for First Circuit information. The First Circuit covers Maine, Massachusetts, New Hampshire, Puerto Rico and Rhode Island. ❑

Credits and Conditions

U.S. Court of Appeals, First Circuit

Geographic jurisdiction: Maine, Massachusetts, New Hampshire, Puerto Rico, Rhode Island

---

The opinions of the First Circuit since November 1995 are brought to you by the Hugh F. Macmillan Law Library, Emory University School of Law, in cooperation with the United States Court of Appeals for the First Circuit. All cases are in full text on the Web, or can be downloaded in RTF format. The files to download are located at the end of each case.

Listing by Month of Decision

1995 Decisions

1996 Decisions

1997 Decisions

Second Circuit

**http://www.law.pace.edu/lawlib/legal/
us-legal/judiciary/second-circuit.html**

Highlights Thanks to a cooperative effort between the Pace University School of Law and Touro Law Center, decisions and orders of the Second Circuit are reported online, along with *summary orders*. A sophisticated search that can find cases by *title, citation, docket number, date, plaintiff, defendant, judge* or by *full text* makes it easy to locate cases. Decisions online are available from September 1995 to present. Summary orders may be searched using free text alone.

The Second Circuit serves Connecticut, New York and Vermont. ❑

U.S. Court of Appeals for the Second Circuit Decisions

Credits and Conditions

These decisions are presented by a joint project of Pace University School of Law and Touro Law Center with the cooperation of the Second Circuit. If anyone would also like to obtain these cases for presentation on the Net please contact the webkeepers mailto:dwilliam@lawlib.law.pace.edu

Search other court cases:

U.S. Supreme Court Federal Circuit Court First Circuit Third Circuit Fourth Circuit Fifth Circuit Sixth Circuit Seventh Circuit Eighth Circuit Ninth Circuit Tenth Circuit Eleventh Circuit

Search Second Circuit Reported Cases

Search Second Circuit Summary Orders

Cases last updated: July 17, 1997.

Third Circuit

http://www.law.vill.edu/
Fed-Ct/ca03.html

Highlights Third Circuit decisions make their way to the Internet courtesy of the Villanova Center for Information Law and Policy. Decisions from 1994 to present can be downloaded from the Web site in HTML, Word 2.0, WordPerfect 5.1 or ASCII format. Look for cases by date or by using the keyword search tool.

The Third Circuit comprises Delaware, New Jersey and Pennsylvania. ❑

Credits and Conditions

United States Court of Appeals
for the
Third Circuit

Accessed Through Hypertext Documents Prepared by
The Villanova Center for Information Law and Policy

The opinions issued by the United States Court of Appeals for the Third Circuit since May 1994 have been acquired from the Third Circuit by the Villanova Center for Information Law and Policy, associated with the Villanova University School of Law. The text of these opinions has been enhanced by the Center with formatting codes and other information so that they can be viewed in HTML format and downloaded in Microsoft Word version 2.0 format, WordPerfect version 5.1 format, and ASCII format. In addition, the formatted opinions can be faxed anywhere in the 202, 215, 302, 609, and 610 area codes.

Listing by Month of Decision

➡ 1994 Decisions

➡ 1995 Decisions

➡ 1996 Decisions

➡ 1997 Decisions
- January
- February
- March
- April
- May

Fourth Circuit

http://www.law.emory.edu/ 4circuit

Highlights Retrieve cases in HTML or RTF (rich text format) from the Emory server for the Fourth Circuit dating from 1995 to present. Cases are located by date, party name or keyword.

The states covered by the Fourth Circuit are Maryland, North Carolina, South Carolina, Virginia and West Virginia. ❑

Credits and Conditions

U.S. Court of Appeals for the Fourth Circuit

U.S. Court of Appeals, Fourth Circuit

Geographic jurisdiction: Maryland, North Carolina, South Carolina, Virginia, and West Virginia

The opinions of the Fourth Circuit since January 1995 are brought to you by the Hugh F. Macmillan Law Library, Emory University School of Law, in cooperation with the United States Court of Appeals for the Fourth Circuit. All cases are in full text on the Web, or can be downloaded in RTF format. The files to download are located at the end of each case.

Listing by Month of Decision

➡ 1995 Decisions

➡ 1996 Decisions

➡ 1997 Decisions

Fifth Circuit

http://www.ca5.uscourts.gov

Highlights Arguably the most sophisticated Web server for a circuit court is this elaborate and information-rich site from the Fifth Circuit. Published opinions in the archive date back to 1985 and are arranged by docket number. A search engine named ISYS can search the database using plain English, command-based or menu-driven queries for all published opinions.

There's far more to this site than just reported decisions, though. Find *Pattern Jury Instructions* and *docket sheets* here as well as such instructive documents as a *Guide to Writing Briefs under the New Rule 32* and an online form for *Appearance of Counsel and Application for Admission.*

Links to other courts lead to the Web sites operated by some of the district courts within the circuit. The Fifth Circuit Web site demonstrates the power that the Web can have in providing judicial materials to the public when the site is thoughtfully and professionally designed.

The Fifth Circuit is Louisiana, Mississippi and Texas. ❑

U. S. Court of Appeals, 5th Circuit

Henry A. Politz, Chief Judge

New Opinions

Opinions Archive

View Docket Sheets NEW

Documents of the Court

Pattern Jury Instructions

Court Units

Links to Other Courts of the 5th Circuit

FTP Site

NEW New documents from the Clerk of Court are available:

*to view or print a PDF file, you must use Adobe Acrobat Reader 3.0, which is available from Adobe's web page at no charge.

- Guide to Writing a Brief under the new 5th Cir. R. 32 - pdf format* NEW

- 5th Cir. R. 32 Notice NEW

- Certificate of Compliance Sample NEW

- Form for Appearance of Counsel and Application for Admission- pdf format*

- Preparing for Oral Argument in the Fifth Circuit

- Notice to Counsel Attending Oral Arguments

All documents are available from Documents of the Court

Search for opinions using the new search engine, ISYS Web

*to view or print a PDF file, you must use Adobe Acrobat Reader 3.0, which is available from Adobe's web page at no charge.

Please send any questions or comments to webmaster@ca5.uscourts.gov

Last updated: 05/6/97

Sixth Circuit

http://www.law.emory.edu/ 6circuit

Highlights The Sixth Circuit is represented on the Internet by Emory University and a bare-bones Web site that, like other Emory reporting services, mounts Sixth Circuit decisions from 1995 to present. The opinions are searchable by date, party name or by keyword searching for terms within the decision.

The Sixth Circuit encompasses Kentucky, Michigan, Ohio and Tennessee. ❑

Credits and Conditions

U.S. Court of Appeals, Sixth Circuit

Geographic jurisdiction: Kentucky, Michigan, Ohio, and Tennessee

---

The opinions of the Sixth Circuit since January 1995 are brought to you by the Hugh F. Macmillan Law Library, Emory University School of Law, in cooperation with the United States Court of Appeals for the Sixth Circuit. All cases are in full text on the Web, or can be downloaded in RTF format. The files to download are located at the end of each case.

Listing by Month of Decision

➡ 1995 Decisions

➡ 1996 Decisions

➡ 1997 Decisions

- January
- February
- March
- April
- May

Seventh Circuit

http://www.kentlaw.edu/7circuit

Highlights Hosting the Seventh Circuit on the Internet is the Center for Law and Computers at the Chicago-Kent College of Law. Court opinions are mounted online daily and date back to May 1995; the Webmasters have announced plans to add cases as far back as January 1993. Cases can be searched by date or by party name.

The Seventh Circuit has jurisdiction over Illinois, Indiana and Wisconsin. ❑

United States Court of Appeals for the Seventh Circuit
Jurisdiction over Illinois, Indiana, and Wisconsin

Resources:

[Browse the 7th Circuit database](#)
[Search the 7th Circuit database](#)
[Index to U.S. Federal Appellate Courts](#)

The Center for Law and Computers at Chicago-Kent College of Law, IIT, is proud to bring you the cases of the United States Court of Appeals for the 7th Circuit. This site is updated daily as new decisions are published.

The 7th Circuit database is maintained by the Center for Law and Computers. You can use the search engine to search cases from May 1995 through the present. You can browse cases from January 1, 1993 through the present (these back cases haven't been added to the database yet, but will be soon!). New cases are added daily. Furthermore, we are working on several enhancements that will make the database more searchable. If you have any suggestions for this site, please contact us!

|| Center for Law and Computers | Chicago-Kent | IIT ||
| Search |

Eighth Circuit

http://www.wulaw.wustl.edu/ 8th.cir

Highlights Washington University School of Law hosts the Eighth Circuit where it reprints daily opinions dating from October 1995, retrievable either by links or by anonymous ftp. The site also includes the court's *calendar* and reprints the *Circuit Rules*, offering the researcher a substantial resource for judicial research.

In addition to the circuit decisions and rules, the site is notable for hosting the first iteration of materials from the Bankruptcy Court, in the current instance, the *Bankruptcy Appellate Panel Rules* and a cal-endar for the same. Also reprinted here are the text of pleadings and motions for Federal Communications Commission cases assigned to the Circuit by the Judicial Panel on Multidistrict Litigation. This is one of the first sites to include all the documents on one site in a suit and should serve as an example to other courts considering the benefits of electronic documents filing. States within the Eighth Circuit are Arkansas, Iowa, Minnesota, Missouri, Nebraska, North Dakota and South Dakota. ❑

United States Court of Appeals for the Eighth Circuit

Bankruptcy Appellate Panel for the Eighth Circuit

Washington University School of Law is pleased to be the home for the United States Court of Appeals for the Eighth Circuit and the Bankruptcy Appellate Panel for the Eighth Circuit.

🔲 Daily circuit opinions issued by the Court since October 30, 1995.

🔲 The circuit court's calendar.

🔲 Circuit Rules of the Eighth Circuit.

🔲 FCC Cases: Text of pleadings and orders in the FCC cases pending before the Court.

Ninth Circuit

http://www.ce9.uscourts.gov

Highlights The Ninth Circuit, curiously, does not publish its opinions on its own Web site but rather delegates that task to the Villanova Center for Information Law and Policy at *http://www.law.vill.edu* The administrators designed this Web site not as a case reporting service but rather as a general information service for the Circuit. On board are publications describing the structure and operation of the court with appropriate links to the courts within the circuit as well as links to administrative offices serving the courts such as the Judicial Council and the Ninth Circuit Judicial Conference.

The Web site is an excellent source for court statistics and for reports on such topics as *Racial, Religious and Ethic Fairness*.

States and territories covered by the Ninth Circuit are Alaska, Arizona, California, Guam, Hawaii, Idaho, Montana, Nevada and the Northern Mariana Islands. ❑

HOME | documents | careers | court links | guestbook | what's new

Office of the Circuit Executive

United States Courts for the Ninth Circuit
a public resource for information on the Federal Judiciary

Welcome. Today is Sunday, 07/20/97. The time is 07:03 PM.

Interested in a career with the Federal Courts?
Careers in the Courts
click here

Info Links...

Thank you for your interest in the United States Courts for the Ninth Circuit. This site has recently been implemented as a public resource for information on Federal Courts in the Ninth Circuit.

The Ninth Circuit, the largest of the 13 federal circuits, includes all federal courts in California, Oregon, Washington, Arizona, Montana, Idaho, Nevada, Alaska, Hawaii, Guam and the Northern Mariana Islands.

This web site is operated by the Office of the Circuit Executive (OCE). The OCE provides administration and staff support to the Judicial Council of the Ninth Circuit, the Ninth Circuit Court of Appeals, District Courts, Bankruptcy Courts, and Probation/Pretrial units.

Welcome! Thank you for visiting the United States Courts for the Ninth Circuit. This site can be used as "jumping off point" for further Ninth Circuit Courts exploration. Maintained by the Ninth Circuit's Office of the Circuit Executive, this site will be updated often, so visit us frequently. And please don't hesitate to send us a comment if you have any suggestions or concerns. If you'd like to know why Ninth Circuit Court of Appeals opinions do not appear on this website, please click here.

Points of interest include the U.S. Courts web site
locator, which has current web-site listings for many federal courts. If you'd like more information on the structure of the federal judiciary, and the Ninth Circuit specifically, visit our Court History and Structure section.

Feel free to explore, keeping in mind new features will be added often. We encourage you to go to our Guestbook area and fill out a survey or leave your comments.

You are visitor **2843** since 03/20/97.

Tenth Circuit

http://www.law.emory.edu/ 10circuit

Highlights Emory University's decisions from the Tenth Circuit follow the same pattern as the decisions it mounts from other jurisdictions: cases are arranged by party name or by date and can be searched using a search engine for keywords contained within the decision.

The Tenth Circuit covers Colorado, Kansas, New Mexico, Oklahoma, Utah and Wyoming. ❑

Credits and Conditions

U.S. Court of Appeals, Tenth Circuit

Geographic jurisdiction: Colorado, Kansas, New Mexico, Oklahoma, Utah, and Wyoming

---

The opinions of the Tenth Circuit since August 1995 are brought to you by the Hugh F. Macmillan Law Library, Emory University School of Law, in cooperation with the United States Court of Appeals for the Tenth Circuit. All cases are in full text on the Web, or can be downloaded in ASCII format. The files to download are located at the end of each case.

Listing by Month of Decision

➡ 1995 Decisions

➡ 1996 Decisions

➡ 1997 Decisions

- January
- February
- March
- April
- May
- June
- July

Eleventh Circuit

http://www.law.emory.edu/ 11circuit

Highlights Another service from the Emory library, this site contains decisions dating from the beginning of 1994 to present; each of them may be searched by party name, date or by key-word searching.

States covered in the Eleventh Circuit are Alabama, Florida and Georgia. ❏

Credits and Conditions

U.S. Court of Appeals, Eleventh Circuit

Geographic jurisdiction: Alabama, Florida, and Georgia

The opinions of the Eleventh Circuit since November 1994 are brought to you by the Hugh F. Macmillan Law Library, Emory University School of Law, in cooperation with the United States Court of Appeals for the Eleventh Circuit. All cases are in full text on the Web, or can be downloaded in RTF format. The files to download are located at the end of each case.

Listing by Month of Decision

➡ 1994 Decisions

➡ 1995 Decisions

➡ 1996 Decisions

➡ 1997 Decisions

Federal Circuit

http://www.law.emory.edu/ fedcircuit

Highlights Like other Emory University courts servers, the Web page for locating Federal Circuit decisions are searchable by party name, by date or by keyword. Decisions are available from the beginning of 1995 to the present month.

The case search function has a controlled vocabulary search engine installed on a scrollable box; use to for quickly locating cases containing commonly used legal terms. ❑

<u>Credits and Conditions</u>

U.S. Court of Appeals, Federal Circuit

The opinions of the Federal Circuit since August 1995 are brought to you by the Hugh F. Macmillan Law Library, Emory University School of Law, in cooperation with the United States Court of Appeals for the Federal Circuit. All cases are in full text on the Web, or can be downloaded in RTF format. The files to download are located at the end of each case.

Listing by Month of Decision

➡ 1995 Decisions

➡ 1996 Decisions

➡ 1997 Decisions

- January
- February
- March
- April
- May
- June
- July

District of Columbia Circuit

http://www.ll.georgetown.edu/
Fed-Ct/cadc.html

Highlights The Georgetown University Law Library hosts a clickable map of all the Federal courts and like Villanova's Federal Court Locator, it makes locating Federal court materials utterly simple. Use the main page as a guide to all the jurisdictions -- but this is also the preferred Web site for the DC Circuit.

Opinions date from the beginning of 1995 to present and can be searched by date, party name or via a keyword search. ❑

United States Court of Appeals
for the
District of Columbia Circuit

*Accessed Through Hypertext Documents Prepared by
Edward Bennett Williams Law Library*

The Edward Bennett Williams Law Library at the Georgetown University Law Center makes the opinions of the United States Court of Appeals for the District of Columbia available to the Internet community on the World Wide Web beginning with March 1995. New opinions are automatically downloaded from the Court's bulletin board each night and converted into several different formats for viewing and downloading. Not all decisions of the Court are available on the Court's bulletin board, and only those that have been made available electronically are available on this Web site. In general, the decisions made available by the Court correspond to those that have been designated for publication.

While the Library works to ensure the timeliness and accuracy of these opinions, it does not make any warranties or representations regarding them. Before relying on any opinion, it is essential for the researcher to use independent means to verify the status of the opinion and determine its precedential value.

The Library does not have access to the Court's docket, and therefore, cannot confirm whether a particular case is pending or provide any information regarding the status of the case. For information about the status of a case, contact the clerk of the Court at (202)273-0310.

Regrettably, the Library does not have the staff resources to answer questions involving research of legal issues from persons not affiliated with Georgetown University. If you have such questions, you may want to go to a law library in your area for additional assistance.

Listing by Month of Decision

➡ 1995 Decisions
➡ 1996 Decisions
➡ 1997 Decisions

U.S. Air Force

http://www.af.mil

Highlights The Air Force flies into the wild blue cyber-yonder with its Web site that connects a library of Air Force weapons systems, publications and speeches with a picture of the world as defended by the USAF in the coming century. Much of the site is designed to highlight recent Air Force achievements and the actual legal information contained here is fairly slim; but it was the Air Force that provided the extensive FLITE database of Supreme Court decisions to the Internet, greatly expanding the available online archive of

Supreme Court opinions.

AirForceLink, as the site is known, mounts news about the service and outlines the careers would-be airmen (and women) may find.

Extensive links provide immediate contact with many branches of the Air Force, including the Air National Guard, Reserve Officer Training Corps detachments and virtually every air base that the USAF commands. It's a big site but it's easy to navigate.
❏

Welcome to Air Force Link, the official site of the U.S. Air Force. View Global Engagement, our vision for the 21st Century.

Let us know what you think about Air Force Link!

Air Force Link is a government computer system
[Home | News | Careers | Library | Sites | Images | Navigate]

United States Army

http://www.army.mil

Highlights Search all that you can search on the Army's Web site. One of the side effects of the end of the Cold War is a greater openness on the part of the military services and the Army is no exception. Connect to thousands of official and unofficial organizations within the Army -- the 8th Army in Korea has a home page as does the 204th Area Support Group of the Louisiana National Guard -- by using the *search for organizations by name* or *keyword* search boxes.

The venerable *Stars and Stripes,* like other newspapers, finds itself sidelined by the Army's electronic journalism that fills the Web site with news from around the service. Use the various links under the frame for *Leadership Organization* to locate information on Army operations. The links found under *Finding Information* are good navigation aids that help in navigating the immense informational tributaries leading to and from this heavy-duty Web site. ❏

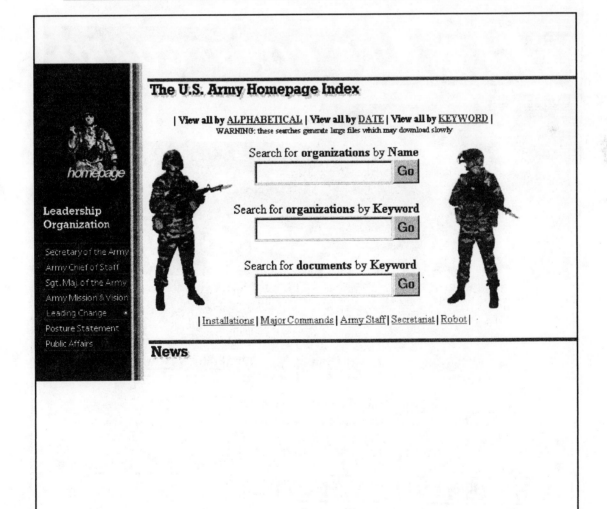

United States Coast Guard

http://www.dot.gov/dotinfo/uscg

Highlights Use the Coast Guard site for its links to *Marine Safety and Environmental Protection*. That's where to find *regulations and notices, licensing, post state control* and information on the *International Maritime Organization*. The Web site is geared for the recreational boater; refer to the *Navigation Center* for local notices to mariners, information on marine communications and locations where nautical charts may be ordered. The Coast Guard only becomes a military service during war; in peacetime, much of its work is the protection of the marine environment. The *National Pollution Funds Center* and the *National Response Center* are both Coast Guard programs to enable the service to respond to oil spills, marine disasters and other threats to coastal waters. ❑

United States Marine Corps

http://www.hqmc.usmc.mil

Highlights As a Web site, this one is field-stripped down to bare essentials. Like a pumped-up Leatherneck, there's no fat on this site -- nor much else of interest to the researcher. A simple collection of links leads to the public affairs division and to the offices of the highest-level commanders. Add to that some logistical information and a directory of Marine Corps bases and that pretty much accounts for the sum total of the service's Internet presence. ❑

MarineLINK > Headquarters, Marine Corps >

Welcome to

Headquarters,

United States Marine Corps

This site is provided as a reference for active duty Marines. If you are searching for Marine Corps information, you are probably looking for MarineLINK.

Commandant of the Marine Corps

Commandant of the Marine Corps   Sergeant Major of the Marine Corps
Assistant Commandant of the Marine Corps

HQMC Staff Agencies

*** Denotes a link to a site off MarineLINK

Marine Corps Uniform Board	Director, Marine Corps Staff
Administration and Resources	***Command, Control, Communication, Computer, and Intelligence
Historical Division	Health Services
Inspector General	***Installation and Logistics
Judge Advocate	Manpower and Reserve Affairs
Morale, Welfare and Recreation	Office of Legislative Affairs
Divison of Public Affairs	Plans, Policies and Operations
Programs and Resources	Marine Corps Systems Command (Quantico)
Marine Corps Combat Development Command	Marine Corps Recruiting Command
***Total Quality Leadership	***Safety Division

This is a government computer system

United States Navy

http://www.navy.mil

Highlights Like the Army, the Navy has produced a large-scale Web site to promote its role as a fighting force and while the legal information for the researcher is fairly slim, there is enough reference information loaded here to make the site a worthwhile destination for such things as *All Hands*, the Navy's magazine and a fact file containing data about ships and aircraft.

Most of the links to the Navy's site are of interest to current members of the service and to potential inductees. The only other substantive information is the reprint of the Navy's biennial budget, the link to *Doing Business with the Navy* and the *Latest News* which carries back and current issues from the *Navy News* service.

For connecting to various Naval commands worldwide, link up to *NavyOnLine*. It provides a central listing and links to the *Bureau of Naval Personnel* and other Navy-related Web sites. ❑

This is the official web site of the United States Navy.
It is provided as a service of the Navy Office of Information, Washington, D.C.

Welcome aboard the website of the United States Navy. You will want to visit often since new features are added or information is updated daily. By the way, the bells you heard are rung aboard ships to announce the arrival of important guests.

The Index pages give you a **comprehensive alphabetical listing** by subject of what's available on this site. Here are some highlights:

America's oldest commissioned ship sails for first time in over a century!
See the Navy up close — the 1997 Great Lakes Cruise

- 1997 Blue Angels Flight Demonstration Squadron schedule
- *All Hands* — the magazine of the U.S. Navy
- Help — Your questions about the U.S. Navy are answered here.
- Biography, Speeches, and Testimony of the Secretary of the Navy
- Biography, Images, and Testimony of the Chief of Naval Operations
- Core Values of the U.S. Navy
- Current status of the Navy - updated weekly

Code of Federal Regulations

http://www.access.gpo.gov/nara/ cfr/cfr-table-search.html

Highlights The body of Federal administrative regulations are now searchable, title by title, on the new Web site for the Code of Federal Regulations at the National Archives and Records Administration.

The newly-designed site is simplicity itself to search: click a check-mark into the box of the title to be searched and then hit the radio button marked *continue*. A subsequent page appears that will correlates the online display to the print version of the CFR: a table graphically displays *Title,*

Volume, Chapter, Parts, Regulatory Entity and reports on the current date of the retrievable text. Use the check boxes underneath the column for *Volume* to make the search more precise.

The task of making the online version of the CFR more responsive to the needs of the legal researcher will take a considerable amount of time. Plans are in the works to improve the hypertext retrieval capabilities of the site and to install editing tools that will allow faster updating of rules as they are amended, added or deleted. ❑

Internet Law Library

The U.S. House of Representatives Internet Law Library Code of Federal Regulations (searchable)

Welcome To the Code of Federal Regulations!

[To skip the introductory material on this page, go to http://law.house.gov/cfr.htm#search.]

The Code of Federal Regulations contains the text of public regulations issued by the agencies of the Federal government. Proposed regulations and regulations issued so recently that they are not yet in the Code of Federal Regulations database, may be found in the Federal Register.

The Code of Federal Regulations does not include statutes enacted by Congress, decisions of the Federal courts, or treaties. Statutes enacted by Congress are available, for the most part, in the United States Code. Some of the decisions of the Federal courts (particularly recent decisions) are available through the Federal Court Decisions and Rules page of the U.S. House of Representatives Internet Law Library. A collection of treaties is also available through the Treaties and International Law page of the Internet Law Library.

Federal Register

http://www.access.gpo.gov:80/ su_docs/aces/aces140.html

Highlights The official publication of all *Notices, Rules and Proposed Rules* as well as Presidential documents and *Executive Orders* is the *Federal Register*. This daily compendium of executive administration now can be searched in full text beginning with January 1994. The text is easy to search: select the appropriate year, include a date range if known and enter free text search terms. Searches can be narrowed with a number of Boolean connectors to make the search more accu- rate. Focus on specific sections of the Code of Federal Regulations by adding quotation marks around the CFR citation. Searches may be truncated as needed. Click on the help link to pull up a list of "stop" (unsearchable) words and some sample searches that aid in finding releases by agency, phrases or relevancy ranking. Searches may also be performed through certain sections of the *Federal Register* like *proposed rules, final rules, notices* and *Presidential documents*.

Federal Register Online via *GPO Access*

Database for the 1995, 1996 and 1997 *Federal Register* (Volumes 60, 61 and 62)

The *Federal Register* is the official publication for Presidential Documents and Executive Orders as well as Notices, Rules and Proposed Rules from Federal Agencies and Organizations. Helpful Hints provide instructions for searching the database.

The 1994 Federal Register (Volume 59) database is also available, however, it contains no fields or section identifers.

Federal Register Issue:

☑ 1997 Federal Register   ☐ 1996 Federal Register   ☐ 1995 Federal Register

Federal Register Sections (If you select none, all sections will be searched, but you may select one or more sections):

☐ Contents and Preliminary Pages   ☐ Presidential Documents

☐ Final Rules and Regulations   ☐ Sunshine Act Meetings*

☐ Proposed Rules   ☐ Reader Aids

☐ Notices   ☐ Corrections

* As of March 1, 1996, Sunshine Act Meetings were incorporated into the Notices section of the *Federal Register*.

Issue Date (Enter either a range of dates or a specific date in the format mm/dd/yy):

Date Range: From [   ] to [   ]

FedWorld

http://www.fedworld.gov

Highlights A cavernous archive of almost half a million government documents make this hodge podge of govdocs almost like an informational flea market. There is no overarching rhyme or reason to the materials that be found here and no discernible pattern to those offices, bureaus and commissions of the Federal government that publish their reports, studies and releases here. Browse the FedWorld Web site by scrolling down the search box: the researcher will find an eclectic menu containing searchable and retrievable documents from the *Davis-Bacon database, the FAA, government job announcements, National Technical Information Service, the EPA Clean Air Act database* and *FBIS Glossary*. One reliable service from FedWorld, however, is its collection of tax forms and instructions. FedWorld becomes an invaluable auxiliary mirror site to the IRS Web at tax time when millions of frantic taxpayers are overloading the server. FedWorld accommodates the overflow. Explore this site; it's odd but useful. ❑

| Work? | Job Opening At FedWorld |

Web Site Revised July 16, 1997
File, Jobs and Web Databases Updated Daily

FedWorld Information Network

Search a FedWorld Web Site
Enter some keywords:

[   ]

Select a Web Site to Search:

[Entire FedWorld Information Network ▾]

[**Website Search**]

Browse a FedWorld Web Site
Select a Site to Visit:

[About FedWorld   ▾]

[**Go!**]

A more Detailed Search Form that lists additional databases is available.

General Information Services

FedWorld FTP Site *(Government information, documents and files)*
    - Access to the **FedWorld File Libraries with more than 15,000 files**, including information on Business, Health and Safety, and the Environment. Now includes East and West coast satellite images that are updated every hour.

Government Information Locator Service (GILS)

http://www.usgs.gov/gils

Highlights In private industry, it's called "info-mining," taking large bodies of data that has been collected and by manipulating it in novel ways creating new uses for the data. That's the idea underlying the Government Information Locator Service which seeks to locate information resources hidden away in the crannies of the Federal government and then, by imposing a standard search engine and retrieval tag on the data, make that information both accessible and more useful.

Not only does GILS try to create a meta-index of government data, it also tries to publicize the existence of little known databanks. Each GILS record reports what information is available and why it was created. The data is then made available for searching using a WAIS database.

GILS is part of a larger, global move to making information not only platform-independent but agency (and even government) independent. The system relies on standard search and retrieval tools used worldwide. ❑

Government Information Locator Service (GILS)

- Search U.S. Federal Sources GPO (Government Printing Office) Access is one source that takes advantage of GILS-compliant servers on the Internet.
- What is GILS? Required under U.S. law and policy, GILS adopts existing international standards and is implemented with specific technologies.
- Contacts for information and discussion related to GILS in areas of policy, services, standards, technology, and other aspects.
- A Demonstration Sampler Here are some examples of how GILS is being applied to help people find information.
- Software Topics in GILS implementation software
- Technical topics and Other Information Useful resources for policy, standards, and technology relevant to GILS.
- Toward a Global Information Locator The free flow of information worldwide is a fundamental goal of the emerging Global Information Society.

Are you looking for help right now on a specific question?
You may wish to contact GSA's Federal Information Center.

December 18, 1996 Press Release, "WORLD'S EXPERTS PLAN GLOBAL LOCATOR SERVICE FOR ENVIRONMENTAL INFORMATION"

Where is this page?

Toward a Global Information Locator

Government Printing Office
GPO Access

http://www.access.gpo.gov

Highlights The Government Printing Office follows the private sector into electronic publication by connecting to Web sites for many of the government agencies it serves. More than 70 government databases can be searched from the GPO Access site including *bills,* the *Federal Register* from 1994 to today, the U.S. Code, *Economic Indicators* and the current and proposed Federal budget.

This is all good and well, but proving the point that the private sector generally does things better than the government, find the same access to government documents in an easier-to-search format from the University of California at their Web server named *GPO Gate.* It provides connections to the same documents on a better Web site with a more flexible and better-designed front end. Find GPO Gate at *http://www.gpo.ucop.edu/search/ default.html* ❏

UNITED STATES GOVERNMENT PRINTING OFFICE

Keeping America Informed

Welcome to the U.S. Government Printing Office Home Page

out the Government Printing Office

ess to Government Information Products
   Superintendent of Documents
      GPO Access: On-line, On-Demand & Locator Services
      Information Available for Free Public use in Federal Depository Libraries
      Information for Sale
   Advisory Commission on Intergovernmental Relations
   Agency for Health Care Policy and Research
   Commission on the Roles and Capabilities of the United States Intelligence Community
   Bureau of Land Management (Colorado Office) NEW
   Congress of the United States
   Department of Interior Office of Inspector General
   Executive Office of the President
      Council of Economic Advisers
      Office of Management and Budget
   Federal Labor Relations Authority NEW
   Food and Drug Administration
   General Accounting Office
   Merit Systems Protection Board
   National Archives and Records Administration's Office of the Federal Register
   National Labor Relations Board NEW
   Office of Compliance
   Office of Government Ethics
   Office of Special Counsel
   Office of Technology Assessment
   Office of Thrift Supervision

Internet Law Library

http://law.house.gov

Highlights The House of Representatives affords the legal researcher a good library of resources with an emphasis on international legal materials at its Internet Law Library. The law-related index pages from law schools and other non-profit organizations do a better job of mounting comprehensive links to law materials Internet-wide but none of them has the simple links to territorial law, the laws of other nations, treaties and international laws that this site does.

The link to laws of other nations is arranged in alphabetical order and while the hypertext links seem to promise an informational Nirvana, the actual materials are usually fairly thin. (The link to Afghanistan is a Turkish-language treaty between Turkey and Afghanistan and some State Department reports on human rights practices in that country.)

Use the Internet Law Library for its connections to the U.S. Code and the Code of Federal Regulations in a pinch. Otherwise, use the other established Internet law servers as outline in Chapter 4. ❑

 Internet Law Library

The U.S. House of Representatives Internet Law Library Welcome!

- About the House Internet Law Library
- U.S. Federal laws (arranged by original published source)
- U.S. Federal laws (arranged by agency)
- U.S. state and territorial laws
- Laws of other nations
- Treaties and international law
- Laws of all jurisdictions (arranged by subject)
- Law school law library catalogues and services
- Attorney and legal profession directories
- Law book reviews and publishers

 FRAMES version of the Law Library

 Fast-loading GRAPHIC-FREE version of our homepage

 Search the U.S. Code

United States Code

http://law.house.gov/usc.htm

Highlights This is what legal research on the Internet is all about: a searchable version of the United States Code is available to anyone who wants to plow through its bulk with an electronic search tool. There are only two major caveats: the text is dated and it's not annotated. It's necessary to refer to the online version of the pocket part and sift through recently signed Public Laws to check on the current language of any particular law section and annotations are still editorial enhancements from commercial publishers. But in an age when Congress -- or more precisely the Library of Congress -- makes these documents immediately available online, updating the U.S. Code is actually easier than making the trip to the law library and thumbing through an already out-of-date pocket part and the classification tables and the recent advance sheets from U.S. Code and Administrative News.

The code is a little tricky to search and first-time users are well-advised to refer to the online tutorial. Searches are easily narrowed to specific title, section or sub-chapter. ❑

Internet Law Library

The U.S. House of Representatives Internet Law Library U.S. Code (searchable)

Welcome To the U.S. Code!

[To skip the introductory material on this page, go to http://law.house.gov.usc.htm#search.]

The United States Code contains the text of current public laws enacted by Congress.

The U.S. Code does not include regulations issued by executive branch agencies, decisions of the federal courts, or treaties. Regulations issued by executive branch agencies are available in the Code of Federal Regulations. Proposed regulations and regulations adopted so recently that they are not yet in the Code of Federal Regulations, may be found in the Federal Register. Some of the decisions of the Federal courts (particularly recent decisions) are available through the Federal Court Decisions and Rules page of the U.S. House of Representatives Internet Law Library. A collection of treaties is available through the Treaties and International Law page of the House of Representatives Internet Law Library.

INTERNATIONAL RESOURCES

The Internet is still very much dominated by the United States and Canada. But other countries, especially English-speaking nations like the United Kingdom, Ireland, Australia, New Zealand, South Africa and former British colonies such as Hong Kong are discovering the power of the Internet as a system for publishing legal information. English is the *de facto* language of international law and trade. Many multilateral and international organizations produce Web sites that are easy for the English speaker to use.

International law is growing and changing rapidly and it is difficult to keep up with the changes as they appear on a global basis. However, a number of index pages have been created to make the resources of the global network readily available to the Internet-equipped researcher.

The U.S House of Representatives **Internet Law Library** at *http://law.house.gov/52.htm* provides links to the *Laws of Other Nations*. The nations are arranged alphabetically from Albania to Zimbabwe; the precise content mounted there varies drastically from country to country. Typically there will be a copy of the nation's constitution and at least a smattering of current statutes. Other links provide access to *Treaties and international law* and *laws of all jurisdictions arranged by subject matter.*

The **International Law Locator** is a service of the Villanova Center for Information Law and Policy; its focus is primarily on European laws but there are interesting links to the full text statutes of Australia, Hong Kong, Hungary, Ukraine, Canada and the U.S. Another project getting underway is the **European Finance, Banking, and Tax Locator** at *http://www.law.vill.edu/international/eetaxurl*

Turn to the leading law-related index pages for the most extensive collections of international law. WashLaw Web at Washburn University operates the **Foreign and International LawWeb** at *http://lawlib.wuacc.edu/forint/forintmain.html* that arranges law by geographic region and by topic. FindLaw hosts **LawCrawler International** at *http://www.findlaw.com/12international/index.html* to give the researcher a search engine to look up international law materials directly. FindLaw has links to individual country pages and a meta-index link to more than one hundred international law sources, including links to primary materials, publications and mailing lists and Usenet groups. Hieros Gamos offers links to **All Supra-National Organizations World-Wide** at *http://www.hg.org/hg.html* and an index to **Every Government in the World**.

Last, one of the most extensive sites for **Public International Law** is the site by the same name created and maintained by Australian law professor Francis Auburn at *http://www.hg.org/hg.html* It's excellent for connections to international organizations and treaties. ❑

State and Local Resources

STATE RESOURCES

Introduction

In the evolution of the Internet, one of the most remark-able transformations has been the explosion of state materials onto the global network. After lagging the Federal government in the breadth and quantity of materials they made accessible to the Internet, state governments are making up for lost time and adding the contents of their public archives onto servers.

While the migration of state law materials from paper-based to electronically stored format is not complete, a significant body of law-related data is now available to the state law researcher. Precisely what information is provided to the Internet varies drastically from state to state. From the informational Nirvana of California's state-of-the-art Web sites to the slim pickings from some of the less technologically-advanced states, state law resources range from complete, searchable access to the state statutory and administrative codes, up-to-the-minute electronic connections to current legislation and seamless links to executive agencies to information-starved pages containing little more than the mailing address for the lieutenant governor.

State Law Index Pages

A number of law-related index pages exist that can provide immediate access to state law resources. These sites are handy and offer the researcher fast links to judicial, executive and legislative materials from easy-to-use Web pages.

Because these sites are so useful for state law research, it's recommended that they all are bookmarked. Multiple index pages are necessary since changes to state law resources can occur quickly and without notice; by using more than one index page, it's more likely that important new developments will not be missed.

State law index pages are useful for checking up on similar legislation or statutory materials from different states or to compare state-by-state variations on uniform laws.

STATE WEB LOCATOR
STATE COURT LOCATOR
http://www.law.vill.edu

From the Villanova Center for Information Law and Policy comes what is arguably the easiest and most complete search service for plugging into state law resources. Ably maintained by Kenneth P. Mortensen, the **State Web Locator** mounts a one-stop search engine on the page that will retrieve every Internet-wired state office nation-wide. Given a choice of one state search engine, this is the one to use. It's up-to-date and reliable. To look up state court decisions and get information on state judges and courts, use the **State Court Locator**.

 THE STATE WEB LOCATOR

The Villanova Center for Information Law and Policy

This is also an excellent source for directory information such as telephone numbers and mailing addresses. The clickable graphic map makes zooming into relevant jurisdictions an absolute no-brainer.

CORNELL UNIVERSITY
LEGAL INFORMATION INSTITUTE
http://www.law.cornell.edu/states/index.html

The Legal Information Institute mounts a gopher-like table of links to all states. It is competently operated but the other state servers offer the researcher significantly more efficient searching because of the availability of built-in search engines.

FEDLAW
http://fedlaw.gsa.gov/intro5.htm

The General Services Administration operates this Web site that mounts a simple, gopher-like table of links to the states. Graphically, the site is dull as ditchwater but it's straightforward and functional.

FINDLAW
http://www.findlaw.com/11stategov/index.html

Pick from two ways to search for state information from FindLaw: there's a search box for fill-in-the-blank text searching or a table of hypertext links to each of the states. Both are equally good at tracking down state materials. FindLaw relies on the AltaVista search, an industrial strength search engine. Searches can be run through the text retrieval box with a high degree of confidence. Clicking on the name of one of the states from the table leads to a page that itself includes a search engine and links to individual resources within the chosen state. Direct links to materials, while current, are not entirely comprehensive, so use the search engine to make sure that relevant sites are not overlooked.

HIEROS GAMOS
http://www.hg.org/usstates.html

In its ongoing bid to become the most comprehensive law site on the Internet, Hieros Gamos provides very detailed and well-maintained links to all state resources. The Webmasters look for connections to each branch of government and reprint links and whatever directory information is available for each state. The links are groomed frequently to keep them current and accurate.

Each state page also bundles search engines on the page. Check for links that don't appear on the page using the built-in FindLaw search box or select one of seven general interest search engines.

INDIANA UNIVERSITY SCHOOL OF LAW-BLOOMINGTON
http://www.law.indiana.edu/law/v-lib/states.html

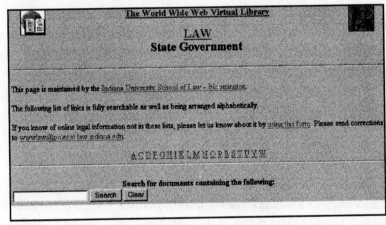

Like many of the other state law index pages, every expense is spared in graphic design, preferring to use simply, utilitarian scroll-down alphabetical gophers to hook up with state links. Indiana University, one of the pioneering institutions in Internet-based law materials, keeps this page fresh and current. Find states by clicking on the corresponding letter or use the WAIS server at the top of the page to zip directly to a state and its sub-agencies.

WASHBURN UNIVERSITY
http://lawlib.wuacc.edu

As one of the leading law-related Internet resources, the framed-Web page with its extensive scroll down menu of law materials can be counted on to provide up-to-the-minute state law searching. Roll the left-hand frame down to the link for *State Law*. Washburn's state entries are structured like most of the other state servers: there is both a search box or a table containing links to the individual states. Either search technique is equally effective; choice of search technique is a matter of individual taste and preference.

National Organizations for State and Local Law

For the state law researcher, national organizations for each of the three branches of state government each have Web sites, each of which is a valuable source of background information on the respective topics. For policy matters and for tracking down elusive state law resources, turn to these pages and their links.

THE COUNCIL OF STATE GOVERNMENTS
http://www.csg.org/

As a national organization for state officials, the Council of State Governments is a clearinghouse for publications and studies of interest to state lawmakers. For a complete description of what the organization does, select the link to *What is CSG all about, anyway?* where the executive director explains CSG's mission to improve the administration of state-run programs. .
The Council pub-
lishes a number of
titles for state offi-
cials including *State*

Leadership Directories, The Book of the States and *Handbooks.* Sales and ordering information are on the Web site.

Find links here to the *States Information Center* which provides free inquiry and reference services to state government officials. Queries may be submitted online to the center where some 20,000 documents on state administration are held online.

The gopher menu is a simple way to connect with CSG regional affiliates, newsletters and look up examples of state contracts.

NATIONAL ASSOCIATION OF COUNTIES
http://www.naco.org

The smallest significant government body in the United States is the county and if, as Tip O'Neill said, that all politics are local, then localities are springing up globally as the political voice of the people. That's nowhere more evident than this national association representing the interests of 3702 counties in the U.S. before the lawmakers in Washington, DC.

NATIONAL ASSOCIATION OF STATE INFORMATION RESOURCE EXECUTIVES
http://www.nasire.org

According to their own description, NASIRE "represents information resource executives and managers from the 50 states, six U.S. territories, and the District of Columbia. State members are senior officials from any of the three branches of state government who have statewide, executive-level responsibility for information resource management. NASIRE associate members are any other state officials and federal, local and Canadian government officials who are involved in information resource management. Private-sector firms and non-profit organizations may join as corporate members." The most interesting features of the Web site are the **state search** search engine and the links to digital signature initiatives nationwide.

NATIONAL CENTER FOR STATE COURTS
http://www.ncsc.dni.us/ncsc.htm

The National Center for State Courts was founded in 1971 at the urging of Chief Justice Warren Burger in order to improve the administration of state courts. The organization now aids state courts by providing models for organizational administration, developing policies to enhance state courts and promoting state court interests at the federal level.

For state court administrators, the Web site operates a listserv called MISForum and publishes a great deal of information about the use of technology in state courts.

The Web site is extensive; one of the most interesting links leads to the *Research Division* where information on caseloads, juries and other court statistics can be located. There is also a schedule of upcoming programs for the *Institute for Court Management*. The *Court Services* division provides technical assistance and consulting services to trial and appellate courts nationwide.

Find a link from this Web site to the *National Association for Court Management,* a members-only Web service containing helpful tips and professional management materials for streamlining state court proceedings.

NATIONAL CONFERENCE OF STATE LEGISLATURES
http://www.ncsl.org

Joining other national organizations to provide a forum in which to speak to the issues of concern to the states at a national level is this solid Web sitre from the National Conferenmce of State Legislatures.

State legislators can confer with their colleagues from other states and share ideas on new legislative initiatives with this site that hooks up statehouses throughout the nation with directories, links and information about state-federal inter-governmental relationships. The NCSL publishes newsletters and updates state lawmakers on current trends. Connect to the states and review information on the Foundation for State Legislatures here.

NATIONAL GOVERNORS ASSOCIATION
http://www.nga.org

Membership in this organization should be fairly exclusive: fifty members to be precise. The site is actually a bi-partisan clearinghouse of information for governors and their staffs and is designed as a forum for the chief executives to share information on state innovations and discuss common problems such as implementing the new welfare reform rules. (In fact, welfare reform resources are abundant on this site.) Press releases from the association and the *Center for Best Practices* make for an informative and useful Web site.

Local and Municipal Resources

In addition to state materials, local governments, municipalities and quasi-governmental organizations are mounting regulations and contact information on Web pages. As a general rule, it's easier to track down city and county information from within an official state Web page or via links from local Web pages geographically close to the local entity.

These are the Web sites created specifically to link to local governments and make for useful starting points for zooming in directly to selected local agencies.

MUNICIPAL CODE CORPORATION
http://www.municode.com/database.html

As presently constituted, this site is mostly of interest to the

Florida researcher tracking down the muni code of the state's cities and municipalities. But there are online codes for a smattering of other cities from around the nation and as this grows into a larger database, it will likely prove to be a valuable resource.

NATIONAL LEAGUE OF CITIES
http://www.cais.com/nlc

Representing some 17,000 municipalities nationwide, the National League of Cities is fundamentally a lobby group that attempts to influence national policy that affect cities and towns. The Web site does not publish much of its material natively but rather provides links to civic and activist organizations throughout the Internet that also have an interest in making local government voices heard at the Federal level.

USA CITYLINK
http://usacitylink.com//default.html

Like the name says, the site connects to American cities and mostly provides Chamber-of-Commerce style information. Some links do connect to municipal codes and regulatory materials but don't count on it.

USA COUNTIES 1996
OREGON STATE UNIVERSITY GOVERNMENT INFORMATION SHARING PROJECT
http://govinfo.kerr.orst.edu/usaco-stateis.html

The most important features of this site are the links to demographic and economic data from around the nation, drawn primarily from Federal statistical sources.

About State and Local Resources

Because the information published to Web sites and gophers at the state and local level varies from jurisdiction to jurisdiction, the reviews for each state were designed to find the following information:

- *The general site for legal information in the state referred to as the* **QuickLink**
- *The governor's home page*
- *A link to the executive agencies and administrative code*
- *Judicial materials including decisions, rules and biographies*
- *Legislative materials including bills, session laws and statutory code.*
- *The state library*
- *Local and municipal resources*
- *Miscellaneous links of interest to the legal researcher*

Because administrations change, no page sponsored by a specific public official is highlighted. Instead, the concentration is on the office. As with all the addresses referred to, they were operative and twice-tested for accuracy; however, materials can change quickly on the Internet, especially at the state level.

Every state has an official home page; so does every governor. They all link to the legislature but what the researcher finds there varies from a paltry index of enrolled bills to an extraordinarily elaborate site that provides all the tools to make creating a state legislative history practical. That's also the case with the judiciary in most states: there are always links but the quantity and quality of retrieveable materials varies greatly.

The legal researcher should actively promote the use of the Internet at the state level. Among the items that states ought to publish electronically but rarely do are *administrative codes, the administrative journals that publish executive rule-makings, administrative law decisions, decisions from courts of limited jurisdiction, all public corporate records* and municipal materials such as *real estate records, mortgages, vital records* and *licenses* for regulated businesses and professionals. States can reduce costs and provide much greater service to the citizen by publishing electronically. It's up to the legal researcher who uses these materials to make sure they are made available. ❑

QuickLink
http://www.alalinc.net

ALABAMA is adding new information regularly to the Internet, and while there are some significant lapses in law resources available -- the state code, for instance, is not yet mounted online-- the legal researcher looking into Alabama state materials will find a fair collection of digitized data.

LEGISLATIVE MATERIALS

Legislative materials are restricted to directory-style information for the various legislators; so far, the text of bills or chaptered laws have not yet been published electronically. The home page for the Alabama State Legislature at *http://www.asc.edu/archives/legislat/legislat.html* links to the House of Representatives and the Senate and provides historical background and a synopsis of how bills become laws.

The Web site for the Alabama State House of Representatives at *http://www.asc.edu/archives/reps_sens/reps.html* is an alphabetical directory of legislators, searchable by district. Entries contain the name and address of the legislator, their district and their resume.

For the Alabama State Senate at

http://www.asc.edu/archives/legislat/senate.html, there is much the same information. The server reprints a list of committee assignments as well as an interesting, if not particularly helpful, list of Secretaries of the Senate.

Bill status information is available by telephone at 1-800-499-3052.

EXECUTIVE MATERIALS

Executive branch materials feature the governor's home page at *http://alaweb.asc.edu/govoff.html* which contains information about the governor's office, his biography, a list of the staff with links to their e-mail addresses, as well as press releases, policy statements and legislative bills that the governor has proposed.

For connections to state executive agencies, head to *http://www.asc.edu/archives/agencies/agencyam.html* where a complete directory of state agencies provides telephone numbers, mailing addresses and connections for e-mail contact. This page reprints the *Alabama Government Manual* and the *State Telephone Directory.*

Alabama provides a nearly complete list of forms and guides for filings with the Secretary of State. The files are stored in PDF format for easy retrieval using the Adobe Acrobat reader. Among the forms available are: *For-profit Domestic Articles of Incorporation; Application for Certificate of Existence; Report of a Domestic Limited Liability Company;* and a *Foreign Corporation Certificate of Authority.* Find the link to the forms at Alabama Secretary of State's page at *http://204.29.92.2/chbin/main/tv?alsecst*

JUDICIAL RESOURCES

Judicial materials are readily available for the State of Alabama and they can be retrieved most conveniently from the Alalinc

Information Network at *http://www.alalinc.net* and by logging in as "guest." Be cautioned that many of the links are still under construction but that when the page is completely functional, it will provide the most comprehensive collection of Alabama court decisions and rules on the Internet.

To get full value from the site, it's necessary to become a member. For information on subscribing to Alalinc, e-mail the Webmaster at *sysop@alalinc.net* for details. Members have access to such materials as the *Alabama Rules of Civil Procedure, Alabama Rules of Criminal Procedure* and the *Alabama Rules of Evidence.*

Non-members will benefit from the *Directory of Trial Court Officials* which offers a county-by-county list of judges, their addresses and phone numbers.

Alabama is in the 11th Circuit; decisions are available from November 1994 thanks to Emory University School of Law. Find them at *http://www.law.emory.edu/11circuit/index.html*

BAR ASSOCIATION

The Alabama State Bar operates a Web site at *http://www.alabar.org* The state-of-the-art Web server features a scrollable menu to navigate the site. The site publishes information about the Alabama Law Foundation, its magazine *Alabama Lawyer* and a referral service. Links exist for members to provide them with information on committees and bar activities. There are also links for law students and *pro hac vice* admission.

MISCELLANEOUS RESOURCES

Among the miscellaneous resources to be found online for the state of Alabama are the Alabama Law Institute, an organization of 150 bar association members, judges and law professors which exists, according to its home page at *http://boots.law.ua.edu/ali/geninfo.html* to "clarify and simplify the laws of Alabama, to revise laws that are out-of-date and to fill in

gaps in the law where there exists legal confusion." To facilitate that noble goal, the ALI page links the status of pending bills, a calendar of events and its publications as well as information about membership and its committees.

The University of Alabama School of Law maintains its home page at *http://www.law.ua.edu* The page provides the expected information about admissions and the faculty; the legal researcher should aim for the links to the law library which provides an online catalog and description of the services the library provides to Alabama attorneys. Unfortunately, research requests must be placed via telephone or fax.

A listserv for Alabama attorneys can be found at *AlabamaAttorneys-l@topeka.wuacc.edu* To subscribe to this list, send the message *subscribe alabamaattorneys-l Your Name* to listserv@topeka.wuacc.edu

LOCAL AND MUNICIPAL RESOURCES

For city information, rely on the collection of links to Alabama's urban centers gathered together on the "Alabama Information Links" page by the UA law library at *http://www.law.ua.edu/ala2.html* Contents lean heavily to Chamber-of-Commerce boosterism, but there may be some useful information here for the traveler.

STATE LIBRARY

The state library hasn't yet migrated online but researchers who need to dig through Alabama's microfilmed archives in the state's academic libraries will find a useful guide compiled by T. Harmon Straighton, Jr. at *http://www.lib.auburn.edu/madd/docs/unionlist.html*
❏

QuickLink

http://www.state.ak.us

ALASKA IS HEADING *NORTH TO THE Future* with a bountiful collection of law-related materials; it's one of the few states that provides historical state materials. Coverage of state offices and resources is thorough and the state's home page is a good starting place for Alaska state research. The researcher can connect effortlessly to state agencies, look up state employees, hook into Usenet groups and search across the state server by subject.

The link to *Agency Directory* is the most information-packed page. Find links to all the major government sites from this subpage at *http://www.state.alaska.us/local/alpha.htm*

EXECUTIVE RESOURCES

For executive branch links, the governor's page reprints such gubernatorial documents as the *State of the State* and the *State of the Budget* addresses. The site also offers a weekly publication titled *Talking Points* which updates citizens on the governor's political initiatives. Also find links to the governor's office in Washington, D.C., a connection to the Office of Management and Budget and of course, online press releases.

The State of Alaska page connects to all executive branch agencies and offices

from *http://www.state.ak.us/local/akdir.htm*

Alaska provides all the major state law resources. the current state code can be searched; so can previous codes from 1993 to 1995. Find links to the different code versions on the legislative server at *http://www.legis.state.ak.us* The site relies on a Folio database search engine to provide full text access to the law. A little practice is needed when using a Folio database for the first time but the knack for effective searching is quickly acquired.

On the same page as the state code are links to *Alaska State Executive Orders*, but be warned that the links have not been updated since March 1996. The *Alaska Administrative Journal*, published weekly by the Lieutenant Governor's office, can be searched in full text as well. It's the official publication for all state agency rulemakings, attorney general opinions, executive orders, administrative orders and for materials about boards and commissions. Find more information on the AAJ at *http://www.gov.state.ak.us/ltgov/aj/table.html* Alaska, to its civic credit, publishes its administrative code online; it's fully searchable.

LEGISLATIVE MATERIALS

Locate the state legislature server at *http://www.legis.state.ak.us* where a comprehensive page of links provides seamless access to the Senate, House of Representatives and the Legislative Affairs Agency, which carries out Legislative Council policy.

Track Alaskan legislation and look up current bill texts from the same page. Available "infobases" are *Bill Tracking and Legislation, Bills and Resolutions, House Journal, Senate Journal* and *Committee Minutes*.

In addition to the current legislative

session, the texts from prior sessions are available online. *Legislative Bill and Resolutions* dating from the 13th Legislature of 1984 can be searched and retrieved via the Internet. The text of the *House and Senate Journals* date from 1987. Committee minutes are searchable too; coverage begins in 1982. Session laws are online from 1981 to present; legislative resolves start in 1983. For general information about the legislature, click on the links to *Legislative Uniform Rules, Research Requests* or connect directly to the *Legislative Library Catalog*. And if none of those resources answers the question, try posting a query to *Lynn_Morley@ Legis.state.ak.us*

JUDICIAL RESOURCES

Judicial resources are plentiful in Alaska. The home page for the Alaska Court System, maintained by the Alaska Court Libraries, is at *http://www.alaska.net/~akctlib/homepage.htm* From this page, links lead to *Supreme Court opinions, Court of Appeals slip opinions* and *Court of Appeals memorandum opinions*. Opinions are current.

Court of Appeals and Supreme Court decisions remain online until they are published in the *Pacific Reporter 2nd*. Most of the opinions can be downloaded in compressed format. Refer to the page for detailed information on how to download and decompress zipped files. Current calendars for oral arguments from both courts are online.

Rules of court can be retrieved in zipped WordPerfect format. There is an extensive library of Alaska court rules mounted here and contains such titles as *Alaska Rules of Civil Procedure, Alaska Rules of Court, Alaska Rules of Appellate Procedure, Alaska Rules of Professional Conduct, Alaska Code of Judicial Conduct* and *Alaska Bar Rules*. Stay up-to-date with the electronic version of *Notice of Alaska Rule Changes* and *Legislative Changes to Rules of Court*. The courts library is at *http://www.alaska.net/~akctlib/libhrs.htm*

BAR ASSOCIATION

Bar association information is abundant and is housed on the server for the Alaska Court System home page at *http://www.alaska.net/~akctlib* Ethics opinions are online from 1990 to present. So too are lists of *Association Section Chairs, Fees and Deadlines*, the current month of *Section News* and a link to the e-mail addresses of the Association's staff.

STATE LIBRARY

The Alaska State Library is at *http://www.educ.state.ak.us/lam/library.html*

MISCELLANEOUS RESOURCES

Other links of interest to the legal researcher include connections to the Alaska Bureau of Vital Statistics where requests for documents such as certificates of birth, death, marriage and divorce can be filed electronically and paid for via online credit card.

The Alaska Judicial Council, the agency that selects new judges and evaluates current justices, publishes its by-laws and membership information at *http://www.ajc.state.ak.us*

The Justice Center at the University of Alaska, Anchorage is an academic, research and public education program serving the state that provides links to all the important state legal resources. Connect here for information on the paralegal certificate program and the Justice B.A. The address for the Justice Center is *http://www.uaa.alaska.edu/just*

The state Department of Law is at *http://www.law.state.ak.us*

Information on legal services to poor Alaskans provided by the Alaska Legal Services Corporation can be found at *http://www.alaska.net/~akctlib/legserv.htm*
❑

QuickLink
http://www.state.az.us

ARIZONA RESEARCH can begin at the governor's page where links to the executive, judicial and legislative branches greet the home page visitor.

EXECUTIVE RESOURCES

Like most governor's pages, the Arizona edition publishes the state of the state address and materials of political interest to the state's chief executive. This one is handsomely designed and provides fast connections from the home page to the *Arizona Department of Commerce*, the *Arizona Congressional Delegation* and the *Arizona Department of Library, Archives and Public Records*.

After the home page, however, there is a big graphical drop-off as the links lead to gopher servers for the different branches of government. The executive branch links connect to barely a quarter of all state agencies; the most important ones mounted on the gopher are *Department of Revenue, Office of the State Treasurer,* the *Secretary of State,* the *Insurance Department,* the *Corporation Commission, Department of Education* and the *Department of Health Services.* The governor's good Web start fizzles quickly with such a slim selection of online connections.

Arizona provides state tax forms online from the state Department of Revenue. They're available in PDF format, so you'll need an Adobe Acrobat reader. Forms included are the 120 Series for Corporate Income Tax, the 140 Series for Individual Income Tax, the 165 Series for Partnership returns, and a number of miscellaneous forms. Instructions are mounted separately. Find tax forms at *http://www.state.az.us/ dor* They're from 1996 and 1995.

LEGISLATIVE RESOURCES

The information story is happier from the Arizona State Legislature. Tune in to the lawmakers' page at *http://www.azleg.state.az.us* where a tidy body of legislative information awaits. ALIS Online is the Arizona Legislative Information Service and provides a dandy, push-button home page with which to navigate the legislature. Keyword searching through the Overviews, Introduced Bills and Engrossed Bills arrives by clicking on the hot button for Bills. The search page allows the researcher to select searches through the 43rd Legislature (1997-1998) or the 42nd Legislature (1995-1996); searches can be limited to all bills in the legislature or to bills from the first of two legislative sessions. Query hints and tips are installed on the page. Helpful accessories on the page include a Floor Calendar, Posting Sheets, a list of Members, a guide to the Legislative Process and a very informative FAQ File.

To search through the full text of the Arizona Revised Statutes, head directly to *http://www.azleg.state.az.us/ars/ars.htm* or click on the links mounted at the home page for the governor or at the legislature. Searching is by keyword; also look around by individual statutes arranged by title. Searches can be limited by title. Pull down from the search box at the top of the page to find a hypertext link to the text of all titles in alphabetical order. Click on the title to produce a search box to look across that particular section of the state code.

Other services from the state legislature are a clickable graphical map to locate *legislative districts*, a list of committees and their agendas and a link to other state legislatures. Also enjoy the online tour of the capitol district.

JUDICIAL MATERIALS

Judicial materials are slowly migrating to electronic servers in Arizona. The Arizona Judicial Department at *http://www.state.az.us/sp/attorn1.htm* divvies up its home page into links depending on interest: there are links of interest to the general public, the court community, attorneys, other government agencies and *students and teachers*. The link labeled for attorneys leads to pages containing the Supreme Court Oral Argument Schedule, Family Issues and Assistance, Judicial Vacancies, Judicial Selection and Performance Survey Results, the Commission on Judicial Conduct and the Arizona General Stream Adjudication.

Court decisions? Court of Appeals, Division 2 is online with *Recent Opinions* published within the preceding 90 days. Also find here case information from its online docket service. (Searching the dockets for particular cases is a little tricky. Be sure to read the instructions thoroughly.) The court mounts judges' biographies and information about the court staff. There's also the *oral argument calendar*.

Under continuous construction, the Arizona Courts page is at *http://www.apltwo.ct.state.az.us/othercrt.html* While all the links may not always be operative, there still is a worthwhile quantity of information to be found here. One interesting link leads to details about the "Courtroom of the Future" project that examines the use of new legal technologies in court settings. This is also the place to look for links to local courts; mounted here are Pima County Consolidated Justice Courts, Superior Court of Arizona in Maricopa County, Superior Court of Arizona in Pima County, Scottsdale City Court and *Tempe Municipal Court*. For quickie links to many legal resources in

Arizona, try the The Arizona Lawyer's Guide to the Internet. It's not earthshaking but there may be materials of local interest for the practitioner.

BAR ASSOCIATION

While the Arizona Bar Association had not yet created a Web site at the time of writing, a summary of the state bar regulations concerning attorney advertising are mounted at *http://www.legaldir.com/pi/bar/az.html*

Links to Arizona's Federal representatives are online. Senators Jon Kyl (*http://www.senate.gov/~kyl*) and John McCain (*http://www.senate.gov/senator/mccain.html*) each have their own home page containing biographies, committee assignments and a link for e-mail. The six Congressional representatives also have home pages. Find links to them at *http://aspin.asu.edu/~pctp/azdeleg.html*

LOCAL AND MUNICIPAL RESOURCES

Local governments are coming online too. There are Web sites for the *City of Phoenix*, the *City of Scottsdale*, *Pima County* and *Maricopa County*. Links to them are at *http://www.ci.phoenix.az.us* Anyone allergic to color and graphics can find an Arizona state gopher server that will spare the researcher all those annoying multimedia fripperies at *gopher://gopher.state.az.us* if it's still operational after 1996.

STATE LIBRARY

The Arizona Department of Library, Archives and Public Records gets handy with the microchips at its Web site at *http://www.dlapr.lib.az.us*

MISCELLANEOUS RESOURCES

For general information about Arizona, turn to the WebHub server at *http://www.rhinonet.com* where the Webmaster has published more than 1900 links to Arizona sites. Links are arranged alphabetically by subject. ❏

ARKANSAS lags the rest of the nation in the amount and quality of the legal materials it publishes online but it is slowly catching up with other, more information-friendly states.

EXECUTIVE RESOURCES

Start Arkansas research at the State of Arkansas home page where links to three branches of government will lead to basic information. The executive branch weighs in with the *Governor's Forum* and features the requisite *State of the State* transcript, governor's biography, calendar of appearances and the ubiquitous press releases. The governor's page is high-tech: download audio and video clips of such historic moments as the swearing-in of the governor and a speech delivered to the Rotary Club. Of such quaint uses is the Web now built and their usefulness to the legal researcher is elusive but ... they're there. For more substantive information, click on the link to *executive branch* from the State home page; the link opens to a fair number of state agencies including the departments of

Education, Employment Security, Health, Human Services, Computer Services, Labor and the State Library. Typical of the information mounted on the departmental servers is that available from the Department of Education: the page provides state-wide *Rules and Regulations, General Information* and *Licensure Information.* There is also a directory for the department and a description of the governing state board.

The Secretary of State hosts a Web site at *http://www.state.ar.us/sos/index.html* that is primarily of interest for election results and its collection of news releases from the Secretary. Look for the various offices under the direction of the Attorney General at *http://www.state.ar.us/ag/division.html* and for an e-mail link to the state's Ombudsman at *BobF@ag.state.ar.us*

The link to the Arkansas Crime Information Center hosts crime statistics for the state and provides links to law enforcement agencies and crime prevention services. Locate the page at *http://www.acic.org/*

Tax Handbook and Revenue Reports can be retrieved from the link to Research Reports. Most helpful for in-depth Arkansas legislative research though, are the links to *Other Research Resources* where connections can be made to the library at the University of Arkansas, Little Rock and its law school library. Other links lead out of state to *Other State Legislatures* and to federal resources.

The Arkansas Code is not available via the Internet as of this writing.

LEGISLATIVE MATERIALS

For legislative information, turn to *http://www.arkleg.state.ar.us* where a well-stocked Web site of data awaits. A link is provided to *Legislators and Committees* which contains member profiles and committee assignments. *Current Session Bills and Resolutions* are online. Search them via *Bill Title, Full Text of the Bill* or for *Specific Text*. Bills can be downloaded in Word or WordPerfect format; links are available to download Word document viewers for those researchers not already equipped with these popular software titles. The link to *Staff Organizations* leads to the Arkansas Bureau of Legislative Research and the Division of Legislative Audit.

The page for the Arkansas Senate at *http://www.arkleg.state.ar.us/data/senate.htm* is sadly, a single, info-starved page. The page for the Arkansas House of Representatives isn't much better nourished; outside of a one-page description of the chamber, there is not much else of value here.

JUDICIAL MATERIALS

The information resources from the Arkansas judiciary is considerably beefier than that from the legislative branch. Head to the *Arkansas Judiciary Home Page* at *http://www.state.ar.us/supremecourt/home.html* where the opinions of both the state's Supreme Court and Court of Appeals are published electronically. Opinions date from Spring 1996 for both courts and are organized by court session. The same page also contains an index to decided cases. Supreme Court decisions are loaded each Monday; corrected opinions with headnotes appear the following Friday. Court of Appeals decisions come online on Wednesdays and appear with headnotes and corrections on the Friday of the following week.

Look here as well for publication of current *Rule Changes* which can be downloaded in ASCII or WordPerfect 5.1 format.

The link to the *Supreme Court* provides a one-page description of functions of the court and a list of the Justices, lacking, alas, any supporting biographical data. Much the same information is available for the *Court of Appeals* on its page. Bibliophiles will appreciate the background information mounted by Arkansas' *Reporter of Decisions*; there's not a great deal of use to the researcher, but it is interesting.

BAR ASSOCIATION

The Arkansas Bar Association maintains its Web site at *http://www.arkbar.com/*

The page is simple but contains all the information the researcher would logically expect from a bar association page. There are links to background information from *About the Association*, a *Calendar of Events* and links to upcoming CLE programs. The Bar Association publishes a series of practice guides, available on paper or electronically, that includes such titles as: *Arkansas Debtor/Creditor Relations, Arkansas Law Office Handbook , Arkansas Bankruptcy Handbook, Arkansas Domestic Relations Handbook & Arkansas Probate Law System*.

Information about the *Bar Foundation*, the charitable arm of the Bar Association, is mounted and contains a description of the Foundation's purposes and its scholarship programs, research fellowships and special projects. Other links from the Bar's page lead to *Membership*, an *Organizational Directory, Committees and Sections, Public Information* and links to *Other Legal Sites*.

For extracts of rules concerning advertising by Arkansas lawyers, go to *http://www.legaldir.com/pi/bar/ar.html* where a simple summary of the regulations are published.

The *Daily Record*, the daily newspaper for the legal profession in the state can be retrieved from *http://www.nerosworld.com/dailyrecord* Links from the *Daily Record* lead to information about cases and e-mail links of interest to attorneys. However, the page is in need of updating since the most current reported court cases were more than four months old. More current reports can be found on the home page for the Arkansas judiciary.

STATE LIBRARY

The librarians of Arkansas check out books online at *http://www.state.ar.us/html/ark_library.html* ❑

QuickLink
http://www.ca.gov/servers.html

ALIFORNIA'S STATE LEGAL RESOURCES online are a model of how legal information can be disseminated electronically. The legal researcher will discover that pleasure of searching for information in the Golden State: it is well-organized, resources are current and professionally maintained and the databases are comprehensive. No other state compares to California when it comes to locating and retrieving state information. State Webmasters in other states are well advised to look at what California has achieved and emulate their success.

EXECUTIVE RESOURCES

Ordinarily, the governor's home page is the best place for taking the first step into any one state's legal materials. However, the executive branch is eclipsed by a specialized Web page headlined the *California State Government WWW & Gopher Servers & Bulletin Boards* at *http://www.ca.gov/servers.html* where links are located to every California state agency. The alphabetical list of agencies starts with the *Alcohol Beverage Control* and doesn't end until the researcher reaches *Water Resources*.

The links don't disappoint. Connections to any particular agency lead to extraordinarily detailed pages containing extensive links to reg-

ulations, news releases and agency directories. A representative state agency Web server is the one from the *State Treasurer's Office* at *http://www.treasurer.ca.gov/* Handsome, push-button links take the visitor to a trove of useful materials including *Boards, Authorities and Commissions, Bond Sales, Redemptions & Official Statements, Financial Statements, Current Budget and Finances, Special Issues, Credit Ratings* and a special report from the State Treasurer on Pacific Rim trade. This single page highlights the way the Internet can be harnessed to deliver public data to the public at a minimal cost. An even more practical use of the Internet will be when the links to the agencies of the *Secretary of State* become fully operational and researchers will be able to hook into *Corporate* filings, *Limited Partnerships, Uniform Commercial Code* filings, executive links and *Information Technology* and then fetch these voluminous files with the click of a mouse.

LEGISLATIVE RESOURCES

The executive branch is not the only division of state government charging headlong into an information-rich future. The California State Legislature is also taking advantage of the powers of Internet technology to make legislative materials readily available online. Start legislative research at *Legislative Counsel* page at *http://www.leginfo.ca.gov/* This is the official site for legislative materials in the state and contains helpful hints on searching for legislation. First-time researchers should turn to *A Guide for Accessing California Legislative Information on the Internet* at *http://www.leginfo.ca.gov/ guide.html* for a simple tutorial that explains the main concepts underlying online legislative research. The Legislative Counsel links to Assembly and Senate bills and is also well-connected with additional links to state legislative sites.

The Senate server at

http://www.sen.ca.gov or the Assembly site at *http://ais3.assembly.ca.gov/acs/default.asp* themselves connect to a breathtaking amount of valuable legislative data. The State Assembly's bill search page not only permits searching across a database of some 100,000 bills, it also allows *Watches* to be set to monitor developments in specific legislative initiatives. The search engine is designed to search bills in either house or both at the same time. Intuitive-to-use scroll boxes help pinpoint searches by *Session, House, Type of Bill* and a variety of informative sub-types. Bill texts are available from 1994 to present. In addition to the searchable bill texts are directory-style entries for legislators, a legislative calendar and links to Republican and Democratic caucuses.

California is unstinting in its access to the State Code. The easiest site for searching through the unannotated statutes is at *http://www.leginfo.ca.gov/calaw.html* Select individual code sections to search -- *Corporations, Penal, Probate*, etc. -- and then plug in the keyword search terms. Searching is fast and painless. To look at the *Table of Contents* of any selected code title, select a code and punch the *search* button without adding any keywords.

JUDICIAL MATERIALS

The California judiciary is no less enthusiastic about the Internet than the other branches of government. A convenient home page for the *Judicial Branch, State of California* at *http://www.courtinfo.ca.gov* is an excellent starting point for accessing court decisions, documents and background information. In particular, look for the link to California Courts at *http://www.courtinfo.ca.gov/cacourts/cacourts.htm* for a comprehensive collection of links to court materials. That page is the single most detailed judicial page available for any state's court system in the nation. From this page, jump to:

- *Opinions of the Supreme Court and Court of Appeals;*
- *An index page leading to California*

court Web sites;
- *Information on members of the Supreme Court, Courts of Appeal, Superior Courts and Municipal Courts;*
- *Commission on Judicial Appointments and Commission on Judicial Performance*

In short, California provides its citizens -- and the citizens of the Internet -- with electronic access to virtually all of its judicial activities. Connections are mounted here for the Judicial Council; and while Judicial Council Forms are not yet online -- a company called Multimedia Abacus Corporation is offering the forms for free at *http://www.mmacorp.com* to promote their other products but that may only be temporary -- but links to the commercial publishers supplying them are.

BAR ASSOCIATION

The State Bar of California maintains its own Web site at *http://www.calbar.org* and is, without question, the most information-packed and informative bar Web site in the country. Highlights of this extensive site include a rundown on the state bar itself and its organization, information resources that include referral services, online member records and links to the *California Bar Journal.* Find up-to-date news about pending legislation and public comment proposals on the page as well. The home page provides a handy search engine to search through this elaborate Web site. It is a superbly well-designed and useful site for all California attorneys.

The amount of information of interest to the legal researcher in California is seemingly limitless. In addition to state materials, municipalities, cities and counties are heading to the electronic world too. City courts, local governments and quasi-public corporations all have -- or shall have in the near future -- their own Web sites. California also leads the nation in the number of wired law firms. Due perhaps to the concentration of high-technology clients in the state, California firms are a substantial presence on the Web and provide newsletters, memos and other information of use to the researcher. ❑

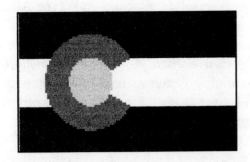

QuickLink

http://www.state.co.us/
gov_dir/govmenu.html

COLORADO'S LEGAL INFORMATION resources on the Internet are not flashy but they are complete. All the basic materials for legal research into Colorado law are available for the researcher. And if Colorado law is not as detailed as that from California, it is still possible to refer to the online resources with confidence in the completeness of the data sources.

EXECUTIVE RESOURCES

Colorado's executive branch is represented by the governor's page at *http://www.state.co.us/gov_dir/governor_office.html* where anyone in dire need of the governor's biography or a transcript of the most recent State of the State addresses will find both prominently published. There are the usual press releases mounted here. So are links to some of the governor's policy initiatives such as the *Responsible Fatherhood Initiative Task Force Report, Child Care* and *Colorado Smart Growth and Development*. Related offices are linked here; most interesting is the *Governor's Advocate Corps* which provides pointers for finding help from government offices in the state.

The office of the Attorney General is getting under way online; the page is under construction. Links are incomplete but it's clearly apparent that the AG will be adding useful materials in the near future.

The Secretary of State provides an online subscription service called *Direct Access* that will connect the agency's *corporation records, UCC filings* and *election information*. This is a fee-based service; details are available from the Secretary of State's home page at *http://www.state.co.us/gov_dir/sos/diracces.html*

Colorado's executive agencies are, for the most part, online. All the major agencies have home pages. Check with the State Government page at *http://www.state.co.us/gov_dir/govmenu.html* for the most complete list of connections to Colorado agencies.

JUDICIAL MATERIALS

The home page for Colorado's state courts is at *http://www.rmii.com/slv/courts/colcts.htm* There the researcher will find links to the Colorado Supreme Court and the Court of Appeals from this page; the Supreme Court page contains biographies of the justices and copies of Supreme Court advance sheets. Direct link to advance sheets -- cleverly called "e-slips" --is at *http://www.cobar.org/coappcts/scndx.htm* Decisions are available for the most recent four month period and generally are mounted on Monday. Court of Appeals decisions are at *http://www.cobar.org/coappcts/ctappndx.htm* and are also current to within the past four months. They usually appear on Thursday. The case decisions are presented thanks to the Colorado Bar Association at *http://www.cobar.org/index.html* and the Colorado Legal Alliance at *http://www.usa.net/cololaw/ index.htm*

LEGISLATIVE MATERIALS

The legislature of Colorado doesn't have an official site, but unofficial state legislative information can be tracked down at *http://www.state.co.us/gov_dir/stateleg.html* Mounted here are the calendars for the Senate and House, status sheets for pending bills, the text of current bills and the latest journals from both houses. The *Legislative Council Staff* prepares research for use by the General Assembly and some of those reports are reprinted in PDF format at *http://www.state.co.us/gov_dir/leg_dir/lcs/index.html* Among the titles mounted here are *Colorado Medicaid Case Load Projections, Department of Corrections Population Projections* and *Preliminary Pre-Kindergarten through Twelfth Grade Enrollment Projections.*

Colorado statutes are online but they are not current. Find older versions of the state code at *http://www.aescon.com/crs95/tables.htm* The current code version can be accessed online for a fee from a company called *iway hyperdocs.* An annual subscription is $40; quarterly access is $15 per quarter. Also find an annotated version of the 1994 code from the Pikes Peak Library District gopher at *gopher://peak.ppld.org:70/11/Government/* Select the link to *Colorado State Statutes.*

Like the statutes, Colorado Rules are available from the same online publisher. Connect to *iway hyperdocs* at *http://www.aescon.com/iway/index.htm* for details.

BAR ASSOCIATION

The Bar Association operates a home page containing a list of committees, sections and links to local bar associations.

This is the page to hit for information on upcoming CLE events, membership benefits and lengthy description of the bar's magazine *Colorado Lawyer.*

The home page for the Colorado Legal Alliance should be bookmarked by any researcher in need of regular Colorado legal materials. The page connects to *statutes, Colorado law by prac-tice area, government agencies* and *Forms.*

Colorado's Federal officials maintain Web sites themselves. Connect to Wayne Allen at *http://www.senate.gov/senate/allard.html* Ben Nighthorse-Campbell is at *http://www.senate.gov/senate/campbell.html* All of Colorado's Congressional representatives have Web sites as well. Find links to all of them at *http://www.state.co.us/gov_dir/COreps.html*

LOCAL AND MUNICIPAL RESOURCES

Local links abound in Colorado. Some of the municipalities online now are the City of Vail at *http://vail.net* and both Boulder City and Boulder County government via the Boulder Community Network *http://bcn.boulder.co.us*

Colorado law firms are joining up to the Internet like firms throughout the nation. Find a listing of Colorado attorneys from the list at Martindale-Hubbell at *http://www.martindale.com* or the list from the Westlaw Legal Directory at *http://www.wld.com*

There is also a good lookup service for local law firms from Washburn's server at *http://lawlib.wuacc.edu*

STATE LIBRARY

Librarians take note: Colorado is home to CARL, the Colorado Alliance of Research Libraries at *http://www.carl.org* This invaluable research facility, now a part of Knight-Ridder Information Service, is a standard tool for reference librarians and should be on every legal researcher's Hot List of must-not-miss sites. Visit the home page for more information on CARL's many services. ACLIN is the *Access Colorado Library and Information Network* which links the state's libraries to provide a comprehensive net of library resources. The home page for ACLIN is at *http://www.cde.state.co.us/aclin.htm* ❏

State of Connecticut

QuickLink
http://www.state.ct.us/

CONNECTICUT MAKES RESEARCH easy by placing links to all the leading law-related sites right on the state's official home page.

The State of Connecticut Web site at *http://www.state.ct.us* joins a list of logically placed links in a columnar frame with a search engine that will zip the researcher directly into any particular state site required. Thanks to such streamlined design, looking up Connecticut legal materials is virtually effortless.

EXECUTIVE RESOURCES

The link to *executive* from the official site delivers a page that will subsequently connect to the home page for the *Governor,* the *Lieutenant Governor, Secretary of State, Treasurer, Comptroller* and the *Attorney General.* The Webs for the Chief Executive and the Lieutenant contain political information for the most part; more practical legal information is available from the other pages.

The Secretary of State's Web site at *http://www.state.ct.us/sots/* does not yet allow electronic access to corporation, limited partnership or other commercial filings, but the office does mount a fee schedule from the *Commercial Recording Division.* A link to *Forms* was under construction when we looked, but when this service is operational, it ought to prove useful in

supplying the requisite forms in electronic format to the public. Most of the other connections lead to directory-style data for the agency and its sub-offices.

The Attorney General's page packs a great of useful material into a simple, frame-constructed Web page. The home page at *http://www.cslnet.ctstateu.edu/attygenl/* produces links to *Formal Opinions, Press Releases, Consumer Tips, Publications, Business Issues* and news on *Child Support.* The page even included a special link in January 1997 to handle complaints against America Online in the wake of their latest service outage. Many of the links are topical and current; the Connecticut researcher should check on the page regularly for updates.

Other executive agency servers are not as well-stocked with useful information as the AG's site nor is the list of agencies online comprehensive. While many Connecticut agencies operate Web sites, most do not. The leading wired offices are such departments as *Agriculture, Banking, Consumer Protection, Corrections, Environmental Protection, Labor, Motor Vehicles, Revenue Services* and *Transportation.* The *Ethics Commission* is also online. Links are on the state's home page.

JUDICIAL MATERIALS

Judicial opinions from the Nutmeg State are not yet on the Internet. Connecticut operates an *Electronic Bulletin Board Service* for the online retrieval of appellate slip opinions, Supreme Court decisions, the weekly publication *Connecticut Law Journal* and selected brochures from the Judicial branch. Information about subscription fees and the requisites needed to access the BBS are mounted at the judicial Web site at *http://www.cslnet.ctstateu.edu/colp/ebbs.htm*

The Commission on Official Legal Publications publishes an online price sheet with ordering information at *http://www.cslnet.ctsta-*

teu.edu/colp/prices.htm Refer to this page to order such official publications as *Connecticut Reports* and *Connecticut Appellate Reports.*

The judicial home page leads to information on the state's courts and a judicial directory. Links to Supreme Court and Appellate Court Judges connect to professional biographies.

LEGISLATIVE RESOURCES

For legislative research, there is a Web page containing a link to search for bills by bill number or title at the state's home page. Connect here for access to legislative journals and bulletins -- though the links were inoperative when we tried them. The Connecticut *General Assembly* has a page containing current *Public Acts* and a *Legislative Bulletin* at *http://www.ntplx.net/~swlewis/* The site is not officially sanctioned but is operated by Stephen W. Lewis, the Committee Administrator for General Assembly's Public Health Committee on his own time at his own expense as a public service.

A useful page for first-time researchers is the *Connecticut Legislative Guide,* published by the Office of Legislative Management at *http://www.ctstateu.edu/state/legislative_guide/legis_guide.html* Also of interest are the Web sites operated by the leading political parties. The Senate Democrats have a site at *http://www.senatedems.state.ct.us/* to highlight the activities of the party's legislators. The Republicans sponsor Web sites for both the House and the Senate.

The Senate Republicans can be found at *http://www.senatereps.state.ct.us/* while the House GOP delegation is at *http://www.senatereps.state.ct.us/* Both sites are most useful for their links to individual lawmakers and the other directory information mounted on the page.

The *General Statutes of Connecticut* are online but the Internet version is seriously out of date. However, it's possible to search the January 1, 1995 edition of the state code at *http://www.cslnet.ctstateu.edu/statutes/index.htm*

To access Connecticut's Federal legislators, head to *http://www.state.ct.us/das/*

ushouse.htm for a list of representatives and to *http://www.state.ct.us/das/ussenate.htm* for its Senators.

BAR ASSOCIATION

Locate the Connecticut Bar Association at *http://www.ctbar.org/index.htm* where a *Calendar of Events* is mounted along with a list of *Publications, Sections and Committees* and selections from the bar association's magazine *Connecticut Lawyer.* The link to the magazine also contains classified and employment ads, making it a useful resource for Connecticut job seekers. The link to *Legal Resources* provides a fair collection of the leading Internet law sites.

While cruising around Connecticut online, don't miss what has to be the most unusual domain name we've seen yet. It's from the New Haven law firm of Early, Ludwick & Sweeney L.L.C. which specializes in the representation of workers occupationally exposed to asbestos The URL? It's *http://www.mesothelioma.com/attorney.htm*

LOCAL AND MUNICIPAL RESOURCES

There's an index page for all Connecticut municipalities at the state home page. The municipality Web site is intended to link all 169 towns and cities in the state from one page. Most, but not all, municipalities are represented. Other states should turn to *Municipality Public Access Initiative* as an example of how to effectively link up town and city halls across each state.

The *Connecticut Development Authority* provides financial assistance to "a broad range of business activities with a focus on economic development and job creation" according to its home page. The page is at *http://www.state.ct.us/cda/*

STATE LIBRARY

Librarians can find extensive links to state libraries at *http://spirit.lib.uconn.edu/ConnState/Libraries.html* ❑

QuickLink
http://www.state.de.us/
govern/intro.htm

DELAWARE IS A SMALL STATE and it should find the Internet to be a means to play on an equal footing with other states, especially in light of Delaware's preeminent position as a national center for corporate law. Unfortunately, the law resources mounted here are disappointing. As the by-word in corporate law, the legal researcher would naturally assume that decisions from the Delaware's influential Court of Chancery would be prominent on Delaware's public Web sites, given the importance to the state -- and the nation's corporations -- of Delaware's business corporation law and body of case law. Sorry to report that the court has not yet mounted case decisions from what is perhaps the most important corporate jurisdiction in the nation and Delaware has not yet mounted its all-important corporate filings. We're hoping this oversight will be quickly corrected.

EXECUTIVE RESOURCES

But, to move from things-that-are-not-there to things that are, head directly to the best

point of entry to Delaware research at the official *State Government* page appearing at *http://www.state.de.us/govern/intro.htm* The researcher can connect to all the leading state resources, from the governor's office to an online phone directory for the State Government. Links to all branches of the state government are available on the page.

For executive branch information, bypass the governor's mansion and head straight to the government page. The link to *State Agencies* produces a list of those offices throughout the state that have wired to the Internet and the list comprises almost all of the executive offices.

The governor's home page is moderately informative, but considering the length of time this megabyte rich page takes to load across an ordinary 28,800 modem, the journey is barely worth the wait. The page is a standard off-the-shelf gubernatorial affair containing the governor's biography, state of the state address, a link to the governor's cabinet and most importantly, a connection to *Delaware's State Government.*

Page content varies. The Public Service Commission, for instance, provides links to *New Orders, Public Notice of Proceedings, Major Issues, Agenda/Calendar* and *Matters Pending,* creating an informative and useful Web site. Other agencies are considerably stingier with the information and restrict themselves to directory data and e-mail links to the Webmaster.

Sorry to report that the Webmasters of Delaware also drop the ball on the executive level by merely reporting a telephone number for the all-important *Division of Corporations,* thereby completely ignoring the Internet's powerful capabilities for delivering the state's corporate archives directly to the public at a minimal cost.

In other departments around the state, the researcher will find other sites to be more helpful. Ever willing to help online users plunge into the revenue stream, locate current state tax forms in PDF format at Delaware's Division of Revenue's gopher at *http://www.state.de.us/ govern/agencies/revenue/form96/*

The *State Government Telephone Directory* is online at *http://www.lib.de.us/gov-law/DE/phone.html*

LEGISLATIVE MATERIALS

For legislative materials, the Delaware General Assembly page at *http://www.state.de.us/govern/agencies/legis/lis.h tm* won't win any prizes for graphic excellence, but access to full-text retrieval of bills from the current and recently completed legislative session is quick and easy. Click on the link to the *Bill Tracking System* to pull up a search page well-furnished with scroll boxes to look up legislation by *Bill Prefix* (*House Bill, House Resolution, Senate Concurrent Resolution,* etc.), *Bill Number, Sponsor, Bill Title* and *Current Status.* Bills are available for the 138th and 139th General Assembly. The page also links to the daily agenda for both houses, committee agendas and meeting notices, and so-called "Ready Lists," the legislature's "To-Do" list.

JUDICIAL MATERIALS

Materials from Delaware's courts are maddeningly scarce. There are no judicial decisions; the links for the courts are simply text narratives of each jurisdiction's workload and court history, thus creating a Web site very like a rhinoceros: very interesting but not practical to keep at the office. Look around, but don't expect any greatly valuable body of common law to pop up from a Delaware server.

The Delaware law firm of Morris, James, Hitchens & Williams maintains a Web site at *http://www.morrisjames.com/* and stocks it with

articles about current issues in Delaware law. They've also published an easy-to-read article that answers the frequently-heard corporate research question, "Why do corporations pick Delaware?" Find the materials along the link for *Newsletters and Legal Commentary.* Also find *Delaware Jury Verdicts and Settlements* from the firm of Morlan & Associates, P.C. at *http://www.morelaw.com/verdicts.html*

STATE LIBRARY

Librarian alert! Connect to DelAWARE, the state's online library system at *http://www.lib.de.us/* Connections can be made to public, state and academic libraries but the one of greatest importance to the legal researcher is the link to *Law and Legislative Libraries.*

MISCELLANEOUS RESOURCES

For a statistical picture of the great state of Delaware, the number-crunchers have re-posted data from the Bureau of the Census at *http://www.state.de.us/govern/agencies/dedo/ dsdc/dsdc.htm* Demographics, economics, geography, quick facts and a *Delaware Statistical Overview* await the intrepid researcher, who is rewarded with a lode of interesting nuggets of data about the state. For clients interested in actually, physically setting up businesses in Delaware, the Delaware Economic Development Office forks over information about its financial assistance packages it makes available to businesses aiming to operate within the state. Find the details at *http://www.state.de.us/govern/agencies/dedo/bsufin.htm*

To get in touch with Delaware's Federal officials, head to the link on the government page for *Elected Officials;* that will escort you to the links for Delaware's Senators and its lone Representative. ❏

QuickLink
http://www.dos.state.fl.us/
fgils/

FLORIDA STATE LAW RESEARCH could not be made any simpler, easier or more elegant. As a rule, Web pages from Florida's public agencies are brilliantly designed and jammed with the type of information all states should be making public on the Web. The Webmasters of Florida have achieved a first-rate network of public data. And thanks to the one-stop shop *Florida Government Information Locator Service*, a self-described "virtual card catalog of government information," finding Florida law resources is a snap.

This plain-Jane page gives no hint of the amount of information waiting for the researcher just beyond the next hypertext link but it's extensive. Find the page at *http://www.dos.state.fl.us/fgils/* set sail to every informational port across the state. Bookmark this page if regular Florida research is necessary. It's a great index.

EXECUTIVE RESOURCES

The hunt for executive branch materials can begin at Florida's Governor's page which is shared in an arrangement unique to Florida with six elected state Cabinet members. As is typical of governor pages, this one contains the usual

array of press releases, budget announcements, biographical information and a link to documents produced by the chief executive's office. The page is at *http://www.eog.state.fl.us/eoghome.htm*

All state agencies are online, furnishing electronic access to commissioners, forms, profiles of the agencies and personnel across the state. The home page for state agencies is at *http://www.dos.state.fl.us/fgils/agencies.html* Find Florida's state commissions and boards at *http://www.dos.state.fl.us/fgils/boards.html*

To see what service a Web site can provide to the legal profession, look at what Florida's Attorney General has published in his page. Here are *legal opinions*, including a searchable database of AG opinions, *news releases*; information on Government in Sunshine; detailed reports on criminal justice initiatives; a report for law enforcement agencies setting out a guide to the use of public records; Florida's *Lemon Law* and other links that the AG from each state ought to provide to the citizens of the Internet.

The Webmaster who designed the page for the Department of State gets our award for graphic excellence; it is one of the best. Not only does the page light up with artistic pizzazz, it's also got links to some of the most interesting sites around the state, such as metalinks to the government, directories, information on Florida's *Digital Signature Act* and information for would-be business owners.

LEGISLATIVE MATERIALS

The Florida Legislature, like other governmental bodies in the Sunshine State, operates a graphically lovely page that overflows with data. The page at *http://www.leg.state.fl.us/* is a good place to begin legislative research; look here for a guide to the hot issues under debate and a calendar guide to the legislature's activities. Florida thoughtfully provides *Lobbyist*

Information, disclosing lobbyist's clients and the linking to relevant lobbying regulations. There are the expected links to state representatives and senators with biographical information and committee assignments.

Cruising for bill texts is a gopherized operation at *http://www.scri.fsu.edu/fla-leg/bills/* There's no fancy graphics like other Florida sites but the links do the job, hooking up with search engines to plow through bills from both chambers dating from 1995 and including the current legislature. Search by chamber. A separate gopher exists for *Bill Information.* Refer to *http://www.scri.fsu.edu/fla-leg/bill-info/* for background information on particular bills.

Statutes? Where some states haven't gotten around to publishing their codes online yet, Florida not only dispatches its code to an HTML server, it also mounts the full text of the code -- with supplements! -- for the past three years. This is an invaluable service to the researcher because it enables the comparative review of changes to code sections for the recent past. Search the entire Florida code at *http://www.leg.state.fl.us/statutes/index.html* Now if only some enterprising state librarian gets around to annotating the text, the researchers of the world would be in information heaven.

The administrative code is not online in its entirety although relevant bits and pieces of it are sometimes available from the home page of those agencies promulgating the rules. however, the *Administrative Weekly* can be searched and downloaded from *http://election.dos.state.fl.us/faw/index.htm*

JUDICIAL MATERIALS

The Florida court system has its own home page called *JOSHUA* (Judicial Online Super-Highway User Access System) at *http://justice.courts.State.fl.us/* Big fat pushbuttons on the page lead to a help menu, an overview of the Florida court system, data on court administration and, most importantly, the full text of opinions from the Supreme Court dating from September 1995. Florida also makes it easy to

comply with court rules; links lead not only to the current *Enacted Rules* but also to *Proposed Rules.*

The Supreme Court runs a terrific page at *http://justice.courts.state.fl.us:80/courts/supct/bookmark.html* with superb links to primary state law resources. Each link is briefed on the page and all of them lead to substantial information sites. In addition to this virtual reference desk for Florida jurisprudence, find links to the state's justices mounted on a frame column.

BAR ASSOCIATION

The *Florida Bar Association* keeps pace with other Florida Web resources with its home page at *http://ww3.pwr.com/LEGAL/FLABAR/toc.html* The page is extraordinarily detailed; there's membership and committee information, links to such agencies as *Florida Board of Bar Examiners,* the *Florida Bar Foundation* and *Judicial Qualifications Commission.* The page also publishes *Rules Regulating the Florida Bar* and *Ethics Opinions.* This is place to go for *The Florida Bar Journal* and related publications.

The *Florida Law Weekly* is available online by subscription. Subscription information is at *http://www.polaris.net/~flw/flw.htm*

STATE LIBRARY

Librarians with a chronic need for Florida information should copy the URL for Florida's Libraries and Library Resources into the bookmark file right now: it's *http://www.dos.fl.us/fgils/library.html* There are catalogs galore here, an archival collection of government records from state and local sources and a link to the state's *Photographic Collection.*

LOCAL AND MUNICIPAL RESOURCES

Local governments within the state can be searched from the Web site from the *Florida Communities Network* at *http://fcn.state.fl.us/fcn/3/index.html* Directories and other reference data are mounted here. ❑

QuickLink

http://www.ganet.org/services/

GEORGIA, LIKE MANY OTHER forward-looking states, is rapidly moving their public documents into the electronic paradigm. And while the legal information selections from Georgia are not as comprehensive as those from California or Florida, there is still a great deal already mounted that the researcher can locate via the Internet.

LEGISLATIVE MATERIALS

Start with *GeorgiaNet* at *http://www.ganet.org/services* where a page connecting to legislative services appears by default. The page is set up to search through the bill text of the current session, however, there is also a scroll box that can provide bill text from sessions going back to 1995. The search mechanisms are simple. Select from on online menu to search by *keyword, bill number, code section* or *by date*. It's also possible to search by *author, committee* and *sponsor*. To track down the number of a bill, refer to the handy index to bills and resolutions from both chambers.

There are two interesting innovations on the page. One is called "Lobbyist-in-a-Box" and provides electronic monitoring of pending legislation. Subscribers to Lobbyist-in-a-Box can create a list of bills to monitor and then receive updated status reports on those bills. The other is a LiveAudio link to the House of Representatives permitting audio-equipped Netizens to enjoy every rhetorical nuance of Georgia's hard-working legislators. There are also the expected calendars, meeting notices and press kits. Novice legislative researchers may turn to the helpful online *Training Manual.* Lobbyist-in-a-Box and the daily press pack are both premium services from GeorgiaNet and require a subscription. Click on the link for additional information at the bottom of the page.

While GeorgiaNet's home page concentrates on legislative materials, refer to the left-hand frame column to find a link to the Georgia Code. The search page pops up to offer the researcher one of two means for searching through the full (unannotated) text of the code: by *keyword* or by *code number*. Either way, searching is fast, accurate and efficient. Results are returned with the header of the code section and a hypertext link to the full text. The administrative code, alas, has not yet migrated to the world of public servers yet.

Georgia has wired up its state agencies. The same GeorgiaNet page contains a clickable icon to state agencies; the page is utilitarian but the links are extensive and most state agencies are represented with a Web site.

There are some other links that make GeorgiaNet worthy of bookmarking. A pay-for service allows researchers to search through *Corporate Records.* (Is Delaware listening?) There's also a link for the *Procurement Registry,* which is of interest to anyone seeking to do business with the state. Last, the *Department of Banking and Finance* maintains a link here to its Web site containing basic information on the institutions it regulates and how the department is organized.

EXECUTIVE RESOURCES

With so many executive branch agencies and services already online at one index page, it may not be necessary even to visit the Georgia governor's home page. However, anyone pinched for a copy of the State of the State address can find an electronic version of the same at *http://www.ganet.org/gov/* along with clicks to the First Lady and gubernatorial programs. More governor-sponsored resources are at *http://www.state.ga.us* at the server for the *Georgia Online Network*.

JUDICIAL RESOURCES

Georgia's courts are up and running on the Web too. The Supreme Court mounts its page at *http://www.state.ga.us/Courts/Supreme/* and fills it with *Case Summaries, Recent Certioraris* and the full text of the *Rules and Procedures of the Supreme Court* and the *Rules and Procedures of the Court of Appeals*. The *Court Calendar* is kept current. That's all very well but the full text of Supreme Court opinions or Court of Appeals decisions have yet to bound onto the electronic scene. Still, this is a good start for reporting judicial information and it's apparent from the state of other public Georgia sites that the judiciary will likely follow suit and add substantial decisions to their Web site. Biographies of the justices and and overview of the operations of the Court are available at *http://www.state.ga.us/Courts/Supreme/scbroch.htm*

BAR ASSOCIATION

The State Bar of Georgia conducts its online business from a server at *http://www.gabar.org* A simple table of pushbuttons connects to the standard links: *Departments and Programs, Sections & Committees, Pro Bono activities, Upcoming Meetings* and a *Directory* for *Bar Staff, Officers and the Board of Governors*. Also click here to get to the *Office of the General Counsel, CLE Information* and an informative *FAQ* file. The *Office of the General Counsel* keeps an index to Formal Advisory Opinions on its Web site, as well as *Disciplinary Charts, Ethics Rules* and *Tips on Setting Up and Maintaining a Trust (Escrow) Account*.

The state bar, however, is not the only place to find information for and on Georgia attorneys. Find the excellent Atlanta Bar Association Web site at *http://www.atlantabar.org/* where the researcher discovers an elaborate and informative page. Membership information and Section Information and News, the staples of a bar association Web site are mounted here. This is also the place to look for CLE programs coming up in the city. Link from the home page to the newsletter, membership applications, the NetForum, a unique bulletin board service/listserv for the Atlanta bar. This prototype ought to be emulated by every other wired bar association because it is a simple, low-cost way for local attorneys to discuss issues of importance in their own jurisdiction.

MISCELLANEOUS RESOURCES

One of the best attorney home pages anywhere on the Internet is run by Georgia attorney Jeffrey Kuester. Kuester operates *KuesterLaw -- The Technology Law Resource* at *http://www.kuesterlaw.com* He's mounted an extraordinary amount of information on his site, including links to Georgia law. In keeping with his practice, most of the links refer to Intellectual Property law; of special interest is his collection of links to articles about Georgia's Internet law. This is also the best place to go for links to local Georgia bar associations

Like Utah, Georgia is addressing the concerns of digital commerce with its *Digital Signature Task Force*. Details are at *http://www.cc.emory.edu/BUSINESS/gds.html*

The Fulton County Law Library at *http://www.mindspring.com/~fclawlib/* is a handy reference page, listing new acquisitions, library hours, details on library services and legal research guides.

Look for the *Atlanta Legal Aid Society* at *http://www.law.emory.edu/PI/ALAS/* Links are artfully arranged under subject headings for *News and Announcements, Departments and Activities, Community Education, People and Operations* and *Contact Information and Special Interest*. ❑

HAWAII (or *Hawai'i* as the official Web sites refers to it) temporarily operated a first-rate legislative service but the Internet connection is no longer available. That's bad news for the legal researcher in need of Hawaiian materials because the replacement data is incomplete and scattered throughout the Web on different servers.

The state government server is weak broth, indeed, but it still is the best centrally located server for Hawaiian legal materials on the network but don't get your hopes up. The page at *http://www.hawaii.gov* does link to all the branches of government

LEGISLATIVE RESOURCES

For aid in legislative research, tune in to the Hawaii Legislative Research Bureau's *Virtual Reference Desk* with its links to Hawaiian information hooked up to a telnet connection -- a telnet client is required. Click on the icon to connect to the telnet session, then select *1. Access* to get to the Hawaii State Legislature. Legislative affairs are sleepy in the islands and the paucity of legislative information is in keeping with the laid-back governing style. The legislature convenes every January for a session

that can last "up to 60 days" according to the gopher page describing the body.

Find a directory of all state, county and federal officials from the Hawaii Legislative Reference Bureau Library at *http://www.hawaii.gov/lrb/dir/dirdoc.html* It's also the page to go for *Reports and Studies, Administrative Rules, Directories and Tables* and a publication for *Bills Passed.*

JUDICIAL MATERIALS

For materials from Hawaii's courts, surf over to the state judiciary's home page at *http://www.hawaii.gov/jud/index.html* but don't expect any overwhelming archive of court decisions. There are only three links on the home page; *Mission Statements* are little more than a gopher-mounted description of Hawaii's various courts. The *Directory* is a more colorful Web site, with in-depth background information on state justices, but still no body of reported law. *What's New* provides news of the courts such as personnel shifts and judicial appointments. "New" is a misnomer since what was mounted when last consulted was at least four months old.

EXECUTIVE RESOURCES

The executive agencies in Hawaii are wired, starting with the governor's office at *http://hoohana.aloha.net/~gov/* Like all governors, the first order of Internet business is republishing the State of the State address on a Web page and this page is no exception. Biographical information and press releases are there too.

To get direct access to the pages mounted by Hawaii's agencies, zip to the gopher page at *http://www.hawaii.gov/icsd/dept.html* Click on the abbreviated links for each agency to call up its page. Most agencies are online; those that aren't should be wired in the very near future, judging by the place-saving inclusion of the not-yet-Webbed agencies on the executive agency roster printed at this page. Agency pages are informative as a rule. There is usually a message from the administrator , press releases, a run-down of what each particular agency does and links to other information. Usually, but not always, a directory for the agency is published on the page.

The Hawaii State Code is not yet avail-able for searching. Neither is the state's adminis-trative code.

MISCELLANEOUS RESOURCES

Hawaii provides a fair body of miscella-neous legal materials.

A selection of state tax forms can be downloaded from the State of Hawaii Depart-ment of Taxation at *http://www.hawaii.gov/tax/96forms.html* Forms are in PDF format and contain instructions for forms since 1995. The department also publishes a quarterly *Tax Facts* and *Tax Information Releases* along with a num-ber of brochures describing the general excise tax, the use tax and withholding of state income tax by employers.

For businesses considering re-locating to the middle of the Pacific Ocean, refer to the *State of Hawaii Data Book* at *http://www.hawaii.gov:8080/databook/* where a 24-section portrait of the state awaits. The state is also thoughtful enough to provide a statistical report on Hawaii's Labor and Employment mar-ket at *http://www.hawaii.gov/workforce/*

With real estate and tourism such impor-tant components of Hawaii's economy, these industries are well-documented online. The *Hawaii Real Estate Commission* has put *General Information for Real Estate License* online (and apparently hiring Charlie Chan's English tutor to write headlines.) The regulations are at *http://www.hawaii.gov/hirec/blue.htm/*

The tourism industry is given a Web site for the Tourism Office and the Visitor's Bureau. In fact, there's even a *Tourism Library*. Find these sites, respectively, at

http://www.hawaii.gov/tourism/
http://www.visit.hawaii.org/
http://www.hawaii.gov/tourism/
Library.html

BAR ASSOCIATION

To connect with the Hawaii Bar Association, aim for *http://www.hsba.org/* There the researcher will find links to an an index of Supreme Court and Intermediate Court of Appeals cases (even though the link promises opinions) and abstracts of cases organized in a subject index. Also mounted at the bar page are *Attorney General Opinions, Corporation Counsel Opinions, Disciplinary Board Opinions* and *Office of Information Practices Opinions*. The link for *Legal Articles and Publications* pro-duces an *index* to the *Hawaii Bar Journal*, arti-cles and index for the Disciplinary Board, ABA publications and other indices. The bar main-tains a bulletin board service called *AccessLine* that requires a subscription; details are published at *http://www.hsba.org/Hawaii/broc.htm*

Hawaii is actively encouraging high-tech companies to locate in the state. The *High Technology Development Corporation*, accord-ing to its home page, exists to "to facilitate the development and growth of commercial high technology industry in Hawaii." To do that, the Web site connects to a series of state-run pro-jects such as the *Manoa Innovation Center*, the *Maui Research and Technology Center* and the *Laupahoehoe Teleservice/Telework Center.*

The *Office of Technology Transfer and Economic Development* seeks to move technical innovations from an academic setting to com-mercial exploitation. Their Web page at *http://www.maui.com/~mandrews/otted.html* out-lines the policy. ❑

QuickLink
http://www.state.id.us

IDAHO GREETS THE LEGAL RESEARCHER with a smile -- and a no-nonsense link that reads *Search the Constitution, Statutes, Administrative Rules and Current Legislation of the State of Idaho.* Legal research doesn't get much easier than this.

Idaho joins the ranks of less-populous states that have embraced the Internet enthusiastically as a means to circulate important law resources to its far-flung citizens. The state's Information Technology Division of the Department of Administration keeps up the Web site and they do a fine job of it. Links are current and comprehensive (in Internet terms) and very simple to navigate.

EXECUTIVE RESOURCES

The bookmark for Idaho is *http://www.state.id.us* and unlike most states, Idaho's index page is not the governor's page. Instead, this page of graphically dull links -- it's basically a gopher -- includes the governor's page as merely one more link in the chain of state information. Bully!

Those interested in the Chief Executive's site can find it at *http://www.state.id.us/gov/govhmpg.htm* where the governor has published the State of the State address, the State of the Budget, a laundry list of press releases and his own weekly schedule. There's also a staff directory and a list of who on his staff is assigned to particular policy assignments.

Most executive agencies are linked to the state home page and the researcher can connect to the leading agencies from there. For those agencies and departments not listed on the home page, refer to the *Agency Directory Search* to fetch a list of telephone numbers and contacts for every state office. Idaho mounts a gopher-style Web page titled *State Government Agencies* at *http://www.state.id.us/state.html* for clickable links to virtually all Idaho agencies.

Such agencies as the Secretary of State at *http://www.idsos.state.id.us/corp/corindex.htm* provide state forms -- corporation, limited liability company and limited partnership forms are online with instructions and fee schedules -- and background information of interest not only to Idaho practitioners but to researchers from outside the state too.

The Attorney General is joining the online revolution with some simple links to *press releases* and a *Consumer Protection* page from the office's own home page at *http://www.state.id.us/ag/homepage.htm* Links aren't very extensive as yet, but from the design promises more information to come, so check back with the site frequently to see what's been added.

The State Treasurer outlines the restrictions on legal investments in the state at the Treasurer's page at *http://www.state.id.us/treasur/sto.htm*

Find tax forms, schedules and tax tables from the State Tax Commission's Web site at *http://www.state.id.us/tax/taxforms.htm* Like most government forms, documents are in PDF format.

LEGISLATIVE RESOURCES

No state has made searching legislative and administrative materials so simple as Idaho. The legislature makes its online home at *http://www.state.id.us/legislat/legislat.html* which is where links appear to search for bill texts and history of laws passed in 1996 and for bill texts, histories and statement of purpose for current legislative documents. Links for the Senate publish information on *leadership, members, committees, administration* and *rules*. A similar link brings researchers to the House of Representatives. Track the progress of bills and floor schedules with the link to *Committee Agendas* and *Reading Calendars*.

The same page links to the Idaho Code. Select from a searchable link to the *Table of Contents* or head directly to a WAIS search engine to search across the full text of the state statutes.

For the administrative rules of Idaho's agencies, head to *http://www.idwr.state.id.us/apa/agyindex.htm* where an alphabetical list of state agencies with links to their regulations is found.

Updating regulations is made easy with an online *Master Cumulative Index of All Rule-Makings* dating from July 1995. Idaho also thoughtfully mounts the full text of the *Idaho Administrative Bulletin* from November 1995.

JUDICIAL MATERIALS

As with the other branches of state government, the Idaho judiciary maintains its own home page that is generous with the material it publishes online. The page lives at *http://www.idwr.state.id.us/judicial/judicial.html* and collects the current sixty days of opinions reported by the Supreme Court and Court of Appeals. Opinions are posted on the day of release by the court.

The Supreme Court reprints *News Releases* on this page; this also the place to find synopses of cases pending appeal. Refer to the home page as well for the *Judicial Staff Directory, Judicial Administrative Newsletter* and *Calendar of Events*.

Idaho court rules roost online at *http://www.idwr.state.id.us/judicial/rulesamd.html* and contain the *Rules of Civil Procedure, Rules of Evidence, Appellate Rules, Administrative Rules* and *Criminal Rules*.

STATE LIBRARY

Idaho's librarians have fashioned a state-of-the-art Web site for hooking up the state and the Internet at large to many services. See the state library at *http://www.state.id.us/isl/hp.htm*

BAR ASSOCIATION

As of mid-1997, Idaho's bar association had not yet created a Web site. However, a handful of Bar Commission rules are available for the researcher's pleasure and convenience at *http://www.idwr.state.id.us/judicial/ibcr.html*

LOCAL AND MUNICIPAL RESOURCES

Local governments are not forgotten in the Idaho state web design. Links from the state home page lead to *Idaho County Information* and *City Home Pages*.

MISCELLANEOUS RESOURCES

Tourist information for Idaho with assorted links to destinations is published on the official Idaho Travel Guide at *http://www.visitid.org*

Also see an interesting collection of organizations and special interest groups at *http://www.state.id.us/orgs.html*

❑

QuickLink
http://www.state.il.us/

ILLINOIS KICKS OFF ACCESS to its state legal materials with a compact table containing all the links a researcher will need to get started at *http://www.state.il.us* From here, almost all state law resources can be accessed, with the notable exception of judicial materials.

EXECUTIVE RESOURCES

The governor gets the ball rolling with a clickable mug shot. Resist the urge to poke him in the eye with the cursor, but double-click anyway to pull up a page drawn straight from whatever workbook the governors of this nation consult to create a home page: *Press Releases, Biographical Statements* of the governor and spouse and *Initiatives and Accomplishments* are the standard features and the State of Illinois does not tamper with the formula. More important are the extensive links to executive agencies. They're accessible from the home page.

Not every agency has been hooked up to the Internet yet, but most major agencies of interest to the researcher are. For instance, the *Office of the Appellate Defender* operates a Web page at *http://www.state.il.us/defender/default.html* that contains extensive publications about the office. There's a *Brief Bank* and a *Handbook on Brief and Oral Arguments* to go along with a *Criminal Law Digest* and a *Summary of Criminal Issues* pending in the

Illinois Supreme Court.

The *Attorney General* weighs in at *http://www.acsp.uic.edu/~ag/* with a page that features AG opinions, press releases and a directory to the office. Web-savvy researchers will be particularly interested in the AG's *Commission on Electronic Commerce and Crime*. This pioneering commission was formed to examine and thwart the expected rise of criminal activity online as electronic commerce moves ever closer to reality. Look for background information on the commission at *http://www.acsp.uic.edu/ag/resource/cecc/cecc.htm* That's also the same place to go to keep abreast of developments pertaining to Illinois' *Electronic Writing and Signature Act*.

The Department of Revenue's Web page is about as pretty as a bureaucratic HTML file can be and the tax collectors of Illinois have provided *tax forms, laws and legislation, statistical information, revenue news, revenue publications* and *revenue mailboxes* on this colorful page. Zero in on the *1996 Practitioners' Liasion Group Questions and Answers* for some quick answers to Illinois tax questions.

LEGISLATIVE MATERIALS

The legislature is poorly represented on the Internet. From the state home page, links lead merely to directory information of the members of the General Assembly. Sadly lacking are bill texts or other legislative documents. Hopefully the state will set up a legislative server like most other states. Neither the Illinois code ("*Illinois Revised Statutes*") nor the administrative code are online, although some executive agencies publish relevant laws and regulations on their respective Web sites.

BAR ASSOCIATION

One of the best sources of legal information in Illinois is from the *Illinois State Bar*

Association Web site at the URL *http://www.illinoisbar.org* In addition to the standard features of bar news, sections and newsletters, the Bar Web site is excellent for hooking up to substantive information that is not linked on other public servers.

Since Illinois legislative materials are not yet available via the Internet, use the punchy and informative weekly *Legislative Bulletins* that are published on this site to stay current with legislative initiatives.

This is also the site for *Courts Bulletin*, a monthly digest of cases reported by the Illinois Supreme Court, Appellate Court and 7th Circuit Court of Appeals. Summaries are grouped by court and law topic.

JUDICIAL RESOURCES

The full text of court opinions can be accessed from the bar's page; the gopher server containing the decisions do not use intuitive file names so it's necessary to first consult the index to Supreme Court opinions and Appellate Court opinions from the page before venturing into the downloading process. Opinions are retrievable in either plain ASCII text or in WordPerfect 5.2 format. Cases are arranged by date filed and by case name. Supreme Court reports date from May 1996. Appellate Court reports, for all districts, date from September 1996 and are listed in filing date order.

A listserv for members of the Illinois State Bar is sponsored by the association. Sign up for membership at *http://www.illinoisbar.org/ subscribe.html*

STATE LIBRARY

Librarians can knock around Illinois' state and public libraries from a convenient index page operated by the Secretary of State.

The page for the Illinois State Library is located at *http://www.library.sos.state.il.us/ isl/isl.html*

LOCAL AND MUNICIPAL RESOURCES

The State of Illinois links up all its cities, counties and municipalities on a large-scale alphabetical page at *http://www.state.il.us/cmmnty/alpha/default.htm* The information available at the end of the links varies from site to site but the selections are for the most part informative and useful for looking up basic data from the remoter corners of Illinois.

The City of Broad Shoulders is also the city of big servers and multitudinous links to the City of Chicago are best found on the *City of Chicago Information* page maintained by the University of Illinois at Chicago. The links are graphically bland but thorough; law-related links, unfortunately, are few. Find the site at *http://www.ci.chi.il.us*

MISCELLANEOUS RESOURCES

One of the leading law libraries in the country, the D'Angelo Law Library at the University of Chicago School of Law maintains a superb Web site under the capable management of librarian and law professor Lyonette Louis-Jacques. The well-stocked *Virtual Reference Desk* provides access to bibliographies, encyclopedias, periodical indices and dictionaries; the *Internet Links* are a tidy list of the leading resources. Use the links to *travel* for information on Chicago and Illinois destinations. ❏

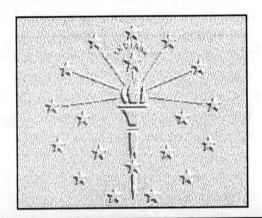

QuickLink

http://www.ai.org/state.html

INDIANA STANDS ALONE among the states in providing access to its public information because of its unique *Access Indiana Information Network (AIIN)*. For a $50 annual fee, a subscriber receives a password which grants electronic access to "state, county, local, association and other public information," according to the AIIN home page. Access Indiana is a superb initiative to make government and the law respond more quickly to the needs of the citizen. but even without subscribing to AIIN, the Internet researcher will find Indiana legal research to be stress-free and resource-rich.

The governor clocks in with a unique audio file of his inauguration speech and the text of his address. The photo collection, State of the State address and biography flesh out the page. As a stop on the legal researcher's ne'er ending hajj for information, this is tiny oasis.

EXECUTIVE RESOURCES

The executive branch agencies, however, line up for inspection at *http://www.ai.org/ stateag.html* There, standing soldier-straight on the page are links to virtually every state office

in Indiana. Its a smartly organized group of sites; the pages themselves are thorough and informative.

The office of the Attorney General is an elaborate site. It contains the to-be-expected press releases and biography of the AG in addition to instructions on how to file claims and complaints with the office. To get AG opinions, follow the links to *Office Publications*. There, resident with the opinions, are copies of Indiana's Public Records Act and its supplement and the Indiana Open Door Law.

Indiana bureaucracies go out of their way to make their forms more computer-friendly. Online at *http://www.ai.org/icpr/ forms/index.html* are Secretary of State forms for such filings as:

Application for Certificate of Authority of a
    Foreign Corporation
Indiana Annual Report of Nonprofit Corporation
Indiana Biennial Report of Business Corporation

The Indiana State Department of Tax eases the pain of paying the boss with its online library of tax forms at *http://www.ai.org/dor/ forms/state.html* Dozens of forms are available in PDF format and include corporate tax forms, individual filings and not-for-profit returns.

While other jurisdictions grapple with the question of notifying communities about the presence of convicted sex offenders released to a neighborhood, Indiana has no qualms about it. Under the auspices of the Indiana Criminal Justice Institute is a publicly-accessible *Sex Offender Registry* at *http://www.ai.org/ cji/index.html* The page links to a selection of searchable public records databases. Choose from:

Offender Release and Registration Information
Records of the Indiana Dept. of Corrections
Records of the Indiana Prosecuting Attorneys
    Council
Records of the Indiana State Police
All Databases

Typical offender records contain the

offender's name, a physical description, Social Security number and a description of the offense.

For a hypertext version of the current Indiana State Code, head to *http://www.law.indiana.edu/codes/in/incode.html* where the Indiana University School of Law at Bloomington has published it. The page publishes a hypertext link to the text of each title. Titles are divided into hyperlinked articles, which lead to chapters and then, ultimately, to the sections.

JUDICIAL MATERIALS

The reports of the judiciary also find a comfortable home among the microchips at a server located at the the IU law school.Find decisions at *http://www.law.indiana.edu/law/incourts/incourts.html* Indiana is one of the rare states to publish online not only its Supreme Court and Court of Appeals decisions but also the reported decisions of the Indiana Tax Court.

Decisions are easy to look up. All materials date from January 1995. From a single page, it's possible to search by *first party, second party, date* or *month* for each of the three reporting courts. Without any citing information, look across the full text of cases using the *subject matter search* or the *word search*. Either style is fast and efficient and should locate the desired cases quickly.

LEGISLATIVE RESOURCES

For legislative information, look no further than the home page for the Indiana General Assembly at *http://www.ai.org/legislative/index.html* Neatly plotted on one page is the current and past year legislative activities. Links will whisk the researcher to the text of bills, committee reports, calendars, committee memberships and to the home pages of the legislators. Bills can be searched by citation or by free text.

The Assembly provides a fee-based service known as *BillWatch* that can monitor legislative activities electronically. Select an unlimited number of bills or keyword subjects to watch; whenever legislative activity occurs concerning the monitored

subject, the Legislative Services Agency dispatches an e-mail message alerting the subscriber to the legislation. E-mail notification is $50 per month. To receive an alpha-numeric page, the fee is an additional $99 per month. Apply for a password at *http://www.ai.org/legislative/billwatch1.html*

The Administrative Code of Indiana has a home in cyberspace at *http://www.ai.org/legislative/iac* where the full text of the code can be searched title by title. Simply click on the link to the relevant code section and the various articles magically appear underneath. Text is mounted in WordPerfect 5.1 format for easy downloading and is current to within a month.

STATE LIBRARY

The State Library of Indiana lives online at *http://www.statelib.lib.in.us/* The page is plain but it connects with a searchable catalog, reference and government services, and a data center. This is also the place to go to check on state archives and find links to other local, state and foreign libraries.

BAR ASSOCIATION

To connect with the Indiana State Bar Association, click the reins on your browser to *http://www.ai.org/isba/* where a high-quality Web site awaits. AIIN subscribers will be at a decided advantage on this page since a password is necessary to access their *Premium Services.* Those nominally-priced services include searches of *driver's license records, title and lien records* and *registration records.*

Non-AIIN researchers will still find the bar's home page informative for getting the e-mail addresses of Indiana attorneys and figuring out who is on which committee. Link to Indiana Continuing Legal Education Forum for practice manuals online, forms on CD and information about the computer lab.

For miscellaneous links to Indiana law materials, look at the Hoosier Lawyer's Gateway to the WorldWideWeb. It's at *http://www.iquest.net*

QuickLink
http://www.webcom.com/piper/state/slia.html

Iowa's legal resources on the Internet won't make anyone turn backflips through the cornfields, but the state has managed to add enough materials since 1995 to give the researcher reason to turn Internet-ward for basic Iowa research. The current harvest of information is relatively thin but time may beef up the available data.

EXECUTIVE RESOURCES

To begin, like governors everywhere, Iowa's chief executive keeps a home page at *http://www.state.ia.us/government/governor/index.html* It is every byte a governor's page: it's got the biography, it's got the State of the State Address and it's got the budget. For variety, this page features press releases, staff write-ups, speech transcripts and media advisories.

Under the governor's supervision are the executive branch Web sites. The most useful link mounted here is the one to Iowa's Secretary of State at *http://www.sos.state.ia.us/index.html* but no one is lining up to hang blue ribbons on the site.

To get the rundown on all the executive offices in the state, load up *http://www.state.ia.us/government/index.html* There, scroll boxes will deliver links to the agencies via your choice of alphabetical listing, functional listing or from a table of hypertext links.

Among the more interesting executive branch sites are those for the Attorney General which hangs "Wanted Posters" of deadbeat dads on its page in addition to Attorney General opinions and that page for the Department of Commerce which leads to information on *professional licensing, insurance, banking, utilities* and *administrative services*.

Other links of interest to the legal researcher include the *Civil Rights Commission,* the *Law Enforcement Academy,* the *Ethics and Campaign Disclosure Board* and a link to Iowa's department of *Information Technology*.

The Department of Revenue and Finance provides electronic filing, current tax forms in PDF format, instructions and a link to Iowa tax news. The page collects the rents at *http://www.state.ia.us/government/drf/index.html*

LEGISLATIVE MATERIALS

For legislative links, find the Iowa General Assembly's page at *http://www.legis.state.ia.us/* This is probably the most information-rich and serviceable page for legal materials in the state. Search here to retrieve bills and amendments from the current legislative session and from prior years. The search mechanism is a no-frills template that permits entering of *file number* for bills from both chambers. Refine searches by scrolling down the search box to select from *file, amendment, resolution, joint resolution, concurrent resolution, study bill* or *conference committee report*. There's also a straightforward hypertext list of directory connections to the same information for the scroll-box-averse.

In addition to the text of bills and amendments, Iowa publishes an *Index of bill history,* the *index of Daily Action Reports* and, when the Assembly is in session, an *index of floor action,* which is updated every half hour according to the Web page.

Both chambers mount pages from their official *journals* on the page along with a weekly brief of legislative actions for the current legislative session. Also find a legislative summary.

The Assembly page is the place to go to search the Iowa Code, available directly by dialing up *http://www2.legis.state.ia.us/Code.html* The code is available from 1995 with supplements and in its most current incarnation. Searching is no mystery: it's an ordinary WAIS database, meaning it supports natural language searching, Boolean operators, truncation, group searching and the ever-popular string search for the literal-minded. Responses can be limited to returns of 10, 20, 50, 100 or 200 items. Look at the link for other *indices* to scout around the *legislative handbook* and all the above-mentioned items from the legislature.

JUDICIAL RESOURCES

For judicial materials, point your browser directly to *http://www.netins.net/showcase/clevad/law.htm* There the researcher will locate links stretching back to November 1995 that will produce decisions of the Supreme, up to and ending with June 1996. Where have subsequent decisions gone? Dunno. Check back with the state page or the home page of the Supreme Court at *http://www.sos.state.ia.us/register/r3/judsupct.htm* to see if later cases are published there. The situation is fundamentally the same with Court of Appeals decisions. There are some online but then coverage mysteriously stops.

STATE LIBRARY

The hard-working librarians of Iowa work just a bit harder now that the patrons of the

Internet can zip their requests to the reference desk via the network. Find a template at *http://www.silo.lib.ia.us/ask.html* whereby inquiries can be forwarded to the State Library of Iowa at the press of a mouse button. (According to librarian Linda Robertson, some 40% of all requests to the library now arrive electronically.) The home page for the State Library is at *http://www.silo.lib.ia.us* The home page links to other library catalogs throughout the state.

Also working late over the HTML editors are the staffers at the University of Iowa Law Library. Their page of links to *Iowa Legal Information* will provide a handy index page for the occasional researcher. It's best used for its links to Iowa law schools, Iowa law journals -- they mount *Transnational Law and Contemporary Problems* and *Drake Journal of Agricultural Law* -- and for the *Bibliography of Iowa Legal Materials*.

BAR ASSOCIATION

The Iowa Bar Association had not yet mounted a Web site as of June 1997.

MISCELLANEOUS LINKS

For a miscellany of Iowa state links, not necessarily law-related, refer to *http://www.state.ia.us/oiid.htm* where links to Des Moines, the *Iowa City Human Rights Commission,* the *Iowa Commission on the Status of African Americans* and the non-profit *Iowa Online* can be found. The *NAACP* maintains a chapter in Cedar Rapids and can be linked from this page.

❑

QuickLink

http://lawlib.wuacc.edu/washlaw/
kansas/kansas.html

KANSAS LEGAL RESEARCHERS are in good hands since Kansas is home to one of the best law-related Web sites on the Internet at the Topeka-based law school at Washburn University. Not only does Washburn monitor the world with accuracy and aplomb, it also keeps close tabs on the local neighborhood as well. Kansas researchers are well-advised to bookmark the Washburn page immediately. The URL is *http://lawlib.wuacc.edu*

And if that's not enough information, try the *Information Network of Kansas* (INK) which itself is a comprehensive collection of state links to legal materials. INK is a subscription service. Frequent Kansas researchers should get a password since INK supplies access to Kansas corporate records, UCC filings, motor vehicle records and other valuable archives of state law information. Subscribers also get to search through the state statutes and the administrative code plus link to local district courts throughout the state.

For the occasional researcher, though, the Washburn site will be more than sufficient. From a single table, links reach out to virtually any point of interest to the legal researcher. The page is embarrassingly easy to use. Connect to government sites, law firms, libraries and the information network of Kansas from here.

EXECUTIVE RESOURCES

So far as substantive materials are concerned, the governor's office is always at the top of the list for state research and Kansas is no exception. Find the ever-important State of the State addresses on the page at *http://www.ink.org/public/governor/#office* accompanied by links to press releases, the governor's weekly address and legislation signed by the governor.

The executive agencies of Kansas are well-represented on the Web. The Kansas Attorney General maintains a Web site at *http://lawlib.wuacc.edu/ag/homepage.html* for publishing little descriptions of the office's functions. Missing are AG opinions and other useful items that the researcher might require.

Pony up the tax dollar on Kansas tax forms which live in PDF format at *http://www.ink.org/public/kdor/taxforms.html* The catalog is virtually complete -- there shouldn't be any problem finding the necessary form and its associated instructions.

Even the gaolers get into the act. The Kansas Department of Corrections has a Web site at *http://www.ink.org/public/kdoc/* notable mostly for the monthly newsletter it publishes on the site.

The complete list of wired executive agencies lies at the end of the hypertext link to *State Agencies* on the home page for the Information Network of Kansas at *http://www.ink.org* but links to some of these agencies are restricted to INK subscribers.

JUDICIAL RESOURCES

For judicial information, the far-reaching pages of the Kansas Judicial Branch Web site at *http://www.law.ukans.edu/kscourts/ksapps.html* will deliver a great deal of court information. The Supreme Court link heads to a page containing a description of the make-up and authority of the court. There are biographies of the justices, photographs and a link to the Supreme Court law library. More important is the link to Supreme Court decisions. They date from October 1996 and can be searched through keywords, docket number, case name or date of release. Opinions are mounted on the site within one hour of release from the Reporter's Office. The page also contains up-to-date docket information. For brief summaries of selected Supreme Court decisions, turn to the materials prepared by the Office of Judicial Administration at *http://lawlib.wuacc.edu/kscases/ojasumm/ojasumm.htm*

The Court of Appeals publishes much the same information as the Supreme Court. The court's home page at *http://www.law.ukans.edu/kscourts/ksapps.html* links to *Purpose, Authority and History of the Kansas Court of Appeals.* Biographies of the judges can be accessed here with a selection of photographs. Two months of docket sheets are published here as are the reported decisions of the court dating from October 1996. Like Supreme Court decisions, texts are searchable by docket number, case name, date of publication or keyword.

The courts' home page is not just for downloading recent decisions. This is the place to go for rules relating to admission and disciplining of attorneys, rules concerning media coverage of judicial proceedings and to see which law students most recently passed the bar examination.

Brief descriptions of district courts -- the trial court in Kansas -- and municipal courts are linked to the Judicial Branch home page.

LEGISLATIVE RESOURCES

Head to *http://www.ink.org/public/legislative/* to get connected with Kansas legislative materials. The full text of bills, calendars, journals from both chambers, bill subject index and the text of enrolled bills are published here. Also get the scoop on state legislators with links to their home pages. As with most legislative Web sites, Kansas posts committee memberships

and the schedules for each of the legislature's committees.

The most useful feature of the legislature's page is reserved for subscribers to INK. A "Lobbyist-in-a-Box" can monitor legislative initiatives for subscribers and deliver *bill tracking* and *bill packets* to their e-mail boxes automatically. And for help with legislative research, consult the *Kansas Legislative Research Department.* The department's home page is accessible at *http://www.kumc.edu/kansas/ksleg/KLRD/klrd.html*

STATE LIBRARY

The Kansas State Library calls its page *Blue Skyways.* Locate the page at *http://skyways.lib.ks.us/kansas*

BAR ASSOCIATION

Kansas abounds in legal associations and organizations. The Kansas Bar Association runs *Kansas CyBar Net,* its Web site at *http://www.ink.org/public/cybar/* Links head in many directions although the information plums are reserved for INK subscribers. The bar's site reprints *ethics opinions* and indexes its publications. There's is information about CLE programs and online briefs for selected subjects of Kansas law. Use this page for attorney referrals and sidebar groups.

For paralegals, the URL *http://www.ink.org/public/ksparalegals/* pulls up a page maintained by the Kansas Paralegal Association. While taking a break from photocopying duties, paralegals can check out the *Code of Ethics, Scholarships, Research Tools, Calendar of Events* and link to the NFPA *National Association.*

Litigators can hang out at the home page for trial lawyers at *http://www.ink.org/public/ktla/* The page features membership information and a link to the association's express mail discount program, professional journal, networking opportunities and the Kansas Attorneys' Litigation Library. ❑

QuickLink
http://www.state.ky.us/ govtinfo.htm

KENTUCKY KICKS OFF its online law resources with a lengthy alphabetical list of the *Kentucky State Government*. All agencies and offices within the state are represented, but not all of them are Web-equipped or linked to this page. Still, coverage is fairly extensive and links to the most important agencies are available.

EXECUTIVE RESOURCES

The governor's electronic mansion welcomes visitors at *http://www.state.ky.us/agencies/gov/govmenu6.htm* and serves guests a buffet of *speech texts* and *press releases,* a *biography* of the governor and links to e-mail and state Cabinet members.

Leading agencies online include the *Kentucky Revenue Cabinet,* the state's tax department. It's a comprehensive site, providing state tax forms in PDF format, instructions and tax schedules. The agency mounts information on filing returns and publishes its strategic plan-

ning. Information on legislation affecting state tax laws can be accessed via the server from the *Legislative Research Commission* at *http://www.lrc.state.ky.us/home.htm*

The Attorney General at *http://www.law.state.ky.us* disseminates *Attorney General Opinions* and reprints selected consumer-oriented laws from the Web site. Look here for links to the AG divisions for *Consumer Protection, Victims' Advocacy* and *Civil and Environmental Law.*

Law students can make tracks to the Kentucky Board of Bar Examiners at *http://www.cris.com/~Kbbe/* for information on admission to the Kentucky bar.

For business entity filings, notary public appointments, voter registration, long-arm service, UCC filings and trademark services, consult the Secretary of State's site at *http://www.state.ky.us/agencies/sos/index.htm*

At the Kentucky Department of Public Advocacy, check out information on the state's death penalty and link to a selection of marriage, divorce and death records. The address for the page is *http://advocate.pa.state.ky.us/*

The rules and regulations governing the insurance industry within Kentucky are reprinted on the Department of Insurance Web site at *http://www.state.ky.us/agencies/insur/default.htm* So is information concerning health care reform, publications from the department, news announcements and a description of the department's organizational structure.

For a complete alphabetical list of Kentucky state agency Web sites, refer to the canonical list supplied by the Kentucky Department of Libraries and Archives at *http://www.kdla.state.ky.us/links/kygov.htm*

LEGISLATIVE MATERIALS

The Kentucky legislature keeps a home page at *http://www.lrc.state.ky.us/home.htm* and it's prim as a circuit board. Under the heading for *Hot Items* are to be found links to the *Leadership and Standing Committees,* the Web sites for the *Legislative Committees* and the *legislative calendar.* There's a tip of the hat to the analog world here with a list of toll-free (800) numbers for the Kentucky General Assembly.

As legislative databases go, this one's a winner. It's easy to navigate, there is clear and complete help available online and materials are kept fresh and current. One significant enhancement to the site is the inclusion of a *conversion table* which helps in tracing citations and determining the legislative history of a given law.

Searching through the Kentucky Revised Statutes means pointing your browser to *http://www.lrc.state.ky.us/statrev/frontpg.htm* As of early 1997 it was only possible to search the code by *Title* and *Chapter* but the Webmasters plan to offer searching by *statute number* and by *full text.* The text is the unofficial version of the code, as the helpful "read me" section indicates, but it does incorporate amendments from the most recent legislative sessions. The code is maintained in PDF format so an Adobe Acrobat reader is necessary.

To search the administrative code of Kentucky, aim for *http://www.lrc.state.ky.us/ kar/frntpage.htm* The instructions and background information will clue in the first-time visitor. The code itself lives at *http://www.lrc.state.ky.us/kar/TITLES.HTM* and is arranged by individual title.

JUDICIAL RESOURCES

For case law written by the Kentucky courts, fire up the home page of the Kentucky Legal Research System. Some 5,000 opinions from the Kentucky courts are available for searching and downloading from the site. The Webmasters estimate that 30 to 50 opinions will be added weekly, depending, of course, on the

workload in the courts. Find the site at *http://www.klrs.com* It's fee-based, with fees varying according to amount of usage. Registration is required and access is restricted to users with valid passwords and IDs. Sample the site from the home page before you sign on the virtual dotted line.

BAR ASSOCIATION

The Kentucky Bar Association is online at *http://www.kybar.org* The Web site describes the association's departments and related organizations, posts a *Calendar of Events* and *gives how-to advice on* handling ethical and personal dilemmas. A review of CLE programs and membership services rounds out the Web site. An associated Web is the Kentucky Bar Foundation, which funds educational programs and seminars throughout the state.

STATE LIBRARY

Librarians can link to the state library at *http://www.kdla.state.ky.us* The online reference service will supply a rundown of what the library does for researchers and archivists and details its public records services.

MISCELLANEOUS RESOURCES

State law schools maintain Web sites too. Locate the University of Kentucky Law School at *http://www.uky.edu/Law* and the University of Louisville Law School at *http://www.louisville.edu/groups/law-www* There's also links to Kentucky law school libraries from the Kentucky Legal Research System at *http://www.klrs.com/links.htm*

A lengthier list of Kentucky colleges and universities is located at *http://www.state.ky.us/colleges.html* ❏

QuickLink
http://www.state.la.us

LOUISIANA, NEVER LACKING IN INTERESTING culture or colorful political institutions, nevertheless serves a decidedly mild gumbo of online resources. We're still waiting for an imaginative Webmaster to step into the job and deliver the legal researcher the electronic *lagniappe* we've come to expect from other states. That's not to say that Louisiana has overlooked the electronic revolution; it hasn't and there are certainly resources worth the researcher's time. They just tend to be info-lite.

EXECUTIVE RESOURCES

The governor's executive office online is addressable at *http://www.state.la.us/gov/gov.htm* There the researcher can retrieve *executive orders* and link to the *press office*, the *Division of Administration* and the *Lifelong Learning* center. Non-operative links are published on the governor's page; many Louisiana agencies operate Web sites. Search them at the InfoLouisiana State Departments home page at *http://www.state.la.us/state/dept.htm*

The Department of Revenue and Taxation runs a tidy Web site and stocks it with *tax data*, information on tax legislation from the most recent legislative session, a *directory of*

services and, most importantly, downloadable *tax forms and instructions* in PDF format. Find the tax page at *http://www.rev.state.la.us/*

Of great service to the researcher is a page containing *Frequently Requested Information Phone Numbers*. Posted here is a searchable telephone directory for state agencies and a list containing the numbers for such oft-used numbers as those for vital records, the Attorney General and the Motor Vehicle Department.

LEGISLATIVE RESOURCES

The legislature maintains separate services for the Senate and the House of Representatives though they may both be approached from the Louisiana Legislature Home Page at *http://www.house.state.la.us/* The Senate server at *http://www.senate.state.la.us/sen/senate.htm* pastes membership and committee information on its gopher-like Web page, along with a legislative map to look up the appropriate legislator in each district. Under the link for committees are online *agendas, committee schedules* and *Senate news notes*. The real value is the hook to bill texts. A click will take the researcher to a summary of bills and their current status; Louisiana's dedication to the Internet as a means of distributing legislative information is suspect since two additional links suggest data is best retrieved via an (800) telephone number or by *LAScribe*, a fee-based subscription service that will deliver to subscribers what most other states provide for free. Details on joining *LAScribe* are available from *http://www.senate.state.la.us/sen/research/legis.htm*

From the House of Representatives comes much the same type of material with the significant addition of links to the *caucuses/delegations*, the *Speaker's Office* and the *Clerk's Office*. Unlike the Senate, the full text of House *bills* and *resolutions* from 1996 regular sessions forward are online and searchable by number and author.

Selected portions of the state's administrative code are available online at *http://www.state.la.us/osr/lac/lac.htm* The monthly *Louisiana Register,* the official reporter of all state agency rules and regulations can be searched as far back as September 1996 at *http://www.state.la.us/osr/reg/register.htm*

So far, Louisiana, the only state in America that still operates according to the Napoleonic Code has not seen fit to publish the unique Louisiana statutes on the Internet.

JUDICIAL RESOURCES

For judicial materials, go to *http://home.gnofn.org/~lasc/* where the Supreme Court of Lousiana makes its online home. Along with biographies of the justices, a history of the court and a review of the constitutional authority of the court, opinions are available dating from 1996.

The link to the year will open a new Web page containing information on *actions,* the text of *opinions* and actions taken by the court on *rehearings.* The full text of the self-extracting compressed opinions can be downloaded in WordPerfect 5.1 format. Decompress the files by exiting to DOS and typing the file name at the DOS prompt. Also find a handy directory of court clerk names, addresses and phone numbers from every parish in the state at *http://www2.linknet.net/lehman/district.html*

BAR ASSOCIATION

The Louisiana State Bar Association does not maintain its own Web both a thorough list of the association's committees and membership and directory information for contacting the Louisiana Bar can be found at the state bar association server operated by Martindale-Hubbell at its site. Martindale-Hubbell's list of state bar associations is at *http://www.martindale.com/profession/statebar*

MISCELLANEOUS RESOURCES

As for miscellaneous links, locate a list of local government servers in Louisiana at *http://www.state.la.us/local/locindx.htm* Find an online magazine for Louisiana Parish Government and an assortment of information about the state's parish system at *http://www.lpgov.org*

STATE LIBRARY

To contact the State Library, dial up *http://smt.state.lib.la.us* Contact information for the state's Law Library in New Orleans also is available from the Supreme Court's home page at *http://home.gnofn.org/~lasc* which is the same place to go for basic directory references to *Judicial Administrator's Office,* the *Judicial Council of the Louisiana Supreme Court,* the *Louisiana Judiciary Commission* and the *Louisiana Judicial College.*

❏

QuickLink

http://www.state.me.us/
agencies.htm

MAINE'S HOME PAGE, cheesy as a road-side lobster shack, is nonetheless designed to provide a maximum of information with a minimum of fuss.

EXECUTIVE MATERIALS

In a no-nonsense state like Maine, the governor sets the tone with his plain-spoken Web site. Unlike high-falutin' governor pages, Maine's chief executive only hands over a bio-graphical statement if the visitor asks for it by clicking on the photograph. There are the expected links to the legislative initiatives and the always-present State of the State address text; there is also a link to the *Communications Office* and *Constituent Services*. A directory of the governor's staff can be pulled up as can general information about the state.

Best link for the legal researcher on the governor's page, though, is the one that hooks into the *State Agency Rules Online*. The Maine Administrative Code (MAC) is organized by chapter, each of which uniquely identifies the Department and sub-agency making and maintaining the regulation. The URL for the code is

http://www.state.me.us/sos/cec/rcn/apa/ depts.htm

In addition to the full text of the MAC, an associated page from Maine's APA Office which handles the Administrative Procedures Act offers an explanation of state rule-making from its home page at *http://www.state.me.us/sos/cec/rcn/apa/apa.htm*

Maine's executive agencies are all online at *http://www.state.me.us/agencies.htm* Typical of the information provided by individual agencies is the page operated by the Bureau of Corporations, Elections and Commissions at *http://www.state.me.us/sos/cec/cec.htm*. It details the fees and deadlines for filing annual reports for corporations, limited liability corporations and limited liability partnerships. The site lists -- but does not e-publish -- the prescribed business corporation forms.

A more elaborate Web site is provided by the Bureau of Banking at *http://www.state.me.us/pfr/bkg/bkghome2.htm* From a table on the home page, the legal researcher can easily pick up *Proposed Legislation, Laws, Rules & Advisory Rulings* and *Directory Information* for the agency. A similar design and information-publication strategy is available from the Bureau of Insurance at *http://www.state.me.us/pfr/ins/inshome2.htm* where the bureau publicizes its *Laws, Rules & Advisory Rulings* along with *Licensing/Registration,* a *Directory, General Information* and links to other insurance sites.

Maine's tax collectors keep a colorful Web page in service at *http://www.state.me.us/ taxation/homepage.htm* where the public can retrieve state tax rules and the law. There are online bulletins for filers and instructional pamphlets for individual tax returns. Curiously, Maine hangs a PDF-formatted *order form* for tax forms on its Web site but not the forms themselves. It's still necessary to get Maine tax forms via snail mail.

JUDICIAL MATERIALS

The Maine judiciary has its home page at *http://www.courts.state.me.us/* The page is simple but elegant and is easy to navigate. The *Chief Justice* provides a biography of the judge and a report on the state of the judiciary. An explanation of the structure of the Maine court system is written for the layperson or juror and is mounted on the judiciary home page. For a more detailed description of how Maine courts are organized, refer to the link for *Directory of Courts* which will connect to the *Maine Supreme Judicial Court,* the *Maine Superior Courts, Maine District Courts* and *Administrative Office of the Courts.*

The most important part of the judiciary's page is its link to *Supreme Court Opinions.* Opinions are mounted in chronological order and can be downloaded in either PDF format or for MacIntosh users, Windows for Mac 3.x. Decisions date from the beginning of 1997.

On the same page as Supreme Court opinions are *advisory opinions* from the justices.

LEGISLATIVE RESOURCES

The Maine State Legislature publishes information about the laws it writes from a page at *http://www.state.me.us/legis/* The link to *Bill Information* does not contain the text of bills but rather leads to a list of bills enacted by the current legislature, reprinted in the *Weekly Legislative Report* and a rundown of the bills introduced in the current session from *Bills Enacted Into Law*; ordering bills is still an analog process relying on old-fashioned telephone calls to the legislature's Document Room at (207) 287-1408.

The link to the House of Representatives at *http://www.state.me.us/legis/house/homepage.htm* leads to a three-frame Web page containing the *biographies* of the legislators, the *Code of Ethics, Joint Standing Committees* and *House and Joint Rules.* Also included are the *Weekly Legislative Calendar, Weekly Legislative*

Report and the cumulative index to the Weekly Legislative Report. The Senate page at *http://www.state.me.us/legis/senate/* contains the same information as the lower chamber.

The Maine statutory code, except for the Constitution, had not yet been posted to the Internet as of February 1997. However, a link on the page containing the Constitution at *http://www.state.me.us/legis/meconlaw.htm* does contain an inoperative place-saving link to *Maine Statutes* that may some day be up and running.

BAR ASSOCIATION

For the Maine State Bar Association, head to *http://www.mainebar.org* It's a simple Web site, providing bar members with information on upcoming CLE events, seminar syllabi, ads for CLE products, committees and section descriptions and an article-of-the-month. More information can be obtained by e-mailing to *info@mainebar.org*

Also of interest to Maine legal researchers is the *Maine Lawyers' Network* at *http://www.mainelaw.net/maine.html*. This service connects to the *Maine Trial Lawyers Association* and the *Volunteer Lawyers Project.* Other links lead to Maine legal resources and to a directory of Maine law firms.

STATE LIBRARY

The State Library can be accessed at *http://www.state.me.us/msl/mslhome.htm* Refer to the *Table of Contents* to pull up a list of links on the site, most notably the reference and research home page. Also find the Nathan and Henry B. Cleaves law Library at *http://www.ime.net/~cleaves* and the University of Maine School of Law Library at *http://www.law.usm.maine.edu/Library.htm*
❏

QuickLink
http://www.mec.state.md.us/
mecmdgov.htm

MARYLAND IS JOINING the ranks of progressive states that are aggressively publicizing the workings of their public agencies and offices. In Maryland, two electronic services are running to make state government desktop-close. Maryland's *Online Public Information Network* called SAILOR is Web-hooked at *http://sailor.lib.md.us* and electronically connects most of the public operations of the state; a project known as *Maryland Electronic Capital* at *http://www.mec.state.md.us* is designed to supply the public with state, county, city and community information throughout the state.

EXECUTIVE RESOURCES

Kick off Maryland research from the governor's mansion by aiming for *http://www.mec.state.md.us/mecexecu.htm*

To locate links to Maryland's executive agencies, head directly to the Web page at *http://www.mec.state.md.us/mecagenc.htm* Virtually every major state office in Maryland is mounted there.

Among the similarly-styled pages linked to this page is one to the Attorney General's office. It's not as richly stocked with informa-

tion as some AG servers, but the researcher armed with the requisite password can still find the office's *organizational structure, origins and functions* and *mandated reports.*

The Maryland Insurance Administration at *http://gacc.com/mia* e-publishes its regulations on the home page and offers a *staff directory, rate guides, glossary of insurance terms* and information on *property/casualty* and *life/health* insurance within the state.

Maryland taxpayers can track down forms from the server from the State Comptroller at *http://www.comp.state.md.us* In addition to the forms, the link to *taxpayer assistance* will produce *administrative releases, bulletins and notices,* aid tax professionals with answers to questions about *electronic tax payments* and deliver the e-publication *ReveNews Online.* The same page leads to archives for *administrative releases* and *bulletins and notices.*

The Secretary of State's home page at *http://www.gov.state.md.us/sos* is the page to hit for data on certifications, pardons and commutations and receipt and service of process.

Corporation information in Maryland is maintained by the State Department of Assessments and Taxation. Find forms and guidelines for business entities on the department's home page at *http://www.dat.state.md.us/charter.html*

JUDICIAL RESOURCES

Turn to *http://www.mec.state.md.us/mecjudic.htm* for judicial information. Links from the judicial branch's home page will lead to *judge's biographies* and a description of the *Court of Appeals, Court of Special Appeals, Circuit Courts* and *District Court of Maryland.*

For decisions from the Court of Special Appeals and the Court of Appeals, head to *http://www.courts.state.md.us/T40* (Per Curiam opinions are not posted online.)

Opinions are arranged by year and date

from 1992. A simple search speeds the looking-up process: click on the search icon to pull up a search box that allows searching for opinions by *topic name, entry subject, keywords, reference* or *all fields*. Searches may also be restricted by time, including new cases or cases posted on a single specific day, week, month or year.

LEGISLATIVE MATERIALS

The Maryland General Assembly's home page at *http://mlis.state.md.us* is the starting point for Maryland legislative research. Background information on the Assembly and its legislative functions is online here. So are links to connect to info about particular bills and their status. The Assembly offers researchers *bill indexes* and *profiles*. The schedule for hearings can be downloaded by *committee* or *date;* an online chart supplies the proceeding index for both chambers.

BAR ASSOCIATION

The Maryland State Bar Association, Inc. lives its online incarnation on a server called *http://www.msba.org* where it serves its 18,000-odd attorneys with a selection of *publications, calendar of events, resources for the public* and *legal links.*

Find the Baltimore County Bar Association online at *http://www.bcba.org* featuring the *Advocate Online Newsletter* and *Lawyer Referral Program;* the Prince George's County Bar Association is available at *http://www.usalaw.net/pg1.htm* along with links to local attorneys and law firms.

The Maryland Institute for Continuing Legal Education of Lawyers, Inc. (more commonly known as MICPEL) provides CLE courses for Maryland attorneys. Details on the courses and publications are available for browsing and downloading at the home page, accessible from *http://www.micpel.edu*

LOCAL AND MUNICIPAL RESOURCES

There are more places in Maryland than Baltimore and Obryki's restaurant as the numerous entries for local government on two State Archives servers attest. Find out where else to crack crabs-- and locate a great deal of government information to boot -- by tuning in to the Maryland Cities Web site at *http://www.mec.state.md.us/meccity.htm* The entry for Gaithersburg, for instance, features information on municipal services, city hall data, civic boosterism and an in-depth picture of the city written in demographic data. A similar service detailing Maryland's Counties can be found at *http://www.mec.state.md.us/meccount.htm*

STATE LIBRARY

Maryland's online information service SAILOR is the fastest way to connect to the libraries of the state including state-run libraries, county institutions and Federal libraries located within Maryland. SAILOR can dead-reckon a path to the major city libraries too; chart the course to *http://www.sailor.lib.md.us/mdlibs/mdlibs.html*

MISCELLANEOUS RESOURCES

Keeping the dust off of records from around the state are the electronic archivists at the Maryland State Archives, whose handiwork can be enjoyed in computerized ease from their Web site at *http://www.mdarchives.state.md.us* Find out about the state's art collection and other government records of permanent value from this interesting Web site.

❑

QuickLink
http://www.magnet.state.ma.us

MASSACHUSETTS IS HOME TO MIT, Harvard Law School and the computer wizards of Route 128 and so it's no surprise that a happy convergence of legal materials and technology make legal research in the commonwealth simple, elegant and orderly. The researcher can find no better starting point for Massachusetts research than the experimental MAGNET (MAssachusetts Government NETwork) server accessible at *http://www.magnet.state.ma.us* It's the official Web site and links to a vast array of state information.

EXECUTIVE RESOURCES

The governor's manse plays host to many agency links; for the governor's own materials, check in on the gubernatorial Web site at *http://www.state.ma.us/gov/gov.htm* In typical governor fashion, the horn that gets tooted is the governor's own: find accomplishments and initatives outlines on the page, along with contact numbers. The complete list of agencies is at*http://www.state.ma.us/massgov.htm*

Corporate information for Massachusetts businesses can be located at the Corporations Division home page at *http://www.state.ma.us/sec/cor/coridx.htm* where forms and instructions can be readily downloaded

As tax collectors go, the revenuers of Massachusetts are downright swinging; at least their Web site is. The home page for the Massachusetts Department of Revenue at *http://www.state.ma.us/dor/dorpg.htm* is billed as the Online Taxpayer Service Center. The page sets off easy-to-figure-out graphical buttons, floating against a groovy starfield background which launch connections to the ho-hum but vital collections of *tax forms and publications, rulings and regulations, child support enforcement, statistical data* and *tax help and filing options*. For the researcher, the regs are are a useful archive and as for the tax forms, they're in Adobe Acrobat PDF format and available for *income, corporate* and *miscellaneous*.

The Attorney General of Massachusetts presides over an elaborate Web system at *http://www.state.ma.us/ag/ago.htm* containing links to the AG bureaus for the *executive bureau, government bureau, business and labor protection bureau* and *criminal bureau*.

LEGISLATIVE RESOURCES

Quaint as a quill pen, the lawmakers of the commonwealth convene a "General Court" of the Commonwealth to consider bills before its august self. The home page lives at *http://www.state.ma.us/legis/legis.htm* By the looks of it, the site might have been designed by a Pilgrim for all its color and action -- there is none -- but a solid Cape Cod house, it's built for utility not show. Humble links roll into a member directory, committee directory and a clickable calendar of committee hearings scheduled for the current week when the general court is in session.

Current legislation is fully searchable by House or Senate bill number or by keyword using simple Boolean searches at the Legislative Tracking System, online at *http://www.state.ma.us/legis/ltsform.htm* (Search tips are a hypertext link away.) Check on a bill number with the link to *numerical list of current legislation.*

Big plans are afoot for the legislature: according to an online wish list, the great and general court will be mounting House and Senate journals, session laws and best of all, the code of Commonwealth of Massachusetts. The statutes and administrative code, as of June 1997, are still not Internet accessible.

JUDICIAL MATERIALS

For judicial information, check in with the Massachusetts Court System at *http://www.state.ma.us/courts/courts.htm*

BAR ASSOCIATION

The publication Lawyers Weekly plays host to the Massachusetts Bar Association home page. There's not a great deal of material mounted on the site other than some press releases and news of interest strictly to the members of the association, a list of officers, and membership information. The Massachusetts Bar Association holds forth, such as it is, at *http://www.lweekly.com/mba.htm*

STATE LIBRARY

Look to the Massachusetts Library and Information Network at *http://www.mlin.lib.ma.us* for a muscle-bound collection of connections to public libraries in Massachusetts and links to their home pages. Check on periodicals and periodical indexes here and wire into the catalogs of the state's online catalogs. The site features links to state, federal and local governments. MLIN also gets reciprocity credits for its collection of links to other state government servers around the Internet.

LOCAL AND MUNICIPAL RESOURCES

The Massachusetts Electronic Atlas, a marvelously sophisticated mapping guide to demographic and sociological information about the Commonwealth, is a high-tech way to pull up information about "communication, crime, economy, education, employment, environmental regulation, health, income, physical features, population, race, real estate/lodging, transportation, voting, and political boundaries for cities and towns." Take a few minutes to become acquainted with how to zoom in and out on the maps to locate the desired information; find the atlas at *http://icg.harvard.edu/~maps/maatlas.htm*

Information on cities, towns and other municipalities is retrievable form the Massachusetts Municipal Association at *http://www.mma.org* The site publishes information, arranged topically, on issues of interest to the smaller government units within Massachusetts and includes such data as unemployment rates, education reports, taxation news and political news from small towns.

MISCELLANEOUS RESOURCES

MassLaw, a service of Lawyers Weekly Publications at *http://www.lweekly.com/masslaw.htm* is a superb online newspaper that bills itself accurately as the "place to go for legal information in Massachusetts." It's the page to hit for connecting to Massachusetts lawyers and law firms via the link to same. As a online newspaper, MassLaw contains classified advertising, a *calendar of events, judge assignments,* and offers links to the Massachusetts Government Network. Like many good legal periodicals, MassLaw features thorough coverage of the state's Supreme Judicial Court and Court of Appeals opinions. And for practitioners in Massachusetts, the *Treasure Chest* of "important documents" usually contains material of timely interest, reporting on regulatory or legislative changes at the state and Federal level. ❑

QuickLink
http://www.migov.state.mi.us

MICHIGAN PROVIDES SUPERB INFORMA-
TION services to the Internet from its
official home page and while no one
will hang a blue-ribbon on the page for pulchri-
tude, the layout is utilitarian and provides the
researcher with fast and easy connections to
information resources throughout the state

EXECUTIVE RESOURCES

The governor's electronic office at
http://www.migov.state.mi.us/migov.html
ensures that the citizens of the Internet are never
at a loss for the Gov's news releases, speeches
or reminders of what hard-working politicians
can achieve. There are also links to the legislature and the courts.

In Michigan, the Secretary of State runs
the Motor Vehicle department and oversees
election results; it does not, however, link up
any information on corporations or other business entities in the state. For that information,
turn to the Corporation, Securities and Land
Development Bureau which maintains a home
page at *http://www.commerce.state.mi.us/corp/*

home.htm Business forms for corporations, limited liability partnerships and companies and
limited partnerships are available for downloading from *http://www.commerce.state.mi.us/corp/
corpinfo.htm* That's the same page where guidelines, policy statements and an index to statutes
and administrative rules can be located.

The Attorney General's office has a link
in place on the Web list of state agencies but it
is not yet operative.

Tax forms are e-printed in Adobe
Acrobat PDF format in conjunction with the
Michigan Electronic Library. Individual, business and fiduciary forms are ready for downloading from the site along with the instructions.
Locate the forms at *http://mel.lib.mi.us/michi-
gan/MI-taxforms.html* Find the Michigan Tax
Tribunal at *http://www.cis.state.mi.us/tax* featuring recent decisions, rules of practice and the
text of the Tax Tribunal Act.

The exhaustive list of links to State of
Michigan Departments and Agencies lies at
http://www.migov.state.mi.us/departments.html

JUDICIAL RESOURCES

Michigan Supreme Court decisions dating from October 1995 can be downloaded from
http://www.icle.org/misupct/index.htm The opinions date from October 1995.and can be
searched by case name; Supreme Court Orders
dating from the beginning of 1996 are searchable and downloadable as well. The Michigan
Court of Appeals also makes its opinions available to the public from the server at
http://www.icle.org/mictapp/index.htm The collection begins with opinions from August 1996.
Amendments and proposed amendments to
court rules are online for review at
http://www.icle.org/rules/mcr/mcr-new.htm

LEGISLATIVE MATERIALS

The online state house can be found at
http://www.migov.state.mi.us/legislature.html

providing a handy starting point for connecting to the Senate and the House of Representatives. The home pages from each chamber reprint directory information: find committee membership, e-mail links and leadership information for the Senate at *http://www.coast.net/~misenate/senhp.html* and for the House of Representatives at *http://www.house.state.mi.us* The text of bills and acts are not yet available via the Internet but a news service at *http://www.icle.org/legsums/leglist.htm* provides updates on recent legislation.

BAR ASSOCIATIONS

The members of the State Bar of Michigan gather electronically at *http://www.michbar.org* Once convened at the Web site, find a full-bodied information service that will lead to court opinions from the Michigan Supreme Court and the Court of Appeals as well as from certain county courts and a *desktop directory* that is essentially a sitemap for this extensive Web. The Bar Association offers online copies of the Michigan Code of Judicial Conduct and the Michigan Code of Professional Conduct. There's also a link for lawyers who are about to start their own practice for both mentors and "mentees."
Michigan is home to many specialized bar associations and professional organizations. Find a directory of county bar associations and a similar list for special organizations at *http://www.michbar.org/affiliates/spo.html*

STATE LIBRARY

First-time visitors to the Library of Michigan at *http://www.libofmich.lib.mi.us* should use the sitemap to become acquainted with the ample services of this terrific server. The law library mounts guides to doing legal research, descriptions of its collections and services and selected Michigan Public Acts from its own server at

http://www.libofmich.lib.mi.us/law/lawlib.html
LOCAL AND MUNICIPAL RESOURCES

A massive Web site, promising more than 10,000 pages of information that links up cities, counties and townships throughout Michigan provides coverage of the smaller communities in the state. MultiMag Michigan at *http://multimag.com/mi* offers connections to the broadest range of information; find state highlights, events, business links, schools. sports teams and hypertext links to Michigan magazines here.

MISCELLANEOUS RESOURCES

The Michigan Electronic Library (MEL) provides electronic access at no fee for such materials as Michigan County Economic Profiles, U.S. Census data for the state of Michigan, data from the U.S. Department of Commerce's Economic Bulletin Board, the Consumer Price Index and information about Michigan's state government. It also links to thousands of other resources, Web-wide. Find a search box that allows searching for Michigan library catalogs, government sources and business resources by surfing through the site from the home page at *http://mel.lib.mi.us*

The Michigan District Judges Association enjoys links to Michigan state and Federal servers. It also mounts an overview of Michigan's district courts and also provides a search engine to help the researcher find a local district judge or court. The site resides on the Web at *http://www.voyager.net/mdja* The Institute of Continuing Legal Education *http://www.umich.edu/~icle/index.html* e-prints cases, statutes, guides and forms. ❑

QuickLink

http://www.state.mn.us/
govtoffice/index.html

MINNESOTA GUIDES ITS INFORMATION resources by the North Star, its state-wide project to bring government information online where it will accessible by the computer-savvy public. North Star is complete and is likely to be the only Internet resource the researcher will need for cruising around the high latitudes of Minnesota.

EXECUTIVE RESOURCES

The governor and the agencies under the control of the chief executive of Minnesota enjoy an expansive online presence. The major agencies, and most of the small ones too, have Web pages where the researcher can find a great deal of useful and timely resources. Like most governors, Minnesota's provides the public with biographical information, a list of official duties and the all-important flattering photograph. There are also the requisite press releases, policy initiatives and reprints of the governor's speeches.

As for executive agencies online, the Department of Commerce is a very large agency that oversees most of the financial services industry within the state. From the home page at *http://www.commerce.state.mn.us*

the researcher can link up to the Division of Financial Institutions, the Division of Insurance, the Division of Securities and the Division of Enforcement and Licensing, among others.

Helping Minnesotans render unto the public coffers more easily is the Web server from the Minnesota Department of Revenue at *http://www.taxes.state.mn.us* Find tax forms and publications online, tax laws and revenue notices (referred to breezily as "The Legal Stuff" on the page) as well as newsletters, research reports and link to tax department help lines.

For information on businesses in Minnesota, turn to the well-wired Business Services Division page at *http://www.sos.state.mn.us/bus.html* The page does not yet permit online searching for corporate or partnership records, but there is a simplified index to the filing fees and a description of the forms required to establish businesses within the state.

LEGISLATIVE RESOURCES

The Minnesota statehouse invites the general public to watch its political horse-swapping online from the Minnesota State Legislature server headquartered at *http://www.leg.state.mn.us*

For keeping up with the lawmakers, peruse the Minnesota State Statutes and Session Laws from the comfort of a Web browser by programming the URL meter to find *http://www.leg.state.mn.us/leg/statutes.htm* Zoom through the text using an Infoseek-based search engine or retrieve entire chapters by clicking on the indicated link from the Office of the Revisor of Statutes. Only the most current version of the state code is printed online.

The administrative code has yet to be released electronically to a public server.

The Legislation and Bill Tracking page maintained by the legislature dramatically simplifies the task of scouting up bill texts and legislative histories. Bill texts can be retrieved by bill number; locate bill numbers by searching through House and Senate archives of bill texts, summaries and introductions or the act summaries. The journals from both chambers are online and searchable. For help in legislative research, refer to the Legislative Reference Library at *http://www.leg.state.mn.us/lrl/lrl.htm*

JUDICIAL MATERIALS

Home port for the courts of Minnesota is the Minnesota State Court System home page at *http://www.courts.state.mn.us* where the courts publish Supreme Court decisions every Thursday at 1 p.m. and Court of Appeals decisions every Tuesday at 1 p.m.

The researcher can enjoy a clickable map of Minnesota outlining its ten judicial districts that will deliver information on those district courts such as address, phone and other directory-style information.

Searchable archives of the Minnesota State Appellate Court and Supreme Court dating from May 1996 to the present are available from *http://www.courts.state.mn.us/ library/archive* The archives can be searched by release number, docket number or case name (first party only).

The server is generous in its publication of proposed rule-makings and surveys. Most materials can be downloaded in WordPerfect or rich text format.

LOCAL AND MUNICIPAL RESOURCES

The land of ten thousand lakes are proud of their end-of-the-Ice-Age inheritance and celebrate the grand diversity of their unique culture with links to all the smaller units of government which populate Minnesota. Find a serious collection of connections to local government agencies at the county, city and township level at *http://www.state.mn.us/local/index.html* (And by Minnesota reckoning, each of them should be able to deliver at least 25 lakes apiece.)

STATE LIBRARY

The Minnesota State Law Library keeps a card catalog open all day long and a valid library card is not even a requirement to search it. Browse the catalog whenever the notion strikes by spurring a browser to *http://www.courts.state.mn.us/library/index.html* The law library home page is a dandy place to link conveniently to other Minnesota law resources; it also publishes a directory of Minnesota county law libraries.

BAR ASSOCIATION

The info-packed Web site from the Minnesota Bar Association is conveniently located off the information superhighway at exit *http://www.mnbar.org* Among the services for the weary traveler are selected articles appearing in the association's monthly magazine *Bench and Bar*, the to-be-expected membership information, classified ads, and a complete rundown of the services to attorneys that membership in the association provides. Members who know the secret electronic handshake can get the MSBA calendar, sections information and practice aids. Enjoy committee information and an outline of sections and districts which are there for the asking from other links on the Web site.

MISCELLANEOUS RESOURCES

The North Star service is the only stop necessary for tourist or travel information in Minnesota. The unified information system provides state directories and connections to hundreds of government offices. General information about the state is available by hitting the link to *Minnesota Connection*, that will dish up a lengthy menu of information containing Minnesota history, economic data, policy issues facing the state and additional links to public and private resources.

❑

QuickLink
http://www.state.ms.us

MISSISSIPPI JOINS THE RANKS of the states pumping out reams of government and legal information onto the Internet, making the network a rich resource for research.

EXECUTIVE RESOURCES

The governor steps up to the plate carrying press releases, speeches, an e-mail link to the governor's mansion and connections to Mississippi Web servers. The governor is not shy: review the administration's achievements humbly called the "Mississippi Miracle."A staff directory is also available.

The Attorney General of Mississippi is very busy but somehow there is time in the day to publish current opinions on an unofficial Web site at *http://www.mslawyer.com/ag/ index.html* The official site at *http://www.ago.state.ms.us* does not yet contain opinions, although the site is promising to e-print a complete collection of opinions in the future. Other information provided by the Attorney General includes press releases, updates on current issues and information written for consumers on filing complaints.

Taxpayers -- or at least legal researchers -- have a friend in the MS State Tax Commission and their Web site which resides at *http://www.mstc.state.ms.us* Click on the colorful logo to enter the site where a framed Web page greets visitors with links to laws, regulations and rules. Tax forms can be ordered online; the forms themselves have not yet been electronically published.

The Secretary of State e-publishes corporate forms, UCC forms, lobbyist registration forms and a promise from the authorities to expand the online offerings.

JUDICIAL MATERIALS

Home for the Mississippi judiciary is *http://www.mssc.state.ms.us* and is the where biographies of the justices of the Supreme Court and the Court of Appeals are the first items to greet the visitor. Hot buttons at the top of the page link to a well-stocked larder of judicial information.

Opinions from both courts may be searched at *http://www.mssc.state.ms.us/decisions/search/default.asp* using a fill-in-the-blank form that allows searching by *case number, date, judge, title, appellant, appellee, category* or *classification*. Rules are online too as is the docket calendar.

Other links connect to the clerk's office which has automated much of the process of filing papers with the court.

LEGISLATIVE RESOURCES

Get to the wired Mississippi statehouse by parlaying the URL *http://www.ls.state.ms.us* into a Web site containing direct links to both the state Senate and the House of Representatives. The same page can connect to a page containing the status of bills; download the bill status in either WordPerfect 5.2 format or plain vanilla ASCII text.

The Senate server gives away a list of its membership, its committees and publishes the Senate rules online. There's also a link to *Joint Rules* and *Constitutional Provisions*. Enjoy all this informational largesse at *http://www.ls.state.ms.us/htms/senate.htm*

The House of Representatives maintains a site containing precisely the same type of information at *http://www.ls.state.ms.us/ htms/house.htm*

STATE LIBRARY

The home page for the Mississippi State Library Commission lives at *http://www.mlc.lib.ms.us* The home page links up to descriptions of the library's services.

The State Law Library can be found at *http://www.mssc.state.ms.us/Library/default.htm* but is considerably constricted in the information it publishes online, restricting itself to history, staff, policy statements and parking info.

BAR ASSOCIATION

Mississippi attorneys have a private club in form of the Mississippi Bar Online. The home page is at *http://www.mississippibar.org* and that's where an easy-to-navigate page will connect researchers to CLE information and bar association meetings. The link to *Ethics and Professionalism* delivers ethics opinions, the *Rules of Professional Conduct*, guidelines of professional conduct and *Rules of Discipline*.

A directory for attorneys and links to the Web sites for the Internet-connected law firms in the state is available from the link to *Bar Directory*. The Mississippi Bar Association is an active publisher and a list of publications is online under the connection to *Publications*.

LOCAL AND MUNICIPAL RESOURCES

Links to schools and universities and to municipalities around the state of Mississippi are featured on a Web site operated by Mississippi State University called, cleverly enough, "Web Sites in Mississippi." A link for *Legal* leads to a small collection of online law firms and services for lawyers.

An interactive map of the state, offering point-and-click access to counties and cities is online at *http://www2.netdoor.com/ ~allred/missmaps*

MISCELLANEOUS RESOURCES

The law library from Ole Miss provides a fair reference page for Mississippi law resources at *http://www.olemiss.edu/depts/law_lib_research/ laws/mississippi.html* Links lead to the Constitution, session laws, state agencies and other public servers.

The Mississippi Code is available online from a fee-based subscription service that incorporates current bills and session laws into the code. The subscription fee is $249 per year or $149 annually for government and non-profit access. Multi-user accounts for up to ten users can obtain passwords for $549 per year; governments and non-profits can get the same service for $249. Find more information on the service from the Web site at *http://www.mississippicode.com*

A commercial online service to disseminate Mississippi legal forms is runs a Web site at *http://www.mslegalforms.com* Known as the Mississippi Lawyers Legal Forms Bank, the site contains more than one thousand forms with instructions that can be downloaded from the site. A complete subscription, which also includes a searchable version of the Mississippi Code updated through the current legislative session is available for $448 per year. Find details on the service and a subscription blank on the home page.

The Mississippi Yellow Pages maintains an online version at *http://yellowpages.mso.net/ main.html*

❑

QuickLink
http://www.state.mo.us

MISSOURI IS FULLY WIRED for the legal researcher. The public services use cutting edge technology and judging by the quantity and quality of electronic information available from the Show Me state, the future will deliver ever-increasing archives of public data. It's easy to find law-related materials from Missouri because the databases are well-organized and the Web pages are built for easy browsing.

EXECUTIVE RESOURCES

Like a good governor, Missouri's chief executive greets visitors to the official Missouri State Government Web with a picture and links to his own Web site. At *http://www.state.mo.us/ gov/index.htm* find a plush Web site upholstered with press releases, copies of speeches, a biography, news from the governor's office and a copy of the State of the State address in both print and audio format. From the home page, find an e-mail and telephone directory for the state.

As for executive branch agencies, the Business Services division of the Secretary of State's office hands out online corporations forms with instructions at its Web site at *http://mosl.sos.state.mo.us/bus-ser/soscor.html*

The Secretary of State's home page also links to UCC forms, commissions and the franchise tax division.

For tax forms and other publications, refer to the home page of the Missouri Department of Revenue at *http://services.state.mo.us/dor* Court case summaries and detailed letter rulings are available from the same address. The State Tax Commission, which oversees property taxation, reprints its regulations electronically at *http://www.state.mo.us/stc/rules.htm*

The Attorney General keeps a tidy Web site that's most notable for its press releases, consumer complaint forms and its list of Missouri's Most Wanted criminals.

JUDICIAL MATERIALS

The Missouri Supreme Court, Court of Appeals and Circuit Courts share a handsome and well-designed Web site named the Missouri Courts Digest: The Electronic Guide to Missouri Courts at *http://www.osca.state.mo.us/ courts/Judicial2.nsf* It is one of the most ambitious Web sites for state court information in the nation; the Electronic Guide provides more information about Missouri courts than any other state court server.

The link for the Supreme Court leads not only to court opinions dating from early 1997 but it also connects to an oral argument docket. The court also Web-publishes other court dispositions such as applications to transfer, extraordinary writs, motions for re-hearing and other matters. Other links lead to biographies of the justices as well as to offices that serve the court: the clerk's office, the Board of Law Examiners, Supreme Court library and Supreme Court publications. Anxious law students can read the results of the bar exam from this same page.

The Missouri Court of Appeals links for the Western and Southern Districts were still under construction in mid-1997 but the connections for the Eastern District offer the researcher immediate access to dockets, opinions and orders, archives, judicial biographies and the office of the court clerk. For a glimpse of Missouri's forward-looking plans to electrify their courts, peek at the Missouri Court Automation Project, also known as Electronic Courts 2004. The plan calls for systematically building connections to all the courts in the state by 2004.

LEGISLATIVE RESOURCES

The Missouri General Assembly gathers down by the old bitstream at *http://www.moga.state.mo.us* and that's where the researcher can find a bill tracking system that can keep tabs on bills in both the House and the Senate.

For both chambers, Web pages detailing their respective memberships are online. The pages contain committee assignments, directories and legislation sponsored by individual representatives.

Locate and browse the full text of Missouri Revised Statutes at *http://www.moga.state.mo.us/homestat.htm* Keyword searching of the entire code is available or retrieve individual sections of the compilation by clicking on the link to *View Missouri Revised Statutes.*

STATE LIBRARY

For checking up on checking out, zip over the Missouri State Library at *http://mosl.sos.state.mo.us/libser.html* where the state librarians outline their reference services, their staff and link up to other libraries throughout Missouri.

BAR ASSOCIATION

When Missouri lawyers say ,"Show me the Web site," point directly to the Missouri Bar Association at *http://www.mobar.org* Chunky search buttons lead the researcher to background

information about the association and to specialized resource materials for attorneys, teacher and the news media. The links available under the connection for lawyers are extensive and include such items as placement services, compensation surveys, CLE requirements, law practice management resources and small firm Internet access guides. There's also a list of bar publications and guides on fee dispute resolution.

LOCAL AND MUNICIPAL RESOURCES

The city home pages offer fingertip access to the smaller communities, regional development corporations and chambers of commerce of Missouri at the click of a mouse. The cities page is located at *http://www.ecodev.state.mo.us/mo/city.htm* From there, links to the various municipalities publish profiles of the towns, economic information and other local business data. Other links on the page branch off to connections for colleges and universities, health services and online publications within Missouri.

MISCELLANEOUS RESOURCES

The Cyberspace Trade Show is an ongoing project of the Missouri Department of Economic Development that provides visitors with virtual tours of business opportunities in the state. Links connect to land sites, buildings and community profiles. (The link to *MO Laws* is a link to the Missouri Revised Statutes service from the legislature.) The online show is at *http://showme.state.mo.us/showme*

An interesting site for geographical research into Missouri sites is provided by the Missouri Spatial Data Information Service at *http://msdis.missouri.edu* The researcher will need some fancy software in order to read the geofiles in ARC/INFO format, but once installed, the system allows downloading of extremely detailed maps by county. The service is useful for real estate research, environmental practice and ag-lawyers.

❑

QuickLink
http://www.mt.gov/gov/gov.htm

MONTANA IS BIG SKY COUNTRY; it's also the land of the big server if the legal resources available to the Internet-wired public are any indication. Montana's government rules in electronic sunshine. The Internet is also an invaluable tool in a geographically immense and sparsely populated state like Montana.

EXECUTIVE RESOURCES

The governor's office is open for business at *http://www.mt.gov/governor/ governor.htm* and that's where the researcher can find the usual Internet trappings that go with the office: press releases and a re-run of the most recent State of the State address, a biography of the governor and First Spouse, a link to the Chief Executive's staff and a judiciously selected collection of speeches.

For companies looking to incorporate in Montana, the Secretary of State's office publishes a long list of available business structures and provides basic information on the formation process. A schedule of fees is available, as are many of the basic forms. The forms can be downloaded in Adobe Acrobat PDF format.

The Department of Revenue is removing bureaucratic stumbling blocks to paying taxes by publishing downloadable tax forms and instructions on its server at *http://www.mt.gov/revenue/rev.htm* That's the same site where the researcher can find information on business tax incentives, the tax structure and get help from the tax authorities. Only thing missing are the tax laws and regulations themselves.

The administrative code of Montana is not yet online but an advertisement for it is; details on purchasing a print version of the regulations for the state agencies can be yours by dialing up *http://www.mt.gov/sos/arm.htm*

JUDICIAL MATERIALS

It's fairly slim pickin's when it comes to judicial materials in Montana. Supreme Court decisions from the current year, arranged by month of publication can be retrieved from the state law library at *http://161.7.121.6/ OPININS.HTM* An informative but not terribly useful annual report is available at *http://161.7.121.6/11.HTM*

There is, however, an interesting Web page published by the Workers' Compensation Court at *http://jsd.dli.mt.gov/work_comp/ table1.htm* The site reprints the text of decisions, court statistics, a trial calendar, court rules and general information about the court.

LEGISLATIVE RESOURCES

The legislature keeps a handsome Web site to deliver fresh laws to the people of Montana. In such a lightly populated place, the legislature doesn't find a need to convene very often (every two years) or for very long (a few months). Still, they get the job done and the results of their efforts can be scanned using the links to online versions of the bills, journals and histories from sessions current and past.

Current laws may be located using a

bills subject index or by perusing a list of bill numbers. The link to *cumulative bill status* updates the researchers on where a particular bill stands in the legislative process. All bills can be downloaded in WordPerfect 5.1 format.

Other information that the Montana researcher will find to be useful are the analysis of the state budget and an interactive legislative district map that helps define who represents who.

Links to the e-mail of all the legislators is on the same page; so too are interim reports by interim sub-committees and statutory legislative committees. A directory of legislative agencies with staff phone numbers and contact information and a FAQ file round out the site. Older legislative materials can be searched through the same sources as current legislation.

Montana publishes a searchable version of its state code online at *http://www.nfoweb.com/folio.pgi/mtcode/doc?* That's where the Constitution of the State of Montana, the text of the statutes of the Montana Code and the Enabling Act reside. It's not all that easy to search -- the site construction is clunky -- but the material is there for the researcher willing to persevere through a series of mouse clicks (which are not exactly as strenuous as say, coal mining or ditch digging.)

STATE LIBRARY

The official state librarians work the reference desk at *http://msl.mt.gov* where links can lead the researcher to statewide library resources including a rundown on staff, services, publications and links to the state's library catalogs. The state is dependent on its natural resources and the state library features a superb *Natural Resources Information System* that will be interest to environmental law researchers. Also find a link to the Montana Talking Book Library.

For law librarians, the state law library of Montana is online at *http://161.7.121.6* Billed as the largest law library in the state, the Web site mounts links to the online catalog, Montana legal

information (court opinions, the state code, the state bar and an annual report from the state Supreme Court) as well as general reference resources, news links and general Montana information.

BAR ASSOCIATION

The Montana Bar Association has not yet published a Web site as of June 1997. However, the Montana Legal Web is a directory of attorneys in the state, searchable by location, area of practice or name. Find the Montana Legal Web online at *http://www.webexmt.com*

LOCAL AND MUNICIPAL RESOURCES

No single source exists online for running down local or municipal sources but the official Montana page is useful for trekking electronically to the more remote areas of Montana.

MISCELLANEOUS RESOURCES

For a taste of Montana via computer, fire up *Montana Online* where road reports, weather conditions, employment data and information about the state's educational system may be browsed. It's also a good place to locate travel and tourism information when planning a Montana excursion.

There's also *MontanaWeb*, an online classified directory of businesses from throughout the state. Entries are indexed by business type: the link to *Legal Services* pulls up hypertext links to those law firms in the state that operate Web sites.

❑

QuickLink
http://www.state.ne.us

NEBRASKA IS THE ONLY STATE IN THE Union with a unicameral legislature, thus reducing legislative lookup time in half. The other branches of government are all well-represented online and there should not be any difficulty in tracking down agency information.

The best Internet resource for the Nebraska legal researcher is Nebrask@ Online. The service is operated by the Library Commission of Nebraska to provide electronic access to the state's information resources. Nebrask@ Online subscribers have (or shortly will have) access to interactive motor vehicle records, interactive title registration and lien searches, corporation records, UCC searches and listservs operated by professional organizations. That's not a bad deal for $50 a year; for more information, see the home page at http://www.nol.org/info/intro.html for subscription information and the complete dossier on the benefits of membership.

EXECUTIVE RESOURCES

The governor of Nebraska keeps an unobtrusive Web server at *http://www.state.ne.us/gov/gov.html* which is where the intrepid researcher can find news releases, the governor's weekly schedule, a biography of the chief executive and a not-terri-bly-shy list of the boss's accomplishments. A reprint of the state of state address and pictures of the esteemed statesman join with a link to the state government Web site to complete the gubernatorial picture.

The Secretary of State reserves the most interesting corporate information databases for the paying customers of Nebrask@ Online. Those subscribers can search through the UCC database and the state corporation and business entity archive. Ordinary mortals will need to be content with the price tag-free collection of corporate and business forms on the SOS's page at *http://www.nol.org/info/intro.html*

The Department of Revenue operates a partly free, partly fee-based service for the general public. Among the freebies are reprints of the revenue statutes, a generous collection of tax forms for individual, fiduciary, partnership, S corporation, and sales and use tax returns and the department's newsletters. The department also hands out electronic versions of its information guides. A password and paid-up account is necessary to access the sales and use tax permits online.

The official list of all Nebraska state agencies linked to the Web is at *http://www.state.ne.us/agency.html* Find a directory of all state employees at *http://www.state.ne.us/statedir/statedir.html*

JUDICIAL MATERIALS

When it comes to the common law of Nebraska, the pickings are slimmer than a cornfield in February. The paucity of Nebraska court opinions is surprising since judicial materials are usually the first public materials that state authorities mount to the Internet. Perhaps the success all the other states have had with electronic publication of court cases will rub off on the judicial Webmasters of Nebraska. Until then, case law research still means hitting the books, not the microchips.

LEGISLATIVE RESOURCES

The aforementioned one-house legislature keeps its online chamber at *http://unicam1.lcs.state.ne.us* There's not so much material on the site that a sitemap is needed, but one is thoughtfully provided anyway at *http://uni-cam1.lcs.state.ne.us/LEGDOCS/CATALOG.HTM* Scroll down the alphabetical listing of information to find links to bill texts, bill status, committee statements, statements of intent, fiscal notes and related documents at once. The legislative work-sheets list the bill numbers and their fate without any editorial interpolation; these sites are hard to decipher for any but the most savvy Nebraska legislative researcher. A directory of lawmakers, helpful explanatory guides on the unique Nebraska legislative process and session calendars are all part of the site. The link to the Legislative Research Division leads to *A Legislator's Guide to Ballot Initiatives.*

Nebraska mounts its statutes on a Folio database that's updated twice a year. The complete code can be searched from *http://unicam1.lcs.state.ne.us/folio.pgi/ statutes.nfo?* There's no sign yet of the administrative code anywhere online.

BAR ASSOCIATION

At *http://www.nebar.com* the Nebraska State Bar Association maintains a home page that comfortably hooks up connections to bar programs and services for members, legislative information and section/committee information. This is also the place to come for a rundown on CLE credits and opportunities and the Nebraska Lawyers Trust Account. Links to judiciary information, a calen-

dar of events (golf tournament anyone?) and list of members round out the site.

STATE LIBRARY

The good-looking home page from the Nebraska Library Commission at *http://www.nlc.state.ne.us* is the clearinghouse for its electronic library, connections to other libraries in Nebraska and a searchable catalog. The link to Nebraska libraries offers hooks to Internet-equipped libraries, depository libraries and OCLC and regional consortia members.

LOCAL AND MUNICIPAL RESOURCES

A comprehensive guide to Nebraska communities is online at *http://www.neblink.com/cit1a/cit1a.htm* The information at the end of the links is underwhelming: it's mostly the mailing address and telephone number of the small-town mayors or city clerks for the burghs and hamlets of Nebraska.

The most thorough and info-packed link is the one for Omaha: it seems that every professional association, civic organization, industry group, hospital, motel and university in the city runs a Web site. Find Omaha's contributions to the WorldWideWeb at *http://www.neblink.com/cit1a/omaha.htm*

MISCELLANEOUS RESOURCES

The general information Web site for Nebraska is NebraskaLink at *http://www.neblink.com* and that's the place to go for connections to the state's newspapers, colleges and universities and travel information. Pluck Nebraska maps from this site as well. ❑

QuickLink

http://www.state.nv.us

NEVADA GAMBLES ON THE ELECTRONIC AGE with a far-ranging collection of legal resources to help the researcher track down the major sources of the law. Sites are all professionally designed though many of them were under construction in 1997; once all the sites are up and running and the electronic shelves have been stocked, there should be no trouble finding the most important law archives in the state.

EXECUTIVE RESOURCES

The Chief Executive has a pleasant home page at *http://www.state.nv.us/gov/gov.htm* that is distinct for its simplicity: it is merely a photograph of the governor and a message of welcome to Internet visitors.

Other agencies are considerably more voluble. The online home for the Secretary of State is *http://jvm.com/sos* but it was under construction in mid-1997. Try back to see what's been made available under the links to *Corporations, Limited Partnerships, & Other Business Entities* and *Uniform Commercial Code* among others. Also under construction was the home page and link to Nevada's Attorney General. Check back with the main

state Web site.

The gambling industry important to the state and the Nevada State Gaming Control Board keeps a no-lose Web site at *http://www.state.nv.us/gaming* that wires the various divisions of the commission and outlines each office's responsibility.

For a comprehensive list of Nevada state agencies and departments, surf to *http://www.state.nv.us/index.htm* where an alphabetical click bar is the guide to navigating the offices.

JUDICIAL MATERIALS

Nevada was still building its judicial services in mid-1997 and there were no judicial links to speak of at that time. But the Nevada Supreme Court library, armed with links to its catalogs and state and federal resources at *http://www.clan.lib.nv.us/docs/NSCL/nscl.htm* promises that Nevada Reports from 1986 to present and Nevada Supreme Court Advance opinions will soon also be published online at the library's Web site.

LEGISLATIVE RESOURCES

The cybergallery for the Nevada State Legislature accepts visitors at *http://www.leg.state.nv.us* The legislature is forthcoming with legislative documents and the link from the home page to the current session allows online access to all bills, resolutions, journal, daily files and revised agendas from both chambers. Reports and histories are available here too and all of the information can be winnowed by using one of the handy search engines to look through documents from the current or previous legislative session.

Nevada's legislators and the committees on which they serve are all connected to the home page.

With little fanfare, Nevada publishes both its statutory compilation and its administrative code to the Internet and both can be searched from the same search engine together. Click on the link for *Search Nevada Law* from the legislature's home page to access the search engine. The only drawback is that the editions of both codes are considerably dated and all chapters and sections should either be thoroughly researched for accuracy or looked up in an official and updated print version.

State Library

To locate the Nevada State Library and Archives, retrieve *http://www.clan.lib.nv.us/docs/NSLA/nsla.htm* for online access to the state's library catalogs. The librarians also supply online directories of libraries, a list of the Federal publications they receive and connections to professional organizations.

Bar Association

It looked like it was still under construction or abandoned in mid-1997 with non-working links, seemingly dummied-up placesavers and very scarce content, but the Nevada State Bar Association Web site at *http://www.dsi.org/state-bar/nevada.htm#nevada* may well be in good working order in the future, though no promises are made.

Local and Municipal Resources

The Nevada League of Cities and its comprehensive links to member and affiliate cities is the place to track down some of the population centers of a sparsely populated state. The municipalities listed here are not all online yet -- in fact, most are not equipped with home pages -- but the site represents the first step in knitting together towns and cities that are geographically remote from one another with the miracles of technolo-gy. The URL is *http://www.state.nv.us/nvleague*

Miscellaneous Resources

Facts and figures about Nevada are what attracts the researchers to the Nevada State Data Center. The center, at *http://www.clan.lib.nv.us/docs/NSLA/SDC/sdc.htm*

Businesses considering re-location to the dry and sunny climes of Nevada can find the requisite details from the Nevada Commission on Economic Development at *http://www.state.nv.us/businessop* The site details Nevada's transportation system, human resources, government incentives, telecommunications and energy infrastructure, real estate and the educational system. The twelve Regional Development Authorities can be reached by browser at *http://www.state.nv.us/businessop/newmap.htm*

Travel planning for Nevada excursions can begin fruitfully with a pre-trip visit to the official online travel guide produced by the Nevada Commission on Tourism at *http://www.travelnevada.com* A complete list of lodging and transportation is online; that's joined by *Nevada Magazine,* a newsy *What's New?* link to goings-on from around the state and a link to request more information from the tourist officials via snail mail.

With its wide-open desert spaces, Nevada is one of the states considered for a nuclear waste dump site. The issue is a charged political concern in the Silver State; keep up with Federal and state parries-and-thrusts at *http://www.state.nv.us/nucwaste* as the wheres and hows of disposing of America's nuclear waste is debated by the authorities.

❏

QuickLink

http://www.state.nh.us

Nᴇᴡ Hᴀᴍᴘsʜɪʀᴇ ᴠɪsɪᴛᴏʀs sᴜʀғɪɴɢ ɪɴ ᴛʜᴇ northern climes are greeted by the state's resident information guru Webster, the New Hampshire State Government Online Information Center. Webster has enough links to keep the researcher happy and if the arguments it makes for complete online access to public documents are half as persuasive as the servers celebrated namesake, the New Hampshire research will indeed be as lucky as Jabez Stone.

EXECUTIVE RESOURCES

The governor holds forth from *http://www.state.nh.us/governor* with a collection of links that included the ever-popular press releases, biographical information and speeches. Bounce from the governor's page to any other government site in New Hampshire with the governor's featured links to all branches of state government.

The Attorney General, Web-present at *http://www.state.nh.us/oag/ag.html* sets out the responsibilities of each division; much of the information is of information to the general public rather than for the professional researcher.

The tax authorities have set up cybershop at *http://www.state.nh.us/revenue/ revenue.htm* to make tax forms, tax laws, administative rules and specific taxes -- business enterprise tax, business profits tax, current use tax, interest and dividends tax, meals and rooms tax, real estate transfer tax and legacy and succession tax -- all fingertip accessible to the Internet-equipped. The Board of Tax and Land Appeals serves online at *http://www.state.nh.us/btla*

See the laws governing professional licenses at the Web site from the New Hampshire Joint Board of Licensure and Certification at *http://www.state.nh.us/jtboard/ home.htm* The board regulates professional engineers, architects, land surveyors, foresters and natural scientists.

For a directory of all state agencies, point the browser to *http://www.state.nh.us/ agency/agencies.html*

LEGISLATIVE RESOURCES

New Hampshire's legislature, known as the General Court, provides the text of chapter laws from current sessions, arranged in chapter law sequence and concurrent resolutions on the home page at *http://www.state.nh.us/gencourt/ gencourt.htm* The Senate's home page at *http://www.state.nh.us/senate/nhsenate.htm* hosts the Senate roster, commitees, calendar and journals and press releases. For the House of Representatives, linked to the General Court's home page, find the same information as well as links to the home pages, where they exist, for individual members. Bills, resolutions and session laws from the previous session are available on the page too. Follow New Hampshire legislation by subscribing to the General Court Information System; details are at *http://www.state.nh.us/gencourt/gcis.htm*

JUDICIAL MATERIALS

Supreme Court slip opinions dating from November 1995 to the present are published on the Supreme Court's server at

NEW HAMPSHIRE
6:66

http://www.state.nh.us/courts/supreme/opin-ions.htm For links to the oral arguments calendar, cases accepted by the court and state Supreme Court orders, refer to *http://www.state.nh.us/courts/supreme.htm* The state's Probate Court hangs probate court forms online as well as administrative orders and procedure bulletins at *http://www.state.nh.us/courts/probate.htm* As a reference service to the courts of New Hampshire, flip to the Administrative Office of Courts home page *http://www.state.nh.us/courts/aoc.htm* for its links to the state courts, justices, judges, marital masters and clerks. They also publish the civil interest rate.

Bar association

While it's distressingly light on substantial information save for links to pro bono activities, a reduced fee referral program and a general referral program, the New Hampshire Bar Association does maintain a skeletal Web site at *http://www.nh.com/legal/nhbar*

State Library

The state library conducts business at *http://www.state.nh.us/nhsl/index.html* where it serves as a depository library for patent and trademark materials and offers online access to the reference desk where the librarians have compiled their picks of the best of the Internet. The library's catalog, NHU-PAC, is fully searchable via a telnet connection at *telnet://199.92.250.12:2000* The *New Hampshire Almanac* offers a general store of state materials, including a picture and description of the ghastly state tartan.

There's also a New Hampshire Law Library available at *http://www.state.nh.us/courts/lawlib.htm* that won't win any awards for

drama but it does provide connection to the leading court sites and e-mail access to the librarians.

Local and municipal Resources

The best link to small-town New Hampshire comes from the official state server at *http://www.state.nh.us/localgovt/cities.htm* An alphabetical list connects to each and every hamlet in New Hampshire with varying degrees of richness in the content.

The New Hampshire Municipal Association has put up a Web site at *http://www.nhmunicipal.org/abous/index.html* to promote their services on behalf of the 200+ municipalities in the state. The association exchanges information among local government officials to help them run local governments more efficiently. The association publishes reference materials, an annual directory of officials and the *New Hampshire Town and City* magazine.

Miscellaneous Resources

NH ResourceNet at *http://nhresnet.sr.unh.edu* is a service to planners, town officials, resource managers and the general public to help project planning. ResourceNet is a joint project of New Hampshire Office of State Planning and the Complex Systems Researcher Center at the University of New Hampshire. The site has information on planning and on a data catalog from the GRANIT server.

The New Hampshire State Archives is beginning to get its feet wet on the Web at *http://www.state.nh.us/state/archives.htm* where a *Guide to the New Hampshire State Archives* is the best feature.

❏

QuickLink

http://www.state.nj.us

NEW JERSEY IS HOME TO THE NEW JERSEY InTouch Home Page, a colorful, punchy and informative official Web site at *http://www.state.nj.us* that loads remarkable amounts of information into a simple package. Place that URL in your bookmark alongside the Web site created by attorney Anne M. Rendall called the New Jersey Law Network at *http://njlawnet.com* and all of New Jersey's online legal and government resources will be yours.

EXECUTIVE RESOURCES

The governor's home page outdoes those of other states by offering the State of the State address not in ho-hum ASCII text, but in your choice of *"outline and text," "text only"* or *"complete with images."* What else is there? It's the usual: press releases, of course, legislative and policy highlights, budget reports and bio-graphical information. Find the electro-mansion at *http://www.state.nj.us/officeo.htm*

An elaborate Web site from the Secretary of State's office is very informative but lacks the true interactivity that would create online value for the researcher; instead, the site deliver numbers-to-call and descriptions of ser-

vices but refrains from providing searchable corporate records or online filing of required documents. That's a major drawback to an oth-erwise well-designed site. Use its reference ser-vices from the Division of Commercial Recording at *http://www.state.nj.us/state/ dcr/dcrpg1.html*

The New Jersey Division of Taxation eases the burden of writing tax checks by pro-viding prodigious links to tax forms, tax notices and press releases on its Web site. Get the com-plete score from the Garden State taxpersons at *http://www.state.nj.us/treasury/taxation*

Like Nevada, casino gambling is a major industry for New Jersey; should you require the rules of blackjack rather than the rules of appel-late practice, refer to the Casino Control Commission curious Web site at *http://www.state.nj.us/casinos*

The monster link to all of New Jersey's online departments and agencies is at *http://www.state.nj.us/njdepts.htm*

LEGISLATIVE MATERIALS

The home page for the New Jersey State Legislature is at *http://www.njleg.state.nj.us* It's the home for text and history of legislative bills. Before the informational pleasures of the New Jersey legislature can be savored, some special software named Envoy Viewer 7.0 must first be downloaded. Get Envoy Viewer 7.0 from Tumbleweed Software at *http://www.tumble-weed.com/download.htm*

The legislature's home page offers an interactive map of legislative districts and links to all members of the Assembly and Senate. Scroll down the page to find links to search bills by bill number, sponsor, subject or keyword in bill synopsis. The full text of the New Jersey State Statutes and the NJ Constitution are accessible from the legislature's Web site as well.

JUDICIAL RESOURCES

The courts of New Jersey maintain their own home page at *http://www.state.nj.us/judiciary* Because the site is so extensive -- it is, in fact, the most elaborate state court site on the Internet -- the Webmasters have installed a site map to aid in navigating the informational crannies stocked on the site.

A slick, professional home page escorts the researcher to court decisions from the New Jersey Supreme Court, Appellate Division and Tax Court. (As one of the few states to provide a Web site for its Tax Court, New Jersey's is a model that should be emulated by the tax courts in other jurisdictions. The New Jersey Tax Court is located at *http://www.state.nj.us/judiciary/tax.htm* The page describes the structure of the court, prints a directory of tax court judges and offers the browsing public a copy of the *Attorneys' Mandatory Settlement Conference.*) Supreme Court cases date from 1994; decisions from the other jurisdictions are available from 1995 to present. Retrieve the cases from Rutgers Law School at *http://www-camlaw.rutgers.edu/library*

The New Jersey Rules of Professional Conduct are published, courtesy of the New Jersey Law Network, at *http://njlawnet.com/njrpc*

BAR ASSOCIATION

The New Jersey State Bar Association keeps its home page at *http://www.njsba.com* and that's where an extensive, subject-oriented collection of local law links will provide a terrific amount of information about practicing law in the Garden State. In addition to the practice area links, there are connections to the New Jersey Institute for Continuing Legal Education at *http://www.njicle.com* and the New Jersey Lawyer Newspaper at *http://www.njlnews.com* Find the New Jersey State Bar Foundation at *http://www.njsbf.com*

STATE LIBRARY

To get to the New Jersey state library, point your browser straight to *http://www.state.nj.us/statelibrary/njlib.htm* Connections mounted on the library site permit searching of the library's catalog and feature links to other New Jersey libraries and libraries in other states.

LOCAL AND MUNICIPAL RESOURCES

Many of the townships and municipalities enjoy a Web presence. Little Egg Harbor, Perth Amboy, Tenafly and Cherry Hill all have Web sites though their contributions to the process of legal research can be very quickly overestimated: they are mostly chamber-of-commerce, boosterific sites that provide scant law-related information. They're more useful for the local information they provide. A detailed collection of local links is available from *http://www.state.nj.us/localgov.htm*

MISCELLANEOUS RESOURCES

In addition to the government's one-stop shopping, try the New Jersey Law Network, brilliantly maintained by Anne M. Rendall. The connections lead to every imaginable law source in the state, as well as plenty of miscellaneous sites for schools, weather, travel and other reference data. The New Jersey Law Network is online at *http://njlawnet.com/index.html*

The Rutgers University School of Law-Camden law library offers a complete Internet reference service to New Jersey and federal resources from *http://www-camlaw.rutgers.edu/library/research.html* The most interesting features of the law library page are its connections to law journals, law schools and general interest newspapers. Also find a fair list of New Jersey newspapers with appropriate links from *http://www.concentric.net/~stevewt/usa/NewJersey.html* ❑

QuickLink
http://www.state.nm.us/

NEW MEXICO IS RAPIDLY ADDING NEW information to the web; there's still a great deal that can be added but the state's first Internet efforts provide the researcher with convenient and timely data.

EXECUTIVE RESOURCES

The governor of New Mexico oversees an unobtrusive presence on the Internet; the governor's page certainly scores with what ranks as the coolest governor graphics on the Internet. As for contents, the page is a simple and dignified convocation of press releases, biographical information, links to other government agencies and political articles titled *Hot Issues*.

Other agencies are as equally accessible. The Department of Regulation and Licensing at *http://www.state.nm.us/rld/ rld_mstr.html* gives background on the regulators and contact numbers.

The State Corporation Commission gathers around the virtual conference table from its Web site at *http://www.state.nm.us/scc* and they do yeoman service with the searchable links to companies within the state, d.b.a. the *Corporation Information Inquiry*. Pop in the name of a company and let it rip: the search engine will pull up basic corporate records of companies established within the state.

The New Mexico Taxation and Revenue Department rakes it in from *http://www.state.nm.us/tax* The site contains a phone list of its various departments and offers downloadable publications and instructions. As for tax forms, there are current forms for individual, business and motor vehicle taxes. Other links lead to federal sources and to out-of-state tax authorities.

A comprehensive listing of all New Mexico agencies reachable via the Internet is online at *http://www.state.nm.us/state/ agencies.html*

JUDICIAL MATERIALS

New Mexico's judiciary is behind the times and is only gingerly adding resources to the Internet. There is very little judicial material online; the only Web site for the New Mexico judiciary is from the Second Judicial District Court at *http://www.cabq.gov/cjnet/dst2alb* where a fine site links up the biographies of justices, local rules, an online suggestion box and a smattering of services to the public. It's a good site, but hopefully New Mexico's court administrators will be logging some HTML time in the near future.

LEGISLATIVE RESOURCES

Debating issues of interest to New Mexico's citizens and making laws to address those issues are the hard-working legislators who show off the fruits of their loquacious labors at *http://www.technet.nm.org/legislature*

A bill finder from the home page will look around for texts from either chamber dating from 1996; restrict searches to all bills, all memorials, memorials, joint memorials, and resolutions. Also search by *keyword, sponsor, category* or *bill number*.

Scroll down a list of *bills passed* arranged in bill order to find bill titles and hypertext links to the bills themselves. Reports from committees on large bills and a daily bill finder are also available.

New Mexico statutes are reprinted in the legislative archives on a Folio database. Find a searchable version of the New Mexico code at *http://www.technet.nm.org/legislature/archives.html* A slightly dated version of the New Mexico administrative code is available for free (after registration) from the commercial publisher Michie at *http://www.michie.com/code/nm/nm.html*

The Senate's Web site links to Senators and committees at *http://www.technet.nm.org/legislature/senate_info.html*

The same information can be had for the House of Representatives at *http://www.technet.nm.org/legislature/house_info.html*

STATE LIBRARY

A top-drawer site awaits the researcher from the New Mexico State Library at *http://www.stlib.state.nm.us* Telnet to the statewide catalog -- the password is *salsa* – or review a lengthy collection of other information resources that include the e-mail addresses of libraries around the state, the *Digital Librarian* and a handy collection of the major links to government sites.

BAR ASSOCIATION

As of mid-1997, the New Mexico Bar Association had not yet mounted a Web site.

LOCAL AND MUNICIPAL RESOURCES

The spread-out towns, cities and small municipalities of New Mexico flock together at one online spot and that spot would, naturally, be browser-accessible at *http://www.nets.com/newmextourism/maps/index.html* Also find a service of the state government at *http://www.state.nm.us/state/city_county.html* that wires up cities and counties from around the state to one browseable Web page.

MISCELLANEOUS RESOURCES

Just on general principle, every researcher should take a look at the QuickTime movie version of New Mexico's tourist pitch to see what can be done with the multimedia applications of the Internet. It has no direct use as a legal research tool, but it counts as an interesting by-way when en route to the other travel planning resources at the NM tourist booth mounted at *http://www.newmexico.org*

Demographic data, county maps, population estimates and simple geographical maps can be found at the New Mexico *Fast Facts Center* at *http://www.state.nm.us/state/FastFacts/Welcome.html* ❑

QuickLink

http://unix2.nysed.gov/ils/executive/g
overnor/governor.html

NEW YORK STATE provides a very thorough collection of materials for state law research. New York pioneered the first Internet publication of state licensing information for professionals and provided one of the first text-searchable gophers for browsing state statutes. Today, New York remains on the forefront of technological innovation; keep up with the latest at the New York State Government Information Locator Service at *http://www.nysl.nysed.gov/ils*

EXECUTIVE RESOURCES

Executive branch research may be started fruitfully from the governor's home page. New York's governor mounts a Web site at *http://unix2.nysed.gov/ils/executive/ governor/governor.html* and fills it with such things as copies of the State of the State Message, budget proposals, and background on the office's "missions and functions." The link to Information Resources leads to a page containing gubernatorial messages and reports.

State statutes can be searched in full-text from the GILS server or accessed directly at *gopher://lbdc.senate.state.ny.us:70/11/.laws/* The code is arranged by individual law title and subdivided into articles and sections, each individually searchable.

For hooking up to state agencies, though, try the server at *http://www.state.ny.us/ state_acc.html* for fast-linking access to some forty state agencies. The helpfulness of the Internet becomes apparent when even the Motor Vehicles Department -- long the single most annoying, frustrating and user-unfriendly government agency in the state to most citizens -- now mounts addresses, a list of necessary information (obviating the previous all-but-compulsory two trips) and even a means of ordering a copy of a driving record abstract.

LEGISLATIVE RESOURCES

Legislative materials are available from both houses. The Senate Home Page is at *http://www.senate.state.ny.us* and mounts a Socratic gopher server that poses questions for researchers in order to answer them. This is the place to go to retrieve the text of bills, find an online version of the Senate's rules or run down the name and committee assignment of particular Senators. A handy zip code search engine can locate a legislator geographically and report back the lawmaker's electronic contact information. The Assembly, too, operates an informative combination Web/gopher site at *gopher://lbdc.senate.state.ny.us:70/ 11/.laws/* In addition to the usual directory-style materials, there is a link to *bill information, the Assembly calendar, hearing schedule, committee agenda, New York State Laws* and *legislative reports.* Don't miss the virtual tour of the State Capitol building in Albany.

JUDICIAL MATERIALS

Court decisions and other court information are available from a number of servers. For basic information about the courts and their administration, try the New York State Unified Court System home page at *http://nyslgti.gen.ny.us/oca/* which links to a department newsletter, court libraries, reference materials, records management, micrographics and provides telephone numbers for additional information. Also find links on this page to court publications, the rules of the Court of Appeals and the New York State Bar Association.

Decisions from the Court of Appeals are available from Cornell University's Legal Information Institute and date from January 1992. Decisions are searchable by date, name, topic or keyword. Cornell also provides an e-mail current awareness service that will automatically alert subscribers with bulletin-like notification within hours after a Court of Appeals decision is released by the court.

Lower court decisions are not yet reported online but some New York State opinions from the lower court make their way into the electronic world thanks to *Law Journal Extra!* that reprints state court decisions of interest. The materials are not comprehensive but it's not a bad idea to check in on the site when in need of a recent, celebrated decision. Find the page at *http://www.ljx.com/courthouse/*

Look for the *Rules of Civil Procedure* and the *Rules of Criminal Procedure* at the gopher server containing the state statutes, where the rules are codified in the Civil Practice Law and Rules and the Criminal Procedure Law, respectively.

BAR ASSOCIATIONS

The New York State Bar Association's self-styled "cyberhome" is located at *http://www.nysba.org* Find an online copy of the *Code of Professional Responsibilities* which contains not only the Preamble and Canon of Ethics, but also the attendant *ethical considerations* and *disciplinary rules*. There are also selected recent *Ethics Opinions*. The Association of the Bar of the City of New York maintains a Web site at *http://www.abcny.org/*

For New York litigators, there is a Web site operated by the New York State Trial Lawyers Association at *http://www.nystla.org* providing membership information, quick tips,

consumer information and reprints of the table of contents of the organization's magazine *Trial Lawyer Quarterly.* The New York State Defenders Association, an association of the criminal defense community, is at *http://www.nysda.org/*

LOCAL AND MUNICIPAL RESOURCES

County government is beginning to appear on the Internet and in New York State, find a handy Web page linking all the wired county governments at *http://www.state.ny.us/mcounty.html* Although resources available vary from one county to another, typical of how local governments are using the Web is Nassau County's server at *http://www.co.nassau.ny.us/* Mounted here are links to the Office of the County Executive, the County Legislature, something called *Crime Stoppers* (which encourages citizens to report crimes to the police), Deadbeat Parents and the Traffic and Parking Violations Agency.

City government appears on the same server. Of all the city governments in the country, none are bigger than New York City; find the official New York City Web site at *http://www.ci.nyc.ny.us/*

STATE LIBRARY

The State Library's Web site at *http://www.nysl.nysed.gov* is most interesting for its links to the research library, in particular, EXCELSIOR, the online catalog of the New York State library. Telnet to EXCELSIOR at *telnet://nysl.nysed.gov*

MISCELLANEOUS RESOURCES

To find process servers in New York State, look at the entry for New York for the home page operated by the National Association of Professional Process Servers. Their page is located at *http://www.napps.org*

For the New York State Archives and Records Administration, refer to the gopher server at *gopher://unix6.nysed.gov* ❑

QuickLink

http://www.sips.state.nc.us/

NORTH CAROLINA IS JUMPING into the Internet world with relish. Although many of its state executive agencies have yet to find a Web presence, many of the other sources of legal information in the state are now at the end of the browser-built rainbow.

EXECUTIVE RESOURCES

North Carolina's chief executive is happily online and hosts the state's official Web site at *http://www.sips.state.nc.us* where the researcher is treated to press releases, biographical information and the usual trappings of First Citizenship.

The North Carolina State agency server warns visitors that the Web site is not comprehensive but rather that it hooks up "all the state agencies known to have information available via the Internet." The list does have some work to do but what's already stocked here makes for a dandy collection of links to NC agencies.

Among the leading agencies online already are the Attorney General's Office at *http://www.jus.state.nc.us/Justice/* where

the researcher can locate formal and advisory opinions and an index of the same.

There's not much online to recommend the tax authorities. Unlike other states that now make tax forms and instructions available online, North Carolina merely reprints telephone numbers to call for such materials at the offices of the Department of Revenue at *http://www.dor.state.nc.us/DOR/*

The Secretary of State's office runs a *Corporation Names Database* that can zip through the state's files to locate the corporate records of business established in the state. Typical records provide the researcher with the entity's *status, category, citizenship, lcoation, name of the registered agent* and the *date of incorporation.*

For a state-wide directory of e-mail, punch up *http://www.sips.state.nc.us/email* The hot-button connections on that page hook up to a great deal of information about business and educational opportunities in the state.

LEGISLATIVE MATERIALS

The North Carolina General Assembly holds forth online at *http://www.ncga.state.nc.us* The online service from the lawmakers links up to the Senate and the Assembly and provides an extensive search service to help in locating bill texts and other legislative documents. Bills can be sifted using a number of filters including *Bill Search, Bills by County, Bills Introduced by Members, Bill History Reports, Bill Status Reports, Bills by Committee, Fiscal Information, Bills Ratified, Presented to the Governor* and *Enacted into Law*. The state server also gives the researcher electronic tools to recreate the legislative history of North Carolina laws by providing basic databases that contain searchable archives of *history of votes, glossary of bill status abbreviations* and *bill status reports codes.* Armed with these signifiers, the researcher should be able to trace recent legislation back from its introduction to its current language.

JUDICIARY

The North Carolina judiciary maintains a Web site that does more than merely publish opinions; it reprints speeches by judges on civic occasions, links to the administrative office of the court and makes connections to the Sentencing Commission, the Dispute Resolution Commission and the Commission for the Future of Justice and the Courts in North Carolina.

Supreme Court opinions for North Carolina date from December 1995 and can be searched by case name or by date of decisions from the judiciary's server at *http://www.aoc.state.nc.us/www/courts/appeals/sc/contents.html* Court of Appeals decisions can be found from December 1995 at *http://www.aoc.state.nc.us/www/courts/appeals/coa/contents.html*

BAR ASSOCIATION

The North Carolina Bar Association operates one of the best bar association Web sites in the nation. It is unstinting in the information it provides to its members and the Internet public alike. Plug in the site at *http://www.barlinc.org* to find retrievable versions of ethics opinions, state court decisions and the best collection of links to other bar associations on the Internet.

STATE LIBRARY

The state library hangs out its reference desk online at *http://hal.dcr.state.nc.us/ncsl-home.htm* The catalog is accessible and browsable; online links create a straight path to univer-

sities in North Carolina.

There's also a clearinghouse of official state publications and links to the library for the blind and physically handicapped.

LOCAL AND MUNICIPAL RESOURCES

The roads to North Carolina cities and counties are paved with data packets as the Web page at *http://ncinfo.iog.unc.edu/nclgovt.html* provides links to dozens of small municipalities across the state. Larger cities have multiple connections.

County profiles reprint data from the State Library and give the researcher one-paragraph civics lessons; a hot-linked map points to the state's numerous local governments.

Another useful resource for local research is the *North Carolina Community Resource Information System* home page at *http://www.cris.state.nc.us* which links to government programs offering assistance to the state's residents.

MISCELLANEOUS RESOURCES

North Carolina's Information Highway is a state-wide initiative to provide high-speed video and data services. Reports and FAQ files on the project are prominent features of the home page at *http://www.ncih.net* The Office of the Comptroller publishes a white paper titled *Statewide Connectivity Report* that should interest the researcher from other states who want to see how the public and private sectors can work together to provide equal access to the benefits of the Electronic Revolution.

The North Carolina Encyclopedia is an overview of the state, told in tones of civic pride. Take the tour through NC history at *http://hal.dcr.state.nc.us/nc/cover.htm*
❏

QuickLink
http://www.state.nd.us

NORTH DAKOTA JOINS THE INTERNET REVO-lution by providing extensive links to its executive agencies and publishing a fair quantity of legislative documents to the Web.

EXECUTIVE RESOURCES

The governor of North Dakota one-ups other governors by publishing a RealAudio version of the State of the State speech and budget message to the legislature on the Web at *http://www.ehs.health.state.nd.us/ gov/index.htm* Other links take the researcher down the electronic path to press releases, major speeches, a rundown on the governor's staff and a gubernatorial biography.

From the cheerful office of the Attorney General at *http://www.state.nd.us/ndag* the researcher can locate press releases, the office's information on in-state gaming and brochures and manuals for the general public on topics such as carrying a concealed weapon. There is a link built in to the home page for AG opinions but it was not functioning in mid-1997.

The taxing authorities of North Dakota have gone electronic with a library of PDF-format tax forms that can be downloaded from the State Tax Department Web site at *http://www.state.nd.us/taxdpt* Forms are available for corporation, fiduciary and individual income tax returns as well as oil and gas tax forms. A list of publications that can be ordered (but not yet downloaded) is also printed on the site with the associated ordering information.

The oil and gas division of the North Dakota Industrial Commission regulates drilling and the production of petroleum products in the state. The quick directory is at *http://www.state.nd.us/ndic/oil.html* Of greater information content is the *Geological Survey* at *http://www.state.nd.us/ndgs/NDGS.HomePage.h tml* The site contains petroleum and sub-strata studies, maps, surficial geological surveys as well as a library and links to staff and publications.

A directory of e-mail addresses for state employees is available at *http://www.state.nd.us/ www/general.html*

LEGISLATIVE RESOURCES

The North Dakota legislature meets every two years but they are always online at *http://www.state.nd.us/lr* except that bill text look-ups are suspended after the legislature ends. Hopefully, the legislature's Webmaster will make bill texts and bill status lookups from the home page available even when the lawmakers are not in session.

Click on *Legislative Assembly Composition* to open a page that features links to leadership, members, standing committees and procedural committees for both the Senate and the House of Representatives.

North Dakota looks forward to the future and has already published legislative deadlines for the yet-to-be-convened 1998 session.

As of mid-1997, North Dakota has not made its state code nor its administrative code available online.

JUDICIAL MATERIALS

The North Dakota Supreme Court keeps its chambers at *http://sc3.court.state.nd.us* and that's where a simple but powerful home page leads to a considerable Web site of judicial information. Supreme Court opinions from mid-1993 can be searched and downloaded; search opinions by *topic, North Dakota citation, regional reporter (NW2d) citation, justice, trial judge* or by full text within the opinion. A copy of the case citation is available at the same page.

No other state prints more of its court rules to the Internet than North Dakota. Under the button link to *Rules,* find copies of the state rules for *appellate, civil, criminal, evidence, judicial conduct, local rules, procedural rules, professional conduct* and *disciplinary rules.*

Track down the district courts within the state at *http://www.court.state.nd.us/COURT/DISTRICTS/NW.HTM* where court location and judicial biographies are in print online.

The North Dakota Supreme Court maintains a link to Federal court sites that is a model of concise Web design.

STATE LIBRARY

North Dakota throws open the cyber-doors to the Internet public from their e-stacks at *http://www.sendit.nodak.edu/ndsl* For prowling around ODIN, the Online Dakota Information Network, telnet to *telnet://odin.und.nodak.edu* where a public access terminal allows visitors to look around the library catalog.

BAR ASSOCIATION

The State Bar Association of North Dakota had still not made the brief but important journey from real world to cyberspace, as of mid-1997.

LOCAL AND MUNICIPAL RESOURCES

Like much of the American West, North Dakota is big and sparsely settled. One of the benefits of the Internet is that it connects small towns and municipalities; North Dakota benefits from these connections as this page demonstrates. Use the Web site at *http://www.tradecorridor.com/cities.htm* to log in to the cities and counties of North Dakota. Information certainly accentuates the positive and legal information may be scarce, but for quickie links to smaller communities, this is a serviceable Web site.

MISCELLANEOUS RESOURCES

A list of North Dakota attorneys is searchable at *http://www.court.state.nd.us/COURT/LAWYERS/INDEX/FrameSet.HTM* Each entry contains the name of the lawyer, address, phone number, bar ID number and date of admission to practice. Search through the list by name or by city. A no-frames version of the site is available and is recommended. For future reference, download a file of all North Dakota Licensed Lawyers to the hard drive to create a local directory. The list of lawyers is supplied by the North Dakota Supreme Court.

Book the North Dakota sojourn with information supplied by the state's Department of Tourism at *http://www.glness.com/tourism/Howto.html* The site provides a guide to lodging, attractions, state-wide activities and prints local maps to aid in trip planning.
❑

QuickLink
http://www.ohio.gov/ohio/index.htm

OHIO WASTES NO TIME UPLOADING statutes, case decisions and executive agency information to the Internet. It is one of the easiest states in which to find legal information thanks to slickly designed Web pages and forward-looking state officials.

EXECUTIVE RESOURCES

Online, the governor of Ohio keeps it simple at *http://www.state.oh.us/gov* A table with links to a biography of Ohio's First Citizen, speeches, announcements from the office and reprints of speeches are e-published to slake the curiosity of the insatiable researcher.

Other public servants in the Buckeye State are also making themselves electronically available to the electronic constituency. The Attorney General at *http://www.ag.ohio.gov* runs an information-rich server that includes AG opinions dating from 1994; the current opinions are in full text and the older ones, now synopsized, will eventually be converted into full text as well. The Attorney General dispatches press releases and reports on such issues as tobacco litigation, death penalty appeals and government-in-sunshine updates on the Web.

For tax forms, phone numbers and answers to frequently asked tax questions, fire up the Web site for the Ohio Department of Taxation at *http://www.state.oh.us/tax* Forms can be downloaded in PDF form and include corporate franchise tax forms, individual income tax, personal property tax and school district income tax. The department e-publishes a list of tax data indices at *http://www.state.oh.us/tax/analysis/index.html*

From the Secretary of State's office, the most interesting information to the legal researcher comes from the link to Business Services Information at *http://www.state.oh.us/sos/buispage.html* A simple Web page delivers general information and assistance on corporations and a basic rundown on forming a corporation. There's also the 411 on other business entities such as limited liability companies, limited partnerships and trademarks and names from the same page. Look here too for filing fees and UCC filings.

The canonical list of Ohio executive agencies provides electronic connections to the state's various offices from *http://www.state.oh.us/ohio/agency.htm* An online directory of state employees lives at *http://www.state.oh.us/ohio/index-sd.htm*

LEGISLATIVE RESOURCES

Each chamber of the Ohio legislature convenes electronically, the House of Representatives at *http://www.knox.net/knox/govt/house.htm* and the Senate at *http://www.knox.net/knox/govt/senate.htm* but the only information making its way to the Internet there are membership lists and links to legislators where available. Session laws, however, can be retrieved from *http://38.223.23.20/stacks/ohioacts* Laws can be searched by full text or by pulling down the House or Senate bill number.

Flip through the Ohio Revised Code at

http://38.223.23.20/stacks/orc where researchers may choose between a frames or an easier-to-search no-frames version. Look through the code by free text search or by retrieving individual titles.

JUDICIAL MATERIALS

The Supreme Court of Ohio at *http://www.sconet.ohio.gov* publishes opinions dating from 1992 to present but getting them requires navigating a gopher server. Use the search engine to look across the various opinions in full text. This is the site where results of the bar exam are published.

STATE LIBRARY

WINSLO, the WorldWideWeb Information Network from the State Library of Ohio at *http://winslo.ohio.gov* connects to the electronic catalog and provides links to Ohio libraries. Select the link to *Ohio and Its Government* to locate newspapers, radio stations, TV stations and newspaper indexes. Other links reach out to state government resources and community servers and an excellent meta-index for international law resources.

BAR ASSOCIATION

As of mid-1997, the Ohio State Bar Association had not yet set up a Web site.

LOCAL AND MUNICIPAL RESOURCES

The best source for local and municipal links in Ohio hails from Ohio Public Library Information Network at *http://www.oplin.lib.oh.us/OHIO/MUNICI* where a clickable map of all the counties in the state provide a vivid graphical means for zoom-ing in to geographical areas. Locate particular communities using a free text search engine as well or scroll down the list of counties using a scroll box.

MISCELLANEOUS RESOURCES

The Ohio CLE Institute at *http://www.ohiocle.org/index.html* offers a CLE calendar and online ordering of its publications. Details on Ohio's CLE credits can be found on the home page along with links to a handful of federal law resources on the Web.

The Ohio State University College of Law Library is online at *http://www.acs.ohio-state.edu/units/law/law3.htm* where a virtual tour of the library is available. Also see a catalog of online research tools from this page. The home page for the School of Law is at *http://www.acs.ohio-state.edu/units/law/index.htm*

The best general reference resource for information about Ohio is the *Discover Ohio* Web site from the Ohio Public Library Information Network. Links lead to business information sources, sports, points of interest, data on health resources and scholarly connections. The URL for *Discover Ohio* is *http://www.oplin.lib.oh.us/OHIO*

Travel planning to Ohio benefits from a quick trip to the Ohio Division of Travel and Tourism at *http://www.ohiotourism.com* Lodging and hot spots from around Ohio are a click away; events and a request line for additional information are all linked to the tourism home page. Pick *Ohio Links* for an extraordinarily detailed list of Ohio diversions such as fishing, golf, historical sites, shopping, universities, weather, zoos and wineries.

❑

QuickLink
http://www.state.ok.us

OKLAHOMA IS OK WHEN IT COMES TO the Internet. The state has made successful efforts to put its judicial information and executive branch resources online and when the state code and administrative rules join the public servers, Oklahoma will be a superbly wired state in which to research.

EXECUTIVE RESOURCES

The Oklahoma governor's home page can be cataloged thusly: state of state address, executive budget, biographies and a weekly online column to the good citizens of Oklahoma. Find it all by dead reckonin' or by pointing the browser to face *http://www.state.ok.us/osfdocs/govhp.html*

The taxman cometh for the Oklahomans at their Web site at *http://www.oktax.state.ok.us/oktax* where forms are downloadable, motor vehicle information is searchable, taxes and fees are reviewable and the Internal Revenue Service and the Federation of Tax Administrators are linkable.

The Oklahoma Corporation Commission runs a robust Web site chock-full of addresses and forms at *http://www.occ.state.ok.us* E-mail the staff and review daily dockets and commission rules and notices here.

The list of state agencies, equipped with the appropriate hypertext links, is at *http://www.state.ok.us/osfdocs/agncs1.html* The state telephone directory is online at *http://www.state.ok.us/osfdocs/phonehp.html* in PDF format.

JUDICIAL MATERIALS

The Internet center for all judicial information is the Oklahoma Supreme Court Network at *http://www.oscn.state.ok.us* This is the site to start judicial research since the page's links head directly to the Supreme Court home page, the Court of Criminal Appeals and to opinions from both courts.

There's a wonderful collection of useful references online here. The network reprints Attorney General opinions, clerk's notices and civil dockets. The roll of attorneys admitted in Oklahoma can be perused. So can court filing fees and a newsletter for the state's judiciary. When the database is fully operational, it will be possible to pinpoint case law and statutory research.

Administrative decisions from the Department of Labor are e-printed at *http://www.onenet.net/oklegal/labor.basic.html*

LEGISLATIVE RESOURCES

The House of Representatives uses the Web to report on its activities at *http://www.lsb.state.ok.us/house/ohorpage.htm* The link to *Highlights* provides narrative descriptions of each of the Acts passed in the most recent legislative session. Click on *Short Title* for links to every bill introduced. Other links point to *members, committees, meetings, staff* and *news* about the House.

The Oklahoma Senate opens its electronic doors at *http://www.lsb.state.ok.us/senate/welcome.html* and provides more elaborate services to the Internet than the House of

Representatives site. Though the texts of bills are not available online, summaries of legislation organized by committee are mounted on the server. The busy home page links up to members, the leadership of the Senate and committees. Issues papers, directories, senatorial biographies and press releases are all online too.

The Oklahoma Legislative Information Service is available via the Web at *http://www.lsb.state.ok.us/docs/legislative1.html*

In spite of the lack of full-text bills on the Internet, find pointers to the three publishers at *http://www.lsb.state.ok.us/docs/billtext.html* that can supply electronic copies of legislative materials. According to the Web site at the Oklahoma Supreme Court Network, the code will be available via the Internet no later than Fall 1997 (which means they've never visited the Oklahoma Bar Association's server known as the *Oklahoma Public Legal Research System* at *http://www.onenet.net/oklegal/statutes. basic.html* where the full text of the code is fully searchable already.) Certain titles of the code also are already available for browsing from the Oklahoma Supreme Court Network.

STATE LIBRARY

The Oklahoma Department of Libraries keeps up an excellent Web site including special links to Oklahoma online legal resources through Cartwright Memorial Library at *http://www.state.ok.us/~odl/lawinfo/index.htm* Other links from the main library page at *http://www.state.ok.us/~odl/weblinks.htm* provide fast connections to the online catalog, comprehensive state government information and the state archives.

BAR ASSOCIATION

As of mid-1997, the Oklahoma Bar Association had not yet created or published a Web site, but it does sponsor the Oklahoma Public Legal Research System with some simple links to the state statutes and case decisions at

http://www.onenet.net/oklegal/index.html

LOCAL AND MUNICIPAL RESOURCES

A directory of Oklahoma' "certified cities" is online at *http://www.state.ok.us/~cc/* to give the researcher entree to the state's online communities, each of which provides varying degrees of useful information. Connections to the counties of Oklahoma can be had from the National Association of Counties Web server at *http://www.com/hpi/okcty*

MISCELLANEOUS RESOURCES

The University of Oklahoma Law Center at *http://www.law.uoknor.edu* is a superb resource for Oklahoma legal research thanks to its collection of state materials, local information and reference services. Of particular use is a metaindex of law-related index pages that allow searching for Internet-based information by legal subject. That index can be accessed directly at *http://www.law.uoknor.edu/ leginfo.html* (This is also a pretty fair index page for international legal links too.)

A service of the Oklahoma legislature is *Oklahoma Facts and Figures* which doles out demographic information, tax and appropriations data, education statistics, health information and statistical reports on the state's prison system at *http://www.lsb.state.ok.us/senate/ F&FTOC.html*

Sunny prose and happy pictures of idyllic life in Oklahoma will also come across with some factual material on the index page for the state local Chambers of Commerce. The puff will be thick but forge on anyway to locate information on the small communities of OK through the eyes of the towns' shopkeepers. The site is at *http://www.state.ok.us/osfdocs/ coclst.html*

The Criminal Justice Resource Center at *http://www.state.ok.us/~ocjrc* links the Oklahoma Sentencing Commission, statistical analysis center and prevention/intervention center on one page. ❏

QuickLink

http://www.state.or.us/governme.htm

OREGON HAS SUFFICIENT MATERIAL already published to the Internet to make research into Oregon legal issues a pleasant task but there are still some significant lapses that will need to be addressed before the legal researcher can consider the Internet to be a comprehensive source of information for Oregon law.

EXECUTIVE RESOURCES

The governor welcomes e-visitors to Oregon at *http://www.governor.state.or.us/governor.html* with a standard governor Web page that is top-heavy with press releases, biographical information, information about initiatives and the ever-riveting State of the State speech transcript.

The Oregon Department of Revenue ponies up tax forms at *http://www.dor.state.or.us/default.html* along with publications, basic tax information written mostly for the taxpayer rather than the practitioner and a FAQ file. Use the built-in search engine or the site map to navigate the Web site.

For corporation information in Oregon, zip over to the Secretary of State's page at *http://www.sos.state.or.us* and hit the link for the *Corporation Division*. Online lookup of names and corporations is on the drawing board for the

future but today's researcher can find registry fees and forms on the site and an official *Oregon Business Guide* to explain how to incorporate in Oregon.

Download UCC forms from the site at *http://www.sos.state.or.us/corporation/ucc/ucc.htm* Use this site to search UCC records for liens and other filings. Tips for filing UCC documents are online alongside links to the UCC of Oregon.

For researchers who need frequent contacts with the Oregon authorities, download a PDF version of the agency referral list at *http://www.sos.state.or.us/corporation/bic/bic.htm*

LEGISLATIVE RESOURCES

The Oregon Legislature takes pains to make legislative documents as easy as possible to retrieve from its server. In addition to directories for the Senate and the House of Representatives containing biographies and e-mail links to the lawmakers, the Web site publishes a flexible legislative gopher that allows the researcher to track down legislative measures and related publications dating from the 1995 session to present.

The link to *Bills and Laws* opens a submenu that can retrieve cumulative and supplemental histories of measures. That page offers a link to *Search Legislative Measures* which provides searching by keyword or measure number.

Oregon places both its statutory code and its administrative code online for the citizens of the Internet to use. The Oregon Revised Statutes live on a plain vanilla gopher server at *gopher://gopher.leg.state.or.us:70/11/ors95.dir* and are fully searchable; be sure to read the preface which explains the new codification system of Oregon's code. In addition to searching by keyword lookup, the code can be searched chapter-by-chapter. Be careful, though; the online version of the code dates from 1995 and requires some legislative tap-dancing through the bill texts and acts of the legislature to bring any single code section up-to-date. For critical applications, refer to the print version for recent updates and amendments to the law text.

For the administrative code of Oregon, turn to *http://arcweb.sos.state.or.us/rules/OAR_1997_default.html* The rules can be searched by chapter number or by agency name. Unlike the state code, the Oregon Administrative Rules are current; rules are easily updated by referring to the monthly *Oregon Bulletin* which reports new rulemakings by the state's agencies at *http://arcweb.sos.state.or.us/rules/bulletin_default.html* Use the *Revision Cumulative Index* in the *Oregon Bulletin* to update rule texts.

JUDICIAL MATERIALS

The home for Oregon Supreme Court and Court of Appeals opinions is the law library at Willamette University. Find decisions for the current year arranged by week of publication at *http://www.imagina.com/webpages/ivysoft/CtSlips/CourtSlipList.html* Other judicial information such as directories and rules have not yet migrated Internet-ward.

BAR ASSOCIATION

The Oregon Bar Association has not yet mounted a Web site, as of mid-1997.

STATE LIBRARY

The Oregon State Library does a facile job of keeping the public informed but also of serving its primary patrons, the state employees of Oregon. As a 1990s library, the OSL can hook up with other libraries throughout the state and so can browse catalogs from other institutions including university libraries, regional consortia, county libraries and the Library of Congress book catalog. Online periodical index lead to the best-known indices; of special interest is the

Oregon Index which tracks Oregon publications and mentions of Oregon in selected magazines. (Passwords are required for certain other index services.) Links head out of the library to the statutes and administrative code and other state government information sources.

LOCAL AND MUNICIPAL RESOURCES

Links to Oregon's towns and villages are found at *Online Highways* at *http://www.ohwy.com/or/homepage.htm*

MISCELLANEOUS RESOURCES

The University of Oregon law library has a home page at *http://netserver.uoregon.edu* that connects to other law schools and law libraries in the state and also provides researchers with a handy subject index to law-related information and resources. It's also the place to go for links to journals such as the *Oregon Law Review* and the *Journal of Environmental Law and Litigation*.

The best source for general information about travel and tourism in Oregon is the aforementioned *Online Highways Travel Guide to Oregon* at *http://www.ohwy.com/or/homepage.htm* Produced jointly by three print magazines, the Web site is the most fact-filled and extensive information service for the state.

The law library from Willamette University, in addition to case law links, also provides one-stop shopping for links to Oregon's statutes, administrative code and government agencies. The URL is *http://www.willamette.edu/law/longlib/* Demographic and economic statistics for Oregon can be found at *http://govinfo.kerr.orst.edu/oregon.html* And last, the *Oregon Index* aids in finding newspaper and magazine articles about the state. Find and browse the index at *http://www.osl.state.or.us/orpac/orindhome.html* ❑

QuickLink

http://www.state.pa.us/govstate.html

PENNSYLVANIA IS IN THE MIDST OF A GENERAL upgrade to the information it makes available to the public on the Internet but it's obvious that the state's policy makers are embracing new information technology to make the most data available to the greatest number of people. The courts and legislative will both soon provide state-of-the-art Web sites.

EXECUTIVE RESOURCES

The governor of the Keystone State presides over a Web site at *http://www.state.pa.us/ PA_Exec/Governor/overview.html* It's a low-key Web site that links visitors via Keystone-shaped icons to policy statements, press releases, current news about the Chief Executive and an overview of the administration. A biography of the governor is, of course, always there for the asking. Executive orders can be retrieved from *http://www.state.pa.us/Regulations/ Executive_Orders*

The Attorney General one ups the boos with a very slick and informative home page at *http://www.attorneygeneral.gov* wherein the AG provides the researcher with press releases, news about criminal prosecutions and information on consumer protection.

The Pennsylvania Department of Revenue operates a "cyberspace district office" on the Web at *http://www.revenue.state.pa.us* It's a sophisticated site that publishes monthly revenue reports, updates to tax regulations and other heads-up news of interest to the tax practitioner. Pennsylvania distributes tax forms in PDF format for personal, corporation and property tax returns. And to let the cyberworld know that they're watching, the tax authorities report on criminal prosecutions from the site.

JUDICIAL MATERIALS

The courts of Pennsylvania are not stingy with their information, as this home page at *http://www.courts.state.pa.us* demonstrates. The Supreme Court posts opinions, memoranda and dispositions on the site; take some time to learn the various file extensions that define the opinions: *.mo* for majority opinions, *.do* for dissenting opinion, etc.

The Appellate Court is moving into the age of electronic docketing; it is now automating its documents filings systems to provide computerized case management.

Amendments and proposed amendments to both the *Rules of Appellate Procedure* and the *Civil Procedural Rules* are available from the Supreme Court committees that maintain the rules of practice. Find the amendments at *http://www.courts.state.pa.us/pub/appeals/rules/index.htm* and *http://www.courts.state.pa.us/ pub/appeals/rules/civrules/index.htm* respectively.

Use the home page for Unified Judicial System to connect to county courts.

LEGISLATIVE RESOURCES

As of mid-1997, the Pennsylvania legislative server was undergoing upgrades in order to provide bill texts, histories, calendars and the other information that is a necessary part of a successful publication agenda by a law-making body. Check back on the Senate's site to see these materials once Pennsylvania's Webmasters have completed their self-appointed task.

Meanwhile, the Pennsylvania Senate home page at *http://www.pasen.gov/senate.html* is filled primarily with directory information to link to members, officers and Senators with e-mail. There's also a list of the standing committees.

Neither Pennsylvania statutes nor the administrative code is yet available on the Internet.

BAR ASSOCIATION

One of the interesting services of the Pennsylvania Bar Association at *http://www.pabar.org* are the online *Judicial Ratings*; ratings are categorized by political party and candidates for election to Pennsylvania courts are rated as "highly recommended," "recommended" or "not recommended" and the explanations for the ratings are published online. Other features of the site are an online legal bookstore, membership benefits and lists of the committees and sections. The connection for *Legal Links* leads to a detailed list of local bar associations in the commonwealth.

MUNICIPAL AND LOCAL RESOURCES

For spelunking the small towns and counties of the grand commonwealth of Pennsylvania, there's no need to look much further than *http://www.state.pa.us/govlocal.html* This is the Pennsylvania's Local Government's page with links to villages and counties governments. The collection of links is not comprehensive, but like most new Internet sites, it's growing quickly.

Also refer to the Pennsylvania League of Cities and Municipalities at *http://pages.prodigy.com/plcm* for a report on the benefits of membership to constituent municipalities.

STATE LIBRARY

For a library-laden state like Pennsylvania, the state library Web site is a disappointment. The links are not very informative nor is the other data mounted natively of great interest to the researcher.

MISCELLANEOUS RESOURCES

The Pennsylvania State Data Center is an electronic repository of official economic and demographic information. Formerly known as the Economic Development Information Network, the State Data Center provides maps, research briefs on selected topics, directories to small chambers of commerce, economic indicators and links to assorted municipal and state information resources. Find the State Data Center at *http://howard.hbg.psu.edu/psdc/psdchome1.1.html*

Plan the next trip to Pennsylvania with the aid of the state's tourist information dealers at *http://www.state.pa.us/visit/paregins.htm* The site features an exploded regional map with appropriate links to accommodations, transportation and a calendar of events from around the state.

For a refreshingly peculiar collection of links that can only be described as "eclectic" look at *309 Useful Links for Lawyers* compiled by attorney Penn B. Glazier. Someone can certainly benefit from links to the *Dog Fanciers' Acronym List* or *German Zip Codes*. Find this pleasantly odd anthology of Web sites at *http://www.acba.org/309_link.htm* thanks to the Allegheny County Bar Association.
❑

QuickLink

http://www.doa.state.ri.us

RHODE ISLAND IS STARTING TO GET WITH the Internet program and wires up its executive agencies very thoroughly. The other branches of government make a fair amount of information available to the researcher but there is still plenty of room in RI's servers for much more to come.

EXECUTIVE RESOURCES

As of mid-1997, the Governor's official home page featured an singularly awful photograph of the office-holder; if the bad .gif file doesn't frighten you away from *http://www.state.ri.us/genoff/almond.htm* an otherwise painless (and linkless) biography of the chief executive can be found there. Hopefully the photo soon will be replaced by a less startling one.

For more substantive legal information, turn to the Secretary of State's site. That office has been instrumental in hooking up all the other public Rhode Island resources to the Internet. Find an extensive Web site, called the Public Information Kiosk at *http://www.sec.state.ri.us* From there, links branch out to all corners of Rhode Island's state government. The canonical hyperlist of all state agencies and departments resides peacefully and

helpfully at *http://www.state.ri.us/ stdept/sdlink.htm*

The details of business regulation in Rhode Island are the province of the Secretary of State too. Find a skinflint directory of phone numbers at *http://www.sec.state.ri.us/stdept/ sd19.htm* Corporation forms and other information are sadly lacking from the otherwise ambitious SOS servers.

Making money flow from citizen to government is an onerous task made simpler by the online tax forms, tax regulations, newsletters and information provided by the Rhode Island Division of Taxation from their Web presence at *http://www.tax.state.ri.us* Forms are downloaded in self-extracting Adobe Acrobat format (except for those StuffIt Macintosh format which require decompression software) and are available back to the 1992 tax season. The scroll bars are easy to figure out: just click, print and file.

LEGISLATIVE RESOURCES

By an act of providence, the Rhode Island legislature now provides the online public with a window on their activities at *http://www.state.ri.us/submenus/leglink.htm* A bi-cameral Web frame divvies up the legislative documents into House and Senate materials. From the Senate side, the bills from current sessions are stacked up in bill number order with associated titles for easy browsing; ditto the House bills. Bills from both chambers can be searched by sponsor or by subject. Both search techniques are equally effective in retrieving the full text of current bills. To determine the status of a particular bill, click on *Action Taken on Bills* or point your browser directly to *http://www.state.ri.us/wwaction.htm*

Get biographical information on lawmakers from *http://www.state.ri.us/ legpages/sort.htm*

Neither the state statutes nor the administrative code have made the metamorphosis from print caterpillar to electronic butterfly. Stay tuned.

JUDICIAL RESOURCES

Judicial decisions are available from from the RI Bar Association at *http://ribar.com/opinions.html* but they are not professionally or thoughtfully published. Links to judges and their professional biographies are mounted for convenience at *http://www.state.ri.us/judges/judglink.htm*

BAR ASSOCIATION

Like most state bar Web sites, Rhode Island's addresses two audiences, members and non-members. From its home page at *http://ribar.com* the Rhode Island Bar Association provides consumer information and lawyer referral services for the general public; for its members (and others in the profession) there are links to CLE programs, court resources including some not-very-well-organized opinions and speedy links to the Secretary of State and the Roger Williams Law School. For members, find by-laws, referral policies and association committees posted on the site.

STATE LIBRARY

Little Rhode Island may be, but it's still convenient to have all of its libraries linked one to the other. Find those connections from the state library at *http://www.dsls.state.ri.us/ genref/rilibs.htm* where telnet and HTML access to the catalogs of municipal and university libraries are there for the browsing. Check out the reference materials linked at *http://www.dsls.state.ri.us/genref/ref.htm*

For the legal researcher, the best link is the one to Roger Williams University libraries

because of its links to periodicals indices and electronic journals.

LOCAL AND MUNICIPAL RESOURCES

Towns and municipalities meet and greet their Internet visitors from a gopher-like page at *http://www.state.ri.us/municipl/munilink.htm* Like most municipal servers, what awaits on the other end of the click is usual an amalgam of town spirit, pictures of city mothers and fathers and telephone numbers for the other upstanding folk and Rhode Island's server is no different.

There's also a good source for local information from *http://www.doa.state.ri.us/ info/cities.htm* The information from that server is more robust and may prove to be more informative than the individual links at *munilink.*

MISCELLANEOUS RESOURCES

The brand-new Roger Williams Law School -- it graduated its first class in 1996 -- is a child of the Electronic Age. One would think that would make it a model of legal scholarship marrying high technology but the page at *http://www.rwu.edu/law/law.html* is decidely ho-hum.

A small law-related index page known as *LegalWorks Online* provides resources to all the New England states, including Rhode Island. Find their simple but informative service at *http://www.legalworks.com*

From the Office of Library and Information Services, fire up the Rhode Island On-Line Sites and Resources for hyperlinks to newspapers, TV and radio stations and a handful of non-profit organizations.

❑

QuickLink

http://www.state.sc.us/gov.html

SOUTH CAROLINA WIRES UP the Palmetto State from east to west; the state is vigorous in its Internet publication. Finding information produced by South Carolina public agencies is a simple matter because the Web servers are properly created and completely stocked.

EXECUTIVE RESOURCES

The governor of South Carolina conducts business online from a very slick Web site at *http://www.state.sc.us/db* The *de rigeur* documents of governorship appear here as press releases, the text of speeches, links to the cabinet and staff and biographical information about South Carolina First Public Servant.
The connections to the state's agencies reach far. All the Internet-smart state agencies are found linked to *http://www.state.sc.us/s tateage.html* and most of the major offices and departments are, indeed, represented by a Web site.

Of the more important executive agencies, locate the State Department of Revenue at *http://www.state.sc.us/dor* where forms and instructions are stocked on the virtual shelf. Among the forms waiting for download are PDF format forms for individual, corporate, fiduciary, partnership, estate and property tax returns among others. The tax authorities haven't as yet published the tax laws and regulations to the Internet yet; what's there are summary instructions and explanations written for non-lawyers. The taxfolk have published what they call "policy documents" consisting of revenue rulings, revenue procedures, private letter rulings, technical advice memos and information letters dating from 1987 to the present at *http://www.state.sc.us/dor/policy.html*

For an old-fashioned analog solution to fetching tax forms, try the DOR's fax-on-demand service; details are available on the otherwise digital Web site.

Knock on the cyberdoor of the South Carolina Attorney General at *http://www.scattorneygeneral.org* The site was under construction in early June 1997 so check back to see what's been added.

In South Carolina, the General Assembly must approve regulations proposed by executive agencies and commissions (except for emergency regulations and regulations promulgated to comply with Federal law) before they have the force of law. Review proposed regulations and executive orders from the General Assembly's server at *http://www.lpitr.state.sc.us/regnsrch.htm* Changes in regulations must first be published in the *State Register* before they are added to the administrative code; find back issues of the *State Register* online at *http://www.lpitr.state.sc.us/register.htm*

LEGISLATIVE MATERIALS

A first-rate legislative server dishes up the bill texts and acts from *http://www.leginfo.state.sc.us* where links swiftly pull up bills, sponsors, committees, actions by both chambers and a legislative index all from the same prim home page. Legislative information in South Carolina goes deep: there's bill information and committee reports on this site dating from 1975, which makes them historical artifacts in Internet terms.

The *Legislative Manual*, accessible from the General Assembly's home page, overflows with useful information from the legislature.

JUDICIAL RESOURCES

Under construction in mid-1997, the judicial server for South Carolina nonetheless links to opinions of the state Supreme Court courtesy of U.S.C. Law Center. Find the presumably working model of the judiciary Web site at
http://www.state.sc.us/judicial

BAR ASSOCIATION

A superbly designed Web site for the South Carolina Bar Association at *http://www.scbar.org* provides members and non-members alike with electronic access to ethics opinions, bar news and terms of the court. The site boasts an excellent selection of pre-screened legal links to the Internet for state-specific and general legal reference materials. Additional links provide a lawyer referral service, information about the Bar Foundation and the association's pro bono opportunities.

LOCAL AND MUNICIPAL RESOURCES

From the General Assembly comes the convocation of counties. Pop on one of the links at *http://www.lpitr.state.sc.us/manual/cntymast.htm* to pull up a down-and-dirty profile of each county with links to county officials, representation, delegations to the statehouse and contact information.

STATE LIBRARY

The librarians of South Carolina staff the online desk with full-service links at *http://www.state.sc.us/scsl* to the state's online databases which include LION (Library Information ONLine) and an electronic bulletin board service. The most useful link for the legal researcher is from the South Carolina Reference Room at *http://www.state.sc.us/scsl/refdesk.html* where an additional connection marked *Government, Law & Politics* creates a path to the leading legal resources in the state. Link up to other libraries in the state at *http://www.state.sc.us/scsl/libs.html*

MISCELLANEOUS LINKS

The South Carolina Information Locator Service at *http://www.state.sc.us/scils/* is under development. It's designed to provide uniform access to the vast amount of data and records collected by the state. When it is fully operational, the SCILS system should act as a *de facto* state card catalog to South Carolina government resources.

The Administrative Law Judge Division keeps a home page at *http://www.law.sc.edu/alj/alj.htm* and that's where to find a handy search engine to locate recent decisions by the ALJs who decide cases brought before them from such agencies as the Department of Insurance, the Department of Revenue and the Department of Social Services.

Thumb through South Carolina daily and weekly newspapers online thanks to the links that appear on the home page of the South Carolina Press Association. The researcher can benefit from the handy link to *Reporter Resources* which enumerates specific information resources in the state and around the nation. The University of South Carolina Law Center keeps a Web site with links to legal resources from around the state and the nation. It's at *http://www.law.sc.edu* ❏

QuickLink

http://www.state.sd.us

SOUTH DAKOTA IS MAKING its first tentative forays into the high-tech world of the Internet. And if the resources online for the legal researcher are not quite ready for prime time, it will only be a matter of time before they are as the first handful of state servers start publishing public data to the network.

EXECUTIVE RESOURCES

The governor posts a list of signed bills containing the bill number, act title and date of signing at *http://www.state.sd.us/state/executive/governor/bills/Signed_1.html* but for other executive information, look to *http://www.state.sd.us/state/executive/governor/* for the chief's press releases, speeches, outline of political initiatives and biography.

The Secretary of State Web site holds promise if the links are updated and some searchable databases are attached to it. As the site stands in mid-1997, the synopses of the duties of the office are all very interesting but there's nothing of substantive interest published on the site to warrant any more than a cursory visit by the average, non-SD researcher.

South Dakota tax forms and applications live in bureaucratic comfort at the server from the Department of Revenue at *http://www.state.sd.us/state/executive/revenue/revenue.html* That's also the place to look up tax laws and quickie capsule descriptions of individual taxes. Other taxes are broken out by category with tax rates published on easy to use tables.

Regulated utilities can be researched from the Web site maintained by the Public Utilities Commission at *http://www.state.sd.us/state/executive/puc/puc.htm* The deftly-designed site hooks up regulations, commission dockets, orders and other regulatory documents and policy statements on the page.

JUDICIAL RESOURCES

Depend on the South Dakota Bar Association for Supreme Court decisions from its site at *http://www.sdbar.org/opinions/index.htm* The decisions date from 1996; older cases can be searched using a handy case summary search tool.

In addition to the case reports, find the South Dakota Supreme Court citation rule on the same page.

LEGISLATIVE MATERIALS

So far as Web sites go, the legislative server for South Dakota earns a C- for a half-hearted service. Yes, it is possible eventually to connect with current legislative information but doing so requires drilling through a number of pages to reach a dimly lit page that contains only the barest of links. Best bet is to skip the preliminary pages and head straight for *http://www.state.sd.us/state/legis/lrc/lawstat/general.htm* where it's still dark and the text is hard to read but where links to the committees and leadership directories for both chambers is e-printed online.

Finding bills is easier. Punch up the bill directory at *http://www.state.sd.us/state/legis/lrc/lawstat/billlist.htm* to retrieve a table of recent bills organized by bill number and title. There's no historic material but finding the small number of bills written by the South Dakota legislature should not present a terribly searing problem for the researcher.

A rather nice touch is the legislator mug book at *http://www.state.sd.us/state/legis/lrc/lawstat/mem.htm* where detailed personal information on the state's lawmakers can be clicked upon.

Neither the state code nor the administrative code is accessible by the Internet at mid-1997.

BAR ASSOCIATION

From its home page at *http://www.sdbar.org* the State Bar of South Dakota publishes opinions and practice guides from a bare-bones Web server. While the site itself is not going to win any beauty prizes, the links to Federal resources within the state and to the state courts are current and effective: who needs ornamentation so long as the other goods are delivered on time and in good working order?

The new citation system for South Dakota is published on the bar site; so too is a lawyers referral service, organized by county. The editorial board prints articles on a variety of topics with titles such as *Punitive Damages in South Dakota, Estate Planning Kits-- Promises and Abuses* and *Common Law Courts: Uncommon and Uncourtly.*

STATE LIBRARY

The State Library coordinates the depository library system and acts as the state publications distribution center, according to the library's Web page at *http://www.state.sd.us/state/executive/deca/st_lib/stinfo1.htm* The South Dakota Library Network offers telnet access to its union catalog which makes for handy searches for magazines and a great number of books. No password is necessary. Link to a list of South Dakota's depository libraries here as well.

MISCELLANEOUS RESOURCES

The University of South Dakota McKusick law library lets researchers browse its online card catalog PALS and reprints decisions from the South Dakota Supreme Court. The most interesting links, the ones for electronic resources and reference, were under construction in mid-1997 but show promise for the researcher who needs answers to nagging questions of South Dakota law.

Find a series of South Dakota listservs at *http://www.state.sd.us/maillist* for general interest mailing lists.

General information from around the state is supplied by the SOuth DAkota POpular Internet Places (SODAPOP). Use it for tourist and travel information. Despite the over-cute nickname, the server at *http://sodapop.dsu.edu* provides comprehensive lists to all of South Dakota's wired world, including businesses, political sites, news media, reference links and a search engine to speed the task of locating elusive South Dakota data.

LOCAL AND MUNICIPAL RESOURCES

Use SODAPOP's links to *Communities* to track down the online brochures for such accretions of South Dakota humanity as Spearfish, Volin, Yankton, Mitchell and Deadwood.

❑

QuickLink

http://www.state.tn.us/governor/

TENNESSEE HAS WASTED NO TIME TURNING over its public resources to the Internet. The government is eminently accessible via browser and the legal researcher will discover a trove of state information that's both sensibly organized and up-to-date.

EXECUTIVE RESOURCES

The governor hosts the state's Web site and promises that the state has opened a gateway to all of its departments and agencies. It's no political bravado; Tennessee is one of the easier states in which to look up the law. Fat icons from the governor's page are good starting points to government sites throughout the state.

With typical governor-like design, Tennessee's First Webmaster gives to the world a State of the State address, news releases, a schedule of activities and biographical information. There's also an annual report.

For corporation forms and fee schedules, fire up the home page for the Secretary of State at *http://www.state.tn.us/sos/service.htm* Forms are in PDF format are available for for-profit and non-profit corporations, limited partnerships and limited liability entities. Corporate records are not yet Internet-accessible in Tennessee.

The tax authorities turn fashionably proactive on their Web site at *http://www.state.tn.us/revenue/links.htm* as they launch information on starting a new business into cyberspace. Also online are tax rulings, legislative summaries and a grand menagerie of forms for the various individual, corporate and excise taxes that the state imposes on its citizens. The site was still under construction in mid-1997 but once it's completely operational, the researcher should have fingertip access to all the most important forms.

The comprehensive collection of links to executive branch departments and agencies is at *http://www.state.tn.us/departments*

JUDICIAL RESOURCES

The Administrative Office of the Courts operates the Web server for the Tennessee Courts and the home page at *http://www.tsc.state.tn.us* is the perfect starting point for digging up the state's court information. Links from the page lead to the Supreme Court, the Court of Appeals, the Court of Criminal Appeals and link to Court Rules. The home page features links to the judicial biographies, a list of cases certified to be heard and links to all the courts within Tennessee. There's also general information and a collection of current press releases.

To locate a directory of opinions, head straight for *http://www.tsc.state.tn.us/OPINIONS/opinopts.htm* The decisions can be downloaded in WordPerfect 6.X format and date back to mid-1995 for all jurisdictions except for Workers' Compensation cases which are online only from 1996.

The page marked for rules only contain changes to the rules. The entire set of rules has not yet made its way to the Internet servers. The court page also hosts links to other sites within the state and from around the nation.

LEGISLATIVE MATERIALS

Home for the Tennessee General Assembly on the Internet is *http://www.legislature.state.tn.us* From the home page, which outlines the structure and schedule of the state legislature, connect to the Senate and the House of Representatives; both chambers proffer the scoop on leadership. Membership, committees and the caucuses from the major political parties are here.

It's the legislative information, though, that's the main reason to visit this site and Tennessee's lawmakers make looking up new and proposed laws very simple. At the Legislative Information page at *http://www.legislature.state.tn.us/Legislative/Legislative.htm* an instructions-laden table provides 1-2-3 lookups for documents produced in the most recent legislative session. Connect here to filed legislation, bills signed into law or call up a search engine for bills that can root through bill texts to locate words or topics. There's also a weekly recap of the legislative session published as the legislative record. Other highlights of the legislative database are schedules, study committees, calendars and a guide to how bills become laws for researchers who ditched social studies class in high school. A glossary of legislative terms rounds out the site.

The legislative library has a general information page at *http://www.legislature.state.tn.us/Legislative/library.htm*

In spite the great strides the state has made in mounting legal information to the Internet, the Tennessee statutes and administrative code remain missing in action.

STATE LIBRARY

The State Library for Tennessee offers a Web-based interface to search its catalog by author, title, subject or notes at *http://www.auto-graphics.com/cgipac/mmx/tns* Other links are directories to libraries within the state.

LOCAL AND MUNICIPAL RESOURCES

Look for cities and counties online at *http://orserv01.ci.oak-ridge.tn.us/orctylnk.htm* from the server for Tennessee City and County Links. Not all cities are represented nor are all the counties in the state, but the site is a start in linking smaller municipalities to the Web.

BAR ASSOCIATION

The Tennessee Bar Association operates TBALink at *http://www.tba.org* and while there's a fair degree of information mounted there for the casual researcher, the real goods are accessible by paid subscription. (Fees are $25 a year for members and $75 per year for non-members.) Members get ethics opinions and judicial opinions in a trice from the courts. There's also CLE Online and Law Forum links which connect to Tennessee-based law-related listservs. Members also get free stripped-down Web sites and discounts on more elaborate ones.

MISCELLANEOUS RESOURCES

Portions of the Tennessee Blue Book, the guide to such Tennessee arcana as where county names came from, state symbols and a listing of such august historical persons as past governors and long-gone constitutional officers can be enjoyed at leisure from *http://www.state.tn.us/sos/blue.htm*

Travelling to Tennessee? Make plans by perusing the online info-kiosks from the Department of Tourism. Brochures and regional information centers provide the 411 to out-of-towners. ❑

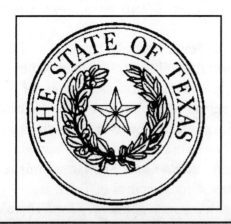

QuickLink
http://link.tsl.state.tx.us/t/txgov.html

TEXAS HAS LONG BEEN the Lone Star State, but it may soon be called the Online State considering the rich legal resources available via the Web for the Texas legal researcher. Texas is one of the most Web-savvy states and provides links and access to all its agencies and law-making bodies.

EXECUTIVE RESOURCES

The governor keeps a virtual office at *http://www.governor.state.tx.us* and like most governor Web pages features the expected welcome messages, speeches, press releases, initiatives, accomplishments and other items of self-approval so dear to the heart of a politician. To the credit of Texas, this is the only gubernatorial site that also includes links to the Texas Music Office (which itself links to some 1,700 Texas music-related sites. Get down!)

Hook up to the state agencies of Texas, locate the complete list of agencies, boards, colleges commissions, courts, departments, offices and universities at the Texas State Agencies page at *http://www.state.tx.us/agency/ agencies.html* Either scroll down the alphabeti-

cal list or hurry the search by clicking on the alphabet bar to zip directly to the agency. Virtually every state office is represented here.

For organizing businesses within Texas, look over the *Business Organization Forms* available from the Secretary of State office. Dozens of forms can be downloaded from the site at *http://www.sos.state.tx.us/function/ forms/index.htm*

The executive agencies of Texas make complying with their myriad regulations now that the Texas Administrative Code can be searched and downloaded from *http://www.sos.state.tx.us/tac/index.html* The *Texas Register*, the official publication for the proposed and adopted rule-makings of the state's agencies is online in HTML or PDF format at *http://www.sos.state.tx.us/texreg/ index.html*

LEGISLATIVE MATERIALS

With an information-efficient home page, the Texas Legislature Online at *http://www.capitol.state.tx.us/* is one-stop legislative shopping at its best. From the home page, links glide effortlessly to searches of bill texts and bill analyses by keyword or phrase. Bills can also be searched by such criteria as *legislative actions, last actions, action date, committee, author* or *co-author*. Bills are fully indexed and contain fiscal notes, captions and other identifying terms.

The legislature's home page provides membership data and connections to both chambers.

The Legislative Reference Library at *http://www.lrl.state.tx.us* sets out the resources it offers the researcher and publishes an informative pathfinder to creating legislative histories titled *Compiling Legislative Intent in Texas*.

Texas statutes are completely searchable from the simple but powerful statutory server at *http://www.capitol.state.tx.us/statutes/statutes.ht*

ml The code can be viewed online or down-loaded in zipped ASCII format.

JUDICIAL MATERIALS

Internet access to Texas state court materials is via a by-subscription service known as *TexLaw*. Details about cost and subscriptions can be found at *http://www.texlaw.com/*

BAR ASSOCIATIONS

Though the Texas State Bar has not yet mounted its own Web site, certain sections of the association have. Find links to the Appellate Practice and Advocacy, Business Law, Computer and Intellectual Property sections at *http://www.texlaw.com/special/sections.htm*

The Texas Law Organizations Resource Center at *http://www.txlaw.com/associa.html* links to the home pages of bar associations, Texas law librarians, legal secretaries and legal assistants.

STATE LIBRARY

The Texas State Electronic Library is a monster information service for the state that makes for convenient links to government resources, reference materials like news, dictionaries, road conditions and subject-oriented lists. The Webmasters of the TSEL also pack the server with listservs, indexes and full-text journals, heavy duty connections to the Library of Congress and an extensive link to Texas regional information. Find this exciting Web site at *http://link.tsl.state.tx.us*

The law librarians of Texas keep up a dandy Web server at *http://ccwf.cc.utexas.edu/~suefaw* that links to all things Texan and law-related.

Many state agencies operate their own libraries. Those libraries, for the most part, are online and a single, unified Web-based browser can search their collective catalogs. Find a link to search these catalogs from the TSEL link at

http://link.tsl.state.tx.us

LOCAL AND MUNICIPAL LINKS

Texas has more counties than any other state and keeping track of them is not simple; that task is made considerably easier thanks to the advent of the Internet. Links to the counties of Texas can be found at a sub-directory of the official state server at *http://www.state.tx.us/county/counties.html* Similar information can be retrieved for the cities of Texas at *http://www.state.tx.us/cities.html* There are also links to Texas cities from USACityLink at *http://usacitylink.com//tx.html*

MISCELLANEOUS LINKS

For general demographic data on Texas and financial information such as revenues and spending, look to the *Texas Fact Book* at *http://notesweb.lbb.state.tx.us/factbook.nsf*

Plan travel to the Lone Star State with an appropriately Texas-flavored travel Web at *http://www.TravelTex.com* Some of the site is pure tourist hooey but there's a good deal of helpful reference information such as maps, lodging and itinerary plans.

State planning regions run a clickable map for the state that fetches up the home page of some two dozen local planning groups and councils of government. Find the map and the links at *http://www.txregionalcouncil.org/mapor.htm*

For a very lengthy list of media outlets in Texas, set your browser to get the page from *http://link.tsl.state.tx.us/t/txnews.html* That's where the researcher can find online newspapers, magazine and some TV and radio outlets from Texas and the rest of the United States. ❏

QuickLink
http://www.state.ut.us

UTAH GREETS VISITORS to the official state server with a Web page that looks more like an online newspaper than a dry-as-dust government information dealer. The site is lively and informative, broadcasting news from state agencies and a calendar of events going on around the state.

EXECUTIVE RESOURCES

Utah's governor hosts a Web site at *http://www.governor.state.ut.us* that in sparkling fashion informs the visitor about the governor's biography and political initiatives and reprints speeches, press releases and articles about the governor. Additional links on this good-looking page lead to spiffed up reports on the state's technology, transportation sector, land issues, health care and to issues concerning education and the family.

Utah has enthusiastically embraced the Internet and the legal researcher should have not trouble finding any public state information from one of the many excellent servers.

From the Attorney General's home page, head directly to opinions from the office dating from 1991 and to the AG's updates for legislators. Links also lead to opinions form the

Supreme Court and the Court of Appeals. The AG is online at *http://www.at.state.ut.us*

The Utah Tax Commission publishes the liveliest Web site of any tax department in the nation and its home page packs an immense informational wallop. In addition to tax forms and publications, which can be downloaded on the spot, Utah links up proposed and current administrative rules, economic reports and tax rates. The Commission even provides a Utah Tax Research Library where the researcher can look around for other tax publications such as appeal rulings, advisory opinions, Tax Bulletins and the Utah Tax Code. Other services from the Utah Tax Commission include a FAQ file and a report for non-Utahans on doing business in the state. Locate the commission's home page at *http://txdtm01.tax.ex.state.ut.us*

As one of the first states to adopt a Digital Signature Act, Utah's State Division of Corporations and Commercial Code now elaborates on this essential element for online commerce at its home page at *http://www.commerce.state.ut.us/web/commerce/digsig/ -dsmain.htm* The site features the text of the Act and associated commentary.

A directory of Utah state employees is maintained at *http://web.state.ut.us/phone.htm*

LEGISLATIVE MATERIALS

Sit in the cybergallery at the Utah State Legislature from its home page at *http://www.le.state.ut.us/welcome.htm* Information about the legislators is linked to the home page; retrieve the text of bills dating from 1996 at *http://www.le.state.ut.us/years.htm* Bills may be searched by bill text or bill status and searches may be run through the House or Senate Journal for a chronological record of the actions and proceedings within each chamber. Enrolled bills that were sent to the governor for signing can be searched separately.

Other research tools available on the legislature's home page are a *Digest of Legislation, Budget, Committees* and *Legislative Rules*.

The Utah Code is completely accessible online in zipped WordPerfect 6.1 format. The code is arranged by title; click on the link to the title to view it on-screen or download the file for later importation into a word processing program. The code is keyword searchable by clicking on the question-mark icon. Find the code at *http://www.le.state.ut.us/~code/code.htm*

JUDICIAL RESOURCES

The Utah State Court System at *http://courtlink.utcourts.gov* has been under construction for most of 1997, but if the smartly designed servers from other branches of the Utah government are any indication, the judiciary should also provide thorough and current reports on the operations and publications of the courts state-wide.

BAR ASSOCIATIONS

Dividing its duties between service to the general public and providing information to its members, the Utah Bar Association Web at *http://www.utahbar.org* offers online lawyers referrals, information about fee arbitration and law-related education links to the outside world and bar journal write-ups, committees and legislative relations reports to its members. Other pages are dedicated to the *Young Lawyers Division, Admissions and Licensing, Lawyer Discipline* and the *Utah Law & Justice Center*.

Find a list with appropriate hypertext connections to county and local bar associations at *http://www.utahbar.org/staff_listings/ LOCAL.html*

STATE LIBRARY

At *http://www.state.lib.ut.us/statelib.htm* the Utah State Library Division keeps shop. Telnet to the catalog by pointing a telnet-equipped browser to *telnet://www.state.lib.ut.us*

and login as *mqpac* using the password HORI-ZON. Choose VT100 as the terminal emulation.

LOCAL AND MUNICIPAL LINKS

The Utah Association of Counties at *http://www.uacnet.org* is a state-wide organization that lobbies for the interests of Utah's 29 counties before the state and Federal government. The Web site is primarily of interest to county commissioners and their staffs, but the researcher can track down useful county information from the link on the association's home page. Plug in to counties and cities from the official state server at *http://www.state.ut.us/ html/counties.htm*

The Salt Lake City Corporation City Code Online represents a rare but welcome instance of a complete municipal code mounted on a server for public convenience. Review the code at *http://www.ci.slc.ut.us/government/city-code/index.html*

MISCELLANEOUS RESOURCES

For statistics on crime within Utah, turn to the Utah Commission on Criminal and Juvenile Justice at *http://www.justice.state.ut.us* The site is laden with other links for crime-related information with connections to the Sentencing Commission, the Board of Pardons, crime legislation and Federal justice links.

The University of Utah law library serves the public from an Internet-based reference desk at reference desk at *http://lawlib.law.utah.edu/refdesk.htm* where links can be located to law sites throughout the network.

❑

QuickLink
http://www.state.vt.us/servers.htm

VERMONT MAY A TINY PLACE but it's not obvious in cyberspace where even one of the least populated places in America can find a home that's as dense with useful information as even the best and most overcrowded states.

EXECUTIVE RESOURCES

The governor maintains a humble site, letting the other official sites in Vermont provide most of the information. From the executive mansion, link to every other public server in Vermont, including the judiciary, the legislature and all the executive agencies.

Of all the executive agencies in Vermont, perhaps the one that's most interesting to non-Vermonters is the one that's responsible for many financial services regulations in the state. Refer to the Banking, Insurance, Securities and Health Care Administration's home page at *http://www.cit.state.vt.us/bis/* for information on the individual divisions and the new laws and regulations each of them has promulgated.

At the Web site for the Secretary of State, a search engine is available to look up UCC filings; there also are downloadable forms for Business Registry filings. The SOS oversees professional regulation and the office publishes press releases and guides to disciplinary procedures online. Find the Vermont Secretary of State at *http://www.sec.state.vt.us*

For the most extensive collection of links to Vermont's state agencies, point your browser to *http://www.state.vt.us/servers.htm* where capsule descriptions of each agency and a link to those offices which have migrated online can be found.

As of June 1997, no tax information, administrative code or attorney general publications were available online.

LEGISLATIVE MATERIALS

The Vermont Legislature is a leisurely body that takes six months between sessions. So with all that down time, state lawmakers have plenty of time to decide what they're going to put on Vermont's legislative server. It's already well-stocked as it is. The home page at http://www.leg.state.vt.us/ starts off the law-writing festivities with links to the current legislative session (if you ever catch them in the act of actually convening), a schedule of committee meetings, and links to bills, acts, resolutions, calendars and journals. Taking the pulse of legislation coursing through the state's committees is most easily done with the link to the Legislative Bill Tracking System which will display the current status and the history of any given bill under consideration.

Actually, during the summer, Vermont's legislators are not entirely idle nor pottering around the mountains; the legislative Web site reprints legislative reports and "summer studies."

In addition to bill texts, find directory information for the members and their committee assignments, reprints of the legislative rules and a FAQ file.

Vermont provides full text access to its statutes, and while the Web site is quick to point out that the online version of the state's laws is not the official source, the site is nonetheless convenient and easy to use; of course, for critical uses, refer to an officially published print source until such time as official versions of compilation appears online. Search for laws either using a Boolean-operator search engine or by selecting the statutes by title. For those researcher creating an Intranet or who otherwise have frequent need for Vermont statutes, a complete set of the statutes can be downloaded from this server in WordPerfect 6.1 format.

JUDICIAL MATERIALS

The Vermont Judiciary maintains its electronic chambers at *http://www.state.vt.us/ courts/index.htm* To track down calendars and basic information from the various state courts — including Supreme Court, Superior Court, District Court, Family Court,Probate Court and the Environmental Court are all online to one degree or another — try *http://www.state.vt.us/courts/vtcourts.htm* In Vermont, only the Supreme Court publishes its opinions to the Internet; the link to them appears on the same page.

BAR ASSOCIATION

The Vermont Bar Association keeps its Web site at *http://www.vtbar.org* The site features advisory ethics opinions, a referral service and links to the Vermont judiciary. The justices are well-wired; links exist for virtually all of the boards and committees that assist in court administration such as the *Board of Bar Examiners, Professional Conduct Board, Judicial Ethics Committee* and advisory committees for rules. Even the Statutory Revision Commission is online at

http://www.state.vt.us/courts/admin/src.htm, though there's not much there but the name and address of commission's chairperson.

STATE LIBRARY

The Vermont Department of Libraries offers access via telnet connections to its library catalogs state-wide. Find Web-based links to the state's repositories at *http://www.state.vt.us/dol/dol.htm* or telnet directly to the sites at *telnet://dol.state.vt.us:23*

The state library features links to *Environmental Decisions, Department of Labor and Industry Workers' Compensation Decisions, Labor Relations Board Decisions* and *Professional Conduct Board Decisions* at *http://dol.state.vt.us/www_root/000000/html/decisions.html*

MISCELLANEOUS LINKS

Tune into a program that provides advanced training for law enforcement personnel at the Vermont Criminal Justice Training Council. It maintains a Web site at *http://www.vcjtc.state.vt.us* where the general public can see what the council is doing to better prepare the police to serve them.

Plan the next leaf-peeping excursion, ski trip or deposition in Vermont using the online state map. Maps are available for the major towns and cities in Vermont — there aren't many — from the *Vermont Traveler's Guide* at *http://www.travel-vermont.com* This is also an excellent site for tourist information in general regarding travel around Vermont. For a virtual tour of Vermont, try the booster-flavored online tour sponsored by the University of Vermont where visitors can flip around a site packed with history, state recreational resources, government information and links to business and education sites. Also online, and pretty as an autumn afternoon in the Vermont countryside is Vermont Life magazine. The magazine publishes feature articles from around the state, real estate advertising and opportunities and travel information. ❑

QuickLink
http://www.state.va.us/home/
governmt.html

V IRGINIA SPORTS A SIMPLE but powerful home page that will serve the researcher well as a first step in looking up the law in the commonwealth.

EXECUTIVE RESOURCES

The Governor of Virginia gives the casual researcher a chance to bail out of reviewing the gubernatorial Web site at *http://www.state.va.us/governor* by requiring a separate click to access the page. Should the chief executive's page hold materials of interest, find a biography of the governor, links to the staff, press releases, transcripts of recent speeches and links to other Web sites. A complete directory of Virginia agencies connected to the Internet is there for the asking at *http://www.state.va.us/home/govvaagy.html*

Other executive Web sites produce a plethora of useful information for the legal researcher. The Virginia Attorney General at *http://www.state.va.us/~oag/main.htm* publishes press releases and official opinions dating from January 1996.

The Virginia Department of Taxation gives researchers access to online tax forms or, alternatively, an online order form for requesting forms from the department. Due dates for vari-

ous forms are published on the site, but tax laws and regulations are not yet there. The Tax Department can be found at *http://www.state.va.us/tax/tax.html*

In Virginia, the Secretary of State has far-ranging responsibilities regulating the insurance industry, financial institutions, securities, corporations, the communications industry and utility companies. Connections to each of these divisions, however, only provide contact numbers, an outline of the Secretary's responsibilities and links to key staff.

Virginia has mounted its administrative code on an Internet-accessible server at *http://leg1.state.va.us/000/srr.htm* A search box on the page lets the researcher zoom through the voluminous collection of state agency rules and regulations. It's also one of the rare states that makes its regulatory journal available. Find the table of contents for the *Virginia Register of Regulations* from the *Register's* home page at *http://legis.state.va.us/codecomm/regindex.htm*

LEGISLATIVE RESOURCES

Find the Virginia General Assembly's online statehouse at *http://legis.state.va.us* From here, push buttons will whisk the researcher to detailed information from each chamber: the pages report leadership, districts, membership biographies, rules and staff information.

The Legislative Information System at *http://leg1.state.va.us/lis.htm* is remarkably thorough. It connects to the status of bills and resolutions, a meeting schedule and a comprehensive index of bills, resolutions and documents. Legislative information can be retrieved dating from the 1994 session.

Search the full text of the *Virginia Code* from *http://leg1.state.va.us/000/src.htm* where a search box allows for simple and flexible searching. To speed searching, click on the *Table of Contents* to access individual titles within the Code.

JUDICIAL MATERIALS

The Virginia Judicial System maintains an elaborate Web site that combines opinions, publications, calendars and documents on one easy-to-click home page at *http://www.courts.state.va.us/*

Use the index on the left side of the page to track down opinions and opinion synopses dating from early 1996 from the Virginia Supreme Court and Court of Appeals. Opinions are archived in WordPerfect 5.1 format or in plain text. (The WordPerfect formats allow for elegant footnotes.)

On the right side of the page, find capsule descriptions of the courts within the state, including courts of limited jurisdiction such as juvenile and domestic relations district court, magistrates and information on mediation.

BAR ASSOCIATION

The Virginia State Bar goes electric at *http://www.vsb.org* Refer to the faux-frame on the left side of the home page to navigate the site which contains an overview of the association, a list of the officers and for the executive committee and the Bar Council and a list of committees and boards. An online brochure outlines the publications available from the bar; ordering them is an analog process requiring the use of a telephone &/or a stamp. A lawyer referral link is installed for use by the general public.

STATE LIBRARY

With its HTML-based online catalog, the Virginia State Library at *http://leo.vsla.edu* is in a class by itself. Search the state library using a word, phrase, combination of words and phrases or Boolean searches. A directory of all Virginia libraries is ready for perusal at

http://leo.vsla.edu:80/directory

One of the services of the Virginia judiciary is an online law library at *http://www.courts.state.va.us/library/library.htm* that features an information desk, links to other Virginia law libraries and a link to the U.S. Government Printing Office.

LOCAL AND MUNICIPAL RESOURCES

A sub-directory of the official Virginia page called *Around the State* is the best bet for drilling down into the informational mines of small-town Virginia. The page is online at *http://www.state.va.us/home/arolocal.html* and connects to counties, cities and regional authorities from around Virginia.

MISCELLANEOUS RESOURCES

Online media in the state can be accessed by heading to *http://www.state.va.us/home/aromedia.html* The resources linked to the page are newspapers and specially designed online versions of radio, television and print sources from around the state.

For making travel plans to Virginia, refer to the *Transportation* links from the state's home page. The links features Amtrak schedules and airport information. The page is available at *http://www.state.va.us/home/arotrans.html*

Take a tour of the law schools of Virginia by connecting to the *Education* links from the same home page. Not all colleges have wired themselves but most have. There's no separate link for the law schools associated with individual institutions but some hunting around should locate them without much exertion.

❏

QuickLink

http://www.wa.gov/wahome.html

WASHINGTON STATE PROVIDES the legal researcher with a complete and detailed universe of law-related resources. The sites of interest are, as a rule, carefully designed and appropriately stocked with the most-used materials.

EXECUTIVE MATERIALS

The governor of Washington, like governors everywhere, serves up a home page furnished with press releases, biographical information, reprints of speeches and position papers on a number of issues and highlights of the proposed budget. But for complete access to Washington State's wired agencies, look at *Home Page Washington's* list at *http://www.wa.gov/state.htm* The researcher can link up to state agencies, judicial and legislative resources, state boards and commissions, councils and special purpose task forces and work groups.

Pay up the taxfolk from Washington by downloading forms, rules and regulations from the Department of Revenue's home page at *http://www.wa.gov/DOR/wador.html* It's also the place to find excise tax bulletins, Washington Tax Decisions and draft rules in progress.

The Washington Administrative Code is Internet accessible and searchable at *http://www.mrsc.org/wac.htm* but the version mounted online is considerably out-of-date. Be sure to consult official sources before relying on the electronic text.

LEGISLATIVE RESOURCES

Begin legislative research from the home page for the Washington state legislature at *http://leginfo.leg.wa.gov* (For the sturdy researcher who likes to do things the hard way, the legislative server may be searched using gopher or FTP.) The legislature comes across with a great deal of bill information and the link to *Bill Info* is the magic portal to laws fresh from the legislative floor. Washington thoughtfully publishes its bill-to-code conversion table which saves untold hours of head-scratching when trying to see what effect new legislation has on current law.

The legislature also reprints committee reports, status reports and initiatives. Access to both houses is available from the legislature's home page.

The Revised Code of Washington is online at *http://leginfo.leg.wa.gov/www/rcw.htm* where it can be browsed and downloaded title by title.

JUDICIAL RESOURCES

The Washington state courts maintain a home page at *http://www.wa.gov/courts/home.htm* The courts provide superb service and make access to judicial resources simple and satisfying. The Web site is extensive and contains just about all court information the researcher may require.

On the court's home page link to opinions, find both officially published and unpublished opinions from the Supreme Court and Court of Appeals. Opinions are kept online for 90 days. To find opinions, refer to *http://www.wa.gov/courts/opinpage/ home.htm* where slip opinions released within the past two weeks can be found using the link to *View a List of the Most Recent Opinions*; for later opinions, use the link to *Enter Search Criteria and Keywords*. The Reporter of Decisions provides a style sheet for opinions and background information on the Reporter's Office.

The administrators of Washington's courts generously provide links to both state and local court rules. Among the state rules e-published here are the rules of *General Application, Appellate Court Administration, Appeal, Superior Court* and *Courts of Limited Jurisdiction*. As for local rules, turn to this page for Superior Court, District Court and Municipal Court rules. Washington is one of the few states to mount court forms and related publications on a Web site. Find the forms themselves and instructions in either Word 2.0 or WordPerfect 5.0 at *http://www.wa.gov/courts/forms/list.htm* Currently online are forms for Domestic Relations, Domestic Violence and Criminal Forms.

BAR ASSOCIATION

The Washington State Bar Association keeps it server open 24 hours a day at *http://www.wsba.org* A welcome message and a guide for first-time visitors makes newcomers feel at home. The association provides information on the services it offers to members, a FAQ file that answers the most basic questions -- *How do I get a new Bar Card? Where can I call for ethics opinions? What is the phone number for attorney referral services?* -- and a link to CLE will keep professional skills in tip-top shape.

Like some other bar associations, Washington takes some of the sting out of waiting for bar results by publishing bar exam results on its home page. Also find links to other Internet resources from the barristers as well as details on the Lawyers Assistance Program (LAP) to aid attorneys who are coping with serious personal problems.

STATE LIBRARY

The State Law Library, with a fine collection of links to aid the researcher in finding a path through Washington research, has its Web site at *http://www.wa.gov/wsl* Telnet-equipped browsers can dial into the library catalog. Track down government information from throughout the state using the online Government Information Locator System (GILS). A list of other libraries in the state is stacked up at the bottom of the Home Page Washington site at *http://www.wa.gov/local.htm#t7*

LOCAL AND MUNICIPAL RESOURCES

Washington State enjoys extensive links to local, municipal and county governments, as well as connections to the tribal governments of Native Americans living within the state. From *Home Page Washington* at *http://www.wa.gov/ local.htm* skip directly to cities and towns, counties, regional organizations, public utilities and ports.

MISCELLANEOUS RESOURCES

Washington State is looking forward to the future of electronic commerce and is now readying laws and regulations in anticipation of the day when such transactions will be routine. Get details on Washington's digital signature law, standards and working group from the page operated by Washington's Secretary of State at *http://www.wa.gov/sec/corps/digsig.htm* A well-considered selection of links to explain the intricacies of public key encryption, international standards and the other issues associated with smoothing the cyberpath to safe and reliable commerce makes this page a worthwhile pit stop for the researcher brushing up on the subject. And to encourage girls to pursue careers in the law, Washington e-publishes *An Online Women's Roadmap to Careers in Law* to highlight the achievements of women in the state of Washington and at the Federal level. ❏

QuickLink

http://www.wvbar.org

WEST VIRGINIA MAY SUFFER from the greatest information deficit of any of the states in the Union. If there is room for improvement in providing information via the Internet, West Virginia is the place to begin.

But compared to what was available to the researcher a scant year ago, this is a drastic increase. Refer to the West Virginia State Bar page at *http://www.wvbar.org* This page is the best starting point for research in West Virginia law.

EXECUTIVE RESOURCES

Tight-fisted though West Virginia may be with information, it still comes as no surprise that the governor gets his state-of-the-state address online, as well as his press releases and biography. The governor weaves his Web at *http://access.k12.wv.us/~governor*

The link to *Agencies* from the state page offers quick connections to the seven offices that maintain an online presence.
have created Web pages.

It's here that the researcher can connect to the *West Virginia Tax and Revenue Department* where only the link to the *Tax Division* is operational. The link makes an

interesting loop-the-loop without ever managing to pit stop at anything more substantial than a biography of the Secretary of the Department.

While none of these sites is likely to knock the socks off the casual legal researcher, the mere fact that the departments have created Web sites is an indication that the state government hasn't completely ignored the digital revolution. Still, the pace of change is slow, especially in light of the breathtaking changes taking place in other parts of the world.

LEGISLATIVE MATERIALS

The West Virginia legislature is online at *http://www.wvlc.wvnet.edu/legisinfo/legishp.html* The legislation of West Virginia is perhaps the easiest area of WV legal research to look up, but don't expect to find bill texts, legislative histories or other routine legislative documents.

Instead, the site provides a calendar of committee meetings and hearings, a legislative session *daily summary* and links to the state's senators and delegates by county, district and committee.

JUDICIAL MATERIALS

The West Virginia Supreme Court of Appeals wields its gavel at *http://www.state.wv.us/wvsca* Opinions are published bi-annually in the spring and fall and are available in WordPerfect 6.1 format dating from Spring 1991. The current year's calendar and docket is posted online, a service that accompanies a staff directory and topical index. A thumbnail history of the court appears on the page as well.

For information on West Virginia state courts, country magistrate courts and the Supreme Court of Appeals, refer to the *WV Court Information* page from the West Virginia State Bar server at *http://www.wvbar.org/barinfo/courts/index.htm*

STATE LIBRARY

The librarians of West Virginia are hip to the Internet and have published a simple but functional Web site called *Infomine* that features a searchable union catalog for the state and mounts links to what government agencies there are online in West Virginia, tourist information and the cultural connections of the state. Infomine can be reached by pointing the browser to *http://www.wvlc.wvnet.edu*

BAR ASSOCIATION

At *http://www.wvbar.org* the researcher can commune with the West Virginia State Bar online, perhaps the best source of Internet-accessible legal information on the state. In addition to the usual features of a bar association Web site -- list of membership benefits, bar committees, news about the association, state bar publications and addresses -- this site also comes across with *TechNet: West Virginia Legal Research*, a by-subscription service for attorneys in the state. There's also an online referral service for attorneys.

Links can be found here to other voluntary bar associations in the state at *http://www.wvbar.org/barinfo/regions/voluntary.htm*

A list of local county bar associations is spelled out at *http://www.wvbar.org/barinfo/regions/index.htm*

LOCAL AND MUNICIPAL RESOURCES

For tourist information on West Virginia attractions like rafting, autumnal foliage and glass factories, snoop through the online brochures at *http://www.state.wv.us/tourism/default.htm*

A directory of state employee phone numbers makes for quick lookups of the direct lines to West Virginia's civil servants. It's searchable at *http://www.state.wv.us/phone*

MISCELLANEOUS RESOURCES

The West Virginia State Law Library is open for business at *http://www.wvlc.wvnet.edu/lawlib/menu.html* That's where the researcher will find a useful collection of Internet links and synopsis of the library's holdings.

Economic data for West Virginia is ready for downloading at *http://www.state.wv.us/wvdev/default.htm* at a page designed to highlight the economic development talents of a consortium of state and quasi-official organizations. Among the publishers here are the West Virginia Development Office, the Small Business Development Center and the Development Office. Of special interest is the *Industrial Properties Database* which helps prospective developers or businesses locate industrial parks, buildings or sites on which to build.

Environmental information about West Virginia receives its own home page at *http://charon.osmre.gov* where the curious can enjoy a very cool shimmering waterfall applet while poking around the abandoned mine database.

❑

QuickLink

http://badger.state.wi.us/

Wisconsin answers neighboring Minnesota's gopher-pride with its own *Badger* server and as a one-stop shop for state information, this badger at *http://badger.state.wi.us* has created a comfortable and information-laden den for looking up state law materials. Everything the researcher needs is here on this page except for links to judicial decisions and other court resources; they're available from the bar association as described below.

EXECUTIVE AGENCIES

Jump right in to Wisconsin research with connections to the Wisconsin State Agency page. This lengthy page, which eventually will be a comprehensive collection of all state agencies, connects to most of the major state departments. It is gracefully simple and satisfyingly fast. Pop on the link to get just about anyplace in the state.

Like governors elsewhere, Wisconsin's likes to see his picture on the Web alongside his state-of-the-state address, state budget and press releases explaining his policies on important state matters. His portrait in pixels dominates.

Among all the state agencies mounted here, the Web site for the Department of Commerce bears special mention for the sheer breadth of the information published there to attract investment to the state. Linked here are dozens of info-leads on business assistance and financing, help for small businesses and entrepreneurs and explanations of other state programs designed to welcome new development to the state. Wisconsin uses Internet technology to roll out a welcome mat for would-be investors.

Other agencies are also sophisticated users of the network. The Office of the Commissioner of Insurance at *http://badger.state.wi.us/agencies/oci/oci_home.htm*, for example, publishes a list of registered agents, as well as news releases and instructions on how to file an insurance complaint. The Department of Regulation and Licensing, for its part, puts up application information, instructions for complaints, publications and a link to the secretary at its site at *http://badger.state.wi.us/agencies/drl*

For Wisconsin tax forms and publications, aim to the penny-iconned home page at *http://badger.state.wi.us/agencies/dor/html/form-pub.html* where forms and publications from 1996 are waiting for download in PDF format. Forms, but not publications, are available for 1995. Wisconsin thoughtfully provides local government forms and publications such as *Real Estate Property Tax* information and a *Guide for Property Owners*.

LEGISLATIVE RESOURCES

The Wisconsin State Legislature lives online at *http://www.legis.state.wi.us* It comes dressed up with a full complement of legislative information and bill tracking firepower. A nine-button home page comprises the console that provides navigation around the site: *Spotlight* is the news service to publish updates on recent legislative activity; *Legislative Information* is a directory containing the legislature's *session schedule, calendar of public hearings* and links to *legislator's e-mail addresses*. The connection to *Bill Tracking* leads to an advanced search system that gives the researcher access to the histories of bills, joint resolutions and resolutions in HTML format. The histories are all linked to the associated text. Bills and acts are mounted in PDF format and so an Adobe Acrobat viewer is necessary.

This site is fully indexed and it's possible to look up current bills and material and material dating back to 1995 from the legislative site at *http://www.legis.state.wi.us/bill-track.html*

Each chamber maintains its own Web site. The Senate site at *http://www.legis.state.wi.us/senate/senate.html* connects to the Senators' *home pages* and *e-mail addresses* and outlines *joint legislative committees* and *Senate standing committees*.

The Assembly's page at *http://www.legis.state.wi.us/assembly/assembly.html* offers the corresponding information for that body. Other links from the legislative pages hook up to *Support Agencies* such as the Legislative Council Staff, Legislative Fiscal Bureau and Legislative Research Bureau.

Wisconsin state statutes are searchable by chapter; the text is mounted in PDF format at *http://WWW.legis.state.wi.us/Statutes.html*

JUDICIAL RESOURCES

For the best links to Wisconsin judicial materials, turn to the Wisconsin Bar Association at *http://www.wisbar.org* This is the place to find Supreme Court opinions and opinions from the Court of Appeals. Local court rules also are published here.

For Supreme Court cases, an archive is available dating from 1995. Cases are indexed by *docket number, petitioner's name, respondent's name* and *date*. There is also a *Case Search Engine* that will plow through recent decisions for the researcher. Recent cases are indexed by the same criteria as the archived cases; cases published after February 20, 1997 are downloadable in Word 7.0 format. Earlier cases are in WordPerfect format.

Decisions from the Wisconsin Court of Appeals are available in the same fashion as the Supreme Court materials. Look on this site to retrieve local court rules on a county-by-county basis at *http://www.wisbar.org/rules*

Wisconsin breaks new ground by publishing its legal notices on the Internet. Look at *http://www.nebweb.com/madison/legals* for such legal notices as *bids/proposals, general notices,* ads from the *Secretary of State* and *construction bids*.

The state also makes its telephone directory online-accessible at *http://badger.state.wi.us/directory.html* giving the researcher instant access to state employees and the legislature.

LOCAL AND MUNICIPAL RESOURCES

County and municipal resources populate the Internet too. Find a stack of links to smaller jurisdictions at *http://badger.state.wi.us/local.html*

BAR ASSOCIATION

In addition to the aforementioned judicial resources, the Wisconsin Bar offers its members and visitors an online legal resource center, CLE books and seminars, discussion groups and the expected lists of committees, member benefits and other coming attractions.

STATE LIBRARY

The electronic reference desk hangs out its shingle at *http://badger.state.wi.us/agencies/dpi/dlcl/*

❑

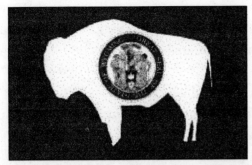

QuickLink

http://www.uwyo.edu/Lib/
Wyoming/index.html

WYOMING, NOT TO BE OUTDONE by the Minnesota gopher, weighs in with its own official state *ferret*. Regional pride aside, the ferret works about the same as the gopher and provides the researcher with either a text-based or graphical interface to the good collection of state law materials mounted on the site.

EXECUTIVE AGENCIES

The best-stocked page for executive agency links is hosted at the Windy Wyoming page at *http://www.uwyo.edu/Lib/Wyoming/index.html* From here, the researcher can connect to the governor's office and its associated pages and to the lightly stocked Attorney General's page (so far containing only directory information for the office and hypertext link to file a missing persons report.)

Wyoming allows public access at no fee to the state's *Corporation Records*. A search page retrieves results by business entity and returns a result containing the corporation's status, registered agent, mailing address, purpose and corporate structure and state of incorporation for all businesses doing business within the state. The URL for the public records search is *http://soswy.state.wy.us/corps1.htm*

Unlike most other states, Wyoming does not have a personal or corporate income tax. The state's Department of Revenue is instead divided into divisions, each of which is charged with the collection of different revenue sources. From the department's home page at *http://www.state.wy.us:80/~revenue/revenue.htm* connect to the divisions for *excise tax, liquor, mineral tax* and *ad valorem*. There are links to the distribution of the *sales tax* and the *cigarette tax*. The department's rules are also accessible from the same site.

The Wyoming government site is equipped with a search engine that will permit searching the contents of all publicly-available WWW documents published on the state's Web site. Find the search engine at *http://www.state.wy.us:80/state/search.html*

LEGISLATIVE MATERIALS

Legislative materials are available beginning with the 1997 legislative session. Link to the connection for *General Session* to pull up a simply-designed page linking to the *rules* of both houses, the legislative *schedule* for the session. For bill information, look to the links that contain *Bill Status Abbreviations*, the *Daily Bill Status Sheet, Bill Titles, Subject Index, Sponsor Index* and *Final Action Sheet*.

Bill texts are arranged in three distinct divisions. *House bills* and *Senate files* ready for introduction merit their own hypertext links. So too do *engrossed bills* from both houses and *enrolled acts*. Wyoming's legislature also publishes a *House Digest* and a *Senate Digest*. This same page also contains links to press releases from the legislature. The *Bill Status Hotline* is still telephone based: call (800) 342-9570 within the state or (307) 777-6185 from outside Wyoming for the status of a pending bill.

The legislative page is the same place to go for searchable *state statutes*. They're in text format and are searchable by title from *http://legisweb.state.wy.us/titles/sitf.htm*

A search page can be pulled up at *http://legisweb.state.wy.us/titles/search.htm*

JUDICIAL MATERIALS

The Wyoming judiciary maintains its own home page at *http://courts.state.wy.us/* and this, of course, is the best place to go to fetch information about the courts and to locate judicial decisions.

The home page offers links to primary materials, including *Supreme Court Opinions.* The opinions date from January 1996 to present and can be searched by month or by using a free-text search box. The link for the *Law Library* connects to useful information on the state's legal materials; among the materials mounted there are the Wyoming Constitution, the statutes, court rules and a telnet connection to WYLDCAT, the law library catalog.

The court system is described in the link to *Wyoming's Court System.* Find biographies of the Supreme Court justices by clicking on the link for the same. Other links on this page provide the researcher with hook-ups to the *Clerk of the Court, Court Administrator, Judicial Directory, Rules of Procedure, E-Mail Addresses* and *Oral Argument Setting,* the last item a calendar of scheduled oral arguments before the Supreme Court.

STATE LIBRARY

The Wyoming State Library is online at *http://www-wsl.state.wy.us* In addition to the catalog connections, the *Statewide Information Services* system will provide assistance "in locating electronic and print information, reference and interlibrary loan, state and federal documents, for State agencies, the public, other libraries and institutions. Through SIS, the State Library provides timely information by responding to questions, conducting database

searches, lending materials, and retrieving documents from its unique collections that are not duplicated elsewhere in the state," according to the SIS home page.

For general information about the State of Wyoming, refer to the extensive and timely Web site operated by the University of Wyoming at *http://www.uwyo.edu*

Also find statistical information from the U.S. Census Bureau -- *Consolidated Federal Funds Report FY 1994* and *Summary of Wyoming State Government Finances: 1991-1993 Census* are online at the Windy Wyoming page. This is also the site to look up standard reference materials on the state such as maps, news, tourist information, recreational links, land status and geological links.

MISCELLANEOUS RESOURCES

Prospective law students in Wyoming will benefit from the online brochure prepared by the dean of the School of Law at the University of Wyoming. It sets out the curriculum, courses, admission information and financial aid programs. The information is mounted at *http://www.uwyo.edu/LAW/adm/bulletin.htm*

BAR ASSOCIATION

As of June 1997, the Wyoming State Bar Association was still living an analog existence at 500 Randall Avenue, P.O. Box 109, Cheyenne, WY 82001 with nary a Web woven. Call the association at (307) 632-9061 and ask them to get with the program.

❏

TERRITORIES AND POSSESSIONS

DISTRICT OF COLUMBIA

The official home page for the District of Columbia is online at *http://www.dchomepage.net/dcmain/index.html* but the contents are surprisingly thin. There's a message from the mayor's office and links to the offices of International Business and Tourism and Promotion and a map of the DC subway but for substantive code information, rely on print sources. Washington D.C. Online is a general information service about the city at *http://www.dchomepage.net*

GUAM

The government of Guam's official page at *http://www.gov.gu/government.html* will provide all the necessary links to the leading agencies and departments, including the Department of Revenue and Taxation and the Office of the Governor. The site also offers a directory of the Guam government.

MARIANA ISLANDS

The Commonwealth of the Northern Mariana Islands keeps up an Internet connection from the middle of the Pacific at *http://www.saipan.com/java.htm* The link to the government connects to the *executive branch, Criminal Justice Planning Agency* and *general information*. A good deal of the site is dedicated to travel and tourism information; there are no statutes, case decisions or other substantive legal information yet online but check back frequently to see what progress has been made.

PUERTO RICO

The official English-language server for Puerto Rico is online at *http://fortaleza.govpr.org/ingles/pris.htm* and the link to *government* provides fairly extensive information about the island. Click there to check the organization of Puerto Rico's government, its municipalities and the Puerto Rico Federal Affairs Administration even though not all of the links are completely operative.

VIRGIN ISLANDS

All branches of the government sprout from the official server at *http://www.gov.vi* and that would be good news except that the links to the executive, judicial and legislative servers don't actually lead to any useful information when clicked just yet. That's not to say that the future won't bring a paradise of data from the territorial court or executive agencies but as of mid-1997, Internet access to Virgin Islands law is elusive.

Booking a vacation on St. Croix, St. Thomas or St. John is easier than looking up the law. Visit the well-stocked tourist Web site at *http://www.usvi.net* for lodging, transportation and shopping information on the islands. Link to the *Community* for local information about V.I. non-profits and local news.

❏

Reference Resources

REFERENCE RESOURCES

Introduction

The Internet abounds with reference information.
In the unstoppable conversion from print to electronic distribution of information, the Internet is rapidly becoming the world's largest online collection of factual data. Materials that either are not copyrighted or works whose copyright protection has expired are now ripe for conversion into digital format for immediate dissemination worldwide.

For the legal researcher, the Internet is a fast and free way to look up quotes, check spellings, find airline schedules, retrieve law journals, create bibliographies, keep up with breaking news and define legal terms. It is a giant library that everyone can now enjoy from any point on the planet.

Reference sources are added every day to the Internet. These Web sites do good jobs at keeping up with the changes; each of them contains links that collectively link to thousands of publications throughout the Internet.

Search Engine Connections

For one-stop retrieval of the most important reference sources, fire up Infoseek, AltaVista, Yahoo! or FindLaw. The leading search engines, especially Infoseek, are wonderful starting points for locating reference sources. All of them have on-page links to the major reference sources, especially for e-mail and address look-ups.

Associations

It's safe to assume that all associations, lobby groups, professional organizations and foundations all have a Web site. These are valuable sources of reference information, either from the information mounted directly on the Web site or because of the immediate contact the sites provide with the organization.

The legal profession abounds in professional associations; this is not a comprehensive list of legal associations, but rather a survey of the leading associations. The links installed on these pages should guide the legal researcher to a large universe of information.

The best list of links to law associations is at *http://www.barlinc.org* from the Bar Association of North Carolina.

American Bar Association
http://www.abanet.org

The nation's preeminent bar association hosts discussion groups, reprints abstracts from the *ABA Journal*, e-publishes newsletters and factbooks

and provides members with news about the association. ABANET is continuously updated and expanded which makes for a dynamic and informative center of information for the profession at large.

Special features are the *LawMart* where vendors can advertise services like software, investigative services and document management systems and *LawLink*, the ABA's (not-terribly-imaginative) suggestions of where to begin legal research.

American Civil Liberties Union
http://www.aclu.org

Controversial, pugnacious and energetic, the ACLU's *Freedom Network* maintains an online library of memos and background information on issues concerning personal liberties and rights for minorities,

women, gays and immigrants. The ACLU is joining with other online groups to fight for rights in cyberspace and is very active in making sure that the same rights guaranteed under the First Amendment extend into the electronic world too.

American Law Institute
http://www.ali..org

Best known for its series of Restatements of the law and drafts on law topics and the practical and scholarly debate that accompany them, the American Law Institute makes available a catalog of their

publications, a bibliography of the ALI in legal literature and a select number of links to other legal resources on the Internet. Drafts of ongoing projects and the restatements with appendices can be ordered from the Web site.

Association of Legal Administrators
http://www.alanet.org

Managing partners, law firm administrators and other administrative managers have a Web site to call their own. Find news about law firm management issues here and a list of members services. In the works are special services that will be accessible only to members with passwords. A *job bank* and a link to *Management Network* discussion groups and forums round out the information mounted on the site.

American Trial Lawyers Association
http://www.atlanet.com

Litigators can find selected articles from the monthly magazine *Trial* online here -- the full text is reserved for dues-paying members -- and connect to the text of some amicus curiae briefs as well. Other links lead to foundations and information about the courts but the real goods are reserved for members. The unwashed public can enjoy the *Legal Links* to other Internet law resources.

American Association of Law Libraries
http://www.aallnet.org

In an effort to automate their membership out of a profession, the largest professional organization of law librarians offers something called *LIBClient* which purports to part the murky waters of the Internet to reveal a world of unadulterated and useful data. Sounds too

good to be true but researchers can test drive it to see for themselves.

More important are the members directory and handbook and the links to member benefits including news alerts about legal publishing that affect librarians.

Corporate Bar Association
http://www.corporatebar.org

The greatest concentration of corporate counsel to Fortune 500 companies live within 75 miles of the border between New York and Connecticut just north of New York City. More than a thousand corporate lawyers -- most of them in-house -- have collected themselves online to create the Corporate Bar Association of Westchester and Fairfield. It's not necessary to live within commuting distance of Darien, CT to enjoy this plain-Jane but informative collection of seminar dates, list of audio tapes and the latest edition of their newsletter. Corporate lawyers are invited to join up online.

Cyberspace Bar Association
http://www.cyberbar.net

Interest in the emerging law of the online world is the common thread at this Web site. The site features seminar announcements, technology articles for the practicing attorney, bulletins and links to other sites. The association is the brainchild of Dallas, TX attorney E.X. Martin III.

Electronic Frontier Foundation
http://www.eff.org

The Electronic Frontier Foundation was one of the pioneers in the world of civil liberties online and it has since grown to be a leader in that role. (According to the EFF, their Web site is one of the Top Five most linked-to sites on the Web.) The foundation aggressively promotes freedom in cyberspace and has

stocked an electronic library full of information about encryption, individual privacy, IP issues and free speech. They boast a large archive of materials on legislation and regulation and reprint law journal articles on the law of the Internet as well as a newsletter. The best part is the cool T-shirt they give away to contributors and members.

National Association of Legal Assistants
http://www.nala.org

Whether they're called "paralegals" or "legal assistants" the job is the same: they help lawyers deliver legal services to the client. Depending on the jurisdiction, legal assistants can help interview clients, fill in basic forms and manage documents. In some states, legal assistants are not permitted to do much more than photocopy and send out faxes. By setting professional standards -- published online at this Web site -- the national organization hopes to raise the standards (and the salaries) of its members. Standards address *communications, ethics, judgment and analytic ability,*  *legal research* and knowledge of substantive law areas. Links include connections to news and Internet law sites.

National Court Reporters Association
http://www.ncraonline.org/

No longer stenographers with a pocket full of sharpened pencils and a notepad, court reporters now are high-tech recorders of court proceedings.
            Like other non-lawyer professional organizations, the NCRA

NCRA NATIONAL COURT REPORTERS A S S O C I A T I O N

seeks to maintain the professionalism of its members and to offer certification in the craft. The library proffers the *Court Reporters Bill of Rights* and a paper titled *The Role of the Court Reporter in the Legal System.*

National Federation of Paralegal Associations
http://www.paralegal.org

            Complementing the National Association of Legal Assistants is this organization (wherein the persons of the occupation are referred to as "paralegals.") The federation is made up of member associations. It seeks to connect paralegals to career assistance and to improve their competence. Online at the Web site are links for discussion groups, public forums and the requisite connections to Internet law resources. The quarterly publication *National Paralegal Reporter* is published online.

National Law Firm Marketing Association
http://www.nalfma.org

            Connecting with clients and raising the profile of the law firm is the task that falls to the marketing department of large law firms. Smaller firms and solo offices rely on personal recommendations and a good reputation to land new business but bigger firms, competing for the legal

NⓍLFMA   National Law Firm Marketing Association

work of big companies and wealthy individuals need specialists in the field. The people who "market" law firms hang out online at their Web site where they publish a job bank and swap tips in a *discussion forum*. Details of committees, chapters and the annual conference are mounted here too.

Practising Law Institute
http://www.pli.edu

PLI is a leading name in legal publishing and reprints seminar transcripts and handouts from the hundreds of conferences they sponsor

Providing the highest quality legal education since 1933

annually. The site gives away some articles about the use of Web by law firms and they reprint archives of the discussion groups; find a list of handbooks, upcoming institutes and programs, AV programs and CD-ROM products on the site.

Bibliography of Internet Publications

Find the best bibliography of books, newsletters and videotapes about the law-related use of the Internet is the "Law-on-the-Internet Booklists" at *http://www.abanet.org/lpm/magazine/ booklist.html* This site is maintained by G. Burgess Allison, himself the author of the American Bar Association's *The Lawyer's Guide to the Internet*. The lengthiest list of books are written for a North American audience but he also includes books about the use of the Internet for law professionals from Japan, Germany, France, the Netherlands, Italy, Australia and the U.K. Allison includes a burgeoning list of newsletters devoted to law resources available via the Internet.

A monthly bibliography of articles appearing in the print press about lawyers and the Internet appears in the newsletter *Internet Law Researcher,* edited by this book's author and published by Glasser LegalWorks of Little Falls, NJ.

For Internet "pathfinders" on an assortment of legal topics, look at the Argus Clearinghouse collection of *Government and Law* guides at *http://www.clearinghouse.net/tree/govlaw.html* The WorldWideWeb Consortium (W3C) keeps up a "Virtual Library" that is a handy guide for subject fields; the link for *Law* refers to the searchable law index from the University of Indiana at *http://www.law.indiana.edu/law/v-lib/lawindex.html*

Books and Literary Sources

As a revolutionary publishing medium, it's no surprise that the Internet is filling up with the texts of books and the great literature of our civilization. As copyright protections expire on leading literary works -- or in instances where copyright is held by a university or other institution -- the text of such works are finding a new home not on the shelves of a dusty library but deep on the drives of some hard-working servers. Literary resources are good for spicing up a legal argument or for tracing an elusive quote to illustrate a point. All of these sources are fully searchable.

The appearance of electronic versions of classic books are a remarkable testament to the generosity of time and spirit of Internet citizens. The texts were input and proofread by volunteers and subsequently uploaded to the server. This is typical entry for the e-text of Sherwood Anderson's *Winesburg, Ohio*:

> *This etext was created by Judith Boss, Omaha, Nebraska.*
> *The equipment: an IBM-compatible 486/50, a Hewlett-Packard*
> *ScanJet IIc flatbed scanner, and a copy of Calera Recognition*
> *Systems' M/600 Series Professional OCR software and RISC*
> *accelerator board donated by Calera.*

Any who uses the e-texts as provided owe a great debt to the thousands of men and women who labored without pay to make these materials available.

Electronic Library
http://www.books.com/scripts/lib.exe

The electronic library promises thousands of titles and by the looks of the directory, that's a conservative estimate. The site contains fiction including novels and short stories, ancient European

ELECTRONIC **L**IBRARY ~ ~ ~ The Electronic Library is provided as a free public service for the dissemination of electronic books (ebooks). We have **thousands** of titles available in a variety of subject areas. Everything from the complete works of William Shakespeare to scripts by Monty Python. Be sure to try out our new Search method which will allow you to look up ebooks by author, title, keyword or ISBN. All ebooks are believed to be copyright-free or used with permission.

literature, Italian literature, poetry and non-fiction. Search by author, title, keyword or ISBN number. The *Directory* is a quick way to browse the site quickly and efficiently.

Project Bartleby
http://www.columbia.edu/acis/bartleby/index.html

Named for Herman Melville's famous law scrivener, Project Bartleby is best used for its searchable ninth edition of *Bartlett's Familiar Quotations* and its fair collection of American poetry. Sponsored by

Columbia University, itself the copyright holder of thousands of literary titles, watch Project Bartleby as its holdings grow.

Project Gutenberg
http://promo.net/pg

"Fine literature, digitally re-published" is the slogan for Project Gutenberg and they're doing a good job of it. It's the best-stocked literature site on the Internet. The Web site is easy to master and with connections to dozens of mirror sites, there should be no waiting to access and download texts. Project Gutenberg offers links to other e-text sites and reprints newsletters and articles.

The On-Line Books Page
http://www.cs.cmu.edu/books.html

The site is utterly utilitarian but within the stacks of links are more than 3,000 English works of literature. This is the meta-index for all literary sites on the network.

Shakespeare: The Complete Works
http://the-tech.mit.edu/Shakespeare/works.html

When stricken with a loss for words or to find a right round phrase to flesh out the poetry of a sentence, it's always helpful to crib from the master. This complete collection of Shakespeare's works is indeed comprehensive and is completely searchable. Never again forget such Shakespearian trivia like the line that precedes "And there cracks a noble heart."

The Universal Library Project
http://www.ul.cs.cmu.edu/

The stated goal of the Universal Library Project is breathlessly advertised on their home page to be "to start a worldwide movement to make available ALL the Authored Works of Mankind on the Internet." That's a fair day's work in any month; this site is coordinating some of the enterprises now in business to bring texts into the electronic age.

Commercial Services

Like thousands of other businesses, all the leading online legal databases are now accessible via the Web. Subscribers to professional databases are assumed to be familiar with the services so only the URL of those databases is printed here. All of these services require service contracts and passwords; contact the individual vendors to establish accounts. Details on pricing and services are available directly from each of the vendors. Also note that to access many of these databases, it's necessary to have telnet client software installed.

BIBLIOGRAPHIC RESEARCH SERVICE	TELNET://BRS.COM
CARL	
COLORADO ASSOCIATION OF RESEARCH LIBRARIES	HTTP://WWW.CARL.ORG
COURTLINK	HTTP://WWW.COURTLINK.COM
COUNTERPOINT PUBLISHING	HTTP://WWW.COUNTERPOINT.COM
DIALOG	
KNIGHT RIDDER INFORMATION SERVICES	HTTP://WWW.DIALOG.COM
DISCLOSURE	HTTP://WWW.DISCLOSURE.COM
DOW JONES NEWS RETRIEVAL	HTTP://WWW.DJNR.COM
DUN AND BRADSTREET	HTTP://WWW.DNB.COM
GLOBAL SECURITIES, INC.	HTTP://WWW.GSIONLINE.COM
IBM INFOMARKET	HTTP://WWW.INFOMARKET.IBM.COM
INTERNET GRATEFUL MED	HTTP://IGM.NLM.NIH.GOV/
LEXIS/NEXIS	HTTP://WWW.LEXIS-NEXIS.COM
LIVEDGAR	HTTP://WWW.GSIONLINE.COM
LOIS LAW LIBRARY	HTTP://WWW.PITA.COM
OCLC	HTTP://WWW.OCLC.ORG
RESEARCH LIBRARIES GROUP, INC. (RLIN)	HTTP://WWW.RLG.ORG
SECURITIES DATA CORPORATION	HTTP://WWW.SDC.COM
THOMSON.COM	HTTP://WWW.THOMSON.COM
VERSUSLAW	HTTP://WWW.VERSUSLAW.COM
WEST PUBLISHING	HTTP://WWW.WESTPUB.COM

Corporations, Companies and Manufacturers

The Internet was seemingly custom-made for tracking down business information and there are some masterful resources for locating information on corporations, companies and manufacturers. With these sites in the research arsenal, there should be very little problem in locating most U.S. business entities.

For corporation information on publicly traded companies, go straight to the EDGAR server at the Securities and Exchange Commission at *http://www.sec.gov* This is where the Commission makes available to the public all the disclosure documents that the agency requires from the companies it regulates. The forms are numerous and researchers who are inexperienced in corporate research should become familiar with the SEC's weighty library of forms mandated by the various securities laws.

The EDGAR server itself (which is slated to undergo a major revision and privatization as this is written in April 1997) can be searched using simple Boolean logic and adjacency connectors or by using the SEC's CIK (Central Index Key) filing system. For basic information on a company, look for the most recent annual report on Form 10K405. Quarterly earnings are reported on Form 10Q. To locate the names of a corporation's directors and officers, refer to the proxy statement, known in EDGAR-speak as a DEF14A. Security registrations are on Forms S-1, S-2 and S-3 for domestic issuers only. (Foreign issuers are still not required to file electronically.) Mergers and business combinations are reported on Form S-4; tender offers and the response are filed on Forms 14D-1 and 14D-9 respectively.

The EDGAR server offers a complete tutorial on effective searching. Use it.

Tracking down companies is made simple by the appearance of the nationwide Yellow Pages called **Big Yellow**. As a business reference,

it's tough to beat this one source. According to Big Yellow, more than 16 million businesses are listed online. Search this superb database at *http://www.bigyellow.com*

The most well-known reference book for manufacturers in the U.S. is the Thomas Register and like other publishers, they now offer a Web-based search engine. Some 155,00 U.S. and Canadian companies appear n the database.

Use the Thomas Register at *http://www.thomasregister.com* to locate manufacturers by product. The service is free; searches return the name of the company and mailing address, along with hypertext links to the company's Web site and e-mail address if they're online.

Current Awareness

Keeping up with the daily changes to the Internet is both time-consuming and confusing. However, there are some Internet services that can keep the researcher current without requiring tedious hours of Web surfing.

Big Ear
Current Legal Resources on the Net
http://barratry.law.cornell.edu:5123/notify/buzz.html

Tom Bruce, d.b.a. "Big Ear" keeps up with the traffic on six of the leading law-related listservs and makes a weekly report of the interesting things he hears. Big Ear listens for new Web sites, announcements of new services of interest to the legal researcher, addresses of resources he thinks others will be interested in visiting and re-prints them in digest form. Big Ear's weekly digest entries each contain the name of the new resource, the URL, the source where the announcement appeared and the full-text of the announcement. This is an excellent current awareness service that should be visited frequently.

Listservs

Every legal researcher should subscribe to at least one or two listservs since they are such an important way of learning about fresh resources and new Internet services. The best place to keep up with the online gossip are **net-lawyers, lawlibref-l** and **lawsrc-l**. (Get the details on how to subscribe from **Law Lists** at *http://www.lib.uchicago.edu/ ~llou/lawlists/info.html*) Listservs fulfill one of their primary functions as the online place to share new discoveries with colleagues; this is where the action is. Check in with subject-specific lists to get the scoop on the Web sites and resources for those areas.

c|net
http://www.cnet.com

As both a Web site and a news service (making C|Net one of the earliest examples of the coming "digital convergence" of technologies), C|Net is a slick, timely and informative news service covering every aspect of the computer, networking and online industries. They got the niche carved out and do a first-rate job of reporting on the ever-changing world. Typical feature articles include software reviews, tips for getting the most out of operating systems and Internet software and wiseguy articles about life on the Internet. C|Net also boasts a software library, glossary and games.

Netscape News
http://home.netscape.com/home/whats-new.html
(or click the *What's New?* button on the Netscape browser)

Netscape Communications clearly has an interest in adding the number of people who use the Internet. One of the ways they do that is by reporting on new and interesting sites. Take the reports with a grain of salt: they're not unbiased. Still, the Netscape news can be informative.

Scout Report
http://wwwscout.cs.wisc.edu/scout/

Net-Happenings
http://www.mid.net:80/NET/

The network administrators from InterNIC produce two current awareness services known as the **Scout Report** and **Net-Happenings**, both free services to the Internet community.

The Scout Report is a weekly newsletter covering new sites and Internet tools, written with an eye for a primary audience of educators and researchers. The report can be viewed online or sent directly via e-mail in either a plain text or an HTML file. Past issues of the Scout Report can be found in the archive linked to the home page. A companion service known as the *Scout Toolkit* provides news about the latest networking tools.

Net Happenings is a daily announcement bulletin board of new and interesting pages appearing throughout the Web. It's a good place to go to find out about cyberevents like real-time chats, concerts and virtual conferences.

Dictionaries

The most popular reference books in any real-world library are the dictionaries and atlases and cyberspace is no different. A selection of legal dictionaries, English language works and foreign language dictionaries can be found and searched via the Internet. There also are technical and computer dictionaries and thesauri to illuminate some of the obscure jargon of the computer world. For a canonical list of all dictionaries and related reference works, refer to http:*//math-www.uni-paderborn.de/HTML/Dictionaries.html*

American Standard Law Dictionary
http://www.e-legal.com/resources/dict

Pop in the word and get a one-sentence definition in return. This is not an ideal dictionary but it will do in a pinch.

Black's Law Dictionary
http://www.alaska.net/~winter/county_tax.html

Extracts from the sixth edition are published here, presumably with permission of the copyright owner.

The Bluebook: A Uniform System of Citation (15th ed.)
http://www.law.cornell.edu/citation/citation.table.html

Parts of the fifteenth edition of the classic reference work on legal citation are included in this online *Introduction to Basic Legal Citation* written by Cornell Law School's Peter W. Martin. That edition has since been superceded by a sixteenth edition, which includes controversial guides to citing Internet sources.

Glossary of Telecommunications Terms
http://www.its.bldrdoc.gov:80/fs-1037/

The most extensive dictionary for telecommunications jargon and online engineering terms is this Federal Standard 1037C. Fully searchable (if not entirely comprehensible to the layman), the site contains thousands of definitions, many of them pertinent to the Internet.

Merriam-Webster Dictionary
Merriam WWWebster Online
http://www.m-w.com/netdict.htm

The Merriam-Webster dictionary has a long history of reliability and authority. The Web-based, ad-supported site can retrieve definitions. It also links to an online thesaurus.

Directories

Like other computer databases, the Internet is a perfect way to distribute directory information. Simple search engines can plow through even the meatiest data compilations with ease. Refer to the Internet to look up addresses, telephone numbers, e-mail addresses and Web site URLs.

411
http://www.four11.com

Four 11 takes the nod from the telephone companies and bills itself as the "Internet white pages." Indeed, this is the first choice for finding e-mail addresses, telephone numbers and, as sign of things to come, videophone and NetPhone numbers. The star-struck can take a peek at the celebrity e-mail links.

BigYellow
http://www.bigyellow.com

What BigYellow did for business directories, it also does for residential listings by cramming the phone directories of the United States into one dandy Web server. Powered by Four 11 technology, the link for

Find People leads to a search page that searches for directory listings on more than 70 million residences in the U.S.

Infospace
http://www.infospace.com

This meta-index for telephone numbers and addresses combines residential and business listings into one immense, searchable database. There are also complete links to federal, state and local U.S. government sites. The site is comprehensive and simple to use.

WhoWhere?
http://www.whowhere.com

The curiously-named *WhoWhere?* makes claims that eclipse even those made by BigYellow and Four 11 by providing look-up services for more than 10 million e-mail users, 80 million residential telephone listings, half a million personal home pages, 14 million businesses, government directories, links to companies online and toll-free telephone numbers. Take their word for it: the database is huge and the response time is fast.

Legal Directories

While many law-related Web sites like Hieros Gamos and FindLaw are establishing attorney directories, the franchise names in attorney directories are Martindale-Hubbell and the West Legal Directory. Until the start-up sites get up to speed completely, rely on these two old stand-bys.

Martindale-Hubbell Lawyer Locator
http://www.martindale.com

Use the link for the *Site Overview* get a feel for the lay of the virtual land. (To look up lawyers, follow the green links.) Except for listings for the state of Iowa where bar rules restrict attorney  advertising and some of the ancillary features of the print service, this is a free and much more portable way to search through the standard reference work. Included on the Web version are links to attorney e-mail addresses and Web sites, where appropriate.

West's Legal Directory
http://www.wld.com

Like the Martindale-Hubbell Lawyer Locator, the West Group
makes looking up lawyers a
simple and expedient process of
filling in the blanks of an online search box. Use this site to locate law
firm Web sites.

FAQ Archives

The *Frequently Asked Question* file is an Internet tradition. In its
simplest form, it is both welcome mat and orientation session rolled into
one simply file that will clue the newcomer in to whatever's going on in
a Web site, on a listserv or in a newsgroup. FAQ files are the *de facto*
instructional manuals for the Internet. Because they're so useful, the
imaginative Web searchers at the Superb Internet site collected all the
FAQs they could find and mounted them on a searchable Web site at
http://ps.superb.net/FAQ Pick the topic from the scrolling frame to locate
the relevant FAQ. The only knock against this site is that it's in need of
more frequent updating.

Forms

Stock up on free legal forms from jurisdictions around the nation
at the lengthy collection assembled at FindLaw at
http://www.findlaw.com/16forms/index.html This site is a meta-index of
forms indices; as new forms sites are added to the Internet, FindLaw
includes them. Direct links to many other sources, some by practice area,
others by government agency, are mounted on the FindLaw site too.

General Interest Magazines

Print publishers can't wait until all their readers have computers;
that way, print costs, mailing and collating costs, bills for paper and ink
all go blithely into the ether and the publishers get to pocket the differ-
ence. The Web is a superb publishing medium and the magazines of the
world realize that; the online researcher enjoys timely access to brand-
name magazines and dozens of other titles slightly lower down the publishing food chain.

Use the Internet for bibliographic research or to locate experts in
a field based on the articles the expert has written. Index pages containing links to magazines and newspapers abound and the researcher should
have no problem finding an electronic publication using the double
whammy of an index page and a search engine.

The Etext Archives
http://www.etext.org/

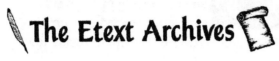 Legal documents and essays are the draw here for the legal researchers. Other links: religion, philosophy, politics and baseball. It's also weighted down with e-books and mailing lists.

CARL
http://www.carl.org

UnCover
http://uncweb.carl.org/

The marquee draw for this online library consortium is its **UnCover** online database of periodicals which be searched for free to create a bibliography or retrieved for a small fee. More than 17,000 journals are available from UnCover, representing some 7,000,000 articles. Passwords are required to order articles.

Electronic Newsstand
http://gopher.enews.com

 More than 2,000 magazine titles are linked to the largest magazine Web site on the Internet. Many of the titles can be browsed online; the **Electronic Newsstand** also can be searched to locate articles or individual titles. Discount subscriptions are available from the site. Search topically for magazines on *Sports & Leisure, Business, News & Politics, Science & Technology, Arts & Culture, Family* and something called *The Edge*.

Pathfinder
http://www.pathfinder.com

The Time-Life family of publications, which include such brand names as *PEOPLE, Money, Time, Fortune* and *Life* are online here along with connections to the electronic news services such CNNfn and the Weather Channel. The site also features a graphically tiny news wire service and slants heavily to entertainment news, celebrity journalism and feature pieces.

Internet Tools for Attorneys

For connections to Continuing Legal Education courses about the Internet nationwide and for links to major research sites online, try **Internet Tools for Attorneys,** operated by Netlawtools, Inc. an Internet training and Web site development company for lawyers. Their site is at *http://www.netlawtools.com*

InterNIC

Every legal researcher should be acquainted with the Internet Network Information Center (InterNIC). It is the clearinghouse for new information about how the network operates and it's where the technical improvements are proposed and debated. More importantly, InterNIC offers some unique reference tools. Its look-up services are far-ranging and comprise registration services, directory services and educational programs; for more details, refer to the Web site at *http://rs.internic.net* Bookmark the site. It's one of the basic Internet reference sites for all researchers.

Law Journals

Law students from generations past will envy the coming ranks of students who will not have to spend hours in the law library trying to locate some scarce law journal or requesting an obscure article mentioned in a footnote. In a world where hypertext is the norm, the very idea of footnotes is obsolete. (Footnotes, in fact, only exist as the print world's solution for linking to information, something that hypertext does with grace and ease.)

Many law journals are now appearing online for the use of legal scholars; some are published only in electronic format. Not all law journals are online yet but the trend to Internet publication of scholarly writing likely will continue until e-publication is the preferred method of disseminating academic materials. Electronic law journals are inexpensive to create, easy to distribute and can respond to emerging trends and current events much more quickly than print publications. E-mail and Web linking can speed up the peer review process and make scholarly work immediately available to the researcher.

These sites are excellent collections of law journal links. For law journals not included here, check the titles on the Web site for the law school or legal organization sponsoring the journal. Use the search engine at FindLaw (*http://www.findlaw.com*) or the link to law journals from Washburn University at *http://lawlib.wuacc.edu* to locate those journals not cataloged at the University of Southern California where the largest collection of law reviews and law journals is mounted.

University Law Review Project
http://www.lawreview.org/

A coalition of online legal information suppliers, among them FindLaw, Stanford, Cornell and the Australian Legal Information Institute operate a searchable database and a free e-mail service that distributes abstracts of new law review articles.

University of Southern California
http://www.usc.edu/dept/law-lib/legal/journals.html

One-paragraph synopses of journal contents describe the hundreds of law journals and scholarly publications linked to this index page, the largest of its kind. The site also features computer magazines and links to other periodical indices.

Law Libraries and Hytelnet

To access law libraries, it's necessary to have telnet software installed as a helper application on the Web browser. Telnet is a very simple program that allows client software to access and navigate through a remote server. Be sure to install a telnet client and link it to the Web browser before trying to connect to catalogs online.

Hytelnet is client software designed especially to browse library catalogs. An easy to understand FAQ file is available from Columbia University at *http://www.columbia.edu/cu/libraries/clio_plus/user_guide/620.html* which includes common Hytelnet commands and tips for navigating the world's libraries.

Hundreds of law libraries (and law schools) are online and accessible from Indiana University's heavy-duty server at *http://www.law.indiana.edu/law/v-lib/lawschools.html* This is the most extensive list of law libraries and associated institutions on the Internet. Law librarians, especially inter-library loan librarians, should bookmark this invaluable Web site.

Galaxy at EINet
http://galaxy.einet.net/hytelnet/US000LAW.html

Galaxy stacks up links to major U.S. law school law libraries in a gopher-like Web setting that's completely graphics-free. The drab, text-only format is a small sacrifice to make for reliable access to dozens of library catalogs. Telnet client software is required; Galaxy provides the requisite link and login information.

Washburn University
http://lawlib.wuacc.edu/washlaw/lawcat/lawcat.html

Second only to Indiana U.'s law library connections, Washburn boasts a huge collection of Hytelnet connections and includes login directions and tips on navigating remote servers.

Newsletters

Newsletter Access
http://www.newsletteraccess.com/

Select *browse* and pick **Legal Links** on this page to connect to more than a hundred law-related newsletters. The site is also useful for its connections to other subjects, totalling more than 5,000 titles.

Miscellaneous Resources

As the world's biggest online library, it's well-nigh impossible to catalog all of the Internet's vast informational riches. That's the job of the search engines!

The resources listed below are included because they have some general application to the legal profession; indeed, any office requires instant access to this information. Herein then is a very brief and very selective representative selection of miscellaneous reference sites that are across-the-board useful.

Area Codes
http://www.555-1212.com/aclookup.html

Telephone area codes by state and city and area and country codes for locales outside of North America are searchable on this site, thanks to Bellcore Communications. Area codes also link to e-mail address lookups courtesy of **411** and **Internet Address Finder**.

Central Intelligence Agency
CIA Factbook
http://www.odci.gov/cia/publications/pubs.html

Statistics, political reports, maps and the lowdown on foreign governments and their potentates put the "intelligence" in the CIA. (The site is not coy about reminding you that your use of their site may be monitored, so watch your online Ps & Qs.)

WEATHER REPORTS

Web site designers love to add weather reports to their sites because it provides popular, in-demand local information at no nominal cost. Because of that, it's possible to belly up to the isobar to get the current weather and forecasts for any spot on earth on innumerable Web sites. These are some of the most popular sites; information ranges from one-sentence meteorologic synopses like "It's 50 degrees and raining" to satellite imagery and official forecasts.

Weather Channel
http://www.pathfinder.com

The online version version of the popular cable TV channel is fully searchable.

CNN
http://www.cnn.com

CNN consistently ranks in the top five most popular Web sites because it's up-to-the-minute and colorful. It's also the best place to look up quickie forecasts for any spot on the globe.

National Weather Service
http://www.nws.noaa.gov/

Our tax dollars predict the future at the National Weather Service, come rain or come shine. Warnings, forecasts, maps and climatological data are onboard here.

ZIP CODES

United States Postal Service
http://www.usps.gov

Look up zip codes and purchase "postal products" (we still call them "stamps") from this state-of-the-art Web site. Simple to use and fast to answer, the Internet-equipped Post Office doesn't deliver the snail mail any faster but it does make figuring out how to address it and how much it costs much easier.

News Sources

The stampede to the world of online news began when the print publishers of the world realized that moving their editorial product from paper to electronic format could save billions of dollars in printing, paper and distribution costs. The Web, whatever else it may be, is a superb publishing medium. Commercial publishers, faced with ever increasing costs for newsprint and delivery, are grasping the obvious advantages of electronic publishing and moving much of their editorial product to the Internet.

So why haven't major publishers discontinued their paper-based publications? The audience for Web news is still not large enough or wide enough to support e-publication alone. News on the Internet is still not a mass medium and has yet to attract a reliable and measurable audience that will generate the advertising revenues to support a Web news site.

The news organizations that benefit most from Web publication are those organizations that never depended on paper distribution to begin with: CNN, other cable TV news services, newswires such as the Associated Press and network television news operations are making the transition to the electronic world with much less anguish than established print newspapers like the *New York Times* and the *Los Angeles Times*. (One exception to this general rule is the *Wall Street Journal*; however, the parent company Dow Jones, Inc. has been a long-time commercial online news producer and the company is well-experienced in the electronic dissemination of news thanks to its own Dow Jones News Retrieval service.)

Still, newspapers have no intention of losing any circulation to the electronic audience. Because of that, the researcher can find most newspapers online, almost all of them available at no cost. The intense competition in the news business, having driven the news media online, provides the researcher with an immense universe of professionally written and edited information.

General News

Thousands of newspapers and magazines are online. The best way to locate titles online is to use an index page containing links to the publications.

INDEX PAGES FOR NEWS SOURCES

All Newspapers Online
http://www.sddt.com/features/newssource/us

The *San Diego Daily Transcript* sponsors this collection of links to American newspapers. Select from a scroll-down frame that lists newspapers by state or click on the U.S. map.

News Central
http://www.everest.simplenet.com/newscentral/

Claiming links to more than 2700 newspapers, News Central is the largest index page for connections to online newspapers. The links are international in scope and can be searched by continent.

Totalnews
http://www.totalnews.com/

As a meta-Web for connections to *Fox News, MSNBC, CNN Interactive, CBS, ABC Radio, Yahoo! News* and the *Nando Times*, TotalNews is a fast link to the leading electronic news services. The site also functions as a news page in itself, with links to subject-restricted news such as *business, politics, sports, national, local* and *international news, weather, entertainment* and *opinion*.

The Virtual Daily News
http://www.infi.net/~opfer/daily.htm

Like TotalNews, the Virtual Daily News is a gateway service to the leading online newspapers and electronic news services. Select from a variety of news topics.

INTERNATIONAL NEWS

Virtual Daily News International
http://www.infi.net/~opfer/world.htm

A short list of the leading titles from around the world is provided by the same site developers at Virtual Daily News.

MAJOR NEWSPAPERS AND TV/CABLE NEWS

Boston Globe
http://boston.com/globe/

Access to the *Boston Globe* is best because of its coverage of the high-tech industries that line the city's Route 128. The Boston area is home to dozens of the best colleges in the nation. The next generation of online innovations will be coming out of these schools and it's quite likely that the newest software may appear in the pages of this august name in American journalism.

CNN
http://www.cnn.com

The CNN Interactive Web site is the most popular news site on the Internet and for good reason. In addition to the authoritative news services, this lively site features background stories, international news, technology and science news and exploits all the capabilities of HTML: the CNN Web service is genuinely multimedia and offers video clips, audio downloads and links to other sites to expand on the news it reports.

There is no single news source as comprehensive or as technologically advanced as CNN. It is also current; news updates are clearly time-stamped and the video vault is a good way to look up older news stories. Coverage of technology and the computer industry is first-rate and the links to national and international news is the equal of all other news organizations. If there is room in the bookmark file for only one news source, make it CNN Interactive.

Chicago Tribune
http://www.chicago.tribune.com

This Chicago institution is not resting on its glorious history nor is it simply slapping Page One into an HTML file and calling it a Web site. The online version of the *Chicago Tribune* is distinctly designed for the electronic age. There are local links to news of suburban and community interest and a *Digital Cafe*.

The online version of the Trib offers stock quotes, headline news and worldwide weather, a significant draw for a city where winter wind chills exceed 25 below zero.

Houston Chronicle Interactive
http://www.chron.com

This is an ambitious and decidedly high-tech site that includes classified ads, news discussion groups, a built-in search engine and directory of maps and telephone numbers for the Houston area.

Los Angeles Times
http://www.latimes.com

Learn how to "thumb" through an online newspaper from the *Los Angeles Times*. Anyone who habitually zips directly to the sports page or the editorials will be happy to find the electronic analogue on the Web site from the *Times*. Scroll boxes whisk visitors to the various sections of the paper, all without a single ink smudge. The coverage of the entertainment industry and aerospace are excellent. A "push" feature allows news to be personalized via PointCast.

MSNBC
http://www.msnbc.com

Microsoft joins with the National Broadcasting Co. to create the Internet version of the popular cable news program. With an emphasis on science and technology and business news, this is a good site for keeping up with breaking news in the high-tech sector.

New York Times
http://www.nytimes.com

The Gray Lady of West 44th Street plugs in the server and fires up a substantial Web site that, despite its annoying series of cookie-set prompts, is a model of simplicity. Realizing that many Web surfers are still hamstrung with slow modems, the *New York Times* site offers a low-graphics version. The site also has forums and special Internet-accented news section called "Cybertimes" which is notable for its fresh and informative coverage of Internet and Web news. Migrating online are all the other features of the newspaper of record; classifieds, editorials, politics and sports are all here. The only thing missing is the crossword puzzle. (Not to worry. Crossword software and puzzles are available from LYRIQ Crosswords at *http://www.lyriq.com/lcwhome.htm*)

USA Today
http://www.usatoday.com

The newspaper designed to be "America's Newspaper" is now the world's newpaper in its Internet incarnation. All the features one would expect from the paper - sports, easy-to-digest headlines, stock prices, colorful factoids and links to the Internet's nether-reaches -- are conveniently installed in this slick-as-ice Web site.

Wall Street Journal Interactive Edition
http://www.wsj.com

Two weeks of the online *Wall Street Journal* are free; after that, annual subscriptions to the e-version are $49 a year (or $29 for print subscribers.) Online here are the popular columns *Heard on the Street, Money and Investing,* the *Front Page* and coverage from Asia and Europe. Interesting feature articles are published online that are accessible to non-subscribers. First-time visitors are encouraged to take the online site tour to get a detailed look at what's available to subscribers and non-subscribers alike.

Washington Post
http://www.washingtonpost.com/

For political coverage, it is hard to beat the *Washington Post* for insightful reporting and unparalleled access to the decision-makers in Washington. The Web site is no different; it's brilliantly designed for maximum impact. A front page search engine aids in navigation; the editorial package is a punchy combination of news, sports, international coverage and cultural features.

WIRE SERVICES

Associated Press
http://www.nytimes.com

Access ten-minute delayed news stories from the Associated Press from the *New York Times* Web site at *http://www.nytimes.com* The site is free to use but registration is required. Click on *Breaking News* from the home page. The headline service is sub-divided into *Top news, news, business, sports* and *entertainment*.

BusinessWire
http://www.businesswire.com

BusinessWire reprints press releases from corporations which makes this a leading Web site for fast-breaking news about companies and corporations. It's especially good for earnings announcements. Other features on the site are links to IPOs, tradeshows, retail reports and links to high-tech companies and news.

Reuters
http://www.yahoo.com/headlines/news/

Yahoo! provides Reuters news service at its Web site at *http://www.yahoo.com*

Legal News

Law publishers, like consumer news organizations, are embracing electronic dissemination of news. With the notable exception of Westlaw's experimental news service, which never caught on with the legal profession, the legal news services are succeeding. The are attracting an audience of lawyers and law librarians and providing timely, accurate reports of breaking news, important decisions and news on leading law topics.

While non-subscribers can benefit from the free news published on the leading law sites, getting the most out of the online legal services means paying for a subscription. Prices and details are set out on each Web site. Also refer to the national news organizations for reports on timely legal topics and court coverage.

CourtTV
http://www.courttv.com

CourtTV covers the drama of headline-making cases on its cable television program, but the companion Web site is more subdued and much richer in background content. There's still plenty of coverage of the big (post-O.J.) trials. The library and case files contain interesting documents on the leading cases and the links to subject-specific law topics feature digests on a variety of subjects.

Law Journal Extra!
http://www.ljextra.com

Still one of the best sources for legal news on the Internet, *Law*

Journal Extra! not
only publishes
breaking news and
feature articles on
current law topics,
it provides an in-
depth archive of

news and newsletters on law topics. The link to *Legal Headlines* is current to the day but the real draw is the collection of articles that can be
found underneath the link on the home page to *practice areas* and
resources.

Lawyers Weekly
http://www.lweekly.com

Lawyers Weekly publishes a national newspaper and seven state
newspapers, each of which features legal news in the state, court opinions, archives and classified advertising. The newspaper is published now
in Massachusetts, Michigan, Missouri, North Carolina, Ohio, Rhode
Island and Virginia.

Software Archives

Software for hundreds of Internet applications is there for the taking from software archives. Software online comes in three flavors:
freeware, shareware and commercial software. Like the name implies,
freeware can be used with no payment required. The most common freeware programs are the Adobe Acrobat reader and stripped-down versions
of commercial programs. Shareware programs can be downloaded and
used for a test period; after a certain period of time, usually a month,
users are expected either to pay a small fee to the developer for the software or erase the program from their computer. Newer shareware programs now self-destruct after a time or severely cripple their critical
functions if no payment is forthcoming. Commercial software releases
require registration and payment of a license fee.

Software is clearly described as commercial or freeware. Some
commercial releases are distributed freely to schools or non-profit organizations; read the pop-up licensing and usage agreements that accompany
all downloaded software.

Consummate WinSock Apps
http://www.stroud.com

Forrest Stroud started it -- he was the first one to create a searchable Web site containing all the software anyone could want that would run over a TCP/IP compliant connection.

Law Office Software List for the Macintosh Computer
http://www.mother.com/~randy/

No one loves the Mac more than attorney Randy Singer. His affection for the operating system translates into the most extensive Web site of Mac-compliant software for attorneys and legal researchers.

Microsoft Corporation
http://www.microsoft.com

The computer world's favorite 800-pound gorilla is also a standard source for software, patches and upgrades. Microsoft can market its services well enough themselves and there's no need to aid and abet here; head to Seattle Bill's little software shoppe-on-the-sound for a large library of software.

TUCOWS
The Ultimate Collection of Winsock Software
http://www.tucows.com

TUCOWS plays Gimbel's to Forrest Stroud's Macy's. If you don't find what you're looking for at one, try the other. TUCOWS is mirrored on more sites that the Consummate Winsock Apps page, so getting through should never be a problem. The software on-board is for Windows 3.X, Windows 95 and Windows NT as well as Macintosh. Pick a platform and find a vast selection of software, some of which is not available from CWA, like parental control software, IP posters and search bots.

Travel

Travel agents of the world are an endangered species. Making travel plans could not be any easier, thanks to the Internet. The neighborhood ticket salesperson may lament the passing of a noble profession, but the rest of the world can now cash in on cheap, instant comparison shopping and enjoy direct links to the reservation desks of all the major air, rail and ground transportation companies. For the legal profession and the near-constant travel it requires, transportation links comprise some of the most valuable reference sources on the Internet.

A few general travel sites provide one-stop shopping for hotels and carriers. Try **TravelWeb** at *http://www.travelweb.com* It's a leading general interest travel site that connects to all the services the traveler needs. **Business Travel Net** at *http://www.business-travel-net.com* specializes, as the name implies, in business travel and connects to hotels, airlines, car rentals, trains and airports and other information.

Don't forget that the major search engines and Web indexes also catalog all the relevant travel information they can find on the Internet; the search engines, especially Infoseek, are a first-rate source of travel information.

AIRLINES

Every self-respecting airline has its own Web site today. Assume that the airline you want is online and except for regional or Third World air services, you'll be right. The leading airlines have intuitive URLs:*http://www.twa.com, http://www.ual.com, http://www.delta-air.com, http://www.americanair.com* etc. will get your where you want to go, or at least, to an online ticket agent.

The mother of all directories to airlines, airports, frequent flyer information and real-time flight information can be had at Infoseek's "Travel" link to *Air Travel*. For reservations and purchasing tickets online, look into **Reservations.com**. Before you plan you first trip, register for free with the site at *http://www.reservations.com* indicate your preferred home airport, frequent flyer accounts and other travel plans. From there, it's a simple matter to plan trips electronically. Reservations.com will search for the lowest fares on all the airlines servicing the selected destinations and travel dates and return a suggested itinerary, including fares, connections and travel restrictions.

CAR RENTALS

Like the airlines, car rental companies have embraced the Internet aggressively and it's a rare car rental company that does not have its own Web site. For making reservations domestically or internationally, the best one-stop car rental Web site is **BreezeNet's** *Guide to Airport Rental Cars* at *http://www.bnm.com/rcar.htm*

HOTELS

Finding a bed at more than 10,000 hotels worldwide is now a task turned into a five-minute chore thanks to **All Hotels on the Web**, a meta-index of online hotels. Find an interactive map of the world and links to cities, states, countries and continents at *http://www.all-hotels.com* Use a search engine to locate individual hotels by name.

<u>MAPS</u>

Although the maps are not all that easy to read, find an excellent U.S. street map service from Infoseek at *http://www.infoseek.com* underneath the left-column list of special services for **Smart Info**.
❑

Glossary

Glossary

The Internet, like many specialized disciplines, has its own jargon. The computer world in general is filled with acronyms and the Internet is no different; those acronyms can be puzzling to the uninitiated. Most acronyms simply substitute for multisyllabic protocols. When an acronym is not clear, it usually can be translated by referring to the relevant FAQ file.

For the most elaborate Internet glossary, refer to the ILC Glossary of Internet Terms at *http://www.matisse.net/files/glossary.html* There's also a dated but still useful hypertext glossary with succinct definitions at *http://www.supranet.com/guide/glossary.html*

For the best collection of telecommunication terms, turn to the Federal Standards 1037C site from the National Institute of Standards and Technology at *http://www.its.bldrdoc.gov:80/fs-1037* The database defines thousands of Internet and telecom terms, but the definitions are written for engineers, not a lay audience, and can be forbiddingly technical.

Two sites for easy-to-understand descriptions of Internet terms and concepts are at C|Net at *http://www.cnet.com* and the PC Webopedia at *http://www.pcwebopaedia.com* The sites are fully linked, professionally designed and offer intuitive, point-and-click navigation. The Webopedia is especially useful and packed to the rafters with definitions and generous links to amplify those definitions.

Last, there is an ongoing project at InterNIC to update the Internet User Glossary. For details on the working group, look in on *http://rs.internic.net/usv/userglos-charter.html*

Acronyms

The Internet overflows with acronyms, especially in the fast-typing world of Usenet. Among the most common acronyms are:

BTW ... by the way
IMHO .. in my humble opinion
ROTFL ... rolling on the floor laughing
TIA ... thanks in advance

An extensive list of Internet acronyms is available at *http://www.hei.com/ ~thong/acronym2.html Also see: Smileys*

Anonymous FTP
See FTP (File Transfer Protocol)

●●●

Archie

An all-but-obsolete search tool, used to find archived files on anonymous ftp servers.

●●●

ARPA; ARPANet
Advanced Research Projects Agency Network

The military network that connected computers at military installations and research centers during the height of the Cold War became obsolete for military use and was turned over to civilian use; the phone lines are the infrastructure of today's Internet.

●●●

AUP
Acceptable Use Policy

A written statement outlining the rules of a newsgroup or a listserv.

●●●

Backbone

The main physical network connections of a network.

●●●

BinHex

Shorthand for *binary hexadecimal*, BinHex is an encoding system used by the MacIntosh operating system to convert text into ASCII.

●●●

Cello

An elegant browser created at Cornell University's *Legal Information Institute* to search the WorldWideWeb but use was eclipsed with the subsequent introduction of Mosaic and then Netscape Navigator.

●●●

Cerf, Vinton

Sometimes called the "Father of the Internet," computer scientist Cerf is credited with creating and championing the *Internet Protocol* that makes the modern Internet possible.

●●●

CGI/BIN
Common Gateway Interface/Binary

Software designed to mediate data between a Web server and an application; on the Web, CGI-BIN forms are used as an interface to receive data, primarly as fill-in-the-blank forms to search a database, order products or subscribe to services.

●●●

Client/ Server

A model of computer network operation in which a user-controlled terminal is the *client* which requests files from or manages data on a remote computer known as the *server.* The Internet is the largest client/server network in the world.

●●●

Cookie

A text file written by a server computer to the client's computer which is returned to the server at subsequent requests. A cookie file contains information about the client's software and provides the server with that information. Generally a server asks permission to set a cookie and the files exist only for a brief time. They're useful for the server but many Internet users find them, at the minimum, annoying and at times a security threat.

●●●

Domains

The group of host computers defined by institutional purpose or geographic location. On the Internet, domains are hierarchical. The upper-level domains are:

Commercial	*.com*
Educational	*.edu*
Government	*.gov*
Military	*.mil*
Network	*.net*
Non-profit organization	*.org*

Host computers in each nation of the world may also use a two-letter country domain such as *.uk* (United Kingdom), *.ca* (Canada), etc. Beneath upper-level domains in the addressing hierarchy are individual server names. Because of the explosive growth of networks connected to the Internet, additional domain names will be added to the original ones, thanks to an agreement signed in April 1997 by 80 organizations in Geneva at an international conference sponsored by the Internet Ad Hoc Committee.

●●●

Domaln Name

The address of an individual server within a domain such as *aol.com,*
mit.edu or *sec.gov*

● ● ●

Domaln Name System (DNS)

A routing system that relies on a hierarchical system of addresses to deliver addressable packets of data to specific servers; the DNS requires access
to servers containing all known addressed and routing information for all
servers connected to the Internet.

● ● ●

Emotloons
See *smileys.*

● ● ●

Eudora

The trade name of a popular e-mail software program, produced by
Qualcomm; named for the author/photographer Eudora Welty, according to
the software designer.

● ● ●

FAQ
Frequently Asked Question(s)

The "instruction manuals" for the Internet, FAQ files are ubiquitous and
are available to answer basic questions about Web sites, newsgroups, listservs and other Internet applications. As a rule, FAQs are very helpful and
should be consulted first before asking a question of the Webmaster, news
group contributors or listserv owner.

● ● ●

FTP
File Transfer Protocol

A means of moving entire files between computers, commonly used to
download or upload large files efficiently. Because many server sites allow
the public to access files on their network and only require a user to login
to that network as *anonymous,* many FTP transactions are known as
"anonymous ftp."

● ● ●

Flame

As a noun, flame refers to a hostile, angry or extremely rude e-mail message; as a verb, it refers to sending such a message.

● ● ●

Frame

A data packet containing user information encoded within an electronic "envelope" containing addresses and other identifying information.

●●●

Frame-Relay

A means of connecting computers via packet-switching on a wide-area network that operates in speeds approaching 1.5 million bits per second.

●●●

GIF
Graphics Interchange Format

A very common, compressible format for graphics materials that relies on bitmapping of images.

●●●

Gopher; Gopherspace

A pioneering client/server software that mounted non-graphical files in a browsable hierarchy for easy review and retrieval. The software was invented at the University of Minnesota, whose mascot is the gopher. Gophers have been virtually replaced by HTML and the Web but they are still an effective means of publishing text-only data; many older databases pre-dating the 1993 explosion of the Web are still in existence. Gopherspace is the sum total of all gophers on the Internet; it's analogous to the WorldWideWeb which refers to the sum total of all HTML pages on the Internet but like the gopher itself, is rapidly becoming obsolete.

●●●

GUI
Graphical User Interface

A picture-based way of issuing commands to a computer that relies on pointing and clicking on an image to issue commands; Windows and the Macintosh interface are both examples of GUIs.

●●●

Home Page

The first page on a Web site. The home page orients the user to the site and usually provides a welcome message, links to help files and links to access the other files that comprise the Web site.

●●●

Host

A server. The host computer contains a file or other desired information that can be retrieved by the client computer.

●●●

HTTP
Hypertext Transfer Protocol

A means of moving a file created in hypertext markup language (HTML) across the Internet between a client and a server computer.

●●●

Internet

The global computer network connecting other networks, characterized by an open architecture and a series of agreed-upon protocols to transfer data between those networks.

●●●

IP
Internet Protocol
See *TCP/IP.*

●●●

ISDN
Integrated Services Digital Network

A network designed to transmit and switch digitized data for telephone, data, electronic mail and facsimile uses. Many telephone companies offer home and office ISDN connections that permit dial-up connections to an Internet Service Provider at speeds of about 168,000 bps.

●●●

HTML
Hypertext Markup Language

A simple, text-based software code that uses a system of switched tags to create rich files that can be decoded by browsers. Files created in HTML can be moved from one computer to another by use of the hypertext transfer protocol which is the basis of the WorldWideWeb.

●●●

InterNIC
Internet Network Information Center
http://internic.net

The record-keeping organization of the Internet created to administer the address registry and to publicize and disseminate technical information pertinent to the successful technical operation of the Internet.

●●●

Link(s); Linking

The defining feature of hypertext documents, links are the textual or graphic devices appearing in HTML files that launch unseen commands which retrieve files from a server either locally or remotely.

●●●

Listserv; Listserver

An electronic mailing list, named for the *listserver* software that controls the operations of receiving and re-broadcasting messages to subscribers.

●●●

Lynx

A non-graphical Web browser designed to read the non-graphic text content of files written in HTML.

●●●

Majordomo

The commercial name of electronic mailing list software used to administer a listserv.

●●●

MIME
Multipurpose Internet Mail Extensions

A format that allows e-mail clients to accept files that are not simply ASCII text files. MIME supports graphics, video files and non-English character sets.

●●●

Moderator; Moderated

A moderator is an individual who exercises some editorial discretion over e-mail posted to a listserv. A listserv so monitored is said to be *moderated*. Unmoderated listservs permit any and all e-mails to appear to all subscribers regardless of the content or the suitability of the message.

●●●

Mosaic

The pioneering Web browser developed at the National Institute for Supercomputing Applications at the University of Illinois Urbana-Champaign that was the immediate freeware precursor to the Netscape Navigator. Mosaic team member Mark Andressen is the founder of Netscape Communications.

●●●

Netiquette

The rules of polite behavior on the Internet, especially important to -- and roundly ignored in -- the unregulated newsgroups and the chatrooms of IRC.

●●●

NetsoapeNavigator
Netsoape Communioator

Very popular Web browsers created and sold by Netscape Communications designed specifically to retrieve and decode HTML files

●●●

NNTP
Network News Transport Protocol

The means by which the messages that constitute Usenet newsgroups are flood-broadcast across the Internet to news hosts.

●●●

Newble

An Internet novice.

●●●

Paokets

A series of binary digits containing a sender's address, a recipient's address, a piece of a message and error control data that can travel as a whole across a switched network.

●●●

Paoket Switohing

Routing and transferring packets of data according to the address included in the packet via a system of routers.

●●●

PDF
See *Portable Document Format*

●●●

POP
Post Office Protocol

An agreed-upon means of transferring e-mail messages from a server to a client computer.

●●●

PPP
Point to Point Protocol

A common technique that allows digital packets of data to be transferred across ordinary analog telephone lines via a dial up connection to a computer that eventually connects the client to the Internet itself. PPP is more stable and sophisticated than its preceding software, SLIP, or *Serial Line Internet Protocol*, but both PPP and SLIP provide the same service.

●●●

Portable Document Format; *PDF*

A graphical file type created by the Adobe Corporation that retains all the fonts and text formatting of the original document no matter what software was used to create the original document. PDF documents are very common throughout the Internet and can be read with the freely distributed Adobe Reader software, available from *http://www.adobe.com*

●●●

Protocol

Technical standard(s) for performing computer operations between two machines that permits computers to share resources on a network. Protocols exist primarily to explain how files and commands are *transferred* between two computers.

●●●

Routers

Computers located throughout the Internet that receive and re-transmit addressed packets to the appropriate server by electronic "consultation" with to a published list of identified Internet Protocol server addresses.

●●●

SMTP
Simple Mail Transfer Protocol

An agreed-upon means of moving e-mail messages between servers across the Internet. **Also see *Post Office Protocol*.**

●●●

SLIP
Serial Line Internet Protocol

A means of sending and receiving digital, packetized data across old-fashioned, analog telephone lines. **Also see PPP.**

●●●

Server

A computer containing a file or files that a client computer would like to download or view and which permits access to that file or files.

●●●

Sitemap

In an elaborate Web site containing many pages, a simplified description of what's mounted on a site.

●●●

Smileys

Also known as *emoticons*, smileys are an annoying grammar based on the clever use of punctuation to indicate in an e-mail message a literary tone such as irony, sarcasm or humor that is more easily conveyed by graceful writing. Common smileys are the colon-hyphen-open parentheses combo **:-)** to indicate happiness and the semi-colon-hyphen-open parentheses to report a sly *bon mot* **;-)** and are to be used sparingly, if at all.

●●●

Spoofing

The grievous, if not fraudulent, impersonation of another person via e-mail or other Internet protocol. Once a harmless prank, spoofing has serious security implications.

●●●

TCP/IP
Transmission Control Protocol/Internet Protocol

A defined means of transmitting data in packet form between networks that relies on a system of addresses and routers. TCP/IP is an open networking protocol that can be used by any developer without the payment of royalties.

●●●

URL
Uniform Resource Locator

The address of a file on the Internet consisting of the *protocol, domain name* and where necessary, the directory and sub-directories on the server where a specific file is located. Thus the URL *http://www.aol.com/~steve/law.html* indicates to the browser that it should use the *hypertext transfer protocol* to ask the *server* known as *aol* in the *commercial* domain to look in the directory *~steve* for a sub-directory titled *law.html*
A URL is a convenience for human users; the browser translates these commands and addresses into numbers which are more readily understood by computers. although occasionally some URLs appear as numbers.

●●●

WAIS
Wide-Area Information Search

A program designed to search through large-scale text databases and return relevant "hits" to the client.

●●●

Webmaster

The individual responsible for maintaining a Web site.

●●●

Web site

A collection of related HTML files on a single site containing links to native materials (files on the same server) and remote materials (files on a separate server).

●●●

WorldWideWeb

The universe of all publicly-accessible HTML files residing on Internet-connected computers.

●●●

Zip; Zipped Files

A colloquialism referring to a process used to compress files for faster transport across the Internet network. Files that have been compressed ("zipped") must be decompressed ("unzipped") after transfer to be useful. Most professionally designed compressed software is now *self-extracting* and does not require the use of a decompression utility program like PKunzip. MacIntosh files are *stuffed* and then *unstuffed*, most commonly with a compression/ decompression utility called *StuffIt*.

❑

Index

INDEX

ABOUT THE *AUTHOR* ...

DON MACLEOD is Manager of Web Applications for Chadbourne and Parke LLP in New York City. He is also the Editor-in-Chief of the *Internet Law Researcher*, a monthly newsletter. Mr. MacLeod lectures frequently around the nation on the use of the Internet and Web-based information systems in the law office. Mr. MacLeod is always pleased to hear from readers. Please send comments, corrections, questions or suggestions for future editions to *dunvegan@panix.com*

ABOUT THE *PUBLISHER* ...

INFOSOURCES PUBLISHING of Teaneck, NJ was founded in 1981 by librarian Arlene L. Eis. Since then, the company has been a leader in publishing legal reference books. In addition to *The Internet Guide for the Legal Researcher, Second Edition*, Infosources Publishing publishes the following titles:

> *Directory of Law-Related CD-ROMS*
> *Law-Related CD-ROM Update*
> *Legal Looseleafs in Print*
> *Legal Newsletters in Print*
> *The Legal Researcher's Desk Reference*
> *The Informed Librarian* (newsletter)

For more information, contact Infosources Publishing on its Web site at *http://www.infosourcespub.com* or by e-mail to Ms. Eis at *aeis@carroll.com*

INTERNET NOTES

INTERNET NOTES

Coming in December 1997!

THE LEGAL RESEARCHER'S

DESK REFERENCE 1998-99

compiled by Arlene L. Eis

Everyone's favorite resource!

RESERVE YOUR COPY NOW.

**1998-99 edition includes thousands of email and www addresses for our listings.

Completely updated, revised and improved

ORDER FORM

Please send _____ copies of **THE LEGAL RESEARCHER'S DESK REFERENCE 1998-99** to:

NAME_____

_____

ADDRESS_____
(No P.O. Boxes, Please)

_____

PHONE _____

EMAIL_____

☐ We wish to receive future annual editions.
  If we already have a standing order, please credit our payment but send only one copy.
  Money Back Guarantee. If not satisfied, we may return unmarked book in 10 days for full refund.

PAYMENT MUST ACCOMPANY ORDER. MAKE CHECKS PAYABLE TO:
INFOSOURCES PUBLISHING, 140 Norma Road, Teaneck, NJ 07666

☐ Please send your latest catalog.

PRICE PER COPY-$58 + $6 SHIPPING $ _____

Additional copies - pay only **$58**
            we pay shipping $ _____

NJ Residents add sales tax $ _____
TOTAL ENCLOSED $ _____

OUR FEIN 22-3244711

Please bill my: ☐ VISA ☐ MasterCard

Acct.# _____

Exp. date _____

Name on card _____

Signature _____

Date _____

MANY NEW ACCESS POINTS

The first and only directory devoted exclusively
to legal, law-related, legislative or
regulatory-related newsletters, bulletins and reporters
in ALL areas and on ALL subjects

LEGAL NEWSLETTERS IN PRINT 1997

Compiled by Arlene L. Eis

Includes the following sections:

❊ **Title List**
❊ **Deletions From Previous Editions**
❊ **Indexes with page references -**
  - Publisher Index
  - Database Index
  - Subject Index
  - Newsletters Available Online
  - Newsletters That Accept Advertising
  - Newsletters Registered With the Copyright Clearance Center

For each newsletter listed, the directory tells you ...

- publisher's name & address
- phone, FAX & toll-free numbers
- e-mail addresses & URLs
- editor's name
- date of first publication
- frequency of publication
- subscription fee
- if offer discounts for multiple copies
- circulation
- number of pages & size
- if it is hole-punched
- former titles
- if advertising & book reviews are accepted

- **DESCRIPTION OF NEWSLETTER** (contents, coverage, readership, special features)
- if it is indexed, & frequency
- where indexed
- which databases it is on
- availability of back issues & reprints
- availability of microfilm or fiche, & from which vendor
- if registered with Copyright Clearance Center
- **CATALOGING INFORMATION:**
  - OCLC control number
  - LC control number
  - ISSN
  - LC call number

Free and fax newsletters are also listed.

A companion volume to **LEGAL LOOSELEAFS IN PRINT**

For Subscribers Only - Free Phone Consultation Service for Newsletter Queries

SAMPLE ENTRY

Law-Related CD-ROM Update
Publ. Co.: Infosources Publishing
140 Norma Road
Teaneck, NJ 07666
(201) 836-7072; Fax: (201) 836-7072
Editor: Arlene L. Eis
Publisher: Arlene L. Eis
Began 3/93; 3x/yr.; $44-U.S., $54-foreign; 12-20pp.; 8-½ x 11;
back issues avail.; CCC.
Provides detailed information on new CD-ROM products in the
areas of law, legislation, and regulation. This is an update in the
Directory of Law-Related CD-ROMs, which is published
annually. Only available to Directory subscribers.
OCLC: 28765233
LCF: sn92-3504
ISSN: 1065-9285

8 1/2 x 11, perfectbound
400 pages

ORDER FORM

ISBN 0-939486-43-1
ISSN 8755-416X

Please send _____ copies of **LEGAL NEWSLETTERS IN PRINT 1997** to:

NAME_____

_____

ADDRESS_____
(No P.O. Boxes, Please)

_____

PHONE _____

PRICE PER COPY - $90 $ _____
NJ Residents add
SALES TAX $ _____

POSTAGE & HANDLING - $6 $ _____

TOTAL ENCLOSED $ _____

OUR FEIN 22-3244711

❑ We wish to receive future annual editions.
  If we already have a standing order, please credit our payment but send only one copy.

Money Back Guarantee. If not satisfied, we may return unmarked book in 10 days for full refund.

PAYMENT MUST ACCOMPANY ORDER. MAKE CHECKS PAYABLE TO:
INFOSOURCES PUBLISHING, 140 Norma Road, Teaneck, NJ 07666
❑ Please send your latest catalog.

Please bill my: ❑ VISA ❑ MasterCard

Acct.# _____

Exp. date _____

Name on card _____

Signature _____

Date _____

"a must purchase for any law library of any size"

LEGAL LOOSELEAFS IN PRINT 1997

compiled and edited by
Arlene L. Eis

LEGAL LOOSELEAFS IN PRINT 1997

➡ is the one and only bibliography of looseleafs.

➡ is now in its 17th annual edition.

➡ provides detailed information on 3,800 looseleafs published by over 270 publishers.

➡ contains 5 easy-to-use indexes with page references. Separate indexes list which looseleafs are online , on CD-ROM, or on diskette.

➡ lists 300 new titles.

Each entry includes information on:

Title	GPO stock numbers	Library of Congress card
Author	Number of volumes	numbers
Editor	Price for the volumes	OCLC numbers
Publisher	Frequency and cost of	LC classification
Edition	supplementation	Availability online, on
Year of publication		CD-ROM, or on diskette

For quick and easy access to information, the directory provides:

Title List	Publisher Index	List of Cessations and Deletions
Publishers' Directory	Subject Index	Electronic Format Index

8 1/2 x 11, perfectbound / ISBN 0-939486-45-8 / ISSN 0275-4088

FOR SUBSCRIBERS ONLY: FREE PHONE CONSULTATION FOR LOOSELEAF-RELATED QUESTIONS

ORDER FORM

Please send _____ copies of **LEGAL LOOSELEAFS IN PRINT 1997** to:

NAME _____

LIBRARY_____

ADDRESS_____

(No P.O. Boxes, Please)

_____

PHONE (_____) _____

PRICE PER COPY - $93 $ _____
NJ Residents add
SALES TAX $ _____

POSTAGE & HANDLING - $6 $ _____

TOTAL ENCLOSED $ _____

Our FEIN 22-3244711

❑ We wish to receive future annual editions.

If we already have a standing order, please credit our payment but send only one copy.
   Money Back Guarantee. If not satisfied, we may return unmarked book in 10 days for full refund.

PAYMENT MUST ACCOMPANY ORDER. MAKE CHECKS PAYABLE TO:
INFOSOURCES PUBLISHING, 140 Norma Road, Teaneck, NJ 07666

❑ **Please send me your latest catalog.**

Please bill my: ❑ VISA ❑ MasterCard

Acct.# _____

Exp. date _____

Name on card _____

Signature _____

Date _____

SPECIAL OFFERS FOR SUBSCRIBERS

Subscribers to THE INTERNET GUIDE FOR THE LEGAL RESEARCHER, SECOND EDITION are eligible for the following special discounts from vendors:

COUNTERPOINT PUBLISHING -

http://www.counterpoint.com (see ad on facing page)

Get a 5% discount on any new (not renewal) one-year subscription to Counterpoint on the Internet.

VERSUSLAW -

http://www.versuslaw.com

Register for your subscription to *V.* from http://www.infosourcespub.com and VersusLaw will grant you a 15% discount on your subscription. Not valid with any other offers or for those who register from the VersusLaw website. Questions? Call 1-888-377-8752 x 3018 or send email to subscrib@versuslaw.com

LOIS -

http://www.pita.com

Get one free week to use all LOIS libraries on the Internet. Also get a free trial CD-ROM from LOIS for any jurisdiction. For your free week, do the following: Go to http://www.pita.com and from the home page, click on the "subscription options and pricing" bar. On the next screen, scroll down to the bottom of the page and click on the "subscribe with a special access code" bar. Complete the on-screen order form. At the bottom of the form in the field labeled "special access code" enter "1week!infosource" (no quotes). When the order form has been completed and you have chosen a password, click on "submit". LOIS will then send you back an email that confirms your order and gives you the User ID and password you will need to gain access to the Member door off the homepage for one week.

To receive a copy of a FREE LOIS trial CD-ROM call 800-364-2512 x152.

*   *   *   *

Your code number to be eligible for these discounts is GK46LWXP. Offers expire 12/31/98.

Check out our website at
http: www.infosourcespub.com